Rose Hill

*the text of this book is printed
on 100% recycled paper*

ROSE HILL

Reed M. Wolcott

HARPER COLOPHON BOOKS
Harper & Row, Publishers
New York, Hagerstown, San Francisco, London

A hardcover edition of this book is published by G. P. Putnam's Sons. It is here re-
printed by arrangement.

ROSE HILL. Copyright © 1976 by Reed M. Wolcott. All rights reserved. Printed in
the United States of America. No part of this book may be used or reproduced in any
manner whatsoever without written permission except in the case of brief quotations
embodied in critical articles and reviews. For information address G. P. Putnam's Sons,
200 Madison Avenue, New York, N.Y. 10016. Published simultaneously in Canada by
Fitzhenry & Whiteside Limited, Toronto.

First HARPER COLOPHON edition published 1977

ISBN: 0-06-090577-8

77 78 79 80 81 10 9 8 7 6 5 4 3 2 1

For the memory of Juliana Knoepfmacher, my teacher, and of Hugh Stuart Johnson, my friend

Acknowledgments

This project began with the help of two people—Ted Irwin, who urged me to explore its possibilities, and Rita Kasky, who introduced me to the town.

Then the citizens of Rose Hill took over. From the day I arrived they were hosts, sources, chauffeurs, antagonists, teachers and friends. It is appropriate and, regrettably, impossible to thank them all.

There are some who must be mentioned for their special cooperation. Dr. W. Dallas Herring and Mister Windsor Johnson provided much initial guidance and opened channels of communication into their respective communities. Anson Lee Baker and Lawrence Hope kept my equipment and, with the help of Dr. C. F. Hawes, my sense of humor in good repair. Jackie and Hugh Johnson and Ginny and Bill Futrell and their large marvelous families were more than hospitable throughout my stays in their homes. My landladies, Mrs. Lilliebelle Brummitt and Mrs. Mary "Bud" Teachey, generously put up with their most erratic tenant. I am grateful to Dr. David Fussell for permitting me to excerpt from his writings and to Mrs. Lucy Farrior, who allowed me to include her renditions of tales told by her mother, the late Mrs. Rachel Southerland. C. T. Fussell, Clerk of Rose Hill, the Duplin County Board of Elections, and the office of Representative David Henderson were kind enough to make various records and statistics available to me.

There were countless others who pointed me in directions I needed to go. And still more, most of whom occupy these pages, who allowed me to share and record their ideas, memories or dreams. Some of these people have asked to remain anonymous. In respect for their wishes the author has invented names for them, made careful alterations to disguise their identity and marked each with an asterisk.

To all who participated, including those who were omitted, go my deepest thanks. In the end, the people of Rose Hill shaped this book. It is as much theirs as mine.

Jerry Bruck performed miracles in the rescue of what would have been inaudible tapes. Ann, Amy and Nina Schulman offered a hideaway at a difficult time.

And finally, some very personal appreciation: to Gloria Lawrence, for her encouragement; to Ellen Colyer, who has been, as always, an invaluable devil's advocate and critic; to my editor, Harvey Ginsberg, for his infinite patience; and most of all, to Jackie and the late Hugh Johnson, for everything.

Contents

9

4. Learnin'

5. Two Successful Men

6. My Angry Don't Count

7. The Good Ol' Boys

8. Three Women

9. Families

10. The Law

11. Praise the Lord

12. The Crow and the Mockingbird

13

Explanatory Note

Rose Hill, North Carolina—population: 1,700 (1970 census, approximate); incorporated 1875; location: southeastern North Carolina, Duplin County; 90 miles southeast of Raleigh, 50 miles from the Atlantic Ocean; area of town: 1.2 square miles; altitude: 94–108 feet above sea level; mean annual temperature: 62.4 degrees; vegetation: pine, oak, hickory, dogwood, cypress, poplar, elm, maple, various kinds of shrubs; crops: tobacco, corn, blueberries; industry: (formerly lumber, turpentine, strawberries), currently poultry; major businesses: Rose Hill Poultry Company, Nash Johnson and Sons' Farms, Watson's Seafood and Poultry Company; tax rate: $1.10 per $100; tax levy 1973–74: $77,000.00; town services: fire department (voluntary), police department (3-man, salaried), sanitation, water supply; government: town board including mayor and five commissioners (voluntary), administrator-clerk (salaried); civic organizations: Chamber of Commerce, Jaycees, Masonic Lodge, Eastern Star, Woodmen of the World, Women's Club, Lions, Tarheel Fine Arts Society; religious institutions: Baptist (1 white, 1 black), Presbyterian, Methodist, Freewill Baptist (1 white, 1 black), Full Gospel Businessmen; educational facilities: Rose Hill-Magnolia Elementary School, Charity Junior High School, Wallace-Rose Hill High School, Harrell's Christian Academy (private), James Sprunt Institute (technical college); recreation: hunting, fishing, swimming (town pool, members only), Rockfish Country Club (golf, tennis); county seat: Kenansville (13 miles northeast); neighboring large town: Wallace (6 miles southeast).

15

Preface: Turn That Thing Off and I'll Tell You Something

When you come to the stoplight at Church Street and highway 117, turn west at the corner by Peanut Scott's garage. If you follow along past the Methodist Church and the post office, you'll discover the town no longer exists. In the old days Rose Hill was a major rail shipping station for strawberries and vegetables and bulbs. Now Watson's Seafood and Poultry Company and Nash Johnson and Sons' Farms haul their chickens on trucks; the old depot is being torn down. One by one the businessmen of Rose Hill constructed large flat buildings and moved out to the highway. Rose Hill Hardware, Waccamaw Bank and Trust, Rose Hill TV Sales and Service. Doc Hawes' son, Charlie, got together some investors and put up a shopping center right off 117 on the way to Wallace. Mr. Masters, the police chief, opened up a Dairyland at the junction of 117 and Charity Road. The people who settled this country have always been attuned to possibilities. They followed the rivers, built a town on the railroad and, when the time came, reorganized themselves around the highway. Turpentine, strawberries and poultry may come and go. The people adapt and survive.

Survival in Rose Hill is a matter of holding your job, which means you take what they pay you and you go on home. "If they don't like workin' for me," laughs Nash Johnson, "they can always leave."

Adaptation is more complicated.

In 1963 the Reverend Lester La Prade arrived. He was an outsider; so he made mistakes. He organized a youth group. He sug-

17

gested to the congregation of the Mt. Zion Presbyterian Church that they pray for "our colored friends." He wore Bermuda shorts downtown. In 1966 a petition was circulated quietly. Most of the congregation knew nothing about it, and when the elders met, they discovered no public support for his dismissal. The subject was closed. A year later Lester La Prade found another assignment, packed up his family and left.

Nobody in Rose Hill has any information. Nobody knows how many people live here. The 1970 census reports 1,700 in Rose Hill township. That, points out town clerk C. T. Fussell, is not to be confused with the town. Nobody knows how many of these people are white or black, male or female, graduated from high school or earn a living.

The town is administered by a clerk, who is appointed and who receives a moderate salary, and by a mayor and a five-member town board who are elected to serve on a volunteer basis. Most of the people who live here would tell you who these men are, but they don't know when they meet and can't figure out what happens at those meetings or how to go about presenting grievances when the sewers are overflowing and the roads don't get paved. When the residents of Yellowcutt, which is one of the two "colored sections," made an appointment to discuss pavement with the mayor and his board, they arrived at the town hall to discover it dark and vacant—which only gives them something in common with the businessmen and professionals who live in the split-level houses on the other side of the highway.

Nobody knows who was responsible for the fact that the old elementary school burned down, or who allowed the Ku Klux Klan to hold a rally, or who organized the boycott that followed. Nobody knows why Rose Hill Poultry and J. P. Stevens have no real problem with unions, or how Representative Tommy Baker, who is generally detested, holds onto his seat in the North Carolina General Assembly, or what Representative David Henderson, who is generally respected, does in his office in Washington. But then, who can say when torrential rains will wipe out this year's tobacco crop, or precisely how the spirit moves us to speak in tongues, or when a farmer might be struck by lightning?

Rose Hill, North Carolina, straddles highway 117, ninety

miles from the state capital at Raleigh, forty-five miles from the coastal city of Wilmington. The country here is flat and wet; most people depend on farming—soybeans, corn, hogs, poultry, tobacco. Everyone else works to supply goods and services of various kinds. When I first arrived in midsummer 1972, Rose Hill was looking forward to four more years.

Knott Teachey, president of the junior chamber of commerce, turned up the volume on Agnew's acceptance speech at the Republican convention. "See that. *They* know what we're thinkin'."

Teachey took one look at a Yankee reporter, hankered for a debate, and finally got one. We sat in his living room, drank Cokes and argued happily. There were hot August afternoons riding out with old Doc Hawes to inspect his quails or his pit bulldogs or his blueberry fields, laying bets on the size of Nixon's margin. It was a quiet town, a pretty town, the kind of town to confirm your most sentimental assumptions about America. There was the Lion's Club and the Eastern Star, choir practice and livestock auctions, the legendary "Mister Nash," who installed an elevator from garage to entryway in the house he built on the hundred-acre man-made lake at his family compound. A go-cart track out on the Lake Tuck Road. There was even the requisite battle for racial justice: the folks out in Yellowcutt wanted their roads paved. Every Sunday morning I awoke to "Little Brown Church in the Vale," courtesy of the Methodist chimes.

It all fell into place; a cheerful, if isolated, community where every home featured either faded reprints of Martin Luther King and the Kennedys on the one hand, or *National Geographic* and *Reader's Digest* magazines on the other. Easy to document, easy questions, easy answers. If you live in Rose Hill, you have your choice of three doctors, two restaurants, four Protestant denominations and ten gas stations. You do your heavy shopping in neighboring Wallace, and take care of official business at the Duplin County seat in Kenansville. Most businesses in Rose Hill close down Wednesday afternoons and stay open half a day on Saturday. In November 1972 three fourths of the registered voters in Rose Hill precinct were Democrats. Richard Nixon defeated George McGovern by slightly less than two to one.

A majority of the people who live here work for one of the two

19

large poultry concerns. By the summer of 1974 each was said to be losing between seventy-five and a hundred thousand dollars weekly. Joe Williams raises hogs, cattle and tobacco. In two years his business expenses went up forty percent. Other farmers were losing as much as twenty dollars a hog. In 1973 it cost Tappie Murray thirty-five dollars a week to feed her family of four. In 1974 she was spending fifty dollars. There were whispers of surplus burnings, baby chicks in their crates, tobacco in the fields. There was gas, but no one expected that to last long. In the fall of 1973 the area's major distributor appropriated four twenty-thousand-gallon tanks, filled them with diesel fuel, and waited for prices to rise. "If we don't go to work an' straighten this mess out," said TV service man Anson Lee Baker, "we're all goin' perish to death." In May 1974, 213 of a possible 1,277 voters turned out for the party primaries. Knott Teachey had just been named Jaycee's Man of the Year, thought the Watergate hearings were soap opera, didn't have much to say. Doc Hawes had no inclination to talk politics. "Pshaw," he dismissed it. "A whole lotta ballyhoo."

To run for office in Rose Hill, North Carolina, you notify the municipal board of elections, then ride over to town hall and pay a ten-dollar filing fee. It seemed simple enough, so one night in the fall of 1973 Lawrence Hope and Perry Whaley sat in the Rose Hill TV Sales and Service, across Church Street from Mayor Ben Harrell's TV Center, and decided that Perry would oppose Ben. They had some cards printed up with Whaley's name on them and spent the Saturday before the election riding around town and knocking on doors. Whaley didn't raise any issues ("I gotta live here an' I didn't wanna stir up too much trouble"), but then neither did Harrell, and Whaley did come within a surprising seven votes of becoming mayor. The insurgents have two theories about the election. One is that Whaley was defeated by the people who came out to vote against a "Liquor by the Drink" proposition—the kind of people who have lived for generations in the big old houses on Main Street. The other is that there was something questionable about the tallies. Lawrence Hope, who carried his appeal for a recount as far as the state board of elections in Raleigh, maintains the contest was stolen. W. S. Wells, chairman of the local board, says he "can't get involved in this petty, penny ante, sour grapes business." But it is Ben Harrell, the mayor, who has the decisive word. "There are," he told me, "no politics in Rose Hill."

It is an interesting observation. If you think of politics in terms of public choices, it is remarkably accurate. You accept the order of things and continue to believe that work and prayer and good behavior will somehow straighten it all out in the end. There is, the Scriptures tell us, power in the blood. There will be wars and rumors of wars. The generations will grow weaker and wiser. We will have the poor among us always. Events, natural and political, just run their course. "It's like catchin' your wife shackin' up," one man told me. "You don't want to admit what's goin' on."

But things go on anyway. The week I returned to Rose Hill in the spring of 1974 the gardens were being planted. By June there were fresh squash and tomatoes behind the house where I stayed. A young girl had an illegitimate baby. A good man died of cancer. A tornado ripped the roof off a house only a few miles down the road. Those were the events worth mentioning. The rest was ballyhoo.

This is country where a coalition of bootleggers and church ladies can fight off liquor by the drink, so you tote your bourbon in a brown bag. This is country where a small group of people opened private schools in the aftermath of integration and, with no sanction from the churches, named them "Christian," where Dr. C. L. Quinn, Republican county chairman, states flatly that freedom is an expendable luxury, one we can't always afford.

"My sweet Jesus," whispers a Klansman, who insists I can only interview him in the middle of a cornfield at two in the morning. "Keep them lights off. They'll all know I been talkin'."

The former union organizer prefers to meet in an old graveyard. "If Mister Nash ever finds out about this, he'll just plain shoot me."

"I believe," the Klansman once explained to me, "in standin' for America. I'm a full-blooded American an' I stand for it." There was little point in mentioning that we had just spent three hours ducking headlights; nor was it possible to discuss contradictions with the housewife who announced that "this is a free country, an' if they hafta spy on me an' my husband to make sure we don't do nothin' to harm it, well then, that'd be just fine."

One of the cheaper places to buy gas is at the self-service pumps in front of the Rose Hill Market, across the highway from the Dairyland. If you stop there on Wednesday evening, some-time after seven P.M., you can hear the people singing in the big white house that belongs to Mrs. Brown. "Sin is to blame," they sing. "This world is full of sorrow." "There'll be mansions and rejoicin'." "I feel like travelin' on." Sometimes there is a guitar and sometimes an accordion, or maybe even tambourines, but mostly what it is, you seek the Spirit, waiting for the Word.

No amount of personal will, let alone accountability, has the slightest effect. When He is ready, the Spirit will claim us. But only at the whim of the Lord. It is a whim that is capricious and not to be questioned, silent and immutable as the big old houses on Main Street, the Democratic executive committee, the rela-tionship between tenant and landlord, chicken catcher and Nash Johnson. The preacher passes the basket, the deputies haul the voters. And all for a greater purpose beyond our understanding. "I've never been so ignorant as to express my opinion," says housewife Tappie Murray. "All them big men up there in Wash-ington—you write a letter, they say 'Who in hell's Tappie Mur-ray?' Why should they listen to *me*?"

"You do what you want," shrugs a local politico. "You just go right on an' ask your questions. I know somethin' about my peo-ple. They talk an' they don't understand a word they're sayin'. An' besides, it don't matter what you write about me. Most of 'em don't read."

"Don't talk to me about *Nixon*," fumed a businessman, then went on to tell me about the time a Hess station operator was un-derselling fuel distributors Tommy Baker and Cecil Worsely. They solved the problem by attempting to buy out the man's supply, and when he wouldn't sell, simply rolled their tankers in front of his driveway.

Q: Didn't it concern you that you were mayor of Wallace at the time?

Baker: No.

Q: No conflict of any kind?

Baker: You hafta wear three or four hats. One was mayor of Wallace. One was that of a private businessman.

Q: But where were the police? Wasn't it illegal?

Baker: I would be the first to admit that it was improper. But you hafta understand the situation. Hess was underselling and we couldn't reach them to discuss it. When you can't reach people, you hafta do something. Besides, that was a long time ago.

Shortly after the incident of the gas trucks, Mr. Baker was elected to the North Carolina General Assembly, where he represents the people who live in the town of Rose Hill. Mr. Baker has had no opposition since his election. That, too, was a long time ago.

It is easy to sit in Rose Hill and imagine the world outside doesn't exist. The most stunning revelations, local and national, have about them an air of unreality, a remote sensation which is at once reassuring and frightening. It is part of a general feeling that "they" have taken over, "they" being the communists, or the Devil, or a combine of banks and big business and insurance companies. It's better not to be black or young or poor, but most of the time it doesn't make all that much difference. I have lunch with a friend. He is a tough, smart, successful businessman. We arrive at the latest bit of landgrab gossip, one involving the purchase and resale of land by a member of the board of education. "Those poor people," I say. "They really don't understand what's going on." My friend, the tough successful businessman, drinks his iced tea. "Yeah," he says finally. "I really got taken this time."

By the late summer of 1974 the House Judiciary Committee had accumulated its evidence. Prices were plummeting at the livestock market in Wallace. Utility rates were climbing. Tobacco was going for under ninety-five cents a pound. Rumors started. The sewing plant might be closing. They were laying off workers down at Watson's. No one at Rural Electric or Watson's would return my phone calls. Neither would Mayor Harrell or Nash Johnson, or the members of the Rose Hill Town Board.

But conversations were no longer suffused with ambivalence. Every encounter led to a litany of corruption, a chronicle of broken promises, of local outrage. Anger became democratic, no longer limited to issues of integration, no longer the property of malcontents and crusaders. At some point there would be a wary silence, a wave at the tape recorder, and then the inevitable command: turn that thing off and I'll tell you something.

There was nothing to do but listen, file it away, try not to choose sides. To take odd comfort in frequent trips to the Dairio down in Wallace and prayer meetings at Mrs. Brown's. "My angry don't count," said former candidate Perry Whaley. Yes. Precisely. I knew more than I cared to about landgrabs and stolen elections, could identify all too accurately which citizens owed on their taxes, which marriages were going awry, and who was going mad with frustration or fear or loneliness. It had been easy not to like a man like Nash Johnson, but it gets a little difficult when you find out that his wife has been crushed to death by a train at the railroad crossing on his land. It became not a question of sides, but a matter of no more distance, a point which was brought home to me with chilling clarity when I found myself sitting in Katie Murray's living room asking her to, yes, to please help me pray. It was a bad afternoon when that happened, and I arrived at that particular interview late and exhausted from a struggle with long-distance static and too much love. But the reasons didn't matter. What mattered was that the vows of silence had been broken and people were hurt and asking for help, and there was no place to go.

"One of these days maybe I'll clean it all up," laughed a prominent politician, one of whom I was respectful and fond. But there was no humor in that laugh, and neither of us thought it was funny, and after a while there was nothing to say.

The Rose Hill Motel is on the west side of 117, catty-corner from the Rose Hill Restaurant, across the highway from Ray Scott's garage. Most of the rooms are empty, but Mary "Bud" Teachey has turned off the VACANCY sign. President Nixon has resigned, and the only air conditioner that works is in the office, so we gather there to watch Gerald Ford take over. There is comfort in numbers, and on top of everything else the sets in the rooms are flickering badly.

Most of the people who stay here are more than transients. By this time we know each other pretty well. I live in room 4. In room 3, next to me, is a structural engineer from Birmingham, Alabama. Every morning he goes to work at a construction site in Wallace, and every afternoon at five he stops at the Mini-Market for two six-packs of Schlitz, and every night I can hear him crying in his sleep on the other side of the wall. To the right of the office lives a girl of fifteen. For some reason that Mrs. Teachey can't quite figure out, her parents have told her she can't stay at home. She leaves her door open, and what you see when you pass by on the way to the drink machine is a bed covered with large, soft stuffed animals. Every night after supper her boyfriend comes by in his pickup truck and they sit in front of the motel, listening to the radio and staring out the window. In the room at the far end is a man who comes and goes, a traveling salesman out of Terre Haute, Indiana. In his wallet he carries pictures of his wife, his children, his grandchildren and his mistress. He doesn't much like being on the road, away from his family, but that's how he earns his living. Every afternoon, late, he offers us a drink, which we mix in paper cups with Sundrop or Mountain Dew from the machine. Every night he polishes off a fifth of bourbon. The man is a diabetic.

It is hot tonight and the evening would be depressing, but the discussion gets lively because another occupant comes to join us. He is passionate about Nixon's innocence and terrified of drugs and atheism and general disorder, most of which he attributes to the Democratic party, specifically such local radicals as Commissioner Fussell and Congressman Henderson. He has some valid reason for concern because he remembers the time, back in the twenties, when a Democratic commissioner took off with his girlfriend. He subsequently got over it and has made some success. He inspires the disgust of Mrs. Teachey by supplementing his social security selling condoms and French ticklers and dildos.

The problem is that the reception on the office set is lousy, so no one can figure out what is happening in Washington because the engineer in room 3 has gone to bed and we can't adjust the picture without him. Everyone drifts off and I stay to help Mrs. Teachey lock up, share a Coke which is lukewarm because by now the drink machine isn't working. Mrs. Teachey worries about the air conditioners, chiefly because her guests won't be comfortable, but also because just yesterday nine people were admitted to Duplin General in Kenansville, struck by lightning.

25

"That Nixon sure fooled a lotta people. I voted for him." We finish our Cokes and put the bottles back in the rack to be picked up in the morning.

"That nigger lady, now. Ain't she sump'n?" We both allow as how Representative Barbara Jordan did quite a job.

Mrs. Teachey tells me that Sue Lynn, who is her daughter, has offered to drive me to the airport at Fayetteville or Wilmington. If only I can make up my mind to leave. We laugh, and I thank her and go to room 4 to start sorting through tapes and documents and the kinds of presents people give you at partings. It's too hot to do much, so I wander out to the drink machine and sit in the rocker in front of the motel with the fourth Coca-Cola of the evening. The parking lot is a mess because it isn't paved, and all week we've had one afternoon after another of sudden, hard-driving rain. The diesel engines are leaking oil, the chicken trucks rattle by half empty on the highway. I remember that I never did make a recording of "Little Brown Church in the Vale" as played by the Methodist chimes. It wouldn't be bad to stay on a couple of days and record it the coming Sunday, but I promise myself that one of these days I'll come back and listen to them. There's always the bus on 117 or the airport at Wilmington or Fayetteville. Right now it's time to leave.

1

Two Views

"It's just a feelin' of security an' belongin'."
—James "Knott" Teachey,
President, Rose Hill Jaycees

"There's a certain pattern of laws here that
you absolutely don't break. . . ."
—Betty McVey

William Dallas Herring

The families that founded this town were from plantations around the area and were descended from the earliest settlers. My mother's people, the Southerland family, came to this country from Scotland in sixteen eighty-four and settled on the northeast Cape Fear River, which comes into this country just east of here. The Herring people settled on the Black River, a tributary of the main branch of the Cape Fear River, which goes upstate. When the railroads came, the population moved from the rivers to the railroad. So the Herrings moved from the Black River and then to Rockfish and then to the railroad, and the Southerlands moved from the northeast to Kenansville and then to the railroad. And they met here and married.

All of my forebears were natives of this region in colonial times, and the end product represents a large number of families. The Herring family had a land grant which was dated, I believe, in seventeen fifty-three, and some of the property is still owned by descendants. My great-great-great-grandfather, Richard Herring, was a planter, and he operated a gun foundry and made cannon for the revolutionary cause. Richard Herring's son, Enoch Herring, lived very near there on a part of the original grant, and he's buried on the old family plantation. If he made any mark for himself, it's not recorded, but I do know that his son, Owen, lived there after him and *his* son, my grandfather, George Dallas Herring, was born and then went to the Civil War from that same plantation. The house was burned by the federal

29

troops during the latter part of the war, and his family was all gone when he came home.

One of my great-grandmothers was a Carr—Lucy Carr—and married a Southerland who operated a general store, a turpentine distillery and a cooper shop to make barrels for the turpentine. During the Civil War he was postmaster at Kenansville, and I have an iron safe that was in the post office when the troops came through. Their son, my grandfather, settled in Rockfish township six miles west of here, some eight or ten miles distant from his father's old place. He married a Williams, who was a member of an old family that inhabited the area from colonial days. The old home was built right after the Civil War and is still standing there on the farm where my grandfather settled with his Williams bride. My father and his brothers and sisters grew up on that old home place and got their education there.

I remember my father telling me about his father rafting turpentine and logs down Rockfish Creek to the Cape Fear River and on down to Wilmington. But when the railroads came along, the turpentine distilleries could be established along the railroad. And this brought on sawmills. The community also developed as a trading center. It was a market for farm produce, in the early days essentially cotton and tobacco, although the ground here is really too lush for growing cotton, and tobacco has never been auctioned in Rose Hill. Before the turn of the century, the people began to grow strawberries and truck crops, and the trains had fifty cars of fresh produce to be shipped to New York or Philadelphia or Boston. In nineteen hundred and six the Bank of Rose Hill was established. There were perhaps twenty-five retail stores, more than we have now. Wallace was developing about the same time, and political favors brought paved roads into Wallace long before we got them. Apparently Rose Hill lost out to Wallace in the race for rural trade and developed as a farming community with some manufacturing.

My great-grandfather was the first mayor here, and his son, my grandfather William Southerland, was mayor later on. My father served as town clerk and my mother as a town commissioner. We had women's lib here in nineteen twenty-six! We had a woman mayor and five women commissioners. The major contribution the ladies made during their administration was to get electric lights from the Tidewater Power Company in Wilmington. Prior to that a local businessman had erected a light plant that was powered by steam. It was very small, and your lights would come on and stay on 'til about ten or ten-thirty and then cut off. I remember going to church before the church was wired, and there were brackets on the walls for oil lamps. The power company came in and began an era of progress that was slowed down some during the thirties because of the Depression. I was elected mayor in nineteen thirty-nine. I was twenty-three years old and the youngest mayor in the country at the time. We built a town hall in nineteen forty, installed water and sewer systems in nineteen thirty-nine, forty, and established a fire department. Then the war caught us and we had to stop that activity. They constructed an air raid warden post down at town hall, and as far as municipal progress was concerned, it was a period in which that wasn't really possible. We paved the streets in forty-seven and built two new churches and consolidated the high school. About the same time Dennis Ramsay and Nash Johnson got started raising poultry as a major industry. Many jobs became available and the population started expanding.

I left the mayor's office in nineteen fifty-one when I was appointed to fill an unexpired term on the county board of education. Governor Hodges appointed me to fill a vacancy on the state board of education in nineteen fifty-five; I was elected chairman in nineteen fifty-seven, and I haven't been able to get shut of the job since. My interest has been two-fold: to try to improve the quality of the public school programs and to develop the community colleges and technical institutes as supermarkets of education to serve the many needs we have. There has been some controversy. The community college movement is a step-ladder, but some of the blacks think that it's a way of forcing them into the vocations and out of the liberal arts which leads them to the professions. I disagree. The objective is to educate young people, the older people, too, for that matter, at the lowest possible cost so we can give them as much learning as we can. I was taught to work with my hands. I still do. There's nothing to be ashamed of. But for the black kid, for so many years, the only way up was through teaching, preaching, being a lawyer or a doctor. Let's face it, there are not many people that are going to

31

go that route. Most of us are going to earn our living in some white-collar or blue-collar job. But that doesn't mean we don't also live. The people here, for example, can attend James Sprunt Institute in Kenansville, which has a college parallel curriculum and a contract relationship with the University of North Carolina at Wilmington. The schools exist for one purpose, and that is to educate *people.* I ask myself one question always: what is best for the child? Not what is best for the teacher or the politically elected officials or the taxpayer. But what is best for the child?

When I sit at the state board of education meetings and listen to all the dull reports, all the figures and statistics, I lean back in my chair and sketch. I don't look upon myself as an artist, but my sketching does play an important part in my life. If it expresses what you think, what difference does it make if it's art or not? Who is to say what contribution something makes? I enjoy watercolors and I'm always giving them away. It pleased my mother; it pleases my friends, my neighbors and a good many strangers who come by. It speaks to them of Dallas Herring and what he thinks of the world he views. I do drawings about my rural background and I hope it makes us think about some great ideas we've had in the past. There's a bit of nostalgia in it. I have consciously tried to do some modern things, and they looked so contrived and so unlike me that I threw them away. That world is foreign to me and I don't really have a desire to live in it. I'm a product of some of the things I'm talking about, and my paintings are a comment on my world.

During the Depression my parents befriended an old Negro woman who didn't have a husband but a house full of children. They provided her with a home. We had a smokehouse down here where we'd keep the meat, corncribs, potato bins, produce of the farm. And the woman's family was fed out of that for several years. She was too old to do much work, but she was competent and she did what she could in gratitude and out of knowing that she'd been provided for.

Well, she brought along some little boys. There were Billy and Charlie and Lester and Matt and James. We'd play outside, ride the marsh ponies, hook up the mule and ride him, go out and gather wood, get in fights, kill snakes, go fishing. I didn't know that we were especially conscious of any strain. We knew that on

Sunday they went to their church and we would go to ours. We had three or four Negro servants in the house in those days—a housekeeper, a cook, a washerwoman, a gardener. Most of them were people who desperately needed food and shelter in the Depression.

When those boys I used to play with got to be teenagers, I went away to college. And we grew apart. I've seen them through the years, and once in a while we'll stop and talk. I'll ask them how they're getting along. They don't have any interest in talking to me. I don't think there's any resentment or hurt, but it's hard to relate to them today as individuals the way we did back then. It's part of the times.

One of them left these parts. He's a bartender in Camp Lejeune over in Jacksonville. He makes more money than I make. I know he owns a better home than I have; he drives a new automobile. He certainly isn't impressed.

The fact is, he doesn't need me anymore. His family does not need my family. We helped when he did need help, and I think maybe that's appreciated. But there's no more corn in the crib. There's no more meat in the smokehouse.

We have some of the new-rich ideas here. You've got to put on a certain amount of show, belong to the right social clubs. I'm indifferent to that. I'm not proud of my social status in a direct sense. I don't belong to the country club. I'm opposed to it. I think it's snobbery. I do respect my family heritage. I know there's such a thing as heredity. I observe it in the animal world and in plant life, and I know it must have something to do with humanity as well. But it doesn't trouble me to take my nineteen sixty Mercury with the license tag forty-five and park it right in front of the Presbyterian Church alongside of all the unpaid-for new models. Some people are conscious of these things, some are not. What counts most about a man is himself.

There are very many things that we're going to lose if we get much larger. I like being able to back my car out of my drive into a side street without having to wait for somebody to get by. I remember when you used to be able to do that on Main Street. You can't do it today. We turned the curbs around the trees. It really is dangerous, but we made them leave those curbs there anyway. We rake leaves in the fall and the government won't let us burn

33

them. Well, nothing could smell as good as leaves burning in the fall. I'm an old-timer in many ways and that's one of them.

I realize most people aren't like me. They want to have a chamber of commerce. They want to cite how many jobs we've got or how many chickens we've slaughtered. We have the Poultry Jubilee and we have a carnival atmosphere and we have the biggest frying pan in the world. What difference does it make? The chicken tastes good. I'd rather be interested in that—the quality of the chicken, the quality of the jobs that people do, the quality of the lives they live. If they work seventy hours a week driving those feed trucks and they come home bored, they never go to church, they never take an interest in their children, they're mad at their wives because they're working at the sewing plant—I don't want to live in that kind of society. I'd rather see them go hungry. I don't mean starve, but have less. Go fishing, for instance.

I've still got my family's factory in the old building that my father built back in the early nineteen hundreds, when he started making caskets. I could fix it up, but it's what I feel comfortable in. It's a protest against all the suave, sleek, powerful Wall Street type of financing and management that J. P. Stevens and the others have. I'm just a little guy. I paint pictures and draw sketches and sell screen printings, and this is what I like to do. It doesn't embarrass me that the governor of North Carolina comes in my office and looks at the building with a strange twinkle in his eye. I get a kick out of it. The building is functional. It has meaning to me because I played in it as a child. It's part of my past and I don't want to tear it down. I like it the way it is.

Betty McVey

When we first moved here 'bout fifteen years ago, all the kids went to this old dump, Rose Hill One, over near the highway. Well, I walked into that schoolhouse to enroll my child in the second grade an' I brought my child out. She didn't go to school for two weeks. I stayed here an' cried an' cried. I could not believe in those years, in this modern day an' time, that people would sit on their damn ass an' send their most treasured posses-

34

sions, their flesh an' blood kids, to a place like that. Take my house, take my husband, take anythin', but mess with my kids an' you've got a wildcat by the ass. I got two hearts an' they got two legs apiece. And baby, they walk an' talk. Touch that an' you ain't never—I'd just as soon put a hole in you *that* big as not. I'd get the Devil himself for my kids. Take my ass, burn me. I don't care.

Constantly, the first three or four weeks Barbara was in school, she ran home without askin' permission to shit an' pee. She wasn't about to use those crummy bathrooms. You absolutely could not imagine. They were abominable. They had a whole damn class of retarded kids an' they never shat in the commode. An' then one would sit herself in the bathroom an' show my first-grader how to finger-fuck herself. We got letters askin' us, the parents, to send donations of soap and toilet tissue. There was a friggin' Sears catalogue in that goddamn bathroom those kids wiped their ass on. The goddamn friggin' janitor made home-made lye soap in the basement and at his home out of discarded fat from the kitchen, an' the school county board of commission-ers gave him money to buy boxes of lye. And my kid used home-made goddamn lye soap to wash her hands. An' wound up at Dr. Howard's in Goldsboro with a seven-hundred-goddamn-dollar allergy.

It was a total firetrap. Hell, it had been legally condemned twice, once in nineteen twenty an' again in nineteen fifty-seven, I believe. The state law says it's to be inspected every thirty days. The inspector didn't even come down. He was a first cous-in of the principal. In the state of North Carolina in a public school plant, if so much as a windowpane is broken, it is to be replaced within thirty days. The check is received by the county superintendent of schools. He gives it to the county commis-sioner, whichever one. Then it's sent to the principal an' that goddamn window's fixed within thirty days. But the man in Ra-leigh told me the goddamn fuckin' checks had been mailed to Kenansville an' they had been cashed, an' nothing happened. Where in the hell did that money go?

I stood up in the PTA meetin' and asked what little I knew. You better believe all hell broke loose when I asked who was guilty of misdemeanor and was to be fined up to thirty thousand bucks, and who could pull five years in prison. They couldn't answer me. Goddamn place jumped up and everybody went crazy. Fire inspector resigned. Honey, goddamn, they trompled each other to death, gettin' out of the damn buildin'.

They cleaned the hell out of that place. An' the man that owned the grocery store, right there where Pratt's is now, he's dead, ol' man Teachey, I won't ever forget. He said, "Betty, if you keep on, those goddamn sons of bitches gonna work themselves to death." The school board members wore dungarees and old clothes, an' rather than let me, livin' this close, see the lights, they scrubbed that sonofabitchin' place an' worked with flashlights at night.

So then I went to kissin' ass, an' I laid quiet for a whole goddamn year to find out what I wanted to know. I cleaned houses just like a goddamn friggin' nigger, an' honey, I can work just like I can talk. There's somethin' I want to find out, I'll go clean that person's house minute I hear he's not feelin' well. Before I leave, they're so indebted psychologically, I can just drop a hint an' get what I'm after. I discovered in a very nonchalant round-about way, through kissin' ass, cleanin' houses, keepin' my damn mouth shut, with all kindsa joinin' in, y'know, that every goddamn fuckin' school teacher was first cousin, blood kin or by marriage, an' not a goddamn son of a bitch out there had more than a B certificate. An' the state law says you cannot teach in the state of North Carolina with less than a B certificate. Not a goddamn one of 'em had renewed their certificates, a couple of 'em in over thirty years of teachin'.

So I wrote to the attorney general and the goddamn governor. Then I went to talk to the congressman. He lives over in the next town, in Wallace, an' he wouldn't even discuss it. And this other little attorney over there, he said he'd rather not touch it, had too many friends involved. That was just before he went on the school board.

An' honey, I raised holy hell, an' let me tell you they sent a man from Raleigh, 'cause Mister Bud Teachey, that owned the grocery store, told me that, too, just before he died. He was dyin' of cancer and he knew it. He said, "Betty, goddamn, they're scared."

I sent Governor Sanford five hundred names on a petition in-

36

vitin' him to speak at our school. What started it, he was goin' to speak at the Kenansville school. They took eighth-graders an' seventh-graders out of class for four weeks and painted every goddamn room an' the auditorium, polished and shined every stick in that goddamn buildin'. I wrote him a letter sayin', "Why not visit *our* school, a school that has not taken two months to prepare, that has not taken one single student out of class, but one that is in dire need of help and in every sense of the word deserves your visit."

He didn't show up. He went to the mayor's house. An' they were so afraid that even a bunch of us would show up over there, they put damn shotgun guards all over the goddamn house. Deputies. On every corner. You couldn't even circle within a radius of three blocks. An' I never got an answer from Governor Sanford.

Constantly, over an' over again, I was told I had no right. I was an outsider. Honey, I got threatenin' phone calls not to let my kids walk to school. It was definitely a well-educated man, the voice. I think if I ever heard it again, talked to it, I'd recognize "goddamn nigger-lovin' dumb. . . ." How was it? *"Outsiders."* Well, I no further let my kids walk to school every day. Honey, they wouldn't touch me with a forty-foot pole. It was as though automatically I had all of a sudden some sort of contagious disease worse than VD. And everyone knew it. I could walk up to a crowd of people and they goddamn scattered like I had syphilis, y'know? "Run for your life" is what I nicknamed myself. And I would absolutely do it for sheer goddamn unadulterated spite an' gall an' damn hilarity.

There is a certain pattern of laws here that you absolutely don't break an' belong. You gotta earn your place in this society. Take one step backwards, one tinge of bad breath, an' sweetie, they'll drop you like a hotcake. There's two kinds of Duplin County, an' that's the haves an' the have-nots. An' the haves won't give you the sweat off their asses, an' the have-nots just keep strugglin'. If they blackball you, the haves, you can't even get a job drivin' a chicken truck. If you're not related by blood or marriage, you're considered an outsider. There is a forgotten people here, an' it's the ones that were not born into the aristocracy an' the old rich.

37

They's the most gods, goddamn gods, in this town I think I've ever encountered. An' everyone you meet wants to play Indians, but not a goddamn one of 'em wants to be an Indian. Every son of a bitch is gonna be a chief or he ain't gonna play. An' he will not even talk to you. An' if he does, he'll give you that nice runaround, goody-goody sugarcoated hunka shit. But he'll never tell you the truth an' the backbone of the whole matter. There's somethin' here that's evil an' it's lyin' dormant, an' you encounter it just like a silent, invisible curtain. An' you can almost mention certain things and watch 'em clam right up. Or it's time to go to work. Or, "I'm sorry, I'm pressured, there's the baby. Oh, there's the phone." Well, the phone didn't ring. Or they put a friend up to let it ring at that particular time.

Mosta these assholes will go along with anythin' that Mr. So-an'-so says an' they'll do anythin' that the majority rules. I can't an' never will go along with a person's opinion just because of who he is. An' I damn admire a man who takes a stand an' will stand up an' tell the world, "Yes, this is my way." I think the gist of Duplin County, the whole damn thing, they're scared to death of controversy. They're scared to death of bein' different. There's a fear here, an unspoken fear. People stand in awe of acceptin' the changes that have taken place in the fifties an' the sixties, in the new space age. They insist on holdin' onto the old way, the old way of thinkin', the old church, the old religion.

I usedta think that in the younger generation, growin' older, becomin' mature, at least one would care enough to want to fight for his own hometown. But incentive seems to be dead. They don't care. They get jobs an' leave an' that's it. Eventually it will be the outsider completely. The Yankee big businessman that moves in, builds a factory. Isn't it a shame that a community can die from within, from lack of care, from complacency?

When I lived up North, a man I had never seen, we lived beside him for a year, died in bed, an' honey, the only way we ever found his body was the smell was so atrocious. And we got the landlady an' the constable to knock the door down and we discovered he had blown up and burst. Had been dead for weeks an' no one knew. An' the same thing is beginnin' to take over the South. That objectivity, that the man next door would live or die, an' the hell with him. It used to be so close and neighborly an' belongin'. But everybody holds an arm's distance and you do not belong if you live here forever. They have their own little clans, their own little cliques, family reunions, an' an outsider is never invited. A family affair is what this whole damn county amounts to. Some of 'em are brother's keepers as long as they've got the fat bank account. To me, there's some things money can't buy.

You can talk to me five minutes an' you know I'm an Aquarius. These damn idiots don't want you to talk about things like that. You can talk about shitty diapers an' what brand of washin' powder do you use an' Sears Roebuck charge plates; they know instantaneously what you're talkin' about, y'know? They seem to have no form of entertainment or outside interests whatsoever except go to school, go to work, go to church. That's it. And everything, every subject an' situation, is "What's in it for me?"

Well, housewifery's great if you're such a damn imbecile that you don't know any better. An idiot with an IQ of two can wash dishes an' make a bed. An' when you've got nothin' but that, it sure as hell can eat at the brains like a cancer. Pretty soon you don't feel you're capable of doin' anythin' but housework.

If you wanna see a professional housewife, you should go see my mother. I suppose if there's not a damn batch of pots an' pans an' no one to cook for an' no flour an' no lard in heaven or hell, my mother's gonna be the most disappointed bitch there ever was. She makes biscuits three times a day. Three meals a day. She washes every Tuesday an' she irons every Friday. Her bowels move at eight o'clock every mornin'. I'm not sure mine'll move without a laxative, an' then I don't know when the urge is gonna hit me. But my mother goes an' sits on the commode at five minutes to eight because she knows they'll move at eight o'clock. She puts biscuits, three big squares a day, on that table. Seven-thirty, twelve o'clock an' seven at night. An' her mother dead, a corpse in the livin' room, she still put three meals a day on that table.

Well, I'll tell you what housewifery consists of in this day an' time: a fiftha liquor, a bottle of tranquilizers, a bottle of pep pills, a carton of fags, a five-pound bag of coffee, a damn private line on the telephone, a good color TV an' a lotta perseverance. A woman's not only a housewife, she's a damn taxi driver, she's a

39

housekeeper, she's a cleanin' woman, she's a prostitute twice a month. Yeah. You hit your forties an' everythin' gets borin' an' tirin'. When you have a partner that is content to get on the couch an' watch two TV programs an' go to bed an' back up at six-thirty, whistlin', life can get to be very everyday an' everyday an' everyday. Damn a jealous husband an' three meals a day an' a sink fulla dishes an' a commode that needs scrubbin'. The hell with it. There'll be houses to clean when I'm dead an' gone.

My husband told me to calm down, stay at home an' be a housewife, or get the hell out. He couldn't take any more of it. An' over an' over again, time an' time again, I got that from the kids. "Ma, all you're doin' is makin' it tough for *me*." An' my kids were not allowed out of the yard, nobody else's kids was allowed in my yard. Until finally, Jackie Johnson let her kids come up. Gradually I became quieter an' quieter. My kids began to belong a bit more an' eventually took part.

No mother in her right mind will make the road of life more complicated than it already is for the kids. An' that is really the pitiful part. I can't do but so much, an' when it hurts your own family, your own loved ones, then damn it, it's time to sit down and shut up and give up. And I did. I had to. But there's days when I feel I have so goddamn much energy, so much to give, so many things this community needs. An' I have absolutely become a recluse, an eccentric to so many people. I know very few people in this town that I can reach mentally. They know nothin' but their own little lives.

Honey, I am the most bored. If I had one wish. I'd wish I would wake up dead first thing in the mornin'. Cold, stiff, y'know? This livin'—shit, man. I been walkin' around dead for years an' didn't even know it. I usedta think I had so much to live for an' to do. But you get in a small town like this, you're just buried alive. I'm thirty-nine goin' on a hundred an' two. Because if experience is the mile-o-meter, I'm a damn old lady. I've been on the road so damn long I think every horse in the world has run through this horseshit. I've been there an' back.

All of a sudden it dawned on me that old age is creepin' in, menopause will shake your hand, that nervous breakdown I'm not over yet, an' what the hell's the use? One day leads to another, an' life ain't nothin' but a struggle. I dunno.

There's so damn many of us itch for things we're just too lazy to scratch for. But life is a cafeteria. It is absolutely cafeteria-style. There's no waiter an' no waitress to bring it to you. An' I found out that change goes by so gradually, that the rewards are just so unrewardin', that the struggle is just too damn hard. An' I have my family. I owe them first. I absolutely cannot fight this complacent attitude, an' when people don't care, one voice in the wilderness doesn't make a damn bit of difference.

2 Back Then

"There's no more corn in the crib; there's no more meat in the smokehouse."
—W. Dallas Herring

Rachel Southerland, 1856–1943

(Courtesy of her daughter, Mrs. Lucy Farrior)

The first thing I really remember about the war was when Pa and Buddie were called to service. Buddie was eighteen that year, but was so small that they sent him home as a patrol to keep the runaway darkies from doing any mischief. Every Negro had to have a pass to go out at night, and if Buddie caught one without a pass, he locked him up. Sometimes he would ride all night long, watching for mischief-makers. Pa was sent back, too, as a home guard for his wife and children and Mrs. Thomas, whose husband was dead and all her sons were in the army.

None of the fighting ever took place in our neighborhood. We didn't have the hardships that some people had. We were never really hungry. We even had a little money all along. We raised turkeys and carried them to Wilmington to sell, and we made tar kilns, grew cotton and raised sheep, and did our own carding and spinning. The only things we lacked were sugar, coffee and flour. We had them whenever a blockade runner would succeed in getting into Wilmington. We would get Uncle Gabe Boney, Mother's brother, a merchant in Wilmington, to get it for us when the runner came in.

The first time I saw any of the soldiers was after the war was over and the Yankees were marching back north.

Mother, Sister Dollie and Rose, the house girl, were in the big hall, spinning. Sister Betsy went out on the porch and said, "Oh, Mother, just look at the soldiers coming down the road." Mother ran out and said, "Oh, my Lord, children, it's the Yankees." Then all the children started screaming and hollering because the Negroes had told us that the Yankees were going to kill all of us white children when they came by and take the Negroes home with them.

The soldiers came to the end of the long lane at the edge of the field and halted, and then two men rode up to the house and saw Buddie out in the field with a horse, plowing. They went up to him and ordered him to undo the horse from the plow. He said he'd never do it. Then one of them told him, "If you don't, I'll blow your brains out." Buddie said, "I haven't got but one time to die. I may just as well die now as any other time." They saw he wasn't going to unfasten the harness and they didn't know how, so they took out their knives and cut the harness from the horse and started away with him.

All the time this was going on everyone was hiding everything they could find. Sister Dollie grabbed the little tin trunk that Pa kept all his important papers in, put it under her apron and ran through the yard full of soldiers to the back of the barn and buried it in some corn shucks that spilled through the cracks.

After these soldiers passed on, the general and his staff officers came. Mother, grand lady that she was, went down to the bottom step and extended her hand and said, "Come in, General." And he came in the house and saw the spinning wheel and wanted to know all about what it was for and how it worked. Mother got some of the fine cloth she had woven and showed it to him. He wanted Sister Mary Ann to spin some for him, and they couldn't find the cards anywhere. Finally, Rose said she had hid them on the sill of the house. Cards were worth fifty dollars, and Rose knew we couldn't get any more. Then Mary Ann carded and spun some more for them. He enjoyed it so much, and Mother and Sister were so nice to the officers that the general gave her a note to show to the other generals as they came by to protect the house. That note saved a lot of trouble. Our house was the only one in the whole countryside that was not ransacked completely. When the general started to leave, he said to Pa, "Send your son up to camp in the morning and I'll give you back your horse."

By daybreak the next morning Buddie was on his way to camp for his horse. When he got there, he asked where the general's tent was and they showed him. The general looked at him like he thought he was the biggest fool in the world. Then he asked, "Are you brother to the girl who spun for us yesterday?" He told him he was, and that changed things. The general told him to go get his horse wherever he could find him and sent a guard for him. Buddie took the horse home and hid him in the smokehouse for a little while.

You know, the first day those Yankees were passing, we children didn't get a thing to eat from daylight until bedtime, except some hardtack the soldiers would give us. As fast as Rose would get anything cooked, they would come in and take it out of the pot. They didn't even want it. One of them took a big piece of meat out of the pot with his hands and went all over the kitchen, squeezing the grease over the floor just for pure meanness. That day we had just had our washing done and hung on the line, and when they found where we kept our sweet potatoes, they stripped the clothesline of everything that would hold potatoes—sheets, tablecloths, pillowcases, dresses, chimer petticoats and even the drawers' legs were tied up and filled with potatoes.

Just before dark the first general left to make camp for the night. After he left, another general came. Mother gave him the note from the first general, and the general and his staff officers stayed in our large reception hall all night before a big fire. Just after night Mother came into the hall with all the small ones with her, crying. She said, "Lord have mercy on us. What shall I do?" The general jumped up and said, "What is it, Madam?" She told him her children hadn't had anything to eat all day and the soldiers wouldn't let anything be fixed for them. They took it all away. He told her to send the girl back to the kitchen to cook supper, and he would give her a guard. Rose swore she wouldn't go back there by herself, she was scared half to death, but she did and the guard stayed right by her.

Just about the time she got supper ready there came a great crowd of soldiers, pushing and shoving. The guard ordered them back, but they didn't pay any attention to him at all. There was a thirty-foot covered passageway with balusters on each side from the house to the kitchen and the dining room. The guard gave about three long leaps down that passageway into the house for the general, and when the men realized what he was up to, they scattered in a hurry. Then we all ate supper in peace.

Our great trouble was after the army passed, going north, and straggling bands of Negroes were left in the neighborhood. Provost Marshal (he called himself), a big Negro man, was the worst among the stragglers we had to contend with. He formed a band of free Negroes, and anything they wanted they took—horses, cattle, food, anything they wanted. They made their headquarters at a common old white man's house, near Mr. John Gilchrist's home, and took three of his Negroes in their band, and his daughter had to leave home for protection. They took all her lovely silk dresses and jewelry and gave it to the Negroes and some common white women in the house they were living in.

One night Buddie, Buddy Coe and Uncle Matt, an old faithful Negro, had been to Willard for the mail, and the gang shut them up in Mrs. Gilchrist's hat shop and had two Negroes guarding them. They heard one of them say , "What 'ud you a'done if he'd a' told you to shoot?"

"I'd a' shot over da head. What 'ud you a' done?"

"I don' know what I'd a' done."

They didn't keep them there very long before they let them go.

Not long after then, Buddie was passing up there one night and heard that old white man talking to Provost Marshal about Cousin Albert Hall, and every now and then he would say, "We'll fix him tomorrow night. We'll fix him tomorrow night." As good as to say they were going to kill him.

The next night a body of masked men on horseback, the KKK, came to the gate and told Pa what they were going to do. Then they went on to Mr. Gilchrist's, called out one of his Negroes they knew was mean and shot him, went on up the road a little further and called out two more leaders and killed them. Then on to Provost Marshal's and killed him, then went back to the Negro quarters at Mr. Gilchrist's and ordered the rest of the Negroes to have those bodies buried before morning, or they would be next. After that there was no serious trouble. That same sum-

48

mer two big Negro stragglers went all through the Negro quarters at our place, then through our house, but failed to find what they were looking for. But when they went down the hill, they met two of Mrs. Thomas' Negroes and they told them where the door to our attic was, and they came back, walked right upstairs, and found some clothes they wanted and left their old filthy clothes up there. One came down with Uncle Tom's high silk beaver hat, strutting like a peacock. Sister told him, "You needn't be so proud. You haven't got on anything but an old, dead Negro preacher's hat."

We all had a time after the Negroes left. All of us, girls and boys, had to work in the field. We couldn't get any help from anywhere, except whenever the neighbors would all go to one place to hull corn or build a barn or roll logs, or something like that, and have a big dinner together. I remember Brother Jimmie and I would each take a row of corn and thin out the small blades with our hands, and Pa would come behind us with the hoe and weed and stir both rows. At times, when we would get tired and want to play, he would say, "Work hard now and I'll get you some candy in Duplin Roads Saturday.

In about a year after the surrender Harriet, one of our darkies, came back with her three children. All of them were almost starved to death. They were so weak they could hardly walk. When Harriet was on her way home, she was so hungry she ate berries and roots along the way, and when she would hear anyone coming, she would hide in the corner of the fence until they passed. When she got home, she begged Mother to keep one of her children. And Mother fed her good and gave her something to put on, and she went on to her sister's house.

Mother had me take a big tub out behind the smokehouse and bathe that little girl and put some of my clothes on her. I used lye soap and scrubbed as hard as I could, and the harder I scrubbed, the bluer she turned. That is the way lye soap turns a Negro. I ran in the house and told Mother I couldn't get her clean. Pa heard me and always teased me and said I couldn't get that Negro white.

The pitiful part of their freedom—they didn't have sense to support themselves. They hadn't been in this country long and didn't know anything; most of them were trained to do just one thing. They didn't seem to be able to think for themselves; they didn't see anything to be done. They had to be told to do it. If you didn't tell them to clean up their quarters or take a bath or make some clothes, they would never do it. Not all of them, but most of them; they didn't seem able to think for themselves.

Mollie Alderman

Down in Pender County there was a man whose daughter got married, an' the man he give my daddy to his daughter for a houseboy. That lady, Miz Sue, she kept him in the house an' he didn't hafta get out with the rest of the slaves. My daddy remembered a lotta things that happened back then, an' I'll tell you what he tol' me. He tol' me the one thing he ever stole in his life, an' that was the Bible 'cause they wouldn't let the slaves have the Bible in those days. An' he'd steal that Bible an' go out at night to the place where he slept, an' he taught himself to read that book from Genesis to Revelations. He couldn't understand the newspapers or nothin' else. But the Bible was the one thing he could read.

The man he worked for was Mister Morgan Alderman, an' my daddy was raised up with his children, an' he took that name. After a while my daddy was a tenant farmer. If you furnished the work an' the seed an' everythin', they furnished the land an' the fertilizer, an' they took half. I growed up workin' for my daddy on the farm. He taught us to read the Bible like he did, an' then I went to school to the sixth grade. Way back yonder we just had a one-room schoolhouse, an' my mama she had so many children that she'd go one day an' I'd hafta stay home, tendin' the other young 'uns the next day. After I got to the sixth grade, I stayed on the farm 'til I was good 'n growed. Mama she was workin' in Wilmington then, cookin' an' workin' in a house, an' I hadda stay home an' care for my daddy 'til he died. Then I took my two l'il children an' went an' moved in with my brother in Rose Hill. That was 'round 'bout nineteen twenty-five.

The white folks my age'll tell you they'd like for it to go back to the way it was. I don' blame them for feelin' that way 'cause then we'd hafta go back an' work for 'em. 'Course I always enjoyed workin', but back then it was like slavery time. An' you hadda take what they paid. I'd go an' do washes, twenty-five cents a washin'; I'd stand out there in that cold all for twenty-five cents a wash load. There was times I'd hang one wash on the line an' go back to get another one, an' the first one'd be hangin' there just stiff as a board. I worked many weeks for two-fifty a week. Not a day, but a week. When I was livin' on the E. R. Bland farm with my brother, I worked in the house with Miz Bland an' helped her with her children, an' then I went to work for other women, an' then I'd come back home. I had two little children, an' you hadda work 'cause you hadda eat. So I kin understand how they'd like for it to go back that way, you see.

The big change for me was when I got a job workin' at Mister Hugh Johnson's. They paid me real good an' treated me like I was a real human bein'. My daughter, Eva, she still helps Miz Jackie some, an' we almost like members of that family. The Johnsons they just be that way. Way back, Miz Jackie she got sick an' stayed in the hospital an' I stayed at that house I don' know how many nights, takin' care of all of 'em. There warn't but two of 'em goin' to school then, Vann an' Tanya, an' the other three, Sarah an' Helen an' Evelyn, woulda been alone, an' I took care of 'em an' cooked an' just watched over it all. That young 'un they call Evelyn, she's a honey. I slept with her right in my arms. 'Course all of 'em young 'uns would start in, "I wanna sleep with Aunt Mollie, I wanna sleep with Aunt Mollie," an' there was times Mister Hugh would come in at night an' they'd all be piled right up there with me. He'd say, "My Lawd, Aunt Mollie, how in the world can you sleep on that cot with all them young 'uns?" But we'd just do it right on.

The Johnsons they was always fine people, an' I think other folks have changed some. I'll tell you what usedta happen here. It ain't happened in a long time. But usedta, white folks would go in there to a store an' buy sump'n for one price an' we'd come in an' we'd hafta pay another price. That's how it was. Times is better now, but things still ain't equal an' it's not just color, I mean. When I say better, I mean it's better just for some. It ain't

51

too good for the other. Now, we get them food stamps. You take me, I'm just by myself, an' I pay more an' gets less a' them stamps than folks I know that pays less'n me an' gets a lot more stamps than I do. I don' know why that is, but it don't make much sense. Things still ain't like they s'posed to be.

When you're talkin' 'bout Negroes, I s'pose it's better, but I'd ruther see some things just like it was. The schools an' things, I'd ruther see it back like it was in the old days. I think folks had more respect for one another back then. I reckon maybe it's just the way I was raised. But I don' think the white folks 'preciates this mix up, this goin' together. See, I usedta read the Bible right smart an' this is what it say. It was a child that was disobedient to his father. He laughed at his father because he seen him naked, an' his father he sent 'im to the landa Nod. He put this curse on his son. An' when the son he got over there, he see'd his wife an' he knowed her, an' the curse was his nation of people would be black, kinky-headed an' flat-nosed. See, it's just a curse that's put on you. I don' feel like it's been a curse in my life or nothin'; I feel like you can get up an' be whatever you wanna be. Cut me an' I bleed red. Cut the white folks an' they bleed red. Flesh an' blood, it all the same. But far's I can see, if God had meant for us to mix, we'd all be brown. You know what I'm talkin'?

I'll tell you one time things wasn't so good for the Negroes in Rose Hill. Back in sixty-four, when President Johnson was runnin'. I was watchin' television an' they called me, an' this man he told me, said, "If he wins, I'm comin' down there an' I'm gonna beat your black so-an-so." I tol' him, "C'mon." I tol' him wouldn't be nobody here but me. 'Course at the time we had a big dog outside, an' he didn't let nobody come in that front door, but I tol' that man if he thought he could do it, he could come on in here. Well, Eva or somebody told Mister Hugh Johnson, an' he musta talked about it right fast 'cause the sheriff he come round here the next day. I tol' that sheriff, said, "There's some dirty white folks 'round Rose Hill. You might not know it, but there is." An' he say, "Well, maybe it was just a child playin' a joke." I said, "I know a man's voice from a child's." An' then I said somethin' else, too. I said, "Y'know, there's somethin' mighty crooked goin' on 'round Rose Hill. 'Cause three nights

52

before the election every light in the colored folks' section was cut out. What you think about that?" Well, that made 'em know I knowed there was somethin' wrong. An' so that evenin', when it come time for the lights to be on, that light was on out there on that street an' it ain't been off since.

These young folks now pretends they know all they need to know. But it's about the wrong things. They got this new sanctification stuff, an' I tells 'em I got the ol'-time religion. Daniel an' the lion, an' the Hebrew children an' the fiery furnace. I asked the Lord to keep me just as I was, an' if this new-time stuff where they ain't got time for nothin' or nobody is the new-time religion, the ol'-time religion is good enough for me. 'Course you know the Bible spoke about the generations gettin' weaker an' wiser. An' they *are* weaker an' they wiser. They go right ahead an' do somethin', knowin' that somethin' might happen to 'em if they do it. They get in trouble. They don't have respect. That ain't wise.

When a person is wise, he knows howta do things. He sees dangers ahead an' he stays away from 'em. Takes a wise person to do that. I wonder if I'm a wise person, an' I s'pose in some ways I am. 'Cause I'll be eighty-two years old my next birthday, an' I been wise enough to live in this world this long an' keep myself goin' an' raise up my children. It ain't always been easy, but it ain't been that hard. First I had one child, an' see, if you had a child the way it was then, folks didn't wanna marry you. An' I didn't wanna marry because I was afraid I'd get somebody that wouldn't be good to my first child. So I said, "I'll go on alone." It's better'n fightin' and sendin' one another to jail an' all like that. It's better just leave the man off an' let 'im go his way an' you go yours. I don't have no enemies nowhere. I never had a fuss or fights or fallin'-out with nobody. An' I don' mind workin', an' in Pender, where I was raised, the lady'd leave me to cook for her husband an' I was so small I hadda stand on the stool to wash them dishes, but I did what I could. Y'know? In Hoover time my sister-in-law's husband gave us a squirrel an' we cooked that squirrel three times. The first time we cooked it we put dumplin's in 'im. Next meal comes along we put pastry on 'im, an' the next time we put rice in there. An' that was the last of that squirrel. That Hoover almost perished us to death.

53

But we made it right on. See, all I know is where I stand. I'm not uneasy 'bout dyin' 'cause I know that one day soon I gotta go. So every day I'm packin' up an' gettin' ready to go home. Way I look at it, life is like a road an' you gotta keep on it. You don' stop to pick the flowers on the way. No matter what, you just keep on goin'. I been down here long enough to know.

Sallie Blanchard

The hotel was built before I can remember. A long time ago this was a very big strawberry market, an' sometimes they'd be lined up from here to at least the highway, waitin' to sell. The buyers came in on the train and they went out an' looked at the strawberries and bid on them, and they all ate at the hotel. Mr. Bradshaw and his wife, Miz Mollie, ran the hotel. When dinner was ready, Mr. Bradshaw would come out on the front porch and he'd ring that bell, you know, like you'd see 'em ring for school, and if they didn't come right away, his temper sometimes would get outta hand.

The strawberry market has almost disappeared from the time it was one of the chief money crops. And when we did not have the market, we did not have the necessity for the hotel, and so it gradually grew less and less until it disappeared. But I've known many days when they fed a hundred people there at once. Strawberry buyers and strawberry sellers and people who came in. A lot of the travelin' salesmen came in on the early train, the *Shoofly*, and had their meals there, and then they went back on the night train, wherever they were headed for.

Then there was Fanny's café. It's been torn down now, but it was right on Railroad Street, on the spot where the new town hall is now. The tiniest little cafe you've ever seen, with a kitchen and the rest rooms, and the dinin' room wasn't probably any bigger than my livin' room. Fanny Brown was a character in this world. She was Miz Scott, but they only spoke of her as Fanny Brown. One time there was a train wreck, not a very serious wreck, but anyway, the train was detained for several hours, so a lot of people went over to the café to get lunch. And one man said somethin' that wasn't very complimentary about Rose Hill,

54

and Fanny charged him seventy-five cents for a sandwich, which was unheard of then 'cause most of 'em got it for fifteen cents.

I remember 'long about World War II, we had a watchtower down right close to where the water tank is now. And that was manned, s'posed to be, twenty-four hours a day. So when it was my husband's time to go, some time at night, I'd go with him and let him stretch out on the cot and sleep and I'd stay awake. One night about two o'clock, it was in the spring when she was havin' a lot of people to eat there, she was workin', dressin' her chickens, gettin' things ready for the next day. And a man came in, wanted her to cook him supper. Well, it was late an' I guess she realized he was drinkin' and she didn't want to do it. I could hear the conversation from the tower. She says, "I ain't got no daddy an' I ain't got no husband an' I ain't gonna cook for no damn man." An' he went on his way.

For a long time that was the only café we had in town, and every Sunday it was just jammed with people from Rose Hill and Wallace. The men loved it because they got there early and did their gossipin' for the day. She served them scrambled eggs an' coffee an' bacon an' toast an' listened to their conversation. She married and her husband drank very heavily and she had a lot to endure. She was good to a lot of people, and when it came to people talkin' bad about Rose Hill, she didn't tolerate that. She ran that little café 'til just before she died.

In our early years we went to school out in a little one-teacher schoolhouse. My sister, Tiny, is two years younger than I am. Then we went to Salemburg to what was called Pine Mount School for Girls, and we both went to Guilford College and finished. Then we both taught in the schools. I wasn't very young when I married, and then I didn't teach anymore except to substitute some. I wanted to keep house. I wanted to cook. I can remember, I was married in nineteen forty, and I think perhaps I had the second electric washin' machine in Rose Hill. Well, you could get a washerwoman to do your washin' at fifty cents a wash. An' I believe that we also had the first air conditionin' unit an' the first home freezer in Rose Hill. Of course, now everyone has them.

When I first married, this Negro woman came; she was cookin' for Miz Elmer Murray right across the street, and she had cooked for my brother and his wife. She came over one Monday mornin', said, "Miz Sallie, I told Miz Murray that I couldn't help her no more, that I hadda come over here 'n cook for you." Well, I really didn't want a cook, but she stayed with us for years. And we started out, I paid her three-fifty a week, an' she came in time to cook breakfast and cook dinner. She did the washin' an' the ironin' an' the cleanin'. Now I hafta pay five dollars for a few hours for just a little bit of help.

Her grandmother was my father's first help when my mother was a bride. She was Aunt Clary, I reckon her name was Clara, but we called her "Clary," and that dear ol' soul bathed and dressed all of Mother's children, all seven of us. And this was her granddaughter come over to me.

When Aunt Clary was old, she drive an ox with a little cart. She would come to spend a day and a night with Mother, and Mother fixed her a feather bed and she cooked the things Aunt Clary liked. Collards. And corn bread. And fat meat cooked with 'em. Whoever got sick in our community, Mother went to see 'em, white or black.

It was difficult to adjust to—this integration. Now really it was. I had worked with 'em an' I'd worked for 'em. I'd sewed for 'em. I'd cooked for 'em. I'd taken 'em to the doctor. A lotta times our closest neighbors were Negroes because they lived in houses on the farm, but there was not that social interminglin' an' they never attended our schools. So then to teach 'em it was a new experience. And you had to do something to *yourself* before you could do it. I felt like at one time I couldn't get over it. That it was somethin' new an' I was at the age, well, you know you get to the age where you don't change as quickly as you do in the younger years. And I thought, "Well now, let's just put it off for a little while." You hafta have these experiences and become adjusted to them before you can take them casually. For instance, we've had a good many ministers that came from the northern areas where there were few Negroes. But they were integrated, and if we were walkin' downtown, I'd find myself bein' very conscious that if I *did* speak to a Negro, I was just puttin' on a show, and if I *didn't*, I was not bein' very kind. But when I walked down by myself, the ones I knew I spoke to and had a good feelin' about it. So that's one of the things. Whatever I felt, I didn't want it to be for show. I wanted it to be real. Then, you know, for a while I was a little hesitant to stop and visit with a Negro man. But I don't mind it now. The people who pick up the garbage and clean the streets, well, one of the men's father and mother lived on our farm. The other day we had a little conversation about the trip Tiny and I took to Alaska. And I had no feelin' inside of me that it wasn't the proper thing to do.

You hafta come to that point slowly, maybe some more slowly than others. I don't feel uncomfortable at all or ill at ease with them now, and I don't think they do with me. And that's been somethin' that I've had to train myself to do, not only be friendly with them and be willin' to do things for them and be grateful when they've done things for me, but to meet them on common ground. The man who was principal of Rose Hill Two, the colored school, Mister Windsor Johnson, called me one morning and asked me to run for mayor. He is a leader of the Negro people, and I thought that was a wonderful compliment.

I never did run for mayor, but one time I did get on the town board. People just kept pesterin' me, an' one day I decided, "I believe I will." My family has always been interested in politics. At the turn of the century my father served as a county commissioner, and we did not have another commissioner from Rose Hill 'til Jiggs Fussell was elected a few years ago. My husband served for many years on the town board. A good many people marveled that we could get elected because Duplin County, as you may know, is a Democratic area, and we're not Democrats. We're registered Republicans.

There are a lot more Republicans in this area than are registered that way because if you want to get into office, if you want to get a road, if you want to get anything, you better be a Democrat. My father had been a Democrat before I can remember, and then he said that in the county things had happened that he just could not tolerate, and so he felt he had to change his registration. Most of the Blanchards are Republicans, but they don't say as much about it as I do. And Nash Johnson. But he's got so much money he doesn't mind sayin' it. I don't have the money. But I say what I think is right.

The things that have been happenin' in our country do not

make me very happy because I think Nixon would have won anyway, and what they say he did isn't a very good way to do. But things like this have been happenin' as long as I can remember anything about it. In the end they will have been too hard on him. When Johnson was President, with all this Bobby Baker scandal, he said, "I don't want to hear no more about it," and that was that. It looks like President Nixon had every opportunity to surround himself with dependable people, and maybe he didn't follow up and find out what their codes of right and wrong happened to be. But sometimes you feel this way: What is it all about? It didn't start out to be this. But they keep pickin' and sometimes nitpickin', and Senator Ervin, he has just been the actor on the stage. And it's been at the expense of our country, sometimes I feel like, because it's been a show. Of course, I'm a loyal Republican. I'll go down fightin'. If they impeach him, I'd be very unhappy. But it bothers me tremendously.

Even now, when I feel that there's somethin' happenin' that isn't right, that the town board can do somethin' about it, I have no hesitancy to go in and say, "Now this is it." We did that when we wanted a full-time policeman. The idea wasn't orginal with me, but I went to see the mayor, who was Mr. Surratt, and he said, "I know what you want, Sallie, and we don't have the money." So the women decided to go to the town board meetin' and state our case. Well, I was old enough so it didn't matter, and I did most of the talkin' as usual, I reckon, and they asked that we not put anything about it in the paper. But we got our policeman. Of course they didn't want to give the women credit. And one of the women's husbands that knew a little bit more about psychology than I did, he said, "Now, Sallie, if there are fifteen women goin', see to it they don't have but ten chairs. If there are twenty women, see to it they don't have but fifteen chairs." Well, there were thirty-five women and they had to continue to bring chairs to the town hall. And I said, "We've got sixty more that woulda come if they had baby-sitters." So, we got our full-time policeman.

For a good many years now, except when I was on the town board, I have served as a judge at elections. And although I was a Republican, I certainly didn't hesitate to yell loud and long when anything wasn't goin' accordin' to the law. And they used to say, "Count on Miz Sallie to straighten 'em out." One time a lady said to me, "Do you realize they don't like you down there?" I said, "Do you realize I don't care?" I would have stayed all night until they did what was supposed to be done. Sometimes those men there just glared at me. I remember one of 'em said, "We've never done it this way. There's no use doin' it now." An' I said, "It's the law, it's been the law, an' you'll do it this way." The last two primaries we had ran as smoothly an' as nearly as accordin' to the law that anybody could get it. I attribute that a lot to my stubbornness.

3

From Sun to Sun

"Reckon the Lord made me like He did a colored person an' a mule. He didn't intend for any of us to get any rest."
—Dr. C. F. Hawes

The Banker: Thomas Murphy

In our immediate area, due to the type of situation we're in, the economy can be very depressin'. We don't consider ourselves a *poverty* area; the average family, man an' wife workin', brings home about two hundred a week. Then there's a few who are makin' real good money an' some that're very poor as well. As for employment, if people really want to work, there's jobs available. But this area *is* low-income, an' with salaries not increasin' an' the rate of inflation, which is hurtin' all over, nationwide, it's pinchin' us and pinchin' us bad.

I'm from Pink Hill, which is fairly close to here, an' you really hafta be that type to understand the people and the situation they're in. Mosta the people here know everyone pretty well, an' about ninety-five percent of 'em know I'm from a rural area, so they don't mind explainin' their problems to me. They know I understand what they're talkin' about an' won't think they're completely Greek or that they're ignorant or won't know what the're sayin'. They'll ask me a lot of questions that are very sensible, an' it works both ways. I learn from them every day.

You hafta be up on all the operations here. You hafta understand when people need money, when the crops get put out an' when they get taken in. There are so many that you just hafta project for, help 'em with their financial needs, show 'em an' advise 'em what to do. We hafta understand the market; in a lotta cases we're just as familiar with it as the producer himself. And we have a lotta people that come in an' ask for advice whether they want us to help 'em with a loan or not. We're here to serve the community an' we try to understand this point. We *have* to understand it or we are behind the eight ball. When we make a loan, we hafta see the customer's situation an' we got to protect the bank at the same time. You hafta understand both sides.

We feel obliged to the people in the area that have been bankin' with us an' we're tryin' to look after the needs of our customers. We're not makin' any outside loans, an' from what I can understand, most of all of the banks are doin' the same as we are. We're lookin' after people's normal needs, but we're tryin' to slow things down. We're not makin' loans for expansion of any type, business or personal. We are not makin' residential loans. We do not float any long term financin'. If a business can get us a letter of commitment from a reliable firm that will take over the loan once construction is completed, we will handle *that* loan on a short-term basis. But we try to discourage this as much as possible. Every individual an' every case is different, so we try to look at it accordin' to what would do for our area. If the community really needs it, we will try to make some arrangements. Yes, we would go that route. In a way we do have a social conscience.

Most of our customers are farmers, an' to them a three- or four-thousand-dollar loan is a necessity. They hafta have it to produce their crops. They've got to have immediate cash at the time that they are housin' the tobacco, for example, because most of this is local labor an' they hafta be paid each day. Two years ago, even last year, most of the fertilizer companies were carryin' their bills until the fall, an' gasoline companies the same way. But this year it's a little different story. There's a shortage in gasoline, a shortage in fertilizer, an' all of the companies wanted their money when they sold it or when it was delivered. The FHA has handled a lotta the larger farmers, which is a great help for the banks, but your smaller farmer has still borrowed the same way he has in the past, an' more. Now he's gettin' most of his fertilizer an' gasoline money from us as well as his labor money. In other words, they got all the expenses in their crops, an' if they can't get money for this, the entire year is wasted. This is why we're makin' loans to them, even at a loss. We feel this is somethin' we have to do.

A lotta people are in a panic situation. I think the reason for this is that the prices have gone completely wild. People can't make any projections of what it's goin' to cost thirty days from now on anythin' that they are buyin', or how much they are goin' to make when it comes time to sell. Mosta the income here is from the poultry industry, which is losin' a lotta money right now. The feed cost is so high an' the sale price of poultry is so low that they're losin' tremendous amounts, an' while they're not layin' off many workers, the salaries aren't increasin'. This affects just about everybody in the community. Even the small farmer's income is not sufficient for him to support his family. Either he has poultry houses on his farm that he is usin' as a sideline, or he or his wife, one, is possibly workin' at one of the poultry plants for additional income. Mosta the farms in the area have cut back fifty percent in production, so this cuts back the growers an' the workers, too.

Then, it's hard to get a lotta the stuff they need—fertilizers or nitrogens. There's never been a shortage of this before. There's a shortage in feed. Now we've got large hog producers in this area. Less than six months ago prices of hogs were sixty-three cents. Within three or four months they've dropped down to twenty-four cents. It took about two to three weeks for 'em to go back to twenty-eight cents. And in nine days they went from twenty-eight to forty-two cents. This really doesn't make any sense. Supply and demand has no control over this. So people are confused. They don't know if they put in livestock today that they can even sell it at the price they purchased it for. They might double their money or they might double their loss.

Your average salaried employee, not farmin', earns approximately a hundred fifty dollars a week. The average female is runnin' possibly ninety to a hundred. Now this is plenty large, but this is *gross*. You hafta take out their deductions. That gives 'em an average income of two hundred a week. Two hundred dollars a week sounds like right much money, but when you've got the kinda expenses people have, it isn't much money at all. People usedta deposit, say, x dollars each month outta their salaries into a savings account. A lotta 'em are stoppin' this because it takes away from the money they need for livin'. They can't save anythin'. Their cost of livin' went up roughly twelve percent in the last year. Even if they got a five and a half percent increase in salary, they probably only get three and a half percent of that as bring-home money, so it stands to reason they are eight percent or nine percent behind.

We get into the matter of expenses when the people come in for a loan, so we're in a position to see some things that most people don't realize. People know what their payments are. But they haven't stopped to think that their grocery bill has doubled, their light bill has gone up probably thirty to forty percent. There are things they cannot control. There's no way you can tell exactly what all the hidden expenses are, but when you add them up, you run into a lotta money. Their expenses are the same amount as their income or greater. An' that's livin' with the bare necessities.

We have a lotta people comin' in now that's wantin' to consolidate their bills into one. Take the average workin' man, the average family. Say they got two kids at home. Their income averages eight hundred dollars a month, an' I think possibly that could be a little high. He's got at least a hundred-twenty-five-dollar car payment, an' he might have a second car, an' that would be seventy-five a month. Even if he's got a large garden he has at least a hundred-sixty-dollar grocery bill. Then he's got a twenty-dollar light bill, a ten-dollar telephone bill, an' you haven't added in anythin' on this for maintenance, repairs, doctors' bills, clothin', this type thing. He's just about got to carry some medical insurance, which is probably costin' him in the vicinity of forty dollars, with some minimal hospitalization on that. He's got a small life insurance policy, at least forty dollars a month. You got at least a tank of gas on each car each week. So even if they don't go anyplace except to work, you're speakin' of a hundred-dollar gas bill. In most cases they have a furniture payment, appliance payments, clothin' store, Master Charge card, some payment of some type that will run in excess of fifty dollars. That's over five hundred dollars for bare necessities, which leaves 'em about four dollars a day. An' that's before the rent or mortgage gets paid. Mosta the average workin' people are in this bracket. They are just about to the hilt as far as they can go.

These are things you have no control over. I handle my own pretty well, but when I feel the pinch on *me*, I can look at the average-income individual an' I can imagine what type pinch he's havin'. I have only one kid an' he works all summer for his own spendin' money. My wife an' myself are both workin' an' we both had increases, but the last increase I got threw me into another income tax bracket. So I'm makin' more money, but most of it's goin' to taxes, an' inflation has surpassed me. I think one thing. We have gotten used to a standard of livin', a *high* standard of livin'. We could get by with less. I really don't need the home I have. There's only three of us in the family an' I got a four-bedroom house, three and a half baths, three carports. We have three cars, a color TV, a stereo at each end of the house. I'm not behind on anythin' I've got. I'm in the wrong position to say this because we preach for savin's accounts all the time, but it's important to spend money on things we like to do. I like to save, but if I can keep my family together an' we can enjoy life together an' do the things we want to together without havin' to go into debt, I feel I accomplished a lot. Money is not the most important thing.

But many people get depressed. They feel it's all uncontrollable. They work five, six days a week an' they don't have anythin' left at the end of the week, an' it's routine over an' over again. They feel they're gettin' nowhere. If it keeps on, they'll be caught again within a year's time, right back in the same situation. All you hear is "recession." I think the recession is just a mild case of the depression, an' I don't see a depression comin' on. But people's income has got to go up. I don't see how it can stop an' be at a standstill. An' if it goes back, then I see no way except a depression. Now this is just my opinion. I don't think it will. I just don't think we can *let* it go back.

The Nurse

The hands of the people who work the lines at the poultry plant look deformed. You see them when they've got an infection, cut their hands on a chicken bone or sump'n like that. Calluses on the first knuckles near the the end of the fingers. Fingernails worn down to the quick as far as they can go. Infections from apparently nothin', yet the ends of their fingers are just pus

67

pockets. Arthritic hands. They probably had arthritis to begin with. But havin' their hands in cold water hour after hour, day after day, there ain't no way to tell 'em they hafta keep their hands dry. They can't. They'd lose their jobs.

The Waitress: Brenda Johnson

Donald's Restaurant is the one place in town that everyone comes together. It seems that it is like an institution in this town. Any kinda meetin' they want to have is held here in one a' the diff'rent rooms. A lotta people come here most every day. The farmers come in an' eat their breakfast or lunch, an if it's rainin', they can't get out to do anythin', so they come to Donald's. An' the salesmen an' them like that, they stop by for a half hour in the mornin', an' then they stop by for another half hour before they go back home. Then there are the ones that work in town, in the hardware, places like that. They pop in an' out for coffee. A lotta 'em they sit at the big table near the door, a shift in the mornin' an' one in the afternoon. The same ones every day. They get here when we get here for work in the mornin', an' sometimes they're outside the door, waitin'. You get tired of 'em sometimes, the cigarette smoke an' the talk, y'know, but some days one of 'em don't show up an' you miss 'im.

Mosta the ones that come often they just drink coffee. They talk about farmin' an' politics, tobacco crops an' things like that. They don't stay but about half an hour an' then they leave. We don't listen to 'em much. When you're runnin' back an' forth an' hear so-an'-so sayin' this or that, you might get everythin' wrong. The girls they usedta sit at the tables with the men an' talk to 'em, but if strangers came in, it didn't look too nice. Anyway, we're busy in here an' I got my own little world an' I wanna stay in it. I figure I can't change what is happenin', so I don't wanna know about it. I don't care about other people's business.

My husband an' his brother do contract work—houses, carpentry, an' stuff like that; an' he did the fireplace here, so he got got to know Donald real well. Donald needed a waitress an' I needed to work, an' I didn't think I could find anythin' else I liked, so I decided to try. I was scared to death, workin' as a

68

waitress. I wasn't usedta bein' around people. I was scared to death of 'em. An' I thought everybody who came to eat here was the Rose Hill society, an' I thought that they were a buncha snobs. I always thought I came from a lower-class family, an' I was sure I would be put down an' be out the door in two weeks. Well, everybody was so good to me I didn't believe it. I've worked in a sewin' plant, an' it was a big place an' nobody cared about nobody. An' I worked in a plant that makes blenders on an assembly line. Those jobs, doin' the same thing all day long, not allowed to talk except at your break, they're terrible. So I quit. But here they tried to help you. They saw that you were scared, an' even if you messed up their meal, they told you that you were good. No matter if you spilled it all in their laps. So it's worked out fine.

Of course you get tired, but that's just human nature. I come quarter to six an' get off quarter to two, an' then my other shift, I come at quarter to twelve an' get off at nine. You work every night for six or seven days in a row, an' then next week you work your regular swing shift, an' then you get one Saturday off every six weeks. One nice thing 'bout workin' here, if you know a girl that is experienced, you can get her to work for you once in a while. If you got any kinda problem, Donald is there. If you need a few days off for some reason, he tries to give 'em to you. As long as you are honest with 'im, you get along real fine. Far as tippin', some people tip fifteen percent of their bill an' some tip more an' some don't tip at all. It's funny. Some of the ladies don't. An' the ones that have all that appearance, they're the ones that usually don't tip too good. The ones that are average or below average they try to do better. I guess the ones that are average know what it is to get out an' work, that's what it is. They realize that you are here for a livin' or you wouldn't be here.

If I had children, I wouldn't work, but I don't, an' so long as I need to work, I'm goin' to. I wouldn't like stayin' home. You do the housework once an' that's it, an' I wouldn't like just sittin' there an' not doin' anythin'. My hours don't seem to bother us much. My husband works 'til five or six, an' by the time he gets home, takes a shower, an' goes out an' eats, it's eight-thirty, an' I'm home by nine-thirty. An' I really hafta keep workin'. In my husband's business everythin' has gone up—materials an' things—an' he had three jobs an' he didn't give a high enough bid, so he lost money on all of 'em. I'm not able to save much money, not like we usedta. We just get by. I'd like to have somethin' put by in case he got sick, an' I think about ol' age sometimes, an' I wonder if we will have money when we get old. That'd be one good thing about havin' children. Maybe they would look after me. But I don't worry about anythin' too much. As long as we can keep our bills paid an' go off, like to the beach every once in a while, it's okay.

Workin' here helped me some. It would help anyone who is shy. There is a story, a girl who was a whole lot worse than I was when she first started. An' the job helped. The people show you they are diff'rent than what you think, an' that helps bring you outta your shell. 'Course you gotta pretend sometimes. I say "Yes, ma'am" when I wanna slap 'em. You gotta do it, that's your job. You can't talk nasty to 'em, you gotta know howta treat 'em. Just go on an' treat 'em like you would anybody else. Give 'em a smile.

The Chicken Catcher: Melvin Johnson

Some people don't like to do this job, but it's not as awful as it seems to be. Main thing is gettin' a person to learn. You hafta know howta hol' a chicken in your hand an' ta keep your hand from crackin' an' hurtin', get your wrist strong. I pick up two 'r three at a time. To me it's kinda easy 'cause I been workin' at it for about sixteen years.

People catch chickens mostly at night, but sometimes the job can run through to the mornin'. Chickens sit kinda quiet in the nighttime. There are lights in the chicken houses, but we cut 'em out an' they can't see. We catch 'em, put 'em in crates an' take 'em to the loadin' machine, stack 'em on the truck. Then they take 'em to the plant to process.

They have trouble gettin' help to do this work, an' so the ordinary chicken catcher can make a hundred twenty-five dollars a week, which is good money for this country. Lotta people don't like the hours. I work five nights a week, all 'cept Friday an' Saturday. I'm a crew foreman, an' mostly my crew consists of nine men, but I'm afraid they'll be cuttin' back on the chicken catchers. Usedta be we had four crews goin' out, but there's only gonna be two 'r three crews startin' round the first of September.

It's never been this bad before, the cutbacks. That worries me some. I have one chicken house of my own, growin' out chickens. Watson's, they give me the baby chicks, a day old, an' they furnishes the feed, an' my main job is to take care of an' feed the chickens. We work on what you call feed conversion, dependin' on how much feed it takes to raise a chicken. If you do a real good job, an' your chicks grow fast, you can get more'n your contract. Right now we're gettin' 'bout six an' a half cents a chicken. Problem is feed is way up now an' we were told they're gonna cut back 'bout half. I dunno too much 'bout the processin' plant, but they say they're cuttin' back on the people workin' for 'em there, too. That's gonna hurt a whole lotta people. But I just don't know what anyone can do.

Some people don't work because they're lazy. I don't think too mucha that. Never have. If I lost my job, I'd go find me another one, if they's jobs to find. I have one child married an' one in the Navy, but still I got six at home. It's kinda hard to make ends meet sometimes, specially when they're in school an' gotta have books an' clothes. But I'm pleased to do it. My father was a sharecropper; he never had enough land to do his own farmin'. An' it was a good feelin' to me when I got my own land. Now I have two girls in college at North Carolina Central in Durham an' I got my son in medical school in Tennessee. So when the company gives me a vacation, I spends most of it workin'. An' my youngest daughter plays the piano. See what I mean? I feel that workin' hard is worth it. I'm doin' it for my family, so I don't mind doin' it at all.

The Druggist: Jerry Cottle

My business is a lot of repeat business, and that's due to the kind of personal attention you can give people in a small town. I keep a medical record of all their allergies, for example. Like if a person is allergic to a wasp bite an' the doctor writes a prescription for this particular person for wasp bite, I write that prescription number down for that thing, an' just in case some day in an emergency they can't get to a doctor an' need some medication, I'll give them six capsules or something like that. We are connected with Gowan's in Wallace. Mr. Gowan, which is my sister's father-in-law, owns part of this store, and he and I have a gentleman's agreement, so that if the people who are in the middle between Rose Hill and Wallace come into his store, he will call me an' ask me what I have on their record an' know I will tell him what it is. I'm not talkin' about tranquilizers or controlled drugs or anything like that. What I mean is personal service. I grew up on a farm out here an' my father used to raise a lot of produce an' supply many of the people who live around town. So they know me. An' in a small town, if a person is sick on Sunday an' the nearest drugstore that is open is forty miles away, you can't very well tell 'em you won't come down on Sunday an' fill a prescription for 'em. See what I mean? If you don't come down on Sunday, durin' the week the person is just goin' to take his tradin' an' go somewhere else. So you hafta do it. The other Sunday afternoon I did about twenty prescriptions. Generally speakin', people from this area are more sensitive, simply because the need arises an' there is no other place to go. I would be sensitive, too, if I had a sick child.

A drugstore is a lot different from other stores because you begin with a basic an' specific item. You start with prescription number one, you start from scratch, an' you keep fillin' an' refillin'. We've been in business two years, an' we've had a tremendous increase in volume. Take, for example, you fill thirty thousand prescriptions. You're gonna have a lotta refills. Then you fill fifty thousand. An' you have a progression. Hopefully. An' that affects the turnover of your other merchandise. I hate to say it, but Rose Hill is too small to support a jewelry store, or strictly a gift shop, or a variety store type thing. So actually a lotta my merchandise is very, very broad. When we opened two years ago, we had nothin' in here compared to what we have now. The first of September we are goin' to have a thousand square feet more of space. We're goin' to hafta turn our stockroom into floor space an' store the extra stuff in some sheds out at my father's farm. Sometimes I think we're carryin' too much surplus, but you hafta take some of it from the distributors, an' you never can tell what people are goin' to need.

In a small town you do a lotta chargin', an' chargin' is not a very good thing, particularly at the moment. You can tell a lot about what's really goin' on in the economy by watchin' the way the payments come in an' watchin' the decrease in sales. You can tell the difference when money is tight by the amount of traffic you have. Well, I'll take that back. Not necessarily traffic, but things like for Father's Day, Mother's Day, by the type of items people buy. Mother's Day is one of my largest gift days of the year, an' we have the biggest gift selection of any store in Rose Hill. Anyway, last year people bought high-price gifts. You're talkin' about fifteen-, twenty-five-dollar gifts. This year they bought one-, two-, three-, four-dollar gifts for Mother's Day. Now what does that mean? People don't care about their mothers less. It's the tight money. In a position like I'm in you can see the people squirming.

My father had a large farm, but he divided it an' there were a lotta brothers an' sisters. I was raised on the farm, an' my parents' income when I was growin' up, I would say it was five thousand a year or less. So I saw it right up close an' I was never interested in bein' a farmer at all. There was no doubt in my mind that I was goin' to college. I just never thought I might not go. In high school you would get into the Monogram Club if you played basketball or any other kinda sport an' got on the varsity team an' played so many hours. Well, I was in the Monogram Club my sophomore year, but after that I just played a lotta Little League baseball an' stuff 'cause I used to work at Harry Rouse, the grocery next door here, every day after school 'steada playin' sports or foolin' around. It's different nowadays. The kids could care less whether they work or not. Back when I was comin' up, which was just a coupla years ago, if you couldn't work when the boss needed you, then you couldn't expect work on Saturdays. Now, if you tell 'em they can't work Saturday, they just say, "'bye." I can't get a kid to work behind the soda fountain. Not dependable. I would be amazed to have a kid work six days in a row, even five days in a row. But me, I saved enough money workin' my last two years of high school, an' my parents borrowed some money an' put me through the first two years of college. When I went off to college, my mother got a job workin' as a teacher's aide. It was somethin' we just felt we had to do.

73

It wasn't all that hard. Big deal. I never could understand people who didn't care. When I got to Chapel Hill, I was amazed at people who were freshmen in college who said, "I don't know what I'm doin' here." The first two years I didn't specify my major, an' then I went ahead an' decided. I gave up a lotta fun, yes. I never got off work Fridays an' Saturdays before eight or nine. I never went to a football game. But I never even thought of not doin' it. I knew I was goin' make a good livin'.

Thre are two drugstores in Rose Hill, an' we're both doin' a pretty good business. Bob Carr moved his out to the shopping center an' I've stayed here in town. Bob was too crowded where he was, an' where was he gonna go? He certainly wasn't gonna move across the railroad tracks. A lotta the businesses moved out to the highway in the last coupla years. Which I think is too bad 'cause I would much rather have seen 'em build up the town. Some of 'em, like Anson Lee Baker's TV store, they moved out there because of the space. But you take the hardware store. It was so long where it was at downtown I can't see any advantage to move out to the highway. Farmers and people like that go to a hardware store. That's a specific need. That store's not gonna get any tourist type of business. I'm not one to say. An' everyone hasta mind their own business. That really is how we do in this town. I'm a member of the Jaycees, but I'm not very active in it. An' I invited myself to a meetin' that I thought was a chamber of commerce meetin', but I never went back. I didn't have the time, to tell you the truth. I've mentioned to people that we oughta get together, fix up the storefronts, that type thing. Like the mess with the railroad station out here. They're tearin' it down an' it looks just awful. An' the grass out in fronta my store. The town is supposed to take care of it, but they don't. They do it on occasion. I called them several times an' then I decided to do it myself. This is a small community an' everybody knows about everythin' that is goin' on. But it's not really such a close-knit thing at all.

It's sad maybe, but I don't feel anymore that I have a real commitment to stayin' in Rose Hill. As much work as my wife an' I have done, if I hadda known that, I don't think I woulda come back. We have two ladies that work basically full-time an' we have my wife, Fay, who works about seventy or eighty or ninety hours a week, an' myself, who is a slave, not an employee, an' works about a hundred. I guess I was curious to see if I could do it, to start somethin' of my own. I enjoyed my work when I was workin' just as a pharmacist, but I was tireder physically. Runnin' my own business, it builds up mentally. It isn't the money. When you start off with nothin', which we did, you know you ain't gonna get much 'til things kinda level off, an' I think things are goin' to be pickin' up businesswise. But then you gotta ask yourself, "Is it worth it?" Fay's been wantin' to go back an' finish her school, an' there's no way now she's gonna be able to go. Far as social life, fun, stuff like that, we haven't done anythin' in two years. You might say we've sacrificed two years of our lives. The best two years, really. I tell myself it takes time. Four years. If I can't make money workin' at my own business after four years, I should be workin' for someone else. But did you ever see somethin' you just would like to see if you can do it or not? Well, that's what this has been like. I'll give you an example. Drugstore labor usually runs twenty and twenty-five percent of your gross sales. Last month mine was twelve percent. I felt good about that. That's really somethin', ain't it? That's how I get my thrills. People get their kicks in different ways.

The Workman: John Henry Ryan*

One day my supervisor an' I was goin' out on the job, an' we went by this Rose Hill Processin' Plant out here an' the colored people were demonstratin'. My supervisor he said, "Y'all know what they're doin', don'tcha?" I knew what they was doin'. They wanted more money. An' I said, "What burns me up is to go into the restaurant an' hear these farmers complain about payin' a damn nigger twenty-five thirty cents an hour, an' yet they'll get together an' hold their hogs or hold their wheat or corn or somethin' for higher prices." An' I said, "What's the diff'rence? Tell me, what's the diff'rence? The man you got workin' for you, you got 'im on a thirty-thousand-dollar tractor an' you're givin' 'im four dollars a day to plow down a patcha beans." But the union was voted out down there. The union sure didn't come in. One time, 'bout two weeks before the election, they was sure it was

75

gonna go, but they beat 'em bad. Nash Johnson's man put thirty thousand in cash money in a basket to show them people the benefits an' stuff they'd be losin', comin' out an' goin' to a union. To try'n scare em. Scare tactics.

At my old job at another company in this county we had a problem with the union. The union was wantin' to come in an' the bosses kinda smoothed things over. The people that worked for the company they was for it, but they was scared to death. The company told 'em that in twenty-four hours after the union got voted in, they'd all get laid off an' there'd be contractors in there doin' the work. Well, things bein' how they was, the men just let it go. 'Course there was one 'r two that was ready to go ahead with it anyway, but they was the type of people that was probably lookin' for a way out. The union situation 'round here, it all goes back to Nash, see. Everybody's not against union, but they all depend on Nash. They don't hafta work for him to depend on 'im, you understan' what I mean? There ain't no union comin' in here for a long, long time.

The Farmer: Joe Williams

Farmin' has changed a whole lot in the last thirty years. It's changed in the last five years. A farmer used to, he took his eggs to the store on Saturday afternoon an' he bought groceries with the eggs. He kept three or four pigs an' he killed 'em for his meat. This is not so now. It's gettin' more mechanized. 'Course you hear a lotta tales about the old days that maybe are not true. See, in the old days, one reason they got up so early was because they went to bed so early, an' after sleepin' for ten hours, there wasn't nothin' to do but get up. They worked back then, an' that was hard work, but you can turn out ten times as much now in a day's work as you used to. I got a tractor that can plow sixty acres a day. An' sixty acres used to take ten mules. An' ten people. You hafta approach farmin' in more or less of a businesslike manner an' a scientific manner if you're gonna keep operatin'. This is the reason your volume of work is so much greater than it usedta be. But a farm doesn't operate on a computer system. A computer can't tell you when a hog's hungry or when the corn needs plowin'. Your management has gotta be close to the land.

Our primary crop is hogs an' we try to grow enough corn to feed 'em on, 'bout ten thousand bushels a year. You either sell 'em at forty or fifty pounds as feeder pigs or you can grow 'em on out, top 'em out as we call it, anywhere from a hundred eighty to two hundred forty pounds. If a person hasta buy mosta his grain, it would be profitable to sell 'em as feeder pigs 'cause there's not much feed involved. Then there are a lotta people, they're in the grain business, an' what they're really doin' is marketin' their grain through hogs. I do the whole business from birth to slaughter. We usually carry 'em to Clinton, to Lundy's Packin' Company. They slaughter'n pack right there in the market. Then I'm in the cattle business, Angus cattle. It's a cow-calf program, you might say, where you keep a herd of brood cows an' raise calves an' sell 'em as feeder calves when they're eight to ten months old. Since this is a registered herd, I keep my male calves as bull calves an' sell 'em as breedin' stock. You can tell if you get a good steak, it's Angus.

The portion of the dollar that you spend for food, the portion of it the farmer gets, I don't think that's gone up any in the last ten years. Everyone is talkin' 'bout the high price a' food, but I don't think there is any way to control it. An' it'll keep right on goin' up unless the housewife raises so much hell that they just won't pay for it. People want meat cut an' wrapped in cellophane. An' this costs. The meat cutter he's organized an' he gets seven or eight dollars an hour to cut meat, an' if he don't get it, he'll strike an' there won't be any cuttin'. This is what makes meat so high.

I won't know 'til the year's over how we're doin', but in the livestock business we're losin' money right now. My business expenses have gone up, I'd say, from thirty to forty percent across the board. Fertilizer—it's up about thirty-five percent. Equipment's up, I'd say, twenty percent above a year ago. Gasoline or fuel of any type—it's up forty or fifty percent. I figure it's costin' me thirty-five, thirty-six cents to produce a pound of pork an' sellin' it for twenty-six cents. So I'm losin' at least ten dollars per slaughter hog. Some people, dependin' on their situation, are losin' up to twenty dollars. So the outlook for the farmer right now isn't at all good.

Last fall, if you recall, the secretary of agriculture asked farmers to go all out on production of everythin'. An' maybe this wasn't quite right. Due to the inflation an' the gasoline shortage, which the government was involved in, a lotta people lost their jobs. An' when you gotta lotta people outta work, it's gonna affect the economy in some respects, an' probably the first thing it's gonna affect is food. Of course, we asked for it. Everybody wanted more of everythin'. Our inflation started after the Second World War an' it kept right on. Now which is worse, a depression or an inflation? In a depression there is no money, or your millionaires 'n your banks have all the money an' the population has none. In inflation everybody has plenty of money an' it's not worth anythin'. I dunno. I wouldn't turn around for the difference.

You probably heard about the book *The Man Without a Country*. Well, I'm the man without a president. In 1972 I was caught between the devil an' the deep blue sea, I reckon, an' I didn't know who to vote for. I'm a Democrat, but I just couldn't go along with McGovern's philosophy. In fact I didn't believe *he* believed what he was sayin'. An' I never have voted for the Republicans. I finally voted for Schmitz, the American party. I knew he didn't have a chance, but Wallace was out an' I didn't like the other two.

About Nixon now, I've got some ideas on some things. How much he knew about what was goin' on or if he gave the orders, I dunno. I don't think anybody else does. But if somebody's workin' for me, I should know what they're doin', an' I probably would. As far as bein' guilty, I don't know what he'd be guilty of exactly. But the whole situation stinks, an' the more they stir it, the worse it stinks, an' it's like spinnin' in a mud hole. The more you spin, the deeper the hole gets. The greatest crime is hard for me to put into words, because the crime Nixon has done is to the thinkin' of the American people, in really provin' that the heads of our government are not real nice people. I never thought they were real nice people necessarily, but what I'm tryin' to say is that it's a great disappointment to the American people that our President, who is supposed to be the leader of this land, could be involved in something as scandalous as Watergate has been. If the President or the FBI had seen fit to bug somebody's office, the FBI should certainly not have their hands tied to the point that they cannot find the enemies of the country. But all this "national security" stuff, that's a lotta malarkey. What is "national security"? Is it to get Mr. Nixon reelected? Could be. But I think what they were concerned about was the security of gettin' him elected, period. An' it was all uncalled for 'cause he woulda been elected anyway. An' look at all he's gained at our expense, his taxes an' his homes an' all. I'm not sayin' that no president has ever took us before, but this is the worst take that's ever been. Maybe the reason that Watergate ever came about is because the average American thinks "Let him run for President, let 'im get his money however he pleases." I mean, people worry about things. They worry about the price of hogs. Well, if we had all the money in the world an' no government, we'd be in bad shape. We hafta go back once in a while an' look at what our forefathers did an' passed on to us. There was a lotta blood an' sweat an' tears that went into that flag an' we've kinda forgotten this. I can't really explain exactly what the crime has been, but it's along these lines. He lied to Joe Williams. That's the main thing.

Farmers don't get ulcers an' take tranquilizers. They just die. My operation today is more confinin' and it's more nerve-rackin' than it was thirty years ago when my father was in my shoes. In the wintertime, in the fall maybe, there wasn't too much goin' on. He could go off an' go huntin' most any day he'd want to. But I can't ever get a day off hardly, unless I just close my eyes an' leave. I got a right good little investment walkin' around out there.

After growin' up on a farm, it was kind of a way of life for me. I enjoyed livestock, I enjoyed seein' plants grow, producin' an' harvestin'. An' then, too, I have a health problem, an' farmin', livin' out in the country, I can control my activities more than doin' some other kinda work. I went to State for four years an' I got a B.S. degree in agriculture. You see more degrees on the farm now than you used to. I don't say that a person with a high school education or a sixth-grade education even couldn't be a successful farmer. They can. Maybe they can be as successful as a college graduate. But goin' to college, it adds a lot to life. Farmin' was a livelihood, but it was a way of life thirty years ago. Now what it is, it's a business.

From Sun to Sun: Hattie Lee Simpson*

Long when I was comin' up, we worked from sun to sun. Labor was cheap back then. They paid the mens forty cents a day. An' the womens, my mother who worked in the house, she got three-fifty a week for housework. The mens worked killin' hogs. The womens they picked strawberries in the summer an' in the winter they just stayed an' kep' house. Once in a while the farmers would have raw peanuts an' the childrens would pick those.

My daddy was a tenant farmer an' sometimes we'd work from mornin' til night an' didn't get nothin' for it, us children. I was workin' ever since I was six years old. We would get out an' do whatever we could do. First thing I learned to do was to pick strawberries. Way back then cotton was the main crop an' there was times I couldn't go to school 'cause I hadda farm the cotton. You'd go in the field early 'cause you were paid by the pound, an' cotton is light an' you'd try to catch the dew, 'cause that made it wet, heavier, y'know? It was bad times, Hoover time, an' everybody was poor, even the white folks. The only thing was that they got the jobs.

I don' know how we lived back then. If we raised hogs, maybe there'd be lard. We had some sugar an' some rice. We raised corn an' my father made cornmeal. They raised chickens in the yard. There was six in my family an' I remember we'd fill up offa bread an' fatback, greens maybe. Still, we lived just like people do. I started school when I was six, an' after the years went on an' I grew larger, I worked on the farm, an' when I was in about the tenth grade, I started helpin' a lady with some work in the house. She was a nice lady. She coulda been my second mother. She taught me an' helped me with everythin' she could.

When I graduated from high school, I tol' her I'd stay an' help her, but I left an' went on to work in Wilmington. I worked a while at a laundry, cleanin', an' then I worked at a café. It was wartime then, an' I moved to Philadelphia. In the summer I worked at the Campbell Soup cannin' company in Camden, New Jersey, an' I worked at a laundry a while in Philadelphia, an' I worked a while at Sears an' Roebuck, fillin' orders. When I worked at Sears an' Roebuck, that was the first big money I ever knew anythin' about. I was makin' fifty dollars a week an' I thought I had money. In Wilmington I made nineteen dollars a week an' I even thought *that* was money. Don't sound like much, but things wasn't so high back then.

I stayed up North 'bout four years an' then I come back home. Been here ever since. My husband farms an' me an' the children help him. We rent the land from Mister Nash Johnson, an' then we pays for our fertilizer an' the people that helps us. Whatever we get, he gets half. We don' make a whole heapa money, 'cause when you get through payin' for labor an' your landlord, that don't leave you much. Our family does the garden work, growin' cucumbers an' squash an' beans, but you gotta have help for tobacco. July an' August are harvesttime. You have some croppers an' they go down the road with tractors an' you have the men haul it to the barn, an' they ties it up an' it dries. Least now we got them tractors. You usedta have mules, way back.

I do some work now like a cleanin' lady, start at seven in the mornin' an' get things goin', then I go back in the afternoon. I worked down at the Rose Hill processin' plant, but sump'n made me sick an' I hadda stay down, an' it was two months before I got up. So I just stayed home an' worked on the farm. My eldest girl she say, "Mama, why do you do what you doin'? You gonna kill yourself, sure." I say, "Who's gonna put the food on the table?" An' I just keeps on goin'. Fact is I wouldn't quit for nothin'. I've worked ever since I was big enough to work. I'm not satisfied less I'm doin' sump'n.

The Mechanic: Alexander McIntyre*

The first week in January 1974 I was informed that I would receive an allotment of eleven hundred twenty gallons per week. Which was two days' supply. Later on, when things really got tight an' people started beggin' for gasoline, it wouldn't even a' been two hours' supply. In the last week an' a half a' March, I got some extra gas, an' the first of April everybody had plenty. People ask me if I think the man who distributes to us done anythin' crooked. I say I can't comment on that. Like the man said hisself, it was his gas an' it was his business. All I say is that I just don' think I was treated fair.

My supplier tol' me, "You are gettin' your fair share of what we are gettin'." That is the absolute remark that come outta my supplier's mouth. Well, I'll put it to you this way. My allotment was s'posed to be based on a nineteen seventy-two usage of what I bought from that company. All right. The lasta seventy-three, sump'n like that, he built maybe a dozen stations of his own which he invested hundreds of thousands of dollars in. That's a lotta money. He's gotta turn around an' keep those stations goin' somehow with some gasoline to try to get some of his investment back. I understand that part. But some of us, we'd been with 'im faithfully for a long time. My regular customers'd come in an' I'd hafta look 'em in the eye an' tell 'em I couldn't help 'em. I had approximately five hundred gallons a week to sell to the public. The rest was for the commercial users. I know I wasn't obligated to nobody, but I'd feel terrible. Sickened. Disheartened. An' I'd watch my customers in the lines at my dealer's places, waitin' an' waitin' to buy gas. An' some a' them got used-ta takin' their business elsewhere. What could I tell 'em? If I didn't have it, I didn't have it. I was afraid that if I got mad an' went down an' raised a whole lotta devil, had I went down to the office an', I'm gonna say frankly, made an ass of myself, he woulda just about tol' me, "I don't care if you close your doors. It don't make no difference to me."

One thing I'm sure of, there wasn't no shortage. They wanted to get the price up, is all. I do feel they're entitled to a little bit of money. But not to what you might say almost double their profits. The gas companies got away with it 'cause the politicians were swimmin' in Watergate. That's all I've heard for a year is Watergate. An' frankly I think this Watergate deal is ruinin' our country. I'm not an educated man. Me, I didn't even finish high school. But I can watch television, I watch the news reports maybe Saturday evenin' an' Sunday evenin', an' I read the paper in the mornin' an' I can put the thing together.

These big people in Washington, they sit around there on their cans an' fool around with the Watergate rather than think about our economy, which is goin' all helter-skelter. Let those prices go up. They allowed this gas shortage, which I never believed in the first place.

A lotta folks come in here an' sit around, that's why I got so many chairs. They drink drinks an' talk about everythin'. They talk about the prices an' the way everythin' is goin' right now. "How'm I gonna make it? My salary hasn't gone up five percent, where the costa livin' has gone up so high." I see people come in here that's had their vacation. "Well, where didya go?" "I hadda stay home. I had no money to go nowhere." There's not a day goes by but there's people after people come in here complainin' about my prices. An' I flatly tell 'em I gotta figure my profits on around twenty percent, an' to me that's hardly enough to get by on. My average earnin's last few years has ranged from seventy-six to seventy-nine hundred. That's what I pay my taxes on. Prices are goin' up an' I don't like it, but what can I do? You take oil. In a two-week period, up a dollar an' four cents a case. Brake fluid, for instance. It's maybe ninety-some-odd cents a can, wholesale. A year ago I paid thirty cents for it. You take anti-freeze goin' up two hundred percent in a period of five months. I just don't know what people are gonna do, an' a little man like myself in a country station, he's in the middle. Right in the mid-dle. I'm the one that catches all the gripes. I can't blame 'em. But my attitude gotta be anybody come in here don' hafta take it. We sell all we can get. An' there you go.

Sometimes things seem crazy to me. I hafta account for every penny on my taxes an' the government spends it like it's goin' outta style. You take people that got money today. If a person's got any money, he's gonna invest it an' live off the interest of it, as high as interest rates got to be. If you had a hundred thousand dollars, you could live off of the interest. Live real good, I be-lieve. An' then I was talkin' to Mr. Murphy down at the bank, an' he was explainin' that people come in for loans an' he figures it out for 'em an' finds out they can't afford to live, let alone bor-row. Who knows what makes sense?

It's like the way the man told me it's his gas an' it's his busi-ness an' he don' hafta sell it to me. It's one of them kinda things you can't talk too much about. When the pinch comes again, I'd be completely left out in the cold. So I never have said anythin' derogatory about him, I've never called him no names. I've never said he was a crook. I never said he was a thief. I never said he done anythin' dishonest. The only thing I ever said was I don't think I was treated fair. You can't go through this world resentin' other people. Now that man he works like a dog. In what way I'm speakin' of work, I mean mentally. His work is in his head. He's made a lotta wise investments an' he sold his investments good an' did very profitable. But I'd say I've worked five times as hard. He doesn't hafta get out an' do his manual. I don't mind a job on the grease rack 'cause I'm standin' up. But when I put the gas in, where the gas tank is under the license plate, I get up sometimes after puttin' twenty gallons in an' I can hardly stand. Like I say, who knows what makes sense?

What I got is this garage here an' my house an' a plot out in the country where my folks are buried. I went out there yesterday an' mowed, I'd say, a hundred people's graves. Kept mowin' 'til I got through, an' I was so tired I could just hardly walk. I looked back an' said to myself, "Maybe God'll bless you for it." When we first started fixin' it up out there, you'd see nobody, maybe 'cept at Easter an' Christmas you'd see a few wreaths out there. Now there's wreaths all over the place. So I put my lawn mower in the back of the truck an' go out there. I'm wishin' that some way or other we could raise the money to have it mowed every week, or fix the tombstones just as clean as the edge of a cabinet. But there's only so much you can do. The missus says I'm foolish for doin' it. Maybe, but I feel like that place oughta be pretty. If you go out there, you'll see I started sump'n.

Woman's Work

I always keep tellin' him the money doesn't matter. He won't listen to me. He just keeps right on doin' the same thing. Ev'ry mornin', up at the cracka dawn, checkin' on this, checkin' on that, doin' his business. Maybe he'll be around at dinner time, but by supper he's so exhausted that it doesn't matter what I fix. He can't taste it anyway. So nothin' matters. I usedta try out all sortsa diff'rent recipes an' stuff like that, put on a new dress, or at least some lipstick. Now I don't bother. He's so tired he wouldn't notice. He's so worried he wouldn't care.

I feel guilty when I watch him workin' hisself to death. I try the best I can. I freeze a lotta corn an' butter beans, an' we get our poultry from the plant, an' I remember all my home economics classes from school, so I can make a lotta things most people hafta buy. But the bills keep gettin' bigger an' bigger. An' clothes. Not for us, just for the kids. You can't send your children out in the world lookin' like poor white trash. An' we hate to say no to them. How are they supposed to understand? But you hafta. That's why I never ask for anythin'. So he never hasta say no to me.

When we were younger, we had all kindsa plans. We looked at the people around us, at my father, at his father, killin' themselves, an' for what? For *what*? A bigger house? A new car? A vacation we never can take because he's too scared that somethin' might happen if he ever for one week left the business. There are a lotta widows in this town, an' some of 'em aren't so old either. Least they weren't when their husbands died. Strokes. Heart attacks. That's what gets 'em. Seems like the more successful a man is, the faster he goes. In some a' them cases, I blame those women. I think they drove their own husbands right into the grave. I honestly don't think I'm doin' that. I really try. But there's nothin' a woman can do when her man can't think of nothin' but his business, 'cept ask the Lord to keep him alive.

The Doctor: Charles Forrest Hawes

When I finished med school, I hadda graduate, come home, get married, take my state board examinations, all in ten days. Well, I went 'round to the dean, asked 'im if I could get off early 'n let 'em mail me my diploma. Said, "You can't do it. All of you hafta be there." Well, I looked around, found out that ol' Dr. Peterson, the one that checked up on us out there, was an easygoin' ol' boy. So I saw Alleycat Burgess. I said, "Alleycat, watcher got on while commencement is goin' on?" He said, "Not a thing, Hawes. Why?" I told 'm just what I was up against. He said, "What you can do, you goin' to get a beautiful cap'n gown t'fit me." Said, "I'm gonna get you your diploma 'n send it right to you. I'll getcha all fixed up."

Well, I got it. But once in a while I bump inta one a' the boys was there for graduation, says, "Hawes, if you'da just been a-watchin' your number, you'da gone right straight down through the floor. Ol' cuss got half lit an' had a big time." They didn't have any foolishness in that place, an' how he got off of it I don' know. Cut up, sho'nuff. Alleycat Burgess. Never have seen 'im since.

I got to thinkin' a while back that since I started practicin' in Rose Hill, I've put in more years 'n got to be older 'n anybody ever practiced here. There was one doctor here when I got started; that was Dr. R. L. Carr. Back then you get anyone cured of syphilis in two'r three years, you were doin' good. An' now, you take pneumonia. The first big change on the pneumonia deal was when sulfapyradine came around. I remember the first time I ever used it, I went out to see this woman. She was down visitin' her parents out 'bout three miles, out there on the George Boney farm. I went in, she had fever 'bout a hundred an' five, she was about gone. I had sulfapyradine in my bag, was gonna use it on the first one I had, an' I looked at her, said, "The Devil, she's gonna die anyway, I'll double the dose." I told her, if she died, to be sure'n let me know so I wouldn't hafta make an unnecessary call out there, an' then I said, "If I don' hear from you, I'll be back tomorra."

When I walked up on the porch, I rapped on the door, she hollered 'n said, "Come in." I looked over there an' it was like somebody dead talkin'. She said, "Dr. Hawes, I don't feel like I did yesterday." I said, "I'll be darned if you look like you did either." She didn't have any fever at all, an' that woman had been *sick*. Since then I haven't had any primary pneumonia cases die on me. Not one.

You stay 'round a place an' you get a chance to watch things a lot better'n you do where you're raised somewhere else an' you move in to practice. I've treated a number of families for generations, an' I already knew everybody 'round here before I ever started practicin'. Some families 'round here, practically all of 'em die off from heart attacks 'n strokes time they're forty-five years old. 'Course a lot more people live on in the bracket where they have strokes an' heart attacks than they used to. You see a lot of 'em check out that you'd like to see live a lot longer. You look around this town, a lot of men are dead 'n gone. You look at Main Street. All widows.

The mental defects you can follow right on down the line in a heck of a lotta cases. You see epilepsy, an' you see families where the insanity runs high. We have, by gosh, schizophrenics, paranoids, maniacs; we have everythin' in the book. We send most of 'em to Cherry Hospital an' we have a heck of a lotta alcoholics we send there. They did lobotomies for a right good while, just go up there in the front part, clip the tracks 'n so forth. I never did think too much of that. Your shock an' your tranquilizers, they're the main things. We have a mental health clinic at Kenansville. Anybody that hasta go to Cherry Hospital, we advise 'em to go to the clinic reg'lar. Some of them go maybe two, three times. That's all. Suicide, the percent you have among the colored people is much lower than white. I'd say we've had 'round a dozen people in thirty-nine years, an' I don' believe I've had but one colored. They always say if a colored person gets to worryin' 'bout somethin', he can sit down an' go to sleep. A white man'll keep on worryin'.

What needs to be done in the case of some of them people who go for generations on welfare, they should be sterilized an' not produce any more of that kind. Wherever there's a heavy tendency for epilepsy or insanity or severe arthritis, stuff like that, they should be sterilized. If you're gonna have children that's not healthy mentally or physically, you're bringin' somethin' in the world that's a deadweight on the taxpayers. Now I don't believe in abortion. If a person has reasons enough to have an abortion, they have reasons enough to have their tubes ligated so they'll be sterile forevermore. If they have health reasons, if it's gonna injure the mother's life, why that's a diff'rent thing. But just because somebody gets in a jam an' don' wanna have the baby, I don't think she should come an' get pregnant later on. I do my very best to get the tubes tied 'n what they call "bows," y'know, those intrauterine outfits, 'n pills 'n so forth. But you never get very far. They use 'em for a while, then they get careless 'n maybe they skip two or three times, or they don't have any pills left, so maybe they take Alka-Seltzer instead. First you know, they're comin' in pregnant again. I had one that was havin' her ninth baby, 'n I asked her was she ever married. She said, "No, suh," She said, "My Lawd, Dr. Hawes, I'm not even engaged."

Some a' these kids stand a good chance of 'em bein' just like their parents an' their grandparents. In one family not any of 'em can hardly talk. We oughta at the least think as much of 'em as we do our own cats, livestock, poultry. We're cullin' everythin' but the human race. But it'll never be done because of your so-called religious angle on it. That's not religion, that's just some darn foolishness, as the man said.

There's a whole lotta 'em roun' here that don't halfway raise their children right. You take a child, you can't get down an' raise 'im like a dev'lish pig or a dog. I'll tell you what I do with practically all of 'em with long hair, I run 'em out, say, "Boy, go out 'n get a haircut. I'll pay for it. Go out'n get your hair cut 'n look like a human bein' an' we'll do some medicine." I'll tell you what I'd do with one a' mine 'fore I'd let 'em grow their hair that way. I'd take one a' my bulldogs, say, "Go get 'im, Spike," an' I'd grab aholda 'im 'n proceed to cut his hair. Right now any of the four a' mine, they'll tell you that the most I've ever done for 'em is teach 'em the necessity of work 'n how to work, then teach 'em how the dollar comes an' how it should go. I would have paid somebody ten dollars a day to work mine for nothin', rather 'n have 'em walk the streets of Rose Hill an' not do a darn thing.

I guess I'm like my daddy. If he told me to stay away from certain people, an' so forth, I knew enough that I'd better do it, an' I don't remember him ever tellin' me wrong. I enjoyed livin', as far as that goes, but insteada goin' tomcattin' aroun', catchin' lotta venereal disease 'n stuff like that, I wasn't the best person in the world, but let me tell you, I was the most scared.

That storkin' is right powerful work. I'll tell you the truth about it. I've been deliverin' babies as much as twenty years, an' I've delivered ten thousand of 'em an' I catch myself when they're havin' pain, I'll be pushin' down the devil myself. It's fascinatin'. I don't spend as much money gettin' things ready, havin' 'em draped nice the way they do in hospitals, an' so forth, but by gosh I can keep things sterile where they don't get any infection. An' I'm way ahead a most of 'em when it comes to that stillbirth/live birth ratio. There's a diff'rence between readin' about it an' gettin' out here an' doin' the real thing.

I deliver two colored ones every time I do one white, an' I hold the price down to a hundred fifty dollars. If you get out an' ask any colored person comes along if Dr. Hawes gives the colored people a square deal, why, they'll tell you, "He's our best friend." I have my reception rooms just like I've always had 'em an' I have some good reasons. If I had a colored person to be out there an' they got there before a white one, there's some whites'll wanna try'n get in ahead of 'im an' you get a lotta trouble. I think I understand their situation an' I think I understand the Negro race, an' I believe they understand me to a great extent. I'll tell you about 'em. They need a lotta help. They're diff'rent people entirely. I don' care what you do, what education, money, religion, what not, he's got somethin' in him you're not goin' to be able to get outta him. We always got along real good. An' I'll tell you what I had thought 'bout doin' for several years 'n I'm liable to do it yet, is close the place here'n go to Africa an' do medical missionary work. I'm not prejudiced. But I'm not gonna squabble 'bout keepin' my reception rooms the way they gonna be. When anybody comes along an' tells me I've gotta make just one room, I'll quit doctorin'.

A man doesn't get rich practicin' medicine. Not the way I practice. I have several thousand patients an' I work about fifteen hours a day. I usually start out nine o'clock, get outta the office twelve, twelve-thirty, make home calls an' go back an' open the office again from two-thirty to six. Then I go out'n do some more visitin'. My fee varies, sometimes five dollars, sometimes three, sometimes a little more, dependin' on the trouble an' if I hafta go way outta town. 'Course I got my hand in some other things. Me an' my son, Charlie, he's my oldest, we've got a coupla thousand acres a' timberland, coupla hundred acres a' blueberries, run 'bout forty thousand chickens every eight to ten weeks. I raise some bobwhites an' Japanese quail an' pheasants. I don' know whether I have the birds or the birds have me. An' I breed Siamese an' Russian Blues, got one tomcat I paid for in Germany. An' then I have some pit bulldogs, go along with the cats.

My wife says I should go a slower pace, but it's hard to do. A lotta trouble with my work is you can't never tell what's goin' to happen. If I'm gonna be outta town, I gets holda Dr. Matthews an' tell 'im to be on the lookout. One time one a' the preachers was a buddy of mine, we had it all planned to go fishin'. An' turned out everyone was away—Dr. Matthews, Dr. Owens, an' all the other preachers. So he said, "Well, Doc, guess we can't go." I said, "Pshaw. Sure we can go. We'll just let 'em all die an' go to hell."

But serious, now, I just can't stop. I get off every two years for ten days or two weeks an' go an' visit my married daughter in Germany. An' I get itchin' to get back. Then I go fishin' 'bout twice a year out in the Gulf Stream, an' I try to sorta sneak down to the beach 'bout once a week, just for a coupla hours. Sunday is always a day for me to get a little rest an' battle with my headaches. They never come along when I'm tired, workin' like the devil, but when Sunday rolls around, that's when I can look out. Reckon the Lord made me like he did a colored person an' a mule. He didn't intend for any of us to get any rest.

The type of work I've done I feel like there was a necessity for it. I've really enjoyed it the most of anythin' in my life. I was thinkin' I'd probably go back an' take a residency in Ob-Gyn, but the money was hard to get back then durin' the Depression, so insteada bein' here two years, I've been here forty-one, an' I'll be here 'til I croak, far's I know. I think I've done as much good as I coulda done anywhere, an' I think on the whole people appreciate it, too. Lotta these boys comin' outta school now, they want bankers' hours. They don't get down an' work hard. They have a right-eye specialist, a left-eye specialist, a right-ear specialist, a left-ear specialist. If I'd a' gone on to a larger place, not known people as well, I would never have enjoyed watchin' a lotta families, a lotta diff'rent types a' sickness an' so forth, an' just everythin' about 'em. The way it follows along, it's right interestin'. I guess I'm just a diff'rent breed.

The Farmer: Tom Knowles

Somebody is gonna wake up one mornin' an' want sump'n t'eat an' there ain't gonna be nobody around to give it to 'im. The little farmers they used to have twenty acres of land an' make a good livin' off of it. Now three quarters of 'em are leavin' the farms. Things are gettin' too high someways, an' the farmer just ain't gettin' enough outta the deal.

The farm was my dad's, an' now my brother an' I we farm it together. We grow tobacco, corn'n soybeans, an' we raise chickens. The main crop is tobacco, but the corn'n soybeans supplement my income. We sell the corn to diff'rent mills around here. We have two of our own chicken houses an' two of my dad's an' we grow 'em out for Mister Nash Johnson. They started to cut back about December, an' it can hurt this area real bad because a lotta people still owe for buildin' their houses an' things. We are lucky enough to have ours paid for. But there are too many people in the middle makin' a profit. We get seven cents for raisin' the chicken, they get 'im from the processin' plant an' put 'im in the meat market an' they'll make ten or fifteen cents off each chicken. Nash is supposed to be makin' a profit, an' he's got an absolute right to make sump'n, an' he's losin'. It ain't his fault the way things are goin'. I feel like if there is any way he can, he will still help us out an' give us more chickens to raise. I dunno who is makin' all the money, the merchants maybe. It don't seem fair to me.

It's been bad for tobacco this year counta the rain. The market is better'n it usedta be. I've hearda people gettin' a dollar per pound an' last year I believe it was about ninety-five cents per pound. But the cost of fertilizer is goin' up so much, won't get as much out of it as last year's. We sell all our tobacco in Fairmont, about ninety to a hundred miles from here. They wouldn't give us enough floor space in the warehouse down in Wallace. It usedta be you could go there an' say you want so much space, you want space for twenty piles. Now they have some kinda rulin', designated or whatever they call it, an' I don' understand it. I think a grower from Duplin County should have priority, but it don't work that way. So a friend of ours he has a large truck an' he just hauls it an' he knows when to carry it on the floor an' when it will be sold an' things like that. That way we don't hafta worry about it. You hafta have connections to sell tobacco.

I've enjoyed farmin'. I like the independence of it, but I never had a choice. When I was goin' to school, I was left-handed, an' the teachers wouldn't take much time with me, helpin' me write an' things like that, so I never got past the sixth grade. I think I done mighty good with whatever education I had, because we got two trucks an' a car an' a pickup truck, an' I even bought a car for my son. Last year we were lucky enough to get ahead where we didn't hafta borrow this year. We are goin' a whole lot better 'n we ever have. You gotta get on your feet. We've been crawlin' a long time.

Our land has been in the family for three generations, an' I do feel attached to it, so I'll leave the land to my son an' he can do what he wants to. I'll say, "Son, you can take it over if you want." And he might work some for a year or two an' decide he wants to go back to the farm. He can do it now if he wants to. Maybe he will. But he's finishin' high school an' he's got a whole lot better education than I got. An' seems like he oughta do a whole lot better'n I done.

The Boss: L. T. Connally*

The unions got too much power, that's a fact. There's two sides of it. There's nothin' gets to be as big as the unions got to be that hasn't got sump'n good about it. That's just common sense. But you see 'em things get so big until too much money an' too much power are gonna put things over that shouldn't be put over. In other words, I don't think that a union should have a say in who should go to Washington to represent us. There's such a thing as havin' too much privilege an' not knowin' how to use it.

I think anybody can have honor enough to do what he says he'll do without havin' a contract with somebody that works with him. If you wanna work for me an' you are satisfied, whadda I care 'bout some man in New York bein' satisfied. If I offend one of the people that's workin' for me, I'd never see him. If I can't be close to the people I'm workin' with, who can? I can do more for the people workin' for me than any union you can find.

The way it is now, there's no trouble in this country gettin' employment. I don't know of anybody wants a job that can't get one. The way my thinkin' is, the way to protect yourself, if I don't treat you decent, go to somebody that will. But don't you go out an' pay some outsiders, some union, to make me decent. Who made the union people as rich as they are? The poor people that need the money. That's made 'em rich, filthy rich. When you tell a man to give you justice an' he's gettin' rich an' you poor, where you startin'? Are you gettin' anywhere?

92

I got the responsibility of my people to a certain extent. It's up to them what they wanna do. That's their privilege. But I'd like for 'em to know what they're gettin' into. A lotta people hear one side of a thing an' don't hear the other. If there is sump'n that I think isn't good for 'em, an' I know it isn't good for 'em, I think I should explain. They got their own mind. But I don't think nobody that works for me is gonna join a union because of me mistreatin' 'em. An' I really don't think the way I treat my people an' the attitude they have toward me an' the attitude I have towards them, that a union could be useful to 'em.

I told that to the union people. I went an' actually met with one a' them. An' I told 'em, "My people are loyal to me. And I'm loyal to them." I said, "If they wanna be unionized, you go down there an' unionize 'em." Said, "If they want it, let 'em have it. But just don't push it on 'em. I think they oughta have a choice." An' I think the people gonna know which way to choose. When you see people goin' union, they're harmin' themselves a whole lot more than they're harmin' the man that runs the business. What can the union do to help them people? Nothin'.

4 Learnin'

"Just because a kid has a high school diploma, that's not any assurance of a bed of roses somewhere."

—Neal Carlton

Open Classroom: Frances Bostic

There have been three elementary schools in Rose Hill, an' I have had the opportunity to teach in all three of them. I taught two years of kindergarten in the old Rose Hill One, which was an old buildin', but I loved it. It was a fire hazard, I'll admit that, but maybe because I was a part of the school I couldn't really see what was wrong. When we started to integrate, even before the school finally burned, the kindergarten department was moved out to Rose Hill Two, which had been the black school over across the railroad. The first year I got all the problem boys. They got modelin' clay stuck in their noses an' got hit on the head. You name it, we had it. I had a black teacher's aide an' we had a wonderful workin' relationship, but then Mr. Johnson, the principal, took her away from me after a month an' put her to workin' with the first grade an' left me with a dropout from high school. That was a hectic year, that first year, but it was certainly a useful experience. We moved into the new buildin', Rose Hill-Magnolia, in nineteen seventy-two an' began a completely open classroom program. It seems to be workin' fine, except there are so many children in here it is sometimes hard to find out just how much they are gettin' out of it.

In our suite we have kindergarten, first, an' second grade, or, as we're supposed to say, five-, six-, and seven-year-olds. Each child works accordin' to his ability, and of course they are not all matured alike. I don't know if it's intelligence or environment or both, but by the time they get into the fourth-grade level, we have a large number of educable mentally retarded children. So it is necessary for us to have two special EMR teachers just in this school alone. Of course we don't have any *correct* readin' level for the five-year-olds when they start out. We just hope we can get them started with the desire to read. But last year most of the sixes an' sevens were below their readin' level, an' if you talk with sixth- and seventh-graders, you'll find their readin' is about the second grade. Some of it might have to do with intelligence, but I do think a lot of it is environment. Parents are workers in Duplin County, and they have to work extra jobs to make ends meet and they have other problems. A lot of them even try to change the birth certificates just to get their children in school earlier, to have a baby-sitter. They don't care how long it takes them to get outta school or anythin'. They just want to get the children away from home. An' then the parents are so busy they don't have time to read to the children when they are little. Maybe that's why we don't have many readers. If you read to a child when he is small, he will have the desire later on.

About ten years ago the federal government started a kinder-garten program in North Carolina. That is a program for the economically and educationally deprived. The importance of this is that in order to qualify for the federal program, you must have a majority of disadvantaged families. So before school starts we interview the children just to see if they know their colors or parts of the body, how many hands they have, their mental maturity, things like that. But we also have to ask the parents questions. Of course we don't actually have to ask about salary, but we can tell if they have TVs or record players, all of those advantages. We aren't supposed to have more than ten percent of the higher-income families, an' Rose Hill has always had more then enough of the deprived to qualify.

When we moved into this new school, we all went in under the open classroom system. Actually, ever since we integrated and some of us moved over to the old Rose Hill Two school, the kindergarten has never really been closed. We would all get together anyway for our films and for our music, an' so the change has not been too difficult. The only problem I have found has been with the age levels because, for example, last year they had me workin' with some seven-year-olds when I felt that I had to be more with the slow five-year-olds. I think you have to pay very specific attention to the problems of the children who need your time.

We have learnin' centers where they learn things like coordination an' concentration. The five-year-olds use three fingers in lacin' beads an' things that will then help 'em hold a pencil later on. They have puzzles and there are also games that are especially for concentration. Then we have listenin' centers with earphones, so that if anybody wants to listen to the television, they can plug it in without disturbin' the other children. I always encourage the children to keep tryin' new things. Basically they select their own activities.

I sometimes feel if I were in my own classroom, I could accomplish more. When the school was planned, they didn't ask the teachers what we needed, an' there are some silly little problems. We have rollin' coat closets, an' I'd much rather have hooks because all the children can't get their coats in there at one time, so all the clothes end up on the floor. We are fortunate that we have a great deal of equipment: the tape recorder, the cassette, the record player, the filmstrip projector and the film projector. There is a *Gateway to Reading* filmstrip series which is very good. To tell you the truth, we have more material than I can possibly get around to, just in the library which belongs to the kindergarten. The equipment is wonderful, but they have spent millions of dollars buyin' it an' really they should have asked us first. There's a viewer which goes with a little math kit that you can show with a tape. It looks like a little television. Unfortunately, mine is broken, so I haven't used it in the last couple of years. I keep puttin' it in the workroom with all the broken things, but it's still not fixed.

Once in a while somebody comes in an' asks, "How many white children do you have; how many black children?" I have to stop an' count. I really don't know. Believe it or not, you don't think about color anymore. We have one big family, an' though I'll admit it gets like bedlam at times, I get a great deal of fun outta teachin', or I wouldn't have been doin' it for sixteen years. When the children start school, they are missin' their mothers for the first time, an' they will come with any little thing to be hugged or to be loved. It's very important an' I pity anyone who is coldhearted toward a kindergarten child. The first teacher makes the most impression, so I hope I've given every little child I've had a desire to learn an' improve. When children learn anythin' new, their faces brighten up an' it's very rewardin'. Last year, when they would see me workin' with another group, they would come over an' whisper, "You come an' work with *me*, Miz Bostic." "I will in just a minute, sugar. I'll get to you." They wanted to work. An' that was very pleasin' to me. I don't want to be structured. I never make 'em sit down. We have problems an' things, but we don't send children to the principal. We settle them right in our own room. We figure if we cannot conquer a five-, six-, or seven-year-old child, an' let him know we deserve his respect, then we shouldn't be in the classroom. You can reach a lotta children more by love than you can by punishment. An' when I talk with a child about a problem an' we whisper about it, it seems to last a whole lot longer than a tap on the bottom.

"Freedom of Choice": Evelyn Chasten

Three days after I graduated from Fayetteville State, I started to teach at ol' Rose Hill Two on the other side of the highway. I was teachin' kingergarten an' we were under the ESEA Title One, which was for disadvantaged children, an' all I can tell you is that ESEA sure bought a lotta unnecessary stuff. We had what you call "supplementary books" that the children couldn't read an' all sortsa googobs of toys an' paint an' paper, an' that was it. Well, the kindsa children we were teachin' weren't even ready for school. In most cases the parents were farmers, an' more 'n likely the lady in the family was workin'. So you spent half the year teachin' the children how to tie their shoes, fix their clothes, try to teach 'em to recognize their names, things like that, things that a lotta children would have had at home. They learned to recognize the alphabet. Mostly we tried to develop their attention span 'cause their attention spans were very short, an' we took 'em to different places in the community an' around. Really, sometimes you would think it was just a baby-sittin' job.

Durin' that time we were supposed to be integratin', but really what it was was "freedom of choice." Some blacks, a few of 'em, were sendin' their children to the white schools, an' the whites weren't sendin' any of their children to the black schools. Then the schools were divided. Grades one, two three an' four went to the Rose Hill Two, the black school, an' five, six an' seven went to the one that burned down near the highway. Well, everyone was wonderin' where we would hafta work. Teachers were bein' shifted around an' people didn't know where they would be goin'. What happened to me was that when I first started workin', they told me there was a possibility that I could get a grammar grade because I have a grammar certificate, but I ended up with kindergarten. Then, durin' my second year, the children really got on my nerves, an' I told them I didn't want kindergarten anymore. To make a long story short, the people who were doin' the hirin' said that since I had said I wasn't goin' to teach kindergarten, there were no jobs available, or somethin' like that. Well, there was an NAACP lawyer, an' I got in touch with him an' called over to the office at Kenansville, an' somehow they assigned me to a school by six o'clock that evenin'. They were still tryin' to get that sixty percent white/forty percent black ratio, so they sent me to teach in Chinquapin, an' I been there ever since. It's funny because when I graduated from high school, I didn't really want to be a teacher, but I did want to go to school an' then come back an' live an' work in Rose Hill. In those days there was only one thing for me to do. Go to college, an' come back here an' start teachin'. So now I'm livin' in Rose Hill an' drivin' back an' forth to Chinquapin.

There are three of us teachin' all subjects: readin', writin', arithmetic, language, math, science, history, physical education—in other words, basically the whole curriculum for third grade. The children are divided into groupin's, an' we alternate so that each of us will have each group for each subject durin' the run of the year. Each child has what you call a "contract," a kinda study plan which is based on the activities that child can do at his own rate. You give a child a contract accordin' to his ability, startin' with the second grade. So at the end of the year one child might have completed one grade, while another might be almost a grade ahead or behind. Each year you start teachin' the child in the beginnin's of the year where he left off. So if he was readin' in the second-grade reader, you start him off where he stopped the previous year, even if he's in the third grade. In our program we have the first three grades, an' if a child hasn't achieved a certain level, we request that he stay another year. But you cannot keep a child in primary grades one, two, three for over four years, so if he hasn't completed his work in that time, he goes on to the next level anyway. The problem is that for the child who is motivated enough to work on his own, this is fine, but contracts don't motivate or help the slow children that well. The contracts were designed so that the child that's accelerated won't hafta wait for the slow ones, an' the slow ones don't feel the pressure of havin' to keep up. We let them work on their contract until they complete it. An' we don't check anythin' wrong. We let the child put a circle around it, an' after he has found out what he did wrong, then he is to go back an' get it right. That's better 'n tellin' 'im. The three of us work as a team, an' we'll give tests an' discuss the child's classroom participation an' try to see if he's workin' at his level before we decide to retain 'im or pass 'im on. If the child has a low IQ, you can't expect 'im to do much, an' there's nothin' left to do but for 'im to go on. The chances are that he will learn more bein' with his peers.

In our teachin' team two of us are black an' one white, an' we never had any problems. There are differences between us in the way we approach things, but that is because there are differences in our own life experiences. Personally speakin', I don't think a white teacher takes as much time with a slow black child, an' really, they are the same way with the slow whites. They haven't got the patience. I think black teachers have a different attitude. When I first started to teach, I wanted to work with handicapped children because I wasn't a smart child myself, an' I know how it is. The things I liked I'd study for, but the things I didn't like I didn't. I got a C in science in the seventh grade, an' I never have liked science since. All children are like that. The one thing they can do, that's what they wanna do. An' the problem with the black child is that he is often limited in what he can do because of his background.

That really is something we hafta deal with. You tend to find more black children on a lower level than you do whites. I'm not sayin' we don't have blacks on a higher level, too, but we don't have as many, an' all of that stems from their background, from

102

those first six years. I don't like to say this but blacks don't provide enough meaningful experiences for their children in their early years. Of course a lot of that depends on the economic status of the family. Now television has done much, an' the cars, to change things for the black kids, but in general in this area there's not that many blacks have taken their children to Disneyland, or even educational places that're here an' easy for 'em to get to. And then, everything is presented in relation to the *white* experience. You can look at all the television you want to, but one of the reasons that people my age went into teachin', for example, is that the only contact we had with what you might call the "professional black" was preachers and teachers. We were isolated. An' that was only a coupla years ago. We didn't see blacks doin' a variety of things on television. Now that's changed somewhat. The materials are changin'. But up until about three years ago you didn't have any books with stories that a black child could associate with his experience. I mean, take readin' a story about goin' out to dinner. Black parents don't take their children out to real dinners. They go to Hardy's an' McDonald's. The whites take summer vacations with the family. The blacks are generally workin' in tobacco. That's why I'm tryin' to provide some of those experiences for my son. He's only fourteen months old, an' he probably won't remember any of the things I do with him now, but I'd like things to be easier for him than they were for me. I've already taken him to the zoo. I didn't go to a zoo before I was twenty years old.

There's been no problem with the children, an' if the older people would leave everythin' alone, we'd be fine. There is more than just color. A lotta people object to the new way of teachin'. They want you to teach their child the way they were taught, an' they don't understand that we have guidelines. We teach accordin' to the way we're told. You need to educate the parents first. About everythin'. The children would learn more if the parent would come to school an' not the child. I don't think that education has had a social effect on the primary children. After school hours we don't find that many black an' white children are playin' together. Just like you don't find many blacks an' whites socializin' after work. I don't think that's so important. What *is* important is that you hafta have some understandin'.

103

In some situations I can relate more to the black kids because I'm black. Usually I have no trouble relatin' to the whites, but when I feel like I'm not, I always ask Arlene, the white teacher, to come over because she can do better in that particular situation. We try to teach the children that you come out better if you say "black" because you gonna make a mess if you say "Negro." Sure, kids are aware of differences. We have a few cases where one'll call the other a nigger, an' some of 'em'll be tellin' jokes that show some prejudice. But that's very seldom. You work things out. They can help you as much as you can help them. You know, I didn't even know why a fawn had spots. I didn't. Well, I found out it's for camouflage. One of the little boys had gone huntin' with his father an' he told me. That was excitin' to me. So you see, things happen slowly. It'll change.

Education is goin' to make a very big difference. Speakin' personally, I can just imagine how my life would have been any other way. My father quit school in the sixth grade, an' he always told us, when we were smaller, he said, "The reason I work like I do is so that you will have it better than I had it, an' you can work an' let your children have it better'n you." I think he's very proud. I was the first in my family to go to college. Then there was my sister. She graduated from Fayetteville State in sixty-nine an' she's workin' for State Employment in Brooklyn. My brother's a sophomore there now, plannin' to major in political science. An' then I have a younger sister that'll be a junior in high school this year, and she's got so much freedom she hasn't even made up her mind what she plans to do or where she's goin'. That's what I mean about things an' how they change.

One thing bothers me. There isn't much standin' up for rights here. But I'll tell you. When they freed us from slavery, a lotta people looked to the preacher an' the teacher for leadership. An' if you had a weak one, you didn't get anythin'. Well, it's still that way. Things were a whole lot better when Mister Windsor Johnson was principal of the Rose Hill Two school. He's a man that is not gonna take no for an answer. Before we integrated, we had the PTA an' we had great attendance, an' he was there to show us the techniques you need to apply to a situation. When he retired, we really lost somethin'.

Sometimes I say, "Well, I'm a teacher, I have a special responsibility." An' one time it mighta been thought that teachers were better'n other people. But I really feel like I'm just a person. I mean, everybody wants the same things outta life. Some just want to do it a different way than others. It's my first responsibility to show that teachers are human. So that has been my decision. We all want the same thing. We all want to live.

The Principal: Neal M. Carlton

When the Negro kid came to my school, I felt that he should have the same opportunity as any other kid. This is the road I've tried to take all this time. The people that really had to bear the brunt of this problem were the principals an' the administrations. It didn't worry me that much, to tell the truth. When we first had "freedom of choice" in Wallace Elementary School, six Negro kids came into a school that had eight hundred whites in it. Now when this was gonna happen, practically every friend I had in town said, "It'll happen over my dead body. They will not set foot in *our* school." But didn't anythin' happen. They came.

At that time I had a little battle with the KKK. I was threatened by the KKK because I punished a kid for doin' somethin' wrong to a black kid. It went all the way to the top, to Shelton. Shelton advised the father of this particular white kid to start his proceedin's, whatever they were supposed to be. But anyway, nothin' ever happened.

My first year at Wallace-Rose Hill there was total integration among the freshmen. At that time we had ninth, tenth, eleventh and twelfth. Then the followin' year they made us into a senior high school an' they made the formerly all Negro school in Charity into a junior high. An' then we were totally integrated. It had its moments, I should say.

When we started out, naturally the black kids who came here from the formerly Negro high school didn't know me, or what kinda treatment they were goin' to get. An' they were very leery, stood off, waited, watched. It was very peaceful because we had student meetin's with representatives from both student bodies an' with our faculty. We called these meetin's workshops, or

105

seminars, an' we had about sixty students from each school. The schools picked the students. I felt it might help if they knew me and a portion of the faculty an' if we knew a portion of the student body. Basically it did because we have never had but very few problems here as far as integration is concerned.

I'll never forget durin' the first year, two or three carloads of white kids came by my house, two o'clock in the mornin'. Made about three or four trips by there. But this didn't get me uptight. I could have almost told you by name everyone that was out there in those cars. I never mentioned it, never said anythin' about it. I knew who they were. I knew what they thought. I knew how they felt. An' there we go back to heritage, deep-seated things. But the change that's taken place in the typical Southerner, these people that said, "Freedom of choice, over my dead body." All right. When we got to the point: "you've *got* to integrate," "No, *sir*. No, *sir. Never do that. Freedom of choice is fine."* You see what I mean? They changed. "Yes. We'll do *this,* we'll do *this,* but don't put *this* on us." We're laggin', yes, we're laggin' but the change is takin' place.

In every kid's life he has had influence on him. I guess I had influences on me from my earliest moments. I came from a Christian home. My mother died when I was five an' my mother was a devout Christian. I was always taught to respect another human bein'. My mother never said to me that I was just to respect whites. We lived in a farm in Warsaw. I worked behind a mule. There were Negro kids at that time that worked with me. They lived on the place as sharecroppers. I can only say that I'm an average Southerner; I am not ashamed of it. I don't know as I'm so proud to be a Southerner, but I'm not ashamed. I'm not a traditionalist. When I say "traditionalist," I'm talkin' about the real hard-core—"keep the nigger in his place" kinda thing. We're all prejudiced. I read somethin' the other day: the trick is not to discriminate in our prejudiced feelin's. Think what you will, but don't discriminate.

I feel it's workin'. Probably the best example is the firecracker in the locker room this mornin'. Okay. This is goin' to hit the streets. The word of it. All right. Now before it's through, we had a bombin' here, you see. A time bomb. An' this is the way things spread.

This is my twenty-first year in school work. An' needless to say, in any school I've ever been in, there've been fights. But since integration, if you have a fight in school, it's a terrible thing. They don't want to find out what the reason is. Nobody seems to understand what a black an' a white kid could fight over the same thing that two white kids used to fight over. Maybe it's a pencil. Maybe somebody dropped a nickel an' they argue about whose it is. It's not because it's black an' white. It has nothin' to do with race. But we have people here in the community that would like to see it not work, an' I think they're a little upset because it's workin'.

In the lunchroom we actually have two lines, a white line an' a black line, but it's their own choosin'. By an' large the blacks sit at tables together, the whites sit at tables together. In classrooms they kinda divide there if the teacher doesn't sit them alphabetically. We have three groups. I don't know how to describe this, except I think every senior high has the same three groups. We have the black, the white an' the hippie. They rarely ever mix, any of these groups. I can only describe it this way: people mingle with those that they have things in common with. There are many various little groups here of four, five, six; they're close friends. They play together, an' naturally everybody else is an outsider. There's maybe a group that consists of six or eight girls. Where you see one, you see 'em all. An' they're together every free minute they have. They're plannin' their little parties an' this an' that an' the other. I don't look at it necessarily as a racial thing. When we were not integrated, it depended on which side of the tracks you lived on, and your problems came from difference between these groups. I'm inclined to think that most of the problems, maybe even throughout the country, is basically, an' maybe always has been, the haves against the have-nots, be it black, white or green. It doesn't make any difference. Class, or caste, is what we have.

We've been close to the Negro in the South, closer than in the North. Well, we talk, "Keep 'im in his place," an' all this, but basically speakin', the families that really cared anythin' had a desire to help anybody in need. I'm reminded of a joke of the southern Negro that got fed up. He couldn't get the price for his crops that a white man could, he couldn't go here, he couldn't go there, an' he heard all these glorious stories about the North. The money is flowin' like milk an' honey. An' so he goes up North. An' he's goin' to get him a job an' then ask his family to come up an' join him. Well, several months passed, no job available. Now this is not a true story, it's a joke, an' it illustrates a point I'm tryin' to bring out. He couldn't get a job, he's hungry, he's cold. Finally he's so depressed he resorts to goin' from door to door, beggin' for food. He's in a fairly nice-lookin' community. He knocks on a door. An' they look an' see 'im an' then the door slams in his face. Goes to the next door. Gets the same treatment. Third door. Same treatment. Finally he gets to this one door. The door opens an' this fella looks out and says, "You black SOB, you get to the back door where you belong." Well, he didn't run away. He was goin' to feed 'im, you see. He was goin' to feed him. The Negro commented, "Home at last."

The point is that with all this man's prejudice, he was still basically willin' to help an individual. We shout all these things, an' I doubt if in the South we even mean them. I'm sure there's prejudice here, there's discrimination, there's everythin' here there is anywhere else. But I think there is a softenin' and I think this softenin' is takin' place faster than in the North.

This generation now, an' I'm talkin' about the middle class, or upper, an' their wall-to-wall carpet, air conditionin', two cars in the garage an' plenty of food. They were brought into the world that way. They don't know an' could care less probably how mama an' daddy got it an' all the sweatin' they did to get it. See, basically we all desire things better for our children than we had. When I talk to my kids about my days on the farm an' how I plowed with-the mule, it's not relevant to them. They don't see any mules now. Everythin's a tractor, or it's mechanized. So I really can't get through to them. They came up with what they see, an' they feel like it will always be this way.

It's peaceful. We have six hundred fifty students. Nice an' small. I really wouldn't like bein' in a large school. I enjoy knowin' my students an' bein' able to call a student by his first name. Since I've been here I've had two cases of people takin' drugs of any kind. Well, I don't know it was drugs, but it was awfully suspicious. An' I guess I'm that much like everyone else, I'm kinda like an ostrich: put my head in the sand an' hope it will go away. At least we don't have the problem here at Wallace-Rose Hill to the extent that it shows. I'm not fool enough to say that drugs aren't used. A kid could go out there an' smoke some marijuana an' probably never be discovered. So I'm sure that more is used than I know. But there again, a small community, we're the last ones it gets to. An' it's gotta grow. Like all cancers, this will grow, too.

There's a feelin' now among kids, there's a runnin' away. I don't know how far the pendulum will swing. "I want to get on with what I'm gonna do for life. I don't wanna mess around with four-year college. All this liberal arts stuff is for the birds. I could care less what Shakespeare does if I'm gonna build bridges. So I'll go somewhere where I can learn to build bridges. And I don't need to know how to talk fancy. I just want to know how to build bridges and the things that make me a good bridge builder." So we have a distinct movin' away from the liberal arts. I'm not sure this is good. Don't like to see it.

We are not basically a comprehensive high school. Maybe we like to say we are, but we're not. We're not reachin' the needs of those kids an' I know it. Money, taxes, everythin' else. We have the same problem anywhere else does. Since I've come we've added courses like automotive mechanics, carpentry, draftin', industrial cooperative trainin', forestry. Specialization is what we're comin' to. Because when we turn a bricklayer out here, he's ready to go out there an' get a job. He'll be an apprentice for a while, but he does a good job. So therefore he can learn a livin' for his family. An' maybe that's what it's all about. Have a person where he can survive in this world. An' if you don't make it on the paycheck, you're not goin' to survive very well.

We're movin' in that direction, because right now when you sit down to apply for a job, they say, "What can you do?" An' you answer, "I have a high school diploma."

"Well, that's not what I asked you. What can you do?"

"Well, I was good in English, pretty good in math."

"That's not what I asked you. What can you do?"

When you get right down to it, the high school diploma, what does it mean? We've got to take another look. Just because a kid has a high school diploma, that's not any assurance of a bed of roses somewhere, you know. Or because he has a college degree;

109

that's not either. "What can you do?" And he better find an answer to that question.

Nowadays the people in my profession, many, many, many, are gettin' out. The problems are tremendous. When you have a locker blown up in your school hall, an' when you have a hundred-forty-somethin' dollars missin' out of the school office, these are things some people can't seem to cope with. But when you get right down to it, theft an' pranks have been with us all the time. So I think, "What are we put here for anyway?" I believe it's meant to be a struggle. It must be. To survive we must struggle. And maybe this is all part of it, the philosophies that an individual takes. Why should I let this run me out?

Three o'Clock in the Morning: Jimmy Bowden

In my classroom I've got a poster that was a key theme last year. The motto on the poster says, "Meet someone halfway. To communicate is the beginning of understanding." And I told my bunch that if they came outta that class an' if they hadn't improved in head an' heart, no matter what they had learned factually, we had missed the boat. That idea doesn't appeal to everyone. All we're interested in now is accountability. We're interested in seein' results. We have standardized tests. The time is comin' in which everythin' is goin' to be so lockstep in education that, here, it's Monday, we're supposed to be *here*, not *there*. We better fly right through "The Love Song of J. Alfred Prufrock" an' give it a lick an' a promise. We're all goin' to use the same texts. They're all goin' to get a taste of *Beowulf*. Well, fine. You can water that down, or you don't hafta go into all the concepts of the tragic hero or destiny an' fate an' all that. It can be a good adventure story. But if you're gonna produce kids who can think an' analyze an' change with the future an' get a little joy outa life, then they need literature. Not just Shakespeare for Shakespeare's sake. But if a test is made up an' it's gonna cover particular technical material an' it kills it for 'em. The impression I'm gettin' is that it doesn't matter about the kids themselves at all.

If you wanna talk about tragedy, you go right through some a' these streets here an', man, we've got it. You don't hafta read Shakespeare to see it in front of you. The kids in the area need to be involved. So many of 'em are gonna be workin' at humdrum jobs the rest of their lives. They're gonna grow old before their time. An' they're the ones who could be reachin' for somethin', who could read somethin' that would get them through. Sure, you spend eight hours doin' this particular thing. But if I'm a whole individual, I can still hack it. I can do that an' then, in my own time, I can grow as a person. What if he doesn't have anythin' but dirty diapers, small paycheck, a car that won't half run. Or s'pose he's blessed with a whole lotta money. That's the same thing. Money won't buy happiness. I'm not sayin' that the basics aren't important. Capitalization an' punctuation are important. And they've gotta be taught that. But what good does it do these kids to spend a year teachin' 'em somethin' that's easy to test because it's easy to grade?

Doris Betts, who is in charge of the Freshman English program at Chapel Hill, wrote an interestin' article, an' she pointed out that the thing that bothers her is not so much the students' writin', grammar an' so forth, 'cause usually it's very correct. But it's sterile. They don't have anythin' to say. It becomes Eng*fish* instead of Eng*lish*. An' this is what so many kids write. They write Eng*fish*. It's dead. It stinks. It's floppy. It has no life at all. It's because they're not turned-on people, for one thing. They're carbon copies. They're gonna give you pretty much what they think you want. They haven't really learned how to see or hear or taste or touch or smell. They sorta drift. They're not really turned on, in that sense. Okay, this is a poor area. An' a lotta kids hafta work. Sometimes it's a case of survival, an' that job hasta come first. So first things first. All right. Let's prepare 'em for a job. An' then let's hope in the future, in the next generation, say, learnin' will be for learnin's sake, to add a little joy to life.

But so many of the kids want to take the easy way. It's a lot more excitin' to sit at the Dairio an' watch all the cars ride around than it is to read a book. You can see it in their writin'.

111

It's pretty dull. There was one fascinatin' one this year called "The Trouble with Goldfish," but the problem is that they don't write *personally*. Okay. It's painful to write about your own personal experience, an' to be an observer of life can be painful, too. So they avoid that. That kinda life, the Dairio an' all, is a safety valve.

For a lotta kids school becomes a game. It's almost somethin' that a kid hasta put up with. So, if we use an approach that what we're after at the end of the year is to see how much progress they have made on this particular test, we've lost 'em. I'm more interested in how much progress they made as a person. For example, last year we did *Jonathan Livingston Seagull, Cyrano de Bergerac* an' *Beowulf.* You might not see the connections in that, an' I'll admit it's sentimental, but in the final analysis the idea is that when you get kicked around, when you're parked at the gas line an' all the gasoline runs out an' you don't get served, what do you do? Do you come apart? Do you blow sky high? Do you scream an' shout? Do you kick an' bawl? How do you face the problems when the goin' gets tough? Are you a loser or do you hang in there an' win a moral victory? A man's true colors are shown when he's really down. That's why literature an' what we're tryin' to do is so important. The thing that bothers me is not the kid that asks, "Why do we hafta study this?" It's the kid that doesn't even care why, because to him it's just a game we play. He's the one that's gonna be tough to wake up, an' if you believe, as I firmly believe, that *that* is dangerous, then you will also see the problems comin'. I can't see the heroic spirit in people. Call it the ol' pioneer spirit if you like. But we're missin' that ol' heroic, unselfish spirit that has brought us through so many problems. When people are goin' to pieces over the gas runnin' out at the pump, they are runnin' scared of the essentials of life.

People in our community might think this nonsense. An' I hope that I am no snob. But when people who are not educators say, "I don't see why my kid oughta hafta take any Shakespeare," or "There's no point in wastin' time sufferin' through classical music or the art museum in Raleigh," or anythin' like that, if so many poeple feel that way, then what's gonna happen? The masses are findin' their voice these days. Well, fine. But when I want to see Shakespeare, I want it to be available. If I want to hear classical music, I want it to be available. If I want to go to the art museum, I want it to be available. Okay. Every man his due. Just so long as I can try to present *my* case. Let's just not throw somethin' out because it's not popular, an' mostly it's not popular in this area because it costs money. That can be dangerous in a democracy. What will happen to our culture if the majority of the people say, "Hey, no, man; that's a waste a' time"?

That's frightenin' to me. I think a lotta people have a gnawin' feelin' inside of 'em. "I'm not satisfied with my life the way it is." It's a good life on the surface, but everybody, regardless of his education or his mentality, wakes up at three o'clock in the mornin' at some time an' hasta look at himself to see exactly "Who am I really?"

In my room, under the poster I mentioned, I have this huge picture of an ape man, an' he's scowlin' an' the caption underneath it is "Find out who you really are." But try to put that across to a kid. That school over there, an' all these courses, are really just so you can graduate an' get a job an' live. People are afraid so many times to run the risk of examinin' things, of really gettin' to know ourselves because it's painful. So we hide it in a lotta activity, a lotta club meetin's, we're busy with people, we make sure not to ask questions or to read or to learn or to know. But at three o'clock in the mornin', when people stop an' look, they do ask, "Who am I really?" An' we all find some dissatisfaction. An' then we think about what the answer to that question really could be.

5

Two Successful Men

"What counts most about a man is himself."

—W. Dallas Herring

Edd Dudley Monk

In the town of Magnolia there was an old man, ol' man Brewster Monk, an' he owned slaves. My great-grandmother was one a' his slaves, an' she had his child, named Dudley Monk, an' the name come on down to my father an' on to me. Well, ol' man Brewster Monk he had a daughter that was named Maggie Monk. She was a pretty woman. She liked Christian work'n she did a lotta missions, an' this woman did such noted things for the town they named Magnolia for her. Magnolia got her name from my great-great-aunt, in a way of speakin'.

Now I'll tell you how innocent those kinda people were. After the white folks got to tradin' slaves, Grampa got sent to another man, an' ol' Brewster Monk he said, "Now take good care a' this child." Well, Grampa was so scared an' innocent, when the ol' man Brewster Monk, which was his father, offered 'im some land, he was scared that the white folks might do sump'n about it, an' he wouldn't take it. No, sir. My father tol' me 'bout how Grampa had told 'im what happened. An' the Monk family owned Magnolia; they owned that whole town. An' now I don' know 'bout no white Monks 'round here at all.

Before we'd go to school, we children'd have a task. We used to make these strawberry cups outta kindlin'. We'd make a thousanda them things for seventy cents. Myself an' my sister, we'd hafta make a hundred cups ev'ry mornin' before we'd go to school, an' then, when we'd come in, we'd hafta make a hundred cups in the evenin'. That was our task. An' our mother'd take us by the fireplace an' call out the lessons an' see that we knew the

117

spellin'. The teacher would give us lessons for the next day an' Ma would make us go over it 'til we got it perfect. The best scholar always stood at the head of the class. That's the way it was. An' I was one a' the good ones.

There was a time they shipped more flower bulbs from Magnolia than 'most any other place in the world. I was hired for a foreman an' I had on my books a hun'red heada people. Ev'rybody got fifty cents a day. Men, women, even the children. I tended all that work, I saw that those bulbs was packed up an' sent straight to the railroad station. We had ninety-eight diff'rent varities an' we hadta keep ev'ry variety true. An' I did all that for nine an' a half dollars a week, an' I hadta work six days a week. The other people worked five days 'n they got two dollars an' a half.

I began to farm on my own. I bought real estate an' had my own farm. One time I remember I had eleven people livin' in one house, an' in another house I had eight people livin', an' they was all tenant farmers. We farmed tobacco, cotton, corn; that was our standard crop. An' soybeans. Then we had truck crops, peppers, tomatoes, cucumbers, watermelons. An' I was takin' care of my mother. My father died an' we buried him right on the farm.

Since then I bought several lots in Rose Hill here. I've bought land so they could start what they call apartment houses for the people that didn't have homes or no place to go. I've got 'bout seventy acres a land in the town an' 'bout forty-five acres right out in the suburbs that I've bought. I've been talkin' with one man on the town board an' he's been aroun' 'n lookin' at some a' the lots, an' he wants to buy three acres to start a buildin' project. If a business concern wanted to come to Rose Hill, first thing they'd wanna know's the population. An' we think if we can get more houses an' get more population, we can get more business an' the town would be a better place to live.

About twenty years ago I had a brother-in-law come to see me one day an' said, "Let's start a funeral home." So we talked with a cousin of ours that was a pretty good businessman, an' we called a buncha people together an' said, "Let's go ahead." We bought the land an' started the buildin' from scratch, an' now I handle the funerals for the colored. When we first went up to get our license, the man that we talked to at Raleigh tol' us we could have a funeral home, but he didn't care what happened, don't bury no whites. Since then this law have come in, this sixty-four law, but we're still segregated, an' I know good an' well we'd start sump'n or other, a riot in the town, if we was to bury other than colored. Some of the white undertakers still has colored, but I don't know a colored undertaker in the state, much less in the county, that buries white.

It don't matter far as the business is concerned. We got plenty a' business. Maybe a family'll come in an' say, "Well, I wanna have a wake, my friends'll be roun' from eight 'til ten." Or maybe somebody'll say from nine 'til sometime. An' then another family might say, "Well, I would like for you to take Mother to the church, this was her favorite church." First Baptist Magnolia or Rose Hill, or wherever the case may be, an' we go up there an' set up an' have soft music an' the families come in an' view, maybe from eight 'til eleven. You begin to get to the place that you have the knack or have the experience of sump'n that could cheer up those kinda people when you been at it so long. You gotta treat 'em in a way that they'll feel that you have their feelin's to heart. It helps in the funeral business, too, if you try'n share the sadness with 'em. Next person in the family dies, they'll call you faster. If you please people, they want you, an' that helps some.

There's not much black business in Rose Hill, but I think that'll change. We got an organization, a buncha farmers, call ourselves the Coastal Growers. It's sump'n I been doin' to help, 'n they appointed me president. That woulda been three years ago. We set it up on this kinda cooperative base. We got an operation in Duplin County, in Sampson County, an' in Pender. Everybody gets paid accordin' to his poundage, fifty cents a hundred. First year we made sump'n like a hundred thousand pounds of cucumbers. I went to work on this thing the next year an' we sold 'bout three million pounds. This organization now, we're tryin' to go into other commodicum, like peppers an' other commod'ies. We built the office, equipped it with which equipment we got, bought the land, paid for that, we don't owe noth-

119

in'. I got the back statement outta the bank day before yesterday, an' we had four thousand dollars in the bank. It's just
sump'n I took on to try'n help somebody.

The government's got all kindsa programs, but the money they
send down here to help people don't go direct to the right places
in my opinion. There's a lotta money 'propriated for diff'rent
things, but you'd be surprised how much money don't go direct
where it oughta go. People in the Agricultural Extension Department, things like that, the big boys, get the money. The fat cats.
Well, there's a lotta boys out in the streets that oughta have good
guidance. If they had a man who wanted to go out there an' start
some kinda project, they oughta put some money in that thing so
the individual could do sump'n to help hisself. Or they could
give guidance to some fifteen head a' young men or young ladies
on some kinda project. That'd be better than they do, bring up a
whole lotta paperwork, whole lotta red tape.

It's parta the history. Just because a man gets to be a certain
kinda successful, don't mean he forget history. My grandfather
an' my grandmother on both sides they worked as slaves. They
did farm work, diggin' an' cuttin' an' splittin' rails, cuttin' wood.
That's kinda rough work, the kind the first settlers hadda do. My
grandfather, bein' ol' Brewster Monk's son, he wasn't treated too
bad. An' on the other side, my mother's people, they wasn't treated too bad. But they were sold off somewhere, sold a family like
you would a horse or a mule, an' carried 'em off to other places.
I've heard 'em tell stories 'bout how bad some of the slaves were
treated. If they did a light crime, they had overseers, they had a
place they'd put their hands, like stocks, an' they'd draw 'em up
'n they'd get 'em barebacked naked an' give 'em twenty-five
lashes with a bullwhip; they'd give 'em the lash 'til they'd bleed.
Well, you can't take revenge. You can't take revenge. You gotta
trust in Providence or some divine power to take care of things
like that. But you gotta think about it an' watch the stuff that's
still goin' on.

Coupla years back I had a white friend. He was a doctor down
in Kenansville. Come to my house an' said they was gonna have
this meetin' down in Rose Hill of the Ku Klux Klan. Said he
didn't know what but they might take a notion to go to the black
businesses, an' he knew I own 'bout the onliest one, an' they

120

might shoot out the windas. I made up my mind if I was payin' tax an' had a place here an' bought an' paid for it, this was mine an' I'd just as soon die. So I came on down an' brought my wife with me. Well, they had their meetin' down there near the highway an' I heard the talk an' some a' the statements. Said the Negro didn't need nothin' but a pair of blue jean overalls an' two dollars an' a half on a Saturday night. You could hear 'em all over town, makin' ridiculous statements like that. We stayed at the funeral home 'til 'bout twelve o'clock that night. To tell the truth, I was a little afraid. 'Cause I didn't know what'd happen. They didn't break out no violence, just flambasted the colored people.

I still think that was plenty bad enough. 'Course the people in this town they say they had nothin' to do with it. Well, how in the world could people get into your town if the authorities don't know nothin' about it? Why, I can't bring a trailer camp in here without I've gotta consult the town authorities. An' I don't understan' how they could put up a camp meetin' with a lotta tents an' block the highway 'n have the patrol force, the law force 'n everythin' to look out for it, an' nobody know nothin' about it. After that, some a' the people here thought some a' the leadin' folks caused 'em to come in, so the black people they boycotted the town.

That was back in the sixties. But talkin' 'bout right now. You don' know a decent job that the colored man gets. Here's Mr. Windsor Johnson, been the principal in the school for a long time. An' there's Mr. Jesse Dafford, also been the principal of a school in Wallace an' helped to make it what it was when it was an altogether colored school. Now the schools are integrated an' both of 'em are out. They wouldn't come out an' say, but pressure. Pressure. Go back to the man hired me to run his bulb business in Magnolia long time ago. I had people there that didn't come up to the respect I thought they should for the job. But do you know what Mr. John, the big boss, tol' me? He said, "Just put so damn much pressure on 'em"—he was a cussin' man—"'til, goddamn it, they can't stand it." Now to be perfec'ly honest, from the papers I been readin' 'bout other principals in other places, there's been so much pressure 'til a man is glad that he get to the age he can retire.

121

Now this is real serious. When you take these kinda people outta the leadership a' the Negro race, you've taken sump'n away from the Negroes. If you can get alla that leadership outta the county, then there's nothin' to look to but the white leadership an' the white principals. There's a lotta jobs the Negro won't apply for. They'll come up with this thing, "You ain't qualified, an' you haven't got the experience." But they'll take a white girl right offa the farm an' put her in that office an' she'll get the experience. White folks don't wanna even communicate with colored people. How many white folks would come in here an' sit down an' talk with me? An' then back yonder, they just didn't wanna talk with you, period. They wanted you to come to the back door, an' on your way as quick as you could. No kinda business of this country here was talked over with the colored people. Why, my first votin', I went to register to vote an' the lady wouldn't let me register. I hadda keep right on.

You take this county development program. There's only one colored man in there, an' that's me, that's myself. They got me on the nominatin' committee. Last night I rushed to a meetin' they had at the Four County Electric office, 'n they give us supper'n all. But there wasn't but one colored man there, an' that was me. I appreciate it, 'preciate it, but there's a whole lotta places that go like that. See, they gotta have a man. Then they go out an' get a man that they think has got some influence, an' they'll put in just enough to say that it's integrated. My point is this: if you're gonna integrate a thing, it would be nice to be five colored an' five white. If you see a diff'rent way, an' they's five white an' one colored, or five white an' two colored, you'd just as well go along with 'em, an' you know it's goin' against your grain.

It's this way: if a colored man he make it in this world, he gotta scrabble for it, an' I reckon some a' that instinct it come from back in slavery time. I didn't get much schoolin', but I knew I hadda pull up my own bootstrap. I had ambition to try to get me this little real estate an' try to get me a little cash so I could have me sump'n, because it disgusted me so bad to see my race havin' to take alla that. An' I've had some mighty bad things said to me as a boy comin' on, like "Don' you do that, nigger," or, "Nigger, go bring me so-an'-so."

What happens, you learn to keep on tryin' an' be better'n everyone aroun'. I'll tell it to you this way: when I was a boy, sometimes I'd hafta miss school to maybe help get up wood for the family. Then you'd hafta go to the foot a' the class. But we'd be spellin' an' I'd just wait for somebody to miss, 'n if you'd spell it, you could just walk on up. You called that cuttin' 'em down. An' I was one that could cut 'em down. An' I'd do it all the time. Me an' another little boy, a first cousin named Jimmy Brown. We wasn't always the best there was, but we ranked in that game. Yessir. We cut 'em down.

Dennis W. Ramsey

In my life I have had one quality, if you want to call it that, of bein' able to leave one thing an' move to another if I think the time is right to make the move. So far this has proved to be a good thing for me. It depends what success really is. For one person it's one thing; for another it's something else. I think that success is, first of all, to reach your objectives. Some people say success comes from stick-to-itness. In other words, select a walk of life an' stick to it. This has proven true for a lotta people. Other people have grown successful because they would grow with one thing for a while an' they would move to somethin' else. I've moved from one to the other a number of times.

Like most other kids, I didn't know what I wanted to do. I was born in New Bern, an' my mother's father helped build one of the railroads in eastern North Carolina, an' my father became a railroad man under my grandfather. I was always interested in what my father was doin', an' so I loved railroads. Anytime the locomotive whistle blew, my ears would pick up the sound. If I was nearby the tracks, I'd watch the trains go by. That's always been the case. I don't know that you can explain the attraction of the railroad anymore than a pilot can satisfactorily explain the fascination of flyin'. It just happens to be one of those things that gets into your blood early an' stays.

In times past I have realized I'd rather be buildin' somethin', that I was never very happy with a static situation. An' this was, perhaps, basically the real pleasure in the railroad business.

123

There was motion. After finishin' at State, I moved to Pennsylvania, where I was employed by the railroad, and I know the greatest satisfaction I got while I was with the company was the first assignment as engine house foreman. I was sent out to a little division point called Derry, Pennsylvania. It was a run-down place in the middle of nowhere. Many of the previous employees had to commute elsewhere to work, and I thought it would be nice if I could build up that engine house an' make it important again, to bring those people back there. Well, it so happened that the war effort was comin' on, an' we were beginning to move more freight, an' by askin' for more work, I was able to induce my boss to send more work from other points to my roundhouse. An' sure enough, we were able to bring these people back. When I left there, it was doin' many times what it was doin' when I first went there. Doin' this an' stayin' within the budget was a real excitin' thing.

Why I gave it up may be a little more difficult to explain. It's true I still love the railroad, but leavin' it hasn't proved to be the worst decision I've ever made. About the time the war was over, my wife an' I began to consider what we should do. Both bein' Southerners, we weren't happy to live so far from home. An' then, I felt I did not fit into a corporate scheme of things. I knew the least about how to politic an' how to get ahead from that standpoint. I knew how to work an' work hard, an' I knew how to do a good job, an' if that wasn't sufficient, I was at a loss. As railroads go, I did have a wonderful opportunity with the Pennsylvania: I had been trained by them to be an officer an' I would undoubtedly have made a fair success. But this didn't seem to be enough, as I could see it. It didn't offer other things that were important to us—havin' a home life, bein' settled, bein' part of a community. To give you some idea what I mean, when I had lived in Rose Hill four years, I had set a new record for myself in stayin' put. I had never lived anywhere four years in all my life. An' now I've lived here since nineteen forty-six. That's a lotta years.

When we first came to Rose Hill, we constructed a motion picture theater. It was quite nice for a town of this size. Havin' known nothin' about the picture show business, we did a lotta things that probably other people would have said couldn't be done. But we succeeded somehow. We had people in Rose Hill, an' I think we still do, that care a lot about the better things: good music, good plays, that sorta thing, which gave us a wide spectrum of shows that we could use. And we had a lotta people that liked the cowboys, too. 'Course we had some rough spots. My wife an' I at times would find ourselves doin' the whole thing. But in the main it did well enough for us to build us a home, raise a couple of adopted children, an' all in all we were very happy to be here. Many times we had an opportunity to sell our business, but it would have meant movin' away from Rose Hill, so we wouldn't do it.

Then along came television. We could see the writin' on the wall, because we knew those very people we depended on to keep us in business would be the ones that would be happy to sit home an' watch the same type stuff on their TV. The time was forcin' me to make a diff'rent choice. I knew a little bit about the poultry business from association—my wife's family had been in it for a few years and had been a success at it. It looked like a pretty good thing, so I began to study it seriously and made my decision. We went into the chicken business.

Up until we started in nineteen fifty-four, chickens were still bein' grown in backyard flocks. No one here had any conception of growin' fryers an' broilers commercially. It was a brand new idea for the area, but I had already seen this in operation an' I thought it would work. I think my engineerin' trainin' stood me well in my business. For one thing it afforded me the ability to organize my thoughts an' get things down on paper in a workable fashion, an' made it possible for me to convey these ideas to other people. In the first year, the year nineteen fifty-four, I sold nine farmers on the idea and built a tenth house myself. I did that both to gain the confidence on the part of the others and in order to learn, too. I tended to the chickens, my wife tended to the chickens, and each employee that came with the company, for some time thereafter, grew a house of chickens. So that when they went out to talk to the farmers, they knew what they were talkin' about firsthand. The need for a feed mill was evident from the beginnin', but we didn't reach that size business until some few months after we had started. At the end, before we sold the company, we were producin' somewhere between four hundred and four hundred fifty thousand chickens in a week, an' had about a hundred eighty-five people on the company payroll, as well as about two hundred contract growers. I would have been happy to have stayed on longer 'til the regular retirement time, but the opportunity came along to sell, and it's not always easy to do this without sufferin' a loss. It's sorta like sittin' in a poker game. You hafta play the cards when they're dealt to you, as they're dealt to you. You may not want to play it right at that moment, but you're sittin' in the game an' the time is now, so you play your hand.

Timin' is a great thing. I know many people who have worked as hard as I have, who have had just as good objectives, had all the ingredients, but they just missed the timin'. It is somethin' you don't always have control of. I had mixed emotions about retirin'. One minute you have a position of some degree of importance, an' the next you have no position of importance, an' this is quite a letdown. And I suppose for one who would just sit an' hold his hands, this might develop into a depression thing. But it's been great. I've been doin' a little bit of everythin', an' almost nothin' at times. I've been involved with my family. I've grown a vegetable for the first time; it's a beautiful thing, you know, to put seeds in the ground an' see them develop. I've actually done some work with my hands an' I'm preparin' to do even more. I love to paint, saw an' nail. An' I've been studyin' paintin' an' drawin', an' while I'm not a particularly good hand at it, it's an outlet. It's a nice hobby. My wife is very good at paintin' an' is a very good artist in ceramics, an' she's been an inspiration to me. I've actually started an' developed on paper another business proposition which I've not put to work, but it could be put to work at a moment's notice. And I've finally had the time to do some readin', an' pay some attention to some of the things that have been goin' on.

This Watergate business bothers me. I've been a lot disturbed about the whole thing. I supported Nixon. He's a man I had confidence in, the kinda president we needed. I'm not convinced Mr. Nixon is at fault; if they don't find him guilty, he's still, as far as I'm concerned, the finest president we've had in a long time. But the things that are happenin' in Washington are due to our lack of interest. Watergate is a revelation of our system. People get so busy they say, "Let Johnny do it." Then Johnny goes ahead an' does it, an' you end up with a dictatorship.

I like havin' some say-so. I like bein' able to participate in the community I live in. I've enjoyed payin' my town taxes because I've been able to go down an' read the budget an' argue about it when I don't agree. When Dan Fussell was mayor, he saw the opportunity to run for county commissioner, which he did, an' this left a void on the town board. I was asked to fill that vacancy and was elected after that. So I served about two and a half terms. My particular area of responsibility was as police commissioner. It had its difficulties at times, but I never was one who abdicated my responsibilities to anyone else. When it came time to run for reelection the last time, I did no campaignin'. As I've said, I just don't know how to politic. I thought if the thinkin' people in town thought I made a good commissioner, they'd come out an' vote for me, an' if they didn't want to bother to vote for me, I had plenty I could do to keep busy. There was an effort made by some of the younger people in town that wanted to have some of their own on the board, which I agreed with. I don't know whether it was particularly to unseat *me*, but it did have that effect. And then many newcomers in town didn't know me and could have cared less who I was. And so these two things together knocked me out. There aren't any hard feelin's, only a little hurt in pride. I thought that I was in a position to serve my community very effectively.

That is the type of thing that happens. An' you can't let it stop you. Just recently I was readin' a discussion on Mr. Nixon. An' the writer said there's undoubtedly three Mr. Nixons: the Nixon his wife an' family know, the Nixon the party knows, that the politicians know, an' the third Mr. Nixon that the people know. An' those three people can be three entirely different people. People in public places have a job to create an image. He might say, "Well, I'm soft on the inside, but I hafta create an image of toughness." What it is, a person must have confidence in himself. But this confidence is somethin' that grows. We're rather insignificant bein's. We're very small in the sight of God, who created all of this. An' I think we need to consider this when we begin to get pompous an' bigheaded. Certainly this realization of smallness should keep us in our place. You go back to what a

127

person thinks of as success. I'm quite happy with the success I've made. Another man might not be. Another man might say, "Well, that was just the steppin'-stone to success." An' he would not be happy. You see, it depends on what your original objectives were.

I wish that I could convey to my children what I feel basically, and that is that I wish I could eliminate the fear of livin' in their lives, as I have. I don't think I have ever been afraid to live. And a lotta people are. They're afraid to make decisions. They're afraid to do this, afraid to do that for fear they'll fail. And if I could just convey to the kids this confidence, that would be the opposite of fear, would it not? Confidence? Confidence in livin'. You find the fear of livin' among the most successful people, as far as we know them. I suppose I'm fortunate. I don't remember a time that I was really afraid.

The thing that would disturb me would be times when I knew there was somethin' more I oughta know about a situation, but I didn't know it an' I couldn't find out. When that happens, that bothers me. But a bad situation, as long as I had all the facts, never really put me down because I always said, "Well, I'll look at the alternatives. An' one of those alternatives will hafta do." This is something that most men who've found it necessary to make decisions have been faced with. We always hafta seek alternatives. The people who become frustrated, generally, are people who can't find them. They can't turn an' go around, they can't detour, they can't make substitutions. There are always new things to do an' to learn an' to see. Which is why, in some ways, I'll never really feel I'm retired. There is always somethin' to keep me busy. Right now I'd like someone to teach me how to play checkers. Then chess. But first, I'd better accomplish checkers.

6

My Angry
Don't Count

Q: Don't you get angry?
A: Yeah. But my angry don't count.
        —former candidate Perry Whaley

The Housewife: Mildred Lawrence*

The big difference between people here is the people who
know how to go about controllin' their lives an' people who have
not the foggiest. We've got huge numbers of people here who
don't know how to ask a question. Don't even know what question it is they oughta ask. Then you've got people who know a
lotta answers because they have learned how to get information
an' how to use that information once they have got it. You've got
Nash Johnson because of his influence over the amounts of jobs
he can offer. You've got the county commissioners an' the board
of education an', to a lesser extent, the town board. You've got
the lawyers around the courthouse. You've got the Democratic
party. You've got the old families. Sounds like a lotta people,
doesn't it? Well, it really come down to just a few. Evidently
they'll let a coupla people kinda crop up an' get into points of
slight influence, so everybody'll feel like that if you keep strivin'
long enough, if you just work *real hard* an' keep at it, the masses'll rise up an' won't be destroyed. But mostly the people in
power make you feel like you shouldn't even aspire. It's sorta
like the divine right of kings.

I've been watchin' this all my life, an' it has made me mad as
fire. I've tried to figure out why I feel this way, because I didn't
grow up any different than any other woman of what you'd call
my age or background. Things were always easy for me. But I remember, even when I was a kid I would see the things they did
to people, an' it would make me sick. I never felt it against *me*,

an' I get along fine, mostly because no one has the slightest idea what I'm thinkin'.

You can have your strong feelin's inside you an' do as much as you can to help people. You can do little undercover types of things. But society here would not accept you if you were terribly pro-poor people, or pro-environment, or even pro-honesty in politics. There are people here who are sympathetic to the black, an' if they came right out an' *said* that, they'd be called "nigger lovers." Even now. When you look at people differently than the majority of people around you, it's kinda dangerous because people would really ostracize you an' you'd be out in the cold.

I tried to decide where I think Rose Hill stands in the spectrum of one to ten, one bein' the worst kinda government you can get an' ten bein' the best, an' I think we would be at about minus twenty. One of the excuses our town government comes up with is that the people aren't interested. Well, the general public would never know what to seek an' how to go about seekin' it. An the result is a type of apathy, but it's apathy that's bred from lack of any input. It's not because we don't care about how things are. It's a kinda deadness from tryin' to find out somethin' an' findin' nothin', an' nobody ever tells an' nobody ever knows.

This whole area, startin' with the town of Rose Hill, is one big corrupt an' inefficient mess. Things are brought up in town government an' disappear, sorta like a vapor that floats out in the air. The town government will say, "The populace isn't behind it, so spit on that program." Well, you've got to present people with ideas, an' then they'll vote whether they want 'em or not. Those people on that board are elected to think about things. But there seems to be no concern for what they need to be doin' to take into account the way Rose Hill is growin'. They don't plan ahead, like by pavin' a little bit or whatever you hafta do as far as keepin' the roads up year by year, or havin' things ready in case money does come available to do somethin'. There's no preventive government, it's always curative government. When there's any government at all. The only time they seem to meet any needs is when the people are screamin' an' yellin' in the streets about it. But people don't know which direction we should be goin' in, so when they do get there, they're all hollerin' from their own little point of view. Nobody even knows the proce-

132

dure. Take the town board meetin'. If you go, you present your plea or your case an' then you leave the room, an' they discuss it an' decide whatever they want to, with you not bein' able to make any defense or take part in the debate about the issue.

When these men run for office, nobody ever discusses issues. An' since the public isn't informed, the quality of some of the men we've got representin' us is very, very poor. We've got a county board of commissioners that seems to do some pretty suspicious types of things, an' the same with the county board of education. Even if they don't do them as a group, which I don't really know about since they keep the records to themselves, they certainly seem to do them as individuals. Our state representative to Raleigh, Mr. Baker, has a history of funny goin's-on right since he started out, I think it was as mayor of Wallace. It looks to me like the only thing he's really interested in is his cousin's oil business. Durin' the time he was mayor down in Wallace, he actually blocked some guy's driveway who was sellin' his gasoline cheaper than they were. 'Course nobody said a word. An' he doesn't even get anybody to run against him. A good example of how people don't even think about issues, or what's goin' on, is somethin' that happened to our congressman, Mr. Henderson. He had some pretty stiff Republican opposition from the northern part of his district a few years back, an' I actually heard people say they was gonna vote for the other man 'cause Dave had been in so long. Nobody ever said what the other man was proposin' to do, but people were gonna vote for him. 'Course, nobody ever told me what Henderson was proposin' to do either, or what he had ever done. So how do you make up your mind? The election did have some effect because since then Henderson's been sendin' out newsletters to give you the impression he's doin' somethin'.

I think it's real serious. An' I don't know if any of 'em care. I think most of 'em are just doin' their job, whatever that means. It looks a lot like they interpret that as a license to do what they wanna do. But as far as really doin' somethin' for anybody in the area, more than their friends, I don't see any evidence of it. I always thought that in a democracy we had representative government, that these men should be workin' for *us*. It starts with the town board an' with Mayor Harrell, an' it goes right on up through all of 'em. The one I liked isn't gonna be with us any-more—Sam Ervin. At least he *stood* for somethin'. I didn't always agree, but he was a man an' he really made me proud. Mosta these men here they seem like they're bein' controlled by somethin' or someone. Commissioner Fussell has all his business dealin's, contractin' an' real estate. Mr. Baker is like a puppet for his cousin an' some a' that crowd down in Wallace. Mr. Henderson he's a pretty boy. Well, all of 'em are disgustin' to me. People here are in a lotta trouble. They're poor an' they're illiterate, an' who's gonna fight for 'em? One thing, they don't seem able to fight for themselves.

I don't think you help the situation much by givin' people handouts. The government comes up with all these programs, which means the money has a hard time gettin' to the people it's meant for. They had a VISTA program here in town for a couple of years, which everyone objected to. I didn't agree with the reasons most people had, which is the VISTA volunteers were outside agitators or communists, which is what we call people we're afraid of. But I also didn't think they did much good. They came in lookin' like hippies an' actin' smart, an' mostly what they did was to stir up more antagonism. They came in, most of 'em, with the attitude that, well, "Here I am in the South, an' look out for the lynchin' an' the cross burnin'" type of thing. The idea was supposed to be to give people the confidence to help themselves.

It's more important to teach a person how to survive than to fund him with money. It's demeanin'. I have had so many experiences with the way social service people treat the poor in this area it makes me sick. After all, these programs are legitimate. I wouldn't hesitate to use Medicare, Medicaid, whatever, if I needed it. But to be treated as though you are a second-rate citizen merely because you need help is an intolerable thing to me. I see people made to wait hours an' then be told sorry, they hafta come back tomorrow because Miss So-an'-so didn't happen to be in the office right then. People who couldn't read had to sit an' wait to get food stamps when there was a sign posted behind the counter which said NO FOOD STAMPS WILL BE GIVEN TODAY. There was a big sorta place where they gave out food, an' you shoulda heard the verbal abuse bein' lashed on this old black man who couldn't read. All sortsa little things go on con-

134

stantly in our society, but I think the most horrible is the treatment of people who need help by people who are just one step above 'em, merely because they've got a decent job. Those county commissioners oughta take a look into these things. I think more people oughta go over an' sit an' watch what happens to people, an' then let 'em say, "All those poor people got an easy ride." It's the most destructive thing. They don't beat 'em up physically. But there are scars on those people who walk outta that Social Security office. There's scars that can't be seen. An' there are scars that the children of those people carry, because when Mama an' Daddy come home lookin' like they don't think mucha themselves, the kids begin to feel like, "Well, I'm not worth much either."

The key to the whole thing is people not bein' human bein's to other human bein's. It isn't easy. Sometimes I pull back inside my shell an' slam it shut because I can't take it. I get too upset about things that happen to people. I can find a lotta things to distract me. I can go to the beach or ride over to Wilmington or play bridge or go out to dinner or somethin'.

But anybody who was been entrusted with public welfare has no right to forget they're responsible. I mean the elected people, the people who work in the offices in Kenansville, the town clerk, all of 'em. I liken 'em to the guards at the concentration camps. They were the kinda people who didn't give a damn about humans. They couldn't have. An' there is nothin' more damagin' or dangerous than a person who doesn't care. I don't care what they care about as long as they've got somethin'. But when you become such a machine that you have no conscience, that anythin' you can do you can justify, you are a dangerous person. An' I think right now in this town, in this county, we got people who are that dangerous.

The Gadfly: Butler Cavenaugh

When I moved up to Duplin County, there was some people runnin' for office, an' they come to see me an' I was very instrumental in gettin' a lotta the voters registered. An' I'd get out an' work for those candidates that I thought were good candidates.

Then after a while I decided I'd run myself, an' I ran for township constable. Well, the crowd in Wallace they controlled the politics in the district, an' the ones in the rural area didn't have a chance, so I didn't get it. But after a while I ran again an' got to be magistrate, an' was magistrate a right good while.

Then they come out an' had a court reform where they changed the system. They put in seven magistrates that I know of, an' outta the seven, five of 'em were alcoholics. They did that to suit the crowd down at Wallace, like they wanted. I don't fool with whiskey. I don't have nothin' to do with it. An' they didn't want me because they couldn't come down an' give me a drink an' tell me what to do.

After a while the political business in Duplin County got even more rotten. They had some tax collector up there in Kenansville. His brother was a lawyer an' another of his relatives was in the real estate business. An' they got to sellin' this land on a book 'n page number. They would sell it an' not give the person's name that the land belong to, an' then the person didn't know what number was that land registered under. They was sellin' other people's land. An' when they did this, this tax collector was hired by the county commissioners to conduct these sales, an' one a' the commissioners went an' bought a piece a' that land cheap 'cause he knew all about it. Now there was an' ol' Negro down there at Rockfish Creek, an' his land was sold. An' a man come an' said to him, "When you get ready to sell your tobacco, I got the sale card. This land belongs to me now." Negro man said, "It don't belong to you. It's my land." Well, the ol' man had struggled an' raised his children; been here all his life. So I went to court for 'im an' got his land back. An' I reported it. We put what they did in the paper, an' the county fired the tax collector. I thought they changed things that way, but things didn't get much better. So I just kept right on, an' they been after me ever since.

Then I ran against this same commissioner I just mentioned. An' I tol' you a while back that Wallace controls the politics. Well, I went by the Wallace town hall where they was votin', an' there's a buncha colored people out there with a table. A load a' colored people'd come in, Negroes, an' they would walk by an' a Negro woman sittin' there would write on the paper who to vote for an' hand it to 'em. My wife an' I were there together an' we walked up an' said, "Is Cavenaugh gettin' any votes here?" They said, "No, sir." Said, "They tol' us if we didn't vote for the commissioner, we'd lose our welfare."

They have been after me ever since. See, I didn't go along an' let 'em push me around with all the low-down dirty deals. Every time they wanted anythin' done, they would send someone up, you know, to see how I felt about it, an' I would always tell 'em exactly how I felt because I was for what was right an' nothin' else.

So after a while, when they were doin' anythin' they wanted to do here in the county, I decided I'd heard some things an' that I'd make an investigation. There was a landfill out here between Rose Hill an' Kenansville, an' I said to one of the county commissioners, "I understand they bought some land for a landfill." He says, "Yep." I said, "Who'd they get it from?" He says, "They got it from one a' the commissioners." I said, "What did it cost?" He said, "Five hundred dollars an acre." I said, "Didn't you know that's a conflict of interest, tradin' with yourself?" He said, "I dunno, I reckon so." I said, "Didn't you know if you're aidin' an' abettin', you're part of it, too?" He said, "Well, the rest of 'em did it. I was just there." He said, "The other four outvoted me." I said, "Well, okay." I didn't say nothin', but after a while I kept hearin' about it, an' so I decided I'd go to Kenansville to the auditor's office an' see for myself. I asked the county auditor about it, an' he had a diff'rent story. Said that, no, they didn't buy it from the commissioner; they bought in from Mr. Dixon. An' he tol' me that it went for three hundred dollars an acre for a hundred an' two acres. Well, I went to see Mr. Dixon. Now he was a mighty fine man, he's dead now, but you could believe whatever he told you. He said, "Mister Cavenaugh, they got the land from my boy." He said, "I turned the land over to my boy an' he got in debt. I had some stuff over there, some personal property, an' the boy hadda sell it. His creditors wouldn't carry him no longer an' it was put up for auction." An' he said that when it was auctioned off, one a' the family of the commissioner is the man got it. Said there was three or four biddin' on it. An' he said, "I went out there an' said sump'n t'other 'bout gettin' my things, an' they wouldn't let me have 'em." An' then he said

137

that it was sold again to the county, an' the timber on it was about enough to pay for the whole deal, an' they got I dunno how much land, tractors an' a home an' chicken houses an' everythin'. All that is a profit.

Well, I went back home an' a day or two later I heard from the boy. An' he tol' me if I went back an' said anythin' else to his daddy what he'd do to me about it. I told 'im, "I've been threatened many times an' I don' scare very easily. I'm willin' to get to the bottom of this thing an' I'm gonna find out anythin' I can about it, an' I mean for the people to know." After this happened, the county commissioner come to my house an' wanted to talk with me, but all he talked about was sump'n that happened two, three years ago. I said, "Listen, I been up there an' found out all about this mess, an' it looks to me like the whole buncha you's involved. An' it looks like you been tradin' with yourself, an' some more have, too. This is the taxpayers' money you're spendin', an' I intend to do exactly what I tol' the people I'd do." A few days later on, I got a letter from a man tellin' me about this member of the board of education who bought a piece of land, an' he turned around an' sold that piece of land to the county for a big profit. An' I think they're gonna use it to build a new school. Well, I went to the Wallace *Enterprise* an' asked 'em to print this, an' I found out they wouldn't print anythin' for me. Now I have been to some lawyers to try to get help, an' everybody said, "I don' wanna get involved." Looks like everybody's scared.

You dunno how much I get outta tellin' people the facts about what's happenin'. I don't get a thing in the world but some satisfaction in knowin' that I'm tellin' the truth about this low-down crooked bunch. I never seen the like of people in my life that don't want the facts made known. When I wanted to tell the public about the landfill deal, I hadda get *The News and Observer* to come down from Raleigh, an' only after they printed it, then the Wallace *Enterprise* picked it up. Seems that the papers here don' wanna do anythin' to offend any of this crowd, the politicians. Don't make sense to me. I think the people oughta know what is happenin', an' this thing oughta be broken up.

People come to me an' tell me, "We haven't got any people like you anymore." They're scared to death. Majority of people today are badly in debt an' they know good an' well that some a' these things that get around might get 'em in a lotta trouble. I don't owe nobody nothin'. I'm not scared a' no man. I'm not afeared an' so I'm gonna tell the people exactly what's happenin' as long as I live.

The condition this county is in is the very reason things are happenin' like they are in this country. The political machine gets involved an' they get around an' they do everything they can to keep their crowd in, no matter how low-down it is. They corrupt anythin' they can. They've destroyed this country. What you have today in Washington an' in Raleigh is lawyers an' business people, an' all the bills they pass or do anythin' about are always sump'n for the big man. There's nothin' to help the little man. Go to the courthouse. Who do you see sittin' up there bein' tried? The poor white man an' the nigger. You never see the big boys up there. This thing's been goin' on too long, an' one a' these days it's gonna blow up. It's gonna come to a head an' then the people'll say, "Well, that man told us so."

The other day I went to a funeral, after all this landfill stuff was in the paper. I saw some a' this crowd involved in politics punchin' each other an' laughin', lookin' toward me. I know I'm the center of attraction when I get aroun' these dirty politicians. The reason they see *me* is because I've exposed 'em an' they can't stand that. They can't stand it. In the past few years they would watch me if I go to town, go to Kenansville. They started in a-whisperin', "Butler Cavenaugh's in town, Butler Cavenaugh's in town, Butler Cavenaugh's in town." Just like I was a lion'r sump'n. Because they know good an' well that I will not go along with no low-down dirt that they carry on, an' they're scared. They dunno what I'll do next. They'll be glad when I'm dead an' gone. Yessir.

A Nest a' Wasps: Johnnie Green*

The colored folks just won't stand up for their rights. Seems they give up. They're afraid. We get together an' talk, but out there where it's gonna do some good, they will not talk. 'Course there's reasons for that. Good reasons. So way things are now,

139

we got leaders, an' they do our talkin' for us. If you're a black man in this country, or a black woman, you get usedta keepin' your mouth shut. Say, "Good mornin', ma'am," an' go right on.

In Duplin County if you are black, you don't have no fair chance for nothin'. That the way it is in this county an' that's the way it is in the town of Rose Hill. The people over in Kenansville, they'll take one colored just to say they hired one, but they will give 'im dirty hard work. They would give me a job in an office scrubbin' one a' the floors, but they wouldn't let me sit behind a desk or do nothin' like that. Nothin' to make you proud.

The whole thing, you can see it in the courthouse. If a black person goes to court, there ain't nothin' up there for 'im. Best way I knows to show it is this marijuana an' our children. The white folks growin' it, an' when the catch 'em, they tell 'em you just don't do it no more. But I know 'bout a black boy they got in a frame-up. Said he had it in his car. Kep' sendin' the black deputy 'round to his house, charged 'im with this thing an' that thing an' cleaned 'im outta a lotta money.

Go to the courthouse an' you get one a' them fancy white lawyers, an' they don't care 'bout nothin' but the money they get paid. Now I respect the law. An' I'd whup the tail a' any a' my young 'uns that gets in trouble. But I wants it to be one law for everybody, like it s'posed to be.

Rose Hill is real quiet. Everybody here gets along real good. That's what *they* say. Yeah. It's quiet. Ain't much good in makin' no noise. Whenever you go up town to say anythin', they say, "Well, the resta them seem satisfied." It make you feel real bad. If there's one 'r two tryin', an' they have it to kick it in your face, "Well, the resta them seem satisfied, *they* ain't kickin' to death." You feel kinda bad out there by yourself, tryin' to do. An' whatever you done, you done for the majority that live here. The way it looks to me, the black people they just ain't got courage sometimes. If a man try to do anythin', look to me like the white man'll try'n scare 'im.

I s'pose that's the reason they brought the Klan in here. Was to scare the colored people. But they shoulda known whatever they do, nothin' they do don't scare me. I always felt that way from the time I was big enough to know anythin' up to now. Coupla years back, when Johnson was runnin', they had a rally of the Ku

140

Klux Klan down near the highway. The Negroes were all surprised. We didn't think the whites in Rose Hill would have done that thing. There was loudspeakers pointin' up the roads that the blacks lived on, an' they was sayin' terrible things. Me, I don' wanna hate nobody. But after that it's been mighty hard. Mighty hard. The white men got themselves up so you couldn't tell who they was, but I know who was over there. The Negroes set up a boycott an' folks didn't go to the big market downtown an' some a' the other stores, an' since then we ain't had no rallies or nothin'. No trouble you can *see*. 'Course the boycott might not a' been fair, but I still think some a' them top whites that acted so innocent coulda stopped it if they wanted to. An' some a' them store owners, they got put up to it. If you ask 'em right now, the whites'll tell you there ain't no more hard feelin's, but the blacks are still mad about it, even if it was ten years ago. All this integration they say we have, it ain't nothin' but a pretty picture they're paintin'. They sell us what we need in their stores an' our children go to their schools, an' if you go to vote or sump'n, they don't dare 'n try to stop you. But that don't mean they think we're human bein's.

Some a' them now, they been real fine. I liked President Johnson an' I liked President Roosevelt. Seem like when he got in, there was a change. But the ones around here, don't matter what they *say*, they ain't for us, not one percent. I dunno what they do up in Washington, D.C., or over yonder in Raleigh, but it ain't for us. Fact is, what I hear about the politicians, you're just lucky if it ain't too much against you. There ain't no way a politician in this country here gonna come out an' say he's for the black folks. Not if he don't want the resta them to go on an' take 'im outta his position. Look at what happens to 'em if they're diff'rent. President Kennedy an' his brother an' Martin Luther King, all of 'em was killed because they was tryin' to help the Negroes. An' you find one of 'em come in here right now an' try an' help us, it's gonna be the same thing.

'Course they got certain ones of us they use. I ain't never been one of 'em. They treat 'em real nice, even go an' sit in their homes an' talk about bringin' everyone together. What they mean is, bring 'em all together for votin' time. I wouldn't say money changes hands; I can't prove that, but there's other things they got to give away. See, everythin' depends on what you got to trade. I don' see it that way. I knows that Martin Luther King worked very hard to get black people where they are today, an' so anythin' I can do to keep it movin', that's what I try to do. Martin Luther King pulled 'em up an' out, got 'em up, an' then they did a lot. All them white politicians got for us is a big packa lies. Usedta be, the right thing for 'em to say was "Hate the niggers." Now they countin' our votes an' wantin' to be friends. Coupla years back there was a place on the town board here in Rose Hill, an' they got together an' somehow decided it'd look nice if they put a colored man on. So they went an' asked Mr. Dafford, who is a retired school principal, an' he did it. 'Course they never would ask Mr. Windsor Johnson, who got a big mouth with 'em, or Mr. Mack Henry out yonder in Yellowcutt. They ain't gonna go *that* far, but still they asked Mr. Dafford an' he did a fine job. Elections come along an' the white folks gets rid a' him, but they can always say they put 'im on, see? They talk real nice, but seems like it ain't there when you get to lookin'. So 'til they can show me sump'n they done for me, ain't gonna get me to them polls.

I think black people gotta fight to win this thing. They gotta set down an' pray, an' then they gotta get together an' be one groupin'. Burnin' down sump'n 'r marchin' somewhere don't get us nothin'. Nothin'. Just like goin' along an' bein' real nice don't get us nothin'. The colored people are movin' on, but sometimes, when you talk to 'em, the first thing they'll say, "Well, it's all right with me, I ain't worryin'." That's the first thing they'll say. A person starts out an' then they frighten you or they buy you, an' if that doesn't work, they gonna kill you. I say we gotta be like a nest a' wasps. Whenever you go after 'em, not only one flies, the whole nest flies away. Me, I don't want nothin' from the white men that own this place. An' they ain't got nothin' they can get from me.

The Candidate: Perry Whaley

There was nothin' really outstandin' that I could see that caused Lawrence an' me to decide that one of us oughta run against Ben Harrell. But we wanted to get interested in politics. Lawrence said he didn't wanna be mayor, an' I tol' him if he didn't want it, I'd do it. So we started talkin' more or less, an' the more we talked, the more we convinced ourselves that we ought-a do it, even if we lost. That we'd let people know we'd been aroun'. We lost by seven votes, but at least we tried.

I work over at Kenansville, an' I thought it would be easier for me to do my filin' over there. So I went up to the elections office an' asked the girl if I could file for mayor of Rose Hill. Well, she signed me up. Two 'r three days later she come back an' told me that Rose Hill had a board of elections, an' I'd hafta file through the board of elections in Rose Hill. So I went over to the town hall to file for mayor. They didn't know what to do 'r say. 'Course they knew I was gonna go down there an' do it, but they didn't wanna see somebody do it, I guess.

We didn't have much money 'cause we could neither one of us afford any, so we talked to people mostly. I made some li'l cards an' passed 'em out an' then we went to everybody in the outer side of town. I didn't bother with anybody in the older part. Anyway, I believe that was on a Saturday, an' I tol' them I was runnin' for mayor an' the election was on Tuesday. Just went out, shook their hands. I mighta talked some, but as far as my inner feelin's goes, I really expected to lose until that Saturday. It was one a' them still things. The people didn't have a whole lot to say, they didn't have a whole lotta questions to ask. They didn't really say they was gonna vote for me, but they didn't say they wasn't gonna vote for me. An' I didn't really ask 'em. I dunno why, but I come back home an' I felt like I had that thing wiped out. It didn't dawn on me 'til about one o'clock on that election day, that Tuesday, that I'd lost the election.

There's somethin' that I think caused me to lose, more'n anythin'. At that same time they was votin' on a referendum for liquor by the drink, an' that issue was the biggest issue in the election. The churches lied to people, in my opinion. They tol' people it was to vote on a law for liquor by the drink, an' it wasn't. It was to vote on a *referendum* to permit people to vote for or against liquor by the drink, if they wanted it. I didn't say nothin' about it, but I think the people who knew me knew damn well that if I got in, I was gonna tell 'em that I knew every-

143

body went to Warsaw an' to Wallace to buy their liquor, an' they might as well buy it in Rose Hill an' let Rose Hill take the benefit of the tax they put on whiskey. The whole damn point right there is that people oughta be honest about what they are.

Now I can't prove that they tried to tie me up with that stuff, an' I sure didn't say nothin' about it. But George, my brother-in-law, an' I rode aroun' town the night before the election, an' the lights was on in some houses that shouldn'ta been on at the time of night we was ridin'—the mayor's house, C. T. Fussell, which is the town clerk, one of the Herrings, an' Jiggs Fussell. What I believe, now I can't swear to it because I wouldn't go out here an' ask somebody personally, an' the people, an' the people they contacted wouldn't be the people who would come an' tell *me*, but I do believe that they called a lotta these older folks that live in town an' told 'em that I was for liquor by the drink an' they need 'em to get out an' vote. I can't prove nothin', understand, but I believe that like the day has twenty-four hours.

I didn't even stay down there an' watch 'em count votes, 'cause I hated to stand there an' see myself lose, so Lawrence was the one on that. They would do things like call out a vote for the mayor, say, an' then they would decide that they shouldn't a' counted that vote for some reason, then they would erase it or they would decide to leave it, whatever they felt like, I suppose. The other thing was that the chairman of the local board, Wells, acted as a referee. I don't guess there was anythin' really wrong with that, but Wells has been around here a right good while, an' the way we felt about it was that they should a' got somebody that was not an interested party bein' the referee. The people who ran the elections were helpin' monitor the count, an' some of 'em would actually tally the count, an' we thought that if they was gonna do all that, they shoulda got somebody other than themselves to monitor the thing. Because they would hafta make decisions if sump'n did turn up that was wrong, an' see, if they did the countin' an' the decision makin', then hell, it hadda be rotten.

After the election Lawrence came over to the house an' tol' me I had lost. Lawrence he was about to cry 'cause he had worked so hard. An' George, my brother-in-law, had already been an' told me, an' he said we could still call for a recount. I said I didn't know whether it would do any good or not. An' they kept on about it for a coupla days an' then found out that accordin' to the county board of elections chairman, we was supposed to have five days or a week, maybe, so I tol' Lawrence if he wanted to call for a recount, I didn't care. I helped 'im write the letter to 'em, but I'd about given up all hope.

What they did, an' it coulda been a good idea as far as I was concerned, was havin' the books open so the people who had recently been incorporated in the town limits could register. But it hadn't dawned on me that what they was doin', see, was gettin' some a' these older people who had been livin in town for years to go down an' do the same thing. When I saw that happenin', I shoulda known I'd lost the election, only I didn't think that it was really against the law until three or four weeks after, an' it was too late. After all this occurred, I got me a recent published election law book, an' that said I hadda have satisfactory evidence. An' I looked an' the law said the registration was for the people who'd just been incorporated in the town.

So Lawrence talked to the county, an' after I found out the county sent a letter to the man at the board in Raleigh, an' I called him an' asked 'im what I could do, since it had gone that far. I wondered if there was maybe a possibility I could go up an' talk to 'em. An' he said they didn't let anybody go up an' talk to 'em on these decisions, but he would be glad to consider any new evidence that I had. I never thought a' gettin' a lawyer until after it went to the state board, an' then I thought it was too late because they was gonna make their decision before I could have the time. An' also it was too expensive. If I had a lotta money, probably I woulda done it. But see, in a way I guess I was new to the thing an' I didn't know what I was doin'. I didn't really have my heart in it, if you wanna know the truth.

The biggest majority of people who have complaints about the mayor feel that he's not progressive enough, an' as far as I know, he don't do too much. He'll do what somebody else on the board wants 'im to, you know, but he's not gonna go out an' try 'n get anythin' done on his own.

There was some things we coulda discussed if anybody wanted to do any discussin'. Take over here where the ol' school was burned down. Some people wanted to put a park over there.

145

Well, I think if the people want a park an' really wanna pay for the damn thing, I don' care. But over there, where everybody is livin', is the wrong place. Then there's the streets. They let Blount Bradshaw an' Marlo Bostic lay out the new section into streets an' develop a new housin' area. An' then someone put about an inch a' tar on the dirt without really good gradin', an' this other stuff. So you go over there an' you find holes *that* deep in the streets. Mention to 'em about pavin', C. T.'ll turn around, look around at the other ones an' say, "Oh, them streets, the ones that *Maaaarlo* built." Like he was real bored with the whole thing. Well, I don' give a damn who built 'em, them streets oughta be fixed. But it's real easy to blame someone else, just laugh an' say "*Maaaarlo.*"

The big thing was they wanted to hire more policemen. Well, the law enforcement, state an' county, has increased five times in the last fifteen years. Why does a li'l town like Rose Hill need to go increasin'? If they had all that type of crime that we need three policemen for Rose Hill, hell, it'd be even dangerous to walk down the street. An' speakin' of streets, Yellowcutt, where the colored people live, has been in town for years an' years an' years, an' still only has two streets paved. Them people in Yellowcutt raised all the kids 'round here, looks like they oughta be good enough to have a street to ride out to the highway on.

But I wasn't gonna say nothin'. One reason I didn't talk about issues was there wasn't anybody else talkin'. Very few issues are ever discussed in town elections. People know what the issues are, but they don't wanna discuss 'em. They're afraid they're gonna hurt somebody's feelin's, an' they don't wanna do that. An' I ain't about to do it 'til I get in a position I'm supposed to be in to fight. I gotta live here an' I don' wanna stir up too much trouble, see.

It wasn't 'til after callin' for a recount an' they wouldn't give me one that I decided I'd run for sump'n else. So that's what I'm gonna do. Four years from this November I'm gonna run against Tommy Baker. But I wanna run against Jiggs Fussell first. Maybe after Baker I'll run against Dave Henderson. An' give the people an opportunity to get someone in a' these offices that got the people in mind. Might be honest when he goes in, might be a crook when he goes out. But they could at least one time put somebody in there who hasn't stole everythin' he got to start with.

I can't offer a whole lot, but I'm damn sure of one thing. If I ever get into office, ain't nobody gonna tell me what to do. The way I'll make up my mind is by listenin' to the people. 'Course *they* say they're doin' *now* what the people want. But they didn't want it 'til the politicians told 'em they wanted it, see. I know it's not a good idea to rock the boat in Duplin County because you're raisin' trouble, you're causin' problems, you're makin' a fuss, you're a rabble rouser, you're a nigger lover, you're all this other stuff. I ain't a perfect candidate, I ain't no elegant man, but I don't see why I should hafta turn my back on where I come from 'cause I got a little better education than some. The words I use at times might not be so dignified, but hell, I ain't interested in that. Words is just a matter a' transportation to get you from one part to another. I'm not sayin I'm such an angel. An' even bein' honest, you can be crooked accordin' to somebody else's standards. So maybe I'm only doin' this to prove I can win sump'n. But see, I think I already won that election for mayor. If I'd lost by *fifty* votes, I'd a' still won the election. Now that sounds crazy, but with me not bein' born in Rose Hill an' still gettin' that many votes, I more than won that election. Some of 'em went to vote against Ben, an' some of 'em went to vote for me, an' some of 'em—who knows why they voted like they did? But one thing about it: they sure was sayin' somethin'.

7

The Good
Ol' Boys

"Let 'em bitch, damn 'em, let 'em bitch. I
wasted my life haulin' 'em to the polls. The
hell with 'em."
—former State Representative
Hugh Stuart Johnson

The Commissioner: D. J. Fussell

Let me just sorta say this: Duplin County people are the finest people in the world. I'm not sayin' this just to be sayin' it. They're close together an' our county government is not perfect, but it is strivin' to be that way. Communication is good, an' as long as you can communicate with people, why, you'll work out your differences. Put it this way: we'll work out our problems. If we have agitators comin' in, you can't cope with these type people.

I'm county commissioner of the fifth district of Duplin County. Six years ago I ran for mayor of Rose Hill, an' I was reelected a second term, an' then I decided that I was interested in our governin' of Duplin County. It's more or less a civic thing. The money is very little, it's a lotta hard work, but when we do somethin' we get a very good feelin' from it. There are five commissioners, an' we're elected every four years. My district, the fifth district, consists of Kenansville, Magnolia an' Rose Hill, which I think is the best district in the whole county. You have a certain amount of pride in your district, but you always have concern for our other districts, too. If they needed a new school in Faison, Warsaw, or Wallace, I wouldn't hesitate to back it one hundred percent.

The job of the county commissioners is more or less to help run the government of Duplin County where the town leaves off. We work in conjunction with the town. We assess the taxes, we collect the taxes, we try to use the money wisely an' spend it back in the county. The assessment is one dollar an' sixty-five

151

cents per hundred. Of course we get some ABC money, liquor taxes from the package stores, an' we also now have the sales tax, which has put a shot in the arm a little bit, you know. Our tax rate on property is high enough. Maybe some of us are able to pay more, but I'm talkin' about the average citizen, the one that's, well, he's drawin' social security, yet he's got a little home. He just can't pay any more taxes. I can see where we could use the money for good things, but there's a limit to what you can do.

I am now chairman of the Duplin County Mental Health Clinic. When I became county commissioner, I realized that maybe I could do somethin' about a clinic, an' I pushed for matchin' money from state an' federal, an' we got us a nice buildin'. We started about two years ago, an' believe it or not we now have about eight hundred seventy-five patients or clients. Three psychiatrists come to Duplin County one day a week, an' we have a director, a psychologist by the name of Dr. Raman, from India. We have a mental health nurse, a vocational rehabilitation counselor, two alcoholic counselors, a clerk an' an assistant clerk. So you see what we've done in just two years. I'm thinkin' it's necessary that we hire more people who have rehabilitated themselves, an' we're tryin' to do this to do something for the alcoholics. The money comes from the ABC stores which we have in Wallace, Kenansville, Warsaw, an' Faison. Actually, Duplin County itself as a whole voted against ABC stores, but there is a law in North Carolina which allows each municipality to vote for or against, an' if they're for, why, they can set up a store in their town. Rose Hill does doesn't have one. We have one of the best religious communities in our county and I don't think that our ministerial association would allow it here. But like I say, the other towns do allow liquor stores, an' the county gets forty-five percent of the profit. We try to use it in the way of counselin' an' so forth.

An agitator doesn't get very far in Duplin County because the people, both black an' white, know what's goin' on. I know some of the blacks have been complainin' about the roads in their part of town here. I have had people come to see me an' ask me to try 'n find out what could be done, an' I have been assured that the town will pave the streets. I asked the boys 'n girls to be patient, but it is comin'. An' let me say, too, that when I became mayor, I broke the tradition an' paved for my colored friends, the only pavement that there has been across the tracks in the town of Rose Hill. Actually, to be frank with you, they're friends of mine, the blacks are. Very much so. I know they don't have so much as some of us, but nevertheless, you gotta remember there's a lotta roads that's not paved in the town of Rose Hill.

Listen, since I've been commissioner, we have a young black girl workin' in the commissioner's office, we have put one in the registry of deeds, we have put one in as our mental health nurse. I have one of 'em on the mental health board with me, an' I think we have quite a few good civic workers in our black community. Without 'em, why, Duplin County would not be as progressive as it is. We had one young black to run for the board of education about two years ago, an' he did a good job an' he got quite a number of votes from the whites. It was not bad at all, an' that's a sign of progress. 'Course you cannot expect these things overnight, but as long as you see that things are goin' forward an' see our community workin' together good, why, the future looks bright. An' that's the way I've always found Duplin County. You don't find a community that works together better than our blacks an' whites.

Just about every person that lives in Rose Hill hates to leave. An' if he is an outsider an' comes in an' stays here for two years, he hates to leave Rose Hill, too. But to keep the young people here, it's more or less an economic situation, an' we just do not have the growin' industry that the Piedmont section or Raleigh have. We have been considered one of the nine most depressed counties in the country, but I don't see it that way. Most everyone could work if he wanted a job. There's any number of jobs that can be created, an' if he's lookin' for a job in Duplin County, he can get one. From an economic standpoint it's just a bit underdeveloped.

I, personally, have enjoyed every minute of it. I was born in Rose Hill fifty-nine years ago an' I was raised here all my life. I worked hard an' now I'm retired. Rose Hill has beautiful churches, nice schools an' a library. We have a good police force here, a nice town hall an' we have intelligent people. As long as you have people like that in your community, you'll have a good community. Businesswise, we may be proud that we are a rural community twenty years from now.

What we want is a community in which we can live together in peace, rather than the hustle-bustle that you've got to do this an' live for money an' money alone. There's other things you can appreciate much more than you can the economic situation. You hafta strive for one or the other, an' maybe we are strivin' for the other. Like I say, I've been satisfied. An' I've been lucky. I was the only county commissioner in a hundred years who's ever been elected outta Rose Hill. I'm a Democrat, but never have been involved too much in politics. 'Course I've never had any opposition, so that's made it easier for me to serve. Can't never tell when that'll happen. I'm sure I've just been lucky in that respect.

Mister Chairman: Gerald Carr

The electorate. You know the electorate. Generally speakin' they don't know what is goin' on. One reason they don't know is because they're not interested in the government process, except to the extent of "What can I get out of it?" Which the average citizen gets nothin' an' could care less. We'd have a greater number of people interested in government. You take across our county. Certainly we'd have a hundred able men that could be commissioner. Two hundred, maybe. Men, women, either race. But I daresay the number that would dare seek that office possibly is as low as twenty, an' I think it's reflected by that lack of concern.

Let's assume you have a mess in county government. I'm not sayin' there *is* a mess now. I'm sayin' we're gonna make that assumption. Well, the percentage of the electorate to be concerned about that would be what? Fifty? Twenty-five? Or less? Here's what people think: "Government, leave me alone. I don't like it anyway. I don't wanna get involved." They never once think that along the line there *must* be government. You can't have a group of people without it. To me, the lack of concern is pathetic. It's America's most dangerous issue.

Now we're gonna hafta define the word "politician." When you use the word in this area, they're officeholders. But if the definition of a politician is a person that tries to influence people in their political thinkin' an' actions, yes, I am a politician. People say politics is dirty. Well, that's a loose word. But it's true in some ways. What's dirty? Oh, all the little lies, some white lies an' some black ones, an' rumors. We all use them. Nixon on a massive scale, but yeah, we do. My participation has been dirty to some degree. An' sometimes I wish I had been more so. Like Tommy Baker's little business about blockin' the driveway in Wallace was used in his opposition, but it wasn't used effectively. It shoulda been. But then there's the ones that are made up. In the governor's race between Richardson Pryor an' Dan Moore, well, Richardson Pryor seemed like he was runnin' around with women, an' Dan Moore was an alcoholic, or his wife was an alcoholic. Well, I didn't think Dan Moore's wife was an alcoholic. I think she isn't. That's very dirty, callin' names an' not knowin'. It's like trickin' the boys in basketball or pushin' the one under the goal, an' the referee didn't catch you. The crookedest part in political doin's is the financin' of the thing. You can be interested in a candidate an' you can send a little token, like you give to the American Red Cross or to the cancer drive. But when you talk about thousands of dollars, well, people are not foolish enough to dump out thousands not expectin' somethin' in return. But really, I don't believe we can use the term "crooked politician." The politicians I know fit right in with the electorate.

The party in this area has been Democratic since ninety years. Recently the Republicans have established some organization, but it'll be quite a few years before a Republican could run as a Republican an' win. However, in this area there's no real difference between parties. If there's any views the Republican party wishes to be carried, they can haul off an' support someone runnin' on the Democratic ticket. The Republicans like to think they're conservative. An' they are. But there's not as much difference between the acts of the ones that are supposed to be liberal as either one would like it to be. I do think the Democratic party lends itself to change, hopefully for the better, more readily than the Republican. An' it means somethin' to to be a Democrat, but it did more so ten or fifteen years ago. Politically I think our people are one-third Democrat, one-third Republican an' one-third wishy-washy. We do have a number of loyal Democrats, like myself, an' we take it as a little game in beatin' the hell out of the Republicans every time, regardless of the candidate. I mean, we'd do it for a stick. We get the po' white trash, as they say, an' the blacks, an' we whisper this an' that around, an' we truly enjoy winnin'. But a lotta people like to be registered as Democrats, because if there's any gravy or political plum come out of it, it would be from the Democratic side. Then in the fall elections they'll vote as they'd well please. There's very little head choppin' or use of the ax between the two parties.

When you speak of the Democratic establishment an' the county executive committee, that's entirely two different things. I mean, there might be some members of the establishment in the executive committee, but for that to be thought of as the same would be an incorrect assumption. I'm not sayin' we aren't unified; we don't have any particular deep factions. Every county has what you call the "courthouse crowd" goin' in one direction an' the little antagonism against the courthouse crowd goin' the other way. But the depth of that division is not too deep, an' it's primarily used in politickin', vote-gettin' business. In other words, this ol' American politickin'—"No, we can't support this candidate because the courthouse crowd is with 'im"—is not because you get particular disrespect or dislike for the courthouse crowd in their directions; it's just a little trick of the trade. Candidates for office very seldom consult or work closely with the party structure. In other words, should a person seek the office of commissioner, after he decides to run, he might possibly consult the party, but it'd be on a pleasant basis. You hear the comment, "Well, a host of my friends asked me to run." That's malarkey. When you decide to run for office, the fewer you can ask is the best.

The elected officials in Duplin County are all registered Democrats, as far as I know. But as between the Democratic executive, which consists of about thirty-five people, an' the board of commissioners, which is the governin' body of the county, there is no relationship at all. Not as far as connections or workin's in power plays or politics. The elected officials are responsible to no one other than the people. They do not seem to know that sometimes. But if you live in Duplin County an' you wanna change somethin', or you wanna initiate somethin', your proper place is to go see the board of commissioners. It might be possible, just maybe, for the Democratic Executive Committee to pass information on to the board of commissioners, but to hold somethin' over their heads is not done. An' for what they do, the party isn't responsible. You can't blame Watergate on the Republican party. Absolutely not. I sorta like to, an' probably will in some conventions, but when you get down to it, no. No, sir. The Republican party didn't tell those crooks to go over there, breakin' into Watergate. Could you say the Republican party is as bad as Nixon? What could the party do about it?

Earlier I thought I'd be interested in participatin' in the political arena, but lately I have my doubts because I sorta think of one of the things Senator Goldwater said that hits me right between the eyes as bein' correct in my self-education. He used the statement, "The runnin' it was fun, the servin' it was hell." In other words, to think I hadda work in Washington or even the state legislature for the six months that it's in session wouldn't be any fun to me at all. I'd have a stand on the issues, an' then that slow an' oftentimes useless debate wouldn't be any fun. I've been a town commissioner an' mayor pro tempore, an' then mayor of Rose Hill, chairman of Rose Hill precinct since fifty-eight or sixty until this time. This year we had eight blacks an' seven whites show up at the meetin', an' the eight blacks voted for Windsor Johnson an' the seven whites voted for me. Which was fine an' dandy. I think Windsor will enjoy bein' precinct chairman. I can't say it had somethin' to do with my becomin' county chairman later on, because I hadn't made up my mind at that time, an' anyway, I think he'd a' helped me in the county even if I had beat him in Rose Hill. An' then, too, those precincts he helped me in, the black precincts, I think I woulda won those anyway. I had me a person sorta picked out for county chairman, an' I was puttin' out some feelers an' I couldn't get any response. Then I was reminded of a kinda loose statement I made in the heat of the previous county convention, which was two years ago. I had some support to run against Craft, an' I begged off an' some of 'em said I had said I'd try next time when it was wide open. They reminded me of it, an' on the mornin' of the convention I found out that I had quite a few precincts, an' I made up

157

my mind. I sorta thought I'd win the thing in the nominatin' committee, but it's my understandin' that Dixon Hall won it by one vote. Then in a little hurried squish-squish we assessed what would be our strength from the floor, an' we decided it'd be pretty good, an' that was it.

I hope it's gonna be fun. There's no advantage to it from a political point of view. Never can I remember takin' any action in a back room or makin' any requests by telephone or personal conversation or letter, askin' any of the people I supported to do a damn thing. The committee itself is powerless, not the individuals on it, but its only power comes from that individual level. An' the committee itself doesn't get together an' pool that individual influence. As Gerald Carr, I have influence. An' I think it will increase by bein' chairman, but it's mostly because of me rather than that chairmanship.

Politics is a funny thing. We talk about issues an' issues an' issues, an' yet you still hafta get the votes. All the issues, all the ideas, all the beautiful things you got goin' for you, all your friends an' associates you're gonna have in an' around you, if you're gonna get defeated, they mean zero. I wanna get the people of Duplin County more interested in their government. Hopefully, to support the ones I like, not the Republicans, but if it must be the other way, the interest itself would be a comfortin' thing to me. The responsibility of government in this land is the people's. If it remains corrupt, it's the fault of the people. We, the party, or I, as chairman, can't do it for them.

The Pro: Hugh Stuart Johnson

When you first come to the General Assembly like I did back in the forties, an' sit in the balcony an' look down on it, it looks like a funny farm. It looks like a three-ring circus. When you first observe it, you think, "Jesus Christ. Is *this* what they're spendin' our money for?" Then after a while you starta learn. When you first get there, first coupla terms, you learn everythin' you can about state government operations. An' you make as many friends as you can among all the new ones an' the old ones; you seek their counsel, their guidance. Without that you're just kinda a lost soul an' you don't accomplish anythin'.

The business of operatin' a legislature is diff'rent from any ball game you've ever been in, or any rat race. A good legislator knows when to compromise every so often. If he doesn't compromise, he's gonna get his head busted in. You hafta horsetrade. You hafta back-scratch. An' that's just parta the principles of government—to trade. You gotta learn the rules. Written rules. Unwritten rules. If a lobbyist takes you outta dinner or has any beverages, why, you enjoy them an' vote like you damn well please. Now that's an unwritten rule. Another one, old one. Usedta be, a young man comin' into the General Assembly, why, when I went there, hell, I didn't even make a speech on the floor. You step outta line, they'd cut you down. An' later on, I got to helpin' cut 'em down. The new ones aren't gettin' that kinda groomin'. They just yak yak yak. Lord, they're the mouthiest damn things you ever saw, yammerin' for the TV cameras or to get their picture in the fish wrapper. In the ol' days, we'd a' let that man talk about three minutes, an' then we'd get up an' move to table the bill.

I never did completely believe in what Sam Rayburn usedta say, that those who go along get along. But it does take teamwork, 'cause nobody does anythin' on their own. It's not a thing in the world but people. You just try to understand 'em an' deal with 'em. You move around like a cat, soft feet. You just hafta learn to spot when you think people are dishonest an' respect those that you think are honest. That's intuition an' observation. It's a visceral feelin'.

You hafta test 'em to grade 'em. I'll tell you one thing. When I went into politics, I thought everyone was honest. It was a rude awakenin'. Now a man can make mistakes with the facts. That's not necessarily a plumb bald-faced lie. But a man tells me he's gonna vote with me on a bill in committee tomorra; then he goes down there an' makes a speech against it. I'm through with 'im. Now you smile at 'im. My point is, never lose your temper, an' if you get whipped, smile an' grin. Don't get mad. Start layin' the wood on 'em, so to speak. Politically. You throw a brick at 'im or run your saber through 'em every time you get a chance. You stay in long enough you learn to read their eyes.

After a while I learned that the committee system is where the General Assembly does its work. Your best product comes from your three-man, five-man subcommittees of the parent commit-

159

tee. It may take weeks to siddown to put those words together to make 'em say what you have in your mind, to make it plain to someone else at another time. Those twenty-six letters of the alphabet are double-edged swords. The first committees that I chaired were the Wildlife Resources an' the State Government. I'm talkin' 'bout back in the late fifties an' then on into the sixties. Then I became vice-chairman of the Rules an' then chairman of the Calendar Committee, things like that. The Calendar Committees are the tough hatchet committees. You clean all the bills that've traveled that far an' see if there's enough merit in 'em to take 'em onto the floor. All committees, except the two money committees, Appropriations an' Finance, generally go outta business at the end of the session an' the Calendar Committee takes over all of it. This is usually a select group of fellas—lawyers, businessmen, insurance people, so forth. Now the last two terms I was chairman of the committee that became known as Rules an' Operations. There was not a good system, never had been, to operate the internal affairs of the General Assembly. So that's when I made this handwritten rough draft of a Legislative Services Commission. That provided a vehicle, of a committee made up of the speaker of the House an' the speaker pro tempore of the Senate, an' some members of each body to act as a commission to make judgments an' decisions. I had no desire to be speaker, now. In this state he serves two years, an' he's so busy, he has so many diff'rent things that it is just a rat race. I never cared for sittin' up there an' bein' a referee. I wanted to be on the playin' field where the action was. He hasta appoint his committees an' route his bills, an' he's pushin' this chairman an' that chairman to move certain pieces of legislation or to block a piece or hold a piece. An' everybody in the world is pullin' his coattail. He has no time of his own to speak of.

You might say that's true of any politician. A politician, he's on the firin' line, he's subject to be shot at. You hafta slip away to rest, even from the phones. The tensions they can build up within you, just mental fatigue an' strain, an' you gotta go relax. Everybody hasta have recreation somewhere along the line. If they don't, they run outta the end of their strength an' they end up buggy. I go work with my dogs. You gotta do that. You get so tired sometimes, so physically an' mentally tired, that you can't even add up a pile a' figures. Then you gotta rest 'n get your head back in order.

It was tirin', but I dearly loved it. I didn't wanna retire, but it was eighteen hundred dollars for a session, which covered two years, plus a little per diem to try an' cover your expenses while you were there. An' then your campaign expenses, all those other things, an' time from your business. The family was sufferin'. With three kids havin' to go to college, there weren't anythin' in the world to do but get out an' go to work an' earn a livelihood.

My title is now, I believe they call it, Administrative Director of the Department of State Affairs for the North Carolina State Optometric Society. Which is just some fancy words for "lobbyist." Legman, I call it. Fella that kinda tracks everythin' around. One of the things that I hafta do is check every bill that's introduced to see whether it touches on health affairs that my people are interested in.

An' then if it does touch, I go research the law an' get a copy of the bill to be sure that they're not steppin' on our toes. 'Cause some of the people do that inadvertently. They don't intend to, now, but sometimes they'll try somethin' that will affect *your* operation. So then you hafta go counsel with 'em, an' they'll say, "Oh, I didn't mean that, write me an amendment." So you draw up an amendment an' give it to 'im, an' he inserts it in the bill an' it relieves your problem. A lotta your lobbyists are former legislators. They know the system an' the people, an' they understand the operations an' the type of people that are there. They're good boys. Some of the boys have been up there thirty, forty years, an' they're still in business because they play it straight. One who's dishonest, one who lies, is just gone.

You're born with it. It's like a damn dog. He better have the instinct or I'll shoot 'im. Politics is people, an' it all depends on instinct. It's been years since I've seen it, but Jefferson once said sump'n 'bout men, by their constitutions bein' divided into two groups—those who fear an' distrust the people, an' those who cherish 'em an' consider 'em not always the most wise, but the most safe an' honest repository of the public interest. An' that's how I feel about it. I guess you might call me a populist. Sam Ervin has a way of sayin' that the Democratic party contains more a' God's bein's than any other political party on earth. An' what's

161

been happenin' is disturbin' to me. McGovern now, I didn't like 'im worth a damn. The crowd said, "Hell, he's not my candidate." Guys who had sweated blood for years, they were out. Those others, the blacks, the women, the kids, every damn thing, never had done a thing. So we said, "poof," and we just let 'em go. It has nothin' to do with not wantin' to be open an' democratic. But the hippie liberals an' stuff like that, it's just too fast a social change for me. Hellfire. I recognize in my mind that what McGovern's positions were in seventy-two may very well be accepted as standard in ninety-two 'cause it's a process of growth. But he's so far ahead of his time, he's leapin' instead of takin' baby steps in change. An' what's happened is a lotta division an' a lotta rowdyism an' vandalism, an' when you've worked all your life to build somethin', you don't like to see it torn apart for nothin'. Now George Wallace comes along an' splinters off. They both scare me, the McGovern people an' the Wallace people. There's an ol' statement that holds in this country that may fit. If it's not necessary to change, it becomes necessary not to change.

Some people go through the route of politics to get to be a judge or to get to be a commissioner of revenue or to get to run for Congress. Just to get exposure. They got a goal in mind. It's like huntin'. Some people like it for the thing itself an' some people for baggin' game. There's more enjoyment for me in fixin' up the breedin' dogs an' determinin' as they grow up if you're gonna kill 'em or keep 'em than in baggin' a buck. If you know what I mean. 'Course if you get a bad one in office, you can't shoot 'im, so you hafta go to work an' get enough support for someone to defeat 'im. We are country, easygoin' political types down here. We move more gently, I suppose, than in metropolitan areas. Here you just hafta drive around the precinct, you catch 'em in the street or in the stores. It's hard work. My first actual experience in politics was gettin' people to the polls an' goin' to see 'em an' haulin' 'em or remindin' 'em to go themselves. First time I ran there was two beside myself runnin'. An' I hadda work like heck. There were more races after that, but they didn't take the effort, because by that time you were better known an' better established with the political leaders in a community who would pass the word, "We're gonna vote for Johnson."

162

I'm not interested in power for the sake of power. Now. You've gotta have friends to help pass a bill, or to vote on a certain thing, or to help elect a certain candidate you're interested in. But power—that becomes corrupt. That surreptitious bastard, Nixon. He's an oppor-damn-tunist, an' I didn't recognize it when he ran against Jerry Voorhees, but then what he did to Helen Gahagan Douglas! Awful. That son of a bitch was creatin' autocratic rule, usin' his agents, federal agencies, the CIA, FBI, Internal Revenue Service, to whip people into line. What is the old sayin'? Power corrupts. Sump'n like that. In the House, I was gettin' in a position of power, an' that was bad to get into. You become too powerful, you become enamored of your own power, an' that's a dangerous thing to happen to a man. I just worked right on. If you had the votes, go. If you didn't, hold back. Now havin' strength, if you call that power, you gotta have strength or you don't accomplish anythin'. It's winnin'. You can have a lotta people for you, but if they don't go to the polls, it don't count. You fight to win.

I don't mean you fight dirty. You hafta set your own rules. You hafta develop your own line. What's legal an' what's illegal is one line. But you talk about what's right an' wrong morally, ethically, you may get different opinions on that. There are things you will not do. I wouldn't attack a political enemy personally. I wouldn't go out an' start attackin' his wife. A lotta people do this, start whisper campaigns. Now if I know somethin' about a candidate that I know is true, or I'm satisfied it's true, I might tell one or two lieutenants an' let them whisper it. But if a principal candidate goes to doin' that, people react an' turn against 'im. An' that's right, now. You deal with the truth. Don't deal with suppositions an' falsehoods. That man, what's his name, Segretti, was tellin' a packa dirty lies. Speakin' about information, I'd want all the intelligence I could get outta the enemy camp. Tappin' phones, that's illegal. But I'd use a recorder, a radio device or sump'n like that if I could hide one, an' the next best thing is to have a live bein'. I don't think you should ever violate a statute of law, even if some of it is just tryin' to legislate morality. These damn campaign financin' bills, buncha boy scout crap. You spend what you hafta spend. You just hafta have the natural tendency to do the things you think are right.

Politics is hell. A man's a damn fool to ever get into it an' subject himself to public abuse. Either that or a damn egomaniac. But you see somethin' in fronta you an' you can't stay away. You're always makin' decisions. You hafta vote like you think is right, an' you hafta vote like they want you to, an' between the two of 'em is leadership an' statesmanship. If I become some half-assed leader, it's because I paid attention to the ol' boys who knew where they were goin'. You sat there almost in awe of the way they were runnin'. A lotta these boys these days, they dance around the issues. Some of 'em, when the votin' gets hot, they head for the bathroom or they head for the office. Somebody pulls a piece of paper out an' says, "Oh my God, I gotta telephone call I gotta make," an' he takes off like a rabbit. Hellfire, sometimes it felt like it would be mighty good to run. But you sit there an' you sweat it out, if you got any good blood in you. There's personal things about it that gave me trouble. The biggest price you pay bein' a politician is loneliness. But if I had my druthers, as they say in this country, I would druther be back in the House. In fact, I didn't wanna leave it. I dearly loved it. If I coulda afforded it, an' if the people would a' continued to send me, I woulda stayed there forever. But those days are behind us.

8

Three Women

"I have been a child and I have been a wife and I have been a mother. Now I'm havin' to be an adult. It's the difference between night an' day."

—Emily Sue Longest

Valeria King

When we were in high school, it was all a big party. Whatever the boys did, we went along with. After every football game we'd have this great big pajama party, an' everybody who'd want to come would come. The boys would stay 'til about one o'clock, two o'clock, as long as we could make it, an' then the girls would stay up all night. It was a lot of fun. We were always plannin' somethin'. In the summer each little church group would take a trip to the beach, an' we'd all plan it so that all the churches would be down there at the same time. Carolina was just *our* beach for that week. We were real close to each other, an' we were all kids with a big future. Kids now are more in tune with reality. We had all sortsa crazy hopes and dreams.

Emily Sue an' I were very good friends, an' we would talk about what we were goin' to do when we got out of college. I wanted to be an interior decorator. I can't remember what Emily wanted to be. A teacher, I guess. I thought that would be dull, an' I wanted to do somethin' excitin'. I didn't plan to come back *here*. Oh, no. I was *never* goin' to come back to Rose Hill. Never in my life. The man I married, Craig, is from Teachey, out in the country, an' I certainly didn't think he was goin' to want to come back here to live. But you know how these things are. To tell you the truth, when the time came, I didn't do a whole lot of serious thinkin'. I just couldn't wait to get married.

Before we got married Craig was at East Carolina in Greenville an' I was at Peace in Raleigh. That was two hours away, so we were apart mosta the week an' he'd come on weekends. Well,

167

just a weekend at that point was not enough. I wanted to be with him every minute. I thought that would be so wonderful. But of course, marriage was not like bein' taken out three or four hours for a date every night.

Neither of us were workin', an' we didn't have a dime, not one penny, an' we loved it. We figured we'd go to East Carolina together for two years, but I didn't graduate. I got pregnant with Melody an' I couldn't take the swimmin' test, an' then, would you believe, the one course I lacked was "Marriage and the Family"? Anyway he graduated an' went on to Raleigh, lookin' for a job. He majored in accountin', but that wasn't what he wanted. He came back home an' now he's in pork producin'. That's what happened in a lotta cases. Mosta the girls from Rose Hill married boys from Wallace or Teachey, an' then we couldn't get away from here. It's the land or somethin'.

Right now I think I could be happy anywhere, but I couldn't say that ten years ago. It was just awful when we first moved back. I thought if we didn't live in Raleigh or somewhere where there were things to do, I'd go outa my mind. Ten years ago you had to go to Wilmington or Goldsboro or Fayetteville just to get a spool of thread or a pattern. I even had to go to Wallace to buy my groceries. Anywhere would have been better than Rose Hill. But that was before I was saved. When I made the decision, somethin' happened to me. Before that I didn't like anybody who had a fault. There was nobody in Rose Hill that was perfect, so I didn't like it. Well, after I was saved, I was able to *love* people for what they are. Now I know I have my friends an' I'm kin to everybody here, an' I feel like we have as good a place as any I know. We have everythin' I need.

At the time I was married I was not attuned with God. I had not been a Christian. 'Course, I grew up in the church an' all these things, but I was interested in myself. But after I was married somethin' like seven years, anyway it was four years ago, I was "saved" an' came to know Jesus Christ as my very personal savior. Then I was able to change my life. Instead of lookin' to please Valeria, now I'm lookin' to please God.

Once you take a partner, life changes. An' once you come to know Jesus an' make a decision to let him rule your life, it is a complete change. That's why it's very hard for a housewife or a

168

person in my place to have a personality of her own. There's very little time left, but this is my role. God comes first. Then your husband comes next. An' then your family. I didn't believe this when I was younger. An' as far as men an' women, I was interested in bein' equal, in fact, I think I believed in the inequality of the man. But now I'm all for femininity. I believe in the Christian view. The Bible says a woman should be home with her family where she belongs. Now that I have a knowledge an' a close relationship, I try to live my life that way. I don't know if God intended it for all people, but since He touched me personally, I am sure this is right for *me*.

When you're talkin' about bein' feminine, I don't mean the way the magazines an' all try to influence us. They do condition you that if you're not beautiful, then you're not to be thought of as a woman. If you make yourself beautiful, you have to be beautiful from the inside. It's gotta be some other reason than outer cover. When I was in high school, I was the Wallace-Rose Hill representative at the Strawberry Festival. I don't even know how that happened, 'cept they elected me. My friend, Boochie Longest, was president of the Student Government, an' I suspect Boochie had a lot to do with it. The fact is I didn't like it very much. It was just a beauty contest an' it didn't have anythin' to do with talent. It was just paradin' up there, wearin' evenin' gowns. The night of it there was a big dance an' they had tables everywhere an' everyone came to dance. There was a band, somethin' like Guy Lombardo. There were the girls from all over the county. Of course I didn't win, but that didn't bother me a bit. I didn't have an idea I'd win to begin with. An' I didn't think it was right for women to get any kinda praise for what God had done.

Now this year they're havin' a Little Miss Rose Hill Pageant, an' Melody might be in it. I would never push her, but if she wants to do it, I would help her because you gotta do stuff that shows your talent or your intelligence, not just paradin'. They have interviews with the judges. They have a little luncheon, or somethin' like that, where they get to be together an' enjoy. It's sorta like goin' to camp. They hafta have the right attitude. Not to go into it to win, but to do it as somethin' you do with your friends. An' that's life. You win an' you lose all the time, an' you hafta learn that, to go in an' do your best. I would never push her. I will give her every chance. But I will never encourage her. If she wants to do it, fine.

I like to have some time to spend with each kid. I hafta figure it out carefully. Melody's eight, an' Deborah's five, so if we're plannin' a birthday party or somethin', I can take them in the kitchen an' they can bake cookies or make a lot of things. Buddy's three, so I still have him while they're in school, an' I can spend time with him readin' books, an' he likes for me to play with him. An' then we have things we do all together, maybe after supper. Like play cards or games. We have our story time. I hafta work out all these things in between, an' it seems like you're always runnin'. When they come in from school, there's always somethin' you've got to take care of. Run them to dancin', run them to Brownies, or music or prayer meetin' or goin' shoppin', goin' to the dentist. Then, of course, Craig'll call with things for me to do. I hafta be ready to leave in an instant. Run to the bank. Come get this, come get that. Carry it to Kenansville. Drop everythin' an' go. It sure beats the washin' an' the scrubbin'. I'd be afraid sometimes for somebody to look around at the nooks an' crannies. But it's a lotta fun. When it's your own family, you don't mind one bit long as you're doin' it for somebody you love.

I'd heard all my life that everythin' falls apart when you turn thirty. It happens. You start lookin' in the mirror an' your hair is not that same baby-fine, curly, beautiful color. The texture, everythin' changes. Seems like overnight. Your teeth. Every little pain you have you think is gonna cause somethin'. I don't know why it's that thirtieth birthday. Of course, it's not true. You know it's been gradual. But all of a sudden you look in the mirror an' you see things that are not as young lookin'—that little sag under there, this little bag under here, those dark places under your eyes. You look at your hands an' you see what detergent an' stuff has done to them. The house starts fallin' apart. All your appliances are breakin'. A bulge here an' a bulge there. You're thirty years old an' you're not the same girl.

Don't misunderstand. I love what I'm doin'. But then I would love to have ten times more time to do some of the things I like to think I would like to do. Those old hopes an' dreams I men-

170

tioned that I had as a teenager. Well, I do think one of these days I'll go back to school. Ten years ago I would have wanted to do somethin' that would make a lot of money, but now I think I would hafta do somethin' that would be useful. I would be more interested in studyin' somethin' like biology or medical science. I'm sure Craig would be perfectly happy to have me doin' somethin' I'd like to do.

But I'll always believe that for a woman a career comes after bein' married. You hafta work at it, an' it's a full-time job. An' you hafta have a little mystery. Like Craig says about me—I mean he tells other people an' I have my spies—there's never a dull day with Valeria. He says he never knows what I'm goin' to come up with next. I'm always fixin' a new dish. He tells people I cook all these crazy things. I don't, but you've gotta keep 'em guessin'. I don't do it intentionally. But if you want to have a good relationship, you can't rely on the damn ol' trusted things that you do. Keep up to date. Keep changin'.

You hafta keep thinkin' about what you're doin' an' what you want. An' that gets hard sometimes when you're busy. It might help to talk about it, but that's somethin' we never do here. I don't think anybody in Rose Hill has a close friend. One of the girls who was in my high school class was my close friend, but we moved away an' then came back an', I don't know, we go in different directions. She's in her world an' I'm in mine. It's part of our upbringin', I guess. We don't confide. It's because we're protectin' ourselves. That's one of the things society puts on us. They made us think that you get an education an' go up an' up an' up an' up, an' success is the dollar mark. That's what they brought us up to believe. An' then society puts down feelin's. They're at the bottom of the list. If you cried at a weddin' in Rose Hill, they'd say, "My, isn't she emotional." You have no control over yourself. An' everythin' was to control yourself at all times. But after you've lived in a state of chaos an' confusion, well, it's been eight years now, you don't have much control. You automatically do things. I've been a housewife for a long time an' done little else, but I don't let other things control me. My housework is my job. To fight dirt an' calories. To keep the house clean. But I can't let it pressure me. I could very easily because I'm the kind of person that likes perfection. I would like a

171

spotless house. But I would hafta give up other things, like goin' to church or doin' somethin' for Craig or the kids. So, you see.

It's like, when you're comin' up as a teenager, you know exactly what you believe in, what you're gonna do. You add it all up an' you go forward. An' then all of a sudden you've got three little responsibilities here, an' a big responsibility out workin' over there an' they're pullin' you in all different directions an' you're goin' from one to the other. You're tryin' to please everybody, an' since I been saved, I know that the only way for Valeria to be happy is to make other people happy, but you can't really have much time to concentrate on what you're doin'. When I'm workin', even though there's a lotta confusion goin' on, there are still quiet times when I think about things I wanna do. Or at nights I sorta say my prayers, an' then I hafta make a list in my mind of things I wanna get done next day.

There's a lot of me that maybe I haven't discovered yet. We're constantly takin' on new roles. When I first got married, I was a wife. An' then I became a mother. Now I think of myself as a Christian-mother-wife. An' there's somethin' else in here that's been dormant, sorta like I been holdin' onto it an' passin' it by. You gotta stop sometimes an' take a look. It's been so long I can't even remember when I was not married. I can't even remember what I was like. I guess I was just a silly little kid. That was so long ago, when I was nineteen. I was just a child.

Pearlenia Lee

I been likin' flowers ever since I was a little girl. I usedta go out in my mother's yard an' cut the flowers an' fix 'em in a jar for the table on Sundays. An' when someone would die, I usedta take little flowers an' take a can an' wrap it with aluminum foil an' arrange the flowers in it an' take it to the funeral an' put it on the grave. An' I would look at the flowers that would come from florists, an' anythin' I see I don't hafta take it with me. I can always form a pattern of what I see within my mind an' I can go back home an' do the same thing. I guess I just have a gift for flowers.

Of course, I have a good many other talents for doin' things.

172

But for a business, give me my flowers. I've been involved in this for six years. I usedta do them in my home, but I live out in the country an' I got a chance of a buildin' here on the highway near town, so I took it. I only rent the store, but I own the business. An' I also own the equipment, the counters, floral stands, tables, lamps; I own all of that. I own everythin'.

When I was out in the country, I didn't have no way of keepin' live flowers, an' that was a lotta trouble to me because whenever I got an order for live flowers, I would have to go about seventy miles to pick up those flowers. But here I don't hafta do that. I have a funeral an' the flowers are to be live for the next day. I can do those flowers this evenin'. An' my coolers, they are large walk-in coolers, so I make the flowers up an' set 'em in the cooler. The next day all I hafta do is deliver the flowers.

I'm a very busy person, but if I didn't do anythin', I would go crazy. Some people don't wanna work. But I don't mind workin' because I been workin' ever since I was a child. I usedta sew for a livin', sometimes until three o'clock in the night, an' when I got sleepy an' would make me some coffee, an' when I got too sleepy an' tired, I would just go to bed. I usedta work doin' housework, an' I made my flowers at night. An' the day that funeral was, I would go to the funeral an' take the flowers, an' then work every day. But since I got here in the store, I can't do that. Because when you're out here with a business, someone might come along or want a flower to take to the hospital or somethin'. So I quit domestic work altogether an' I'm here every day.

My grandmother raised us; there wasn't a man in the house. Just as fast as one of us got large enough to work, we hadda go out an' work. We worked for other people on their farms, pickin' strawberries an' dewberries an' cotton, an' choppin' an' housin' tobacco an' things like that. An', I mean, people back then, they worked from sun to sun. When the school season come, we would still hafta work. We girls, as soon as we would get large enough, we hadda do the housework. We would scrub the wood floors. They didn't have no linoleum or things, an' those wood floors, we'd shine them just like those hardwood floors shine now. 'Cause that floor be shinin' when you got outta there or you went back an' done it all over again. That's just how strict my grandmother was. She always learn us children, anythin' you do,

173

you do a good job of it. Don't you slubber over nothin', she say. Because "slubbliness" show sorriness. She say, "I don't want you to grow up in life like that." An' she was very strict.

It takes a smart person to be independent. Very smart. That's right. He don't have no lazy streaks nowhere. I have two girls. I tried to learn 'em howta work, 'cause I'll tell you, that's the best thing you can do for a child. You hafta let a child know how things come. That they are not handed out to you. An' people now, they say, "I don't want my child to come up like I did." I say, "It don't matter to me. I *want* mine to come up like I did." I say, "It didn't hurt me. It made a woman outta me."

'Cause there ain't nobody cut no more wood an' worked in no more farmin' than I have. I started tyin' tobacco when I could hardly throw the tobacco 'cross the horse. An' when I got married, I could string a barn a' tobacco a day. That's a thousand sticks. That's how swift I usedta be with my hands. Anythin' that I learned, I tried to do the best. I don't care what it is. I always have to be the best.

I dunno why I got married, but I got married when I was sixteen. You know how children, when they get along sixteen or seventeen years of age, they get that marryin' streak. Nowadays, the way people courts now, they be together a lot. When I come along, you very seldom saw your boyfriend. Well, I lived with my husband from thirty-nine to fifty-five. I'm separated from my husband now. That man has more respect for money than he have for anythin' in his whole life. All he care about is the dollar an' a woman. I mean women. Not woman, women. That's all. That's the reason why I don't be bothered. 'Cause I have nothin' for 'im. Nothin'.

For the things an' the way he treated me I don't have no hard feelin's. I love him, just like I love anybody else. But to see him now is like seein' somebody I've never had no contact with. But the onliest break that there is in there for a woman is that the man is to die. Facts is facts. Actually, that's the only hope she's got. If he dies, she come into possession of everythin' he own. I'd give my husband a divorce anytime he wants, providin' he pay off. Because everythin' I worked for is there. I hafta have sump'n or other. Because I got out here an' tried to make me a

174

start on my own. An' I feel like. if he goin' to get a divorce, I should have sump'n. I got out. I worked an' I got me a home. An' I paid for it. Everythin' I got, I worked it out with these two hands.

Like the woman say on television, I'm for anythin'll get me outta the kitchen. I feel like every woman should be independent. Because I feel like that mens should be taught a lesson. They were put here to rule the earth, but they're not rulin' it right. A woman was put here for a helpmate. I can't tell you exactly where it's at in the Bible, but I've read it. But see, the women ruined themselves; they ruined the men. Because they workin', takin' care of the men. Let the men work an' take care of themselves.

In these days an' times, even if you goin' with a man an' he buy you lunch a coupla times, he think he has some authority. But I let him know he don't have no authority here whatsoever. 'Cause I pay my bills an' I live here. An' you don't rule my house. The same door you come through you can go out. I'll never have anybody else tell me what to do. I'm gonna stay like that as long as I live. 'Cause I don't want nobody tellin' me when to come an' go. I go when I get ready. An' I come back when I please.

Bein' a woman is hard. Because the weak-minded part of our womens don't think a woman can do as good a job as a man. An' a man definitely don't think so. Through life I don't think that my color have had anythin' to do with me, because I've always been a woman an' I've always been a person. An' I've never had any trouble goin' anyplace I've wanted to go.

My place is anywhere I feel like I'm nice enough to be. I've always tried to carry myself decent. You can be somebody whether you black, white or gray. But as a woman, the odds are against you. Then mens are against you an' the biggest majority of the womens. Because you know women'll give you a hard time if you have two pairs of shoes an' they don't have but one. So if you learn two alphabets an' they don't learn but one, they're against you.

I feel like every girl should oughta live some. Learn the factsa life. Go places. See things. Learn things. When you done alla

175

that, then there's plentya time to get married. I know, I been through it, an' I know. If it was possible for me to live my life over again, I'd be a whole new person.

Sometimes I look back an' I wonder why I don't have more than I do have. 'Cause I been workin' so long, ever since I was a child. I mean I have worked hard. I haven't picked my jobs. I did the bad jobs as well as the good jobs. An' I sometimes wonder, why do I still hafta have it so hard? But I say that was in God's plan.

I think He knows what we need. He goin' to give his children what He see fit that they need. I believe that. So I say, "Thank you, Jesus," an' hol' my head up an' go ahead on. Gets pressure sometimes, but you know you have a God above an' He say He never let His children go lackin'. So we don't have to worry 'bout new dollars, 'cause new dollars are here when we come, an' new dollars belong to Him. An' He distribute 'em out like He see fit, right? So I wouldn't worry, always make it over somehow. He may not come when I think He oughta come, but He always on time. He really always on time.

Sue Lynn Bowden

All my life I was very, very shy, 'specially when I was young. But I always made lotsa plans. Only children have more time, probably. You don't have people to bother you. I had some friends that were as close as a brother an' sister could be, here in town, at least until we got into high school, where we became sorta spread out in our friendships. So I never felt lonesome. We weren't a demonstrative type family as far as affection, but there was a deep feelin' for each of us. I always loved animals, an' everybody thought I was crazy 'cause I loved animals more than I did people. I would talk to an animal rather than play with a doll or things like that. When I was in the first or second grade, I used to be a ventriloquist an' I developed that ability, talkin' to the animals we had around. I have always enjoyed doin' that type of thing, carryin' on, makin' puppets. I still have good rapport with animals an' I still talk to 'em. I guess that's a carry-over from when I was real little an' not havin' any brothers an' sisters.

176

When I was a kid, the only people on the block were boys, mainly, so I was a tomboy. We were a very imaginative group. We played war, we dug foxholes, we hung from trees an' fell out of them. My parents bought some dolls, but they very quickly learned that I'd rather have a set of cap pistols. Mother would worry, "Why won't she play with the doll, why won't she?" Daddy said, "Oh, let her do what she wants to do. Don't bug the kid." Here's the only thing he always said. He said, "I don't care what you make in school. I'd like for you to do well. But don't worry. If you're dumb, you're dumb. Just do your best, an' whatever you do, don't make a D in conduct. Just keep your mouth shut." Well, I couldn't keep my mouth shut, then or now. I was always bein' called down to the office. I still have that problem.

I think I appreciate livin' a lot more because I never developed a specific role I felt I had to play. I guess that's because I was allowed to be *me*. Somethin' very sad happened to a lotta my friends. They got so conditioned that now you can't ever get to that person they really are. Underneath all that sugar there's a real human bein'. It was important to be allowed to grow up an' be yourself an' have a good time. You just were you, whatever that was. Whether it was weird or normal, you were allowed to express a personality. I never did give a happy what anybody thought. I was happy to be Sue. I mean, remember when everybody was bein' real cute an' all? Well, we all wore crinolines an' junk like that, but I never was that conscious that I hadda be somethin' I wasn't. I remember one or two times that maybe I was kinda miserable because I didn't understand why I didn't wanna be stupid an' ignorant. That always turned me off. I guess I always had a strong sense of myself.

One thing I remember is that I never appreciated anybody spankin' me. I knew when I was wrong, an' I didn't think physical abuse was the way to correct that. For example. When I was little, one time my mother broke a switch in the yard an' spanked me with it. When she finished, I said, "Are you through?" She said, "Yes." I said, "May I have the switch?" She gave it to me, I took it an' broke it in about fifteen pieces, an' I said, "Don't ever do that again." It really stunned her. I musta been about eight or nine. But it insulted my intelligence for anyone to beat on me. I figured if you got somethin' to tell me, tell me. An' I would talk

Daddy outta spankin's. I would promise the moon to just "don't put no bodily harm on me." I remember one Sunday we were carryin' on, just pickin' at each other, watchin' TV or somethin'. The Redskins game. We'd sit in the dinin' room part of the house where we had the TV set. We had this great big heater in that room an' we'd bundle up with the blankets an' watch the game. Anyway, we were sittin' there an' I said somethin' smart, evidently, an' it hit Daddy wrong, an' all of a sudden it turned into "What do you think you are sayin'?" type of thing. Daddy never did get mad much, but when he did, he was furious, an' I saw that he was goin' to spank me, so I hopped up an' ran around the other side of the dinin' room table. Daddy was on one side an' I was on the other, an' he said, "Don't you move," an' he started comin' around an' I would run. Mother was fixin' lunch, an' she heard this commotion an' she walks in an' there we are, runnin' full force as hard as we can run, goin' round an' round. All of a sudden we were just standin' there an' looked at each other an' realized what ignorant fools we were. We never were too open with each other, but we always were close. We all had a temper, an' when we talked we got loud; the more excited we'd get, the louder. We were all a lot alike, an' we got mad an' things, but we could laugh about it. Mother can't see herself in me. She'll do the same things I do an' then she'll jump all over me about doin' 'em. We've had some real knockdowns, an' we'll slam outta the house an' won't speak to each other for two or three days, an' then we'll both get hysterical about it. The main thing was, I think, that they thought of me as a real person.

Right at the present I'm workin' on a Ph.D. in science education at the University of North Carolina. Then this summer I'm employed as a teacher in an in-service workshop for elementary teachers at Campbell College, an' if I can't get a job teachin' in Duplin County, it looks as if I'll be teachin' at Campbell this fall. When I get my degree, I would love to work in this county, in-service types of things with people who are already teachin', in a local school, settin' up curriculum. What I really would love to do would be to be a principal sometime an' have a school the way I wanted it. I would love to have that power once. My big hang-up is that I want to be involved with people, an' that's where I blew it, I guess. I spread myself too thin. I'm a photographer, portraits an' weddin's mostly. I do a lotta church work with young people. I'm chairman of the recreation commission in the town of Rose Hill. I'm a jack-of-all-trades.

When you got an advanced degree, people think you're tryin' to be snobbish, so you're feared. That's one assumption they make immediately, about a woman especially. Jimmy, my husband, is very positive about what I'm doin', an' I'm glad because I know men that we wouldn't last ten minutes because they're very role-conscious. His idea is like mine, that a person should develop to the most he wants to be. Jimmy teaches at Wallace-Rose Hill an' has a B.S. in English, an' though he would like to get a master's, he couldn't care less about a doctorate. He takes courses constantly an' buys books all the time an' keeps up, an' he's probably as informed as I will be with a Ph.D., but that has no appeal for him. We're very lucky because whatever makes each one of us feel good about ourselves, that's fine. So again, it's a matter of what I am as a person. But it isn't always that simple, an' when you hafta deal with the world as it is, it can get frustratin'.

It's hard for a woman in a workaday situation. First of all you've got two strikes against you. You're a woman an' you're basically in a man's situation. You constantly are faced with the fact that you've got to prove yourself over an' over, whereas other people, I mean men, don't seem to. This is somethin' I've run into in grad school an' I've run into it every time I've applied for a postition. Someone who has lesser qualifications, or maybe really isn't committed, gets the job an' you are considered an' gracefully pushed aside. In my case it's been frustratin' because the whole idea has been to become a person who has enough knowledge an' ability to contribute somethin'. An' a person who wants to make a difference doesn't want to do a halfway job. To come back to your own home an' not be able to get a job is frustratin'. Of course it's true that women are findin' it a little easier to get their foot in the door, but on the whole it's still very difficult an' we're findin' questions about our abilities, whereas men who are less qualified are assumed to be fine.

It isn't just as a woman, it's a certain type of person. It's very difficult when you see things you want and become committed to a particular goal, an' the people around you don't give any signs of commitment or are willing to say, "Just get it done." Most people are willin' to settle for someone who's just a warm body, whether the person can contribute or not. It's sorta like a kid told me one time in a Sunday school class: "I don't wanna think. Don't make me think when I come here. Just open my mind an' pour in what you want me to know." That's the sorta reaction you get from a lotta people. "Don't try to turn me on."

Thinkin' is very painful, but it's somethin' you can't stop doin'. You can't keep from gettin' involved. You can say, "This time I won't care. I'm just goin' to go on an' do my job." But the first thing you know, you go in an' see that everythin' isn't quite clickin', an' before you know it you're in the same situation again. You more or less hafta put on a show of great nonconcern an' nonthought as a protective measure. Other people don't seem to appreciate thinkers or people with goals. Maybe it's because we make them be more than they want to be. It's very hard to cope with. We get ulcers, people like us.

I would never have classified myself as a "different" type of person. But I see things differently. I don't know whether it's so much intelligence or perception. There's a difference. You can be intelligent without havin' much perception. There are people who are highly intelligent who go through life blunderin' through people's feelin's an' emotions with no insight at all. An' then there are other people who have empathy. It's like you're in tune with people, whether you want to be or not. You can't learn how to do it. You seem to have always had it. An' you can't turn it off an' you can't turn it on. You find yourself, when you meet people, sensin' things that other people are totally oblivious to. You pick up little body language. It seems like you have a special sense of things.

Some people are acutely aware of all the little movements, for some unknown reason. An' if you don't know what someone's talkin' about when they say that, there's no way you can understand. It's just there. You can be in a situation an' you can stand over here an' look at it at the same time. It's almost schizoid. There are certain points, or peak moments, that you have, an' you see things an' you can't see why everybody can't see them.

But you can't go out tryin' to make disciples. An' there are certain periods when you realize that people do look to you an' you do cast those shadows. It's sorta like, "I'm not important as a physical person, but it's the reality I can give other people through bein' with 'em." But before you ask, "What shadow am I castin'?" you gotta be satisfied with yourself. Then it's sorta like Peter Pan. Suddenly you got your shadow back.

Families

"A lot depends on which family you belong to."

—Horace Ward

Horace Ward

The importance of the families is that is the way we came into this world. And here a lot depends on which family you belong to. If you are a Fussell or a kin of the Fussells, you are in. If you are a Southerland and a kin to the Southerlands, why, then you are in. Or Herring. Or Boney. Or, of course, Ward. The other extreme is that if you name some other families, if you belong to them, you don't stand a chance at all.

Your name means a great deal here, and there probably is some basis for that. The basis goes way back. Characteristics. The Ward family, for example, came to this country from England in the sixteen hundreds. One of our ancestors was a soldier in the Revolutionary War. They brought with them a lot of the customs and a lot of the traditions and the language of the English. Perhaps some of these characteristics continue to apply. Our family is different in some ways. The original old man Ward was a Universalist and most of his children and the majority of his grandchildren have been Universalist, and I think that has contributed to their ardent joy for life and their feeling for each other and their independence. We are perhaps more independent mentally and emotionally than most people. We are unique in this area in that the majority of the family have been Republicans. Then there is a cousin who is an outspoken Democrat, liberal for around this country. You might say it is characteristic of our family that we don't depend too much on somebody else's thinking.

Over the years the families who belong to the same social strata tend to intermarry with each other, sometimes over four or five generations. A Blanchard married one of the granddaughters of the original William Ward. The Southerlands, Williamses and Wellses have intermarried quite a bit, and some Carrs have intermarried with them. The Boneys generally live in Wallace, but there were some Boneys here and they are related to the Herrings and the Southerlands. My wife is a Herring, so we have to go to a Boney reunion. The McMillans belong to Teachey, down between here and Wallace, but they are members of or related to some of the families here. There are quite a few Rouses, but they come from over Charity way. Some of the Teacheys claim kin to Blackbeard Teach, the pirate. There is some question about that, but it's just part of the history that people like to talk about, or don't like to talk about, depending on what the story might be.

You can go too far with what family you come from. You are not somethin' because you belong to a certain family. You are somethin' because you are a human bein'. But there are characteristics. There are families that like their liquor. There is an expression I've heard, "Your uncle stole my granddaddy's horse." That means I don't trust you. My daddy, for example, had a good business, and people had a great deal of respect for him. Anything he said you always took at face value. He was very honest in his business dealings. And he was morally a very good man. So this reputation, you might say, this certain character, was inherited by his family, his children and his grandchildren. Whereas a lot of people who are thieves, the families might be thieves, and you take for granted you can't trust his children or his grandchildren far.

William Ward married Elizabeth Robinson. They raised eight children and those children raised about fifty-six other children altogether. The group of first cousins, one of which was my father, were rather unique in that they cared about each other. From fifty-six children the grouping became in the next generation, with in-laws, about sixteen hundred people. We have a family association and every year we have a reunion. It started about fifty years ago, when my father invited all his cousins to come on a certain day for a picnic lunch. They enjoyed it and they started doing it each year. Now we have officers—president, vice-president, secretary, treasurer, and committees to take care of various things. They keep up with the lists, with deaths, marriages and so forth, and they report any of those that they know about. Our biggest financial undertaking is that we sponsor a publication which was first done twenty-five years ago and which my sister has just brought up to date. It took a lot of time and effort, but with the old book as a basis, it was easier to find out about sixteen hundred people, the basic facts about who they married and who their mother and father were, what kind of work they do and what church they go to. Of course there are some things that are naturally omitted. But disgrace to the family—so far that hasn't happened. If it did, we would just forget about it, I suppose. Some things which other people would call a disgrace maybe we would accept and understand as being part of the human being.

The family is probably more of an important unit here than in other areas. It is part of the way things are done. Of course there is a kind of competition. In the churches you will find that one family dominates and another family wants to dominate. This is probably true in politics as well, but it is not so obvious. There is certain competition between family businesses which have been around from generation to generation. But there is a general tendency here to want to preserve things. Pleasantness might be the best way of putting it. There is a lot in the way you do a thing. It is as important as what you do. Some rules come out of fear, I think. There is a law against alcoholic beverages. Most people break it. Most people who don't have a fear of becoming alcoholic. I don't know that I could put into words what is being protected or how. But I think there is a matter of learning to deal with your old fears and bugaboos. And it is my theory that when one learns to deal with all his fears, he will start living. I think I learned something of that in my four hundred and seventy days of combat in the Second World War. I compare the things that frighten people here with what I went through there, and it seems so very insignificant that I find it amusing. I'll admit that new and outside ways can seem frightening. But some of the things that are upsetting to people here are ridiculous to me.

Some may worry that the families are getting weaker, but it doesn't seem that way to me. New people move here, but I don't think the intermarrying with outside families will weaken the old. We have been intermarrying with outsiders for generations and new families have been forming all the time. It may be that as this happens my old grandfather gets pushed further and further back into history, that he is going to loom less important to the present and future generations. But the families are going to be important for a long time. My children may not find the family as important as I do. They might when they reach my age. Of course conditions are different now. When I was a youngster we lived in the country, and Cousin Charlie and Uncle Bob would come and visit and sit and spend the evening. When the kinfolk would visit, there was no place for me to go, and I would sit and listen. So in that respect the average kid is going to have a different feeling about his kinfolk. He won't know them as well. But it doesn't bother me that the kids might not keep it going.

When you are young, you rely on yourself more. But as you grow older, your mind begins to reach back. A family is a place in which a child shall be born. It might break up to a certain extent. I could name dozens of our people who have moved away, and we've lost sight of them. But, for example, there is someone coming from south Georgia to our family reunion. His father was one of the fifty-six cousins, and he moved to Georgia when he was a young man. Periodically he came back and he brought his family, and the children have kept in touch. And as far as the next generation, I am sure some of them will move away and forget about it, and we won't know about cousin so-and-so and what he is doing. But I have a feeling there will be those who will carry on the tradition and keep in touch and will be glad of it. It is good to feel that you have sixteen hundred people associated with you in the world. It gives you a sense of belonging. I think everybody needs to know who he is, in one sense or another, and where he comes from. So I think that those who carry on these traditions will find life a little bit richer because they do.

The Futrells

Robert

I got married when I was twenty-four. I fell in love with her the day I saw her, an' I ain't never been down there more'n four times afore we got married. She wasn't my first girlfriend. I was engaged with girls a whole lotta times. But I just turned 'em down. I guess I loved her in a way that was different.

I always been poor, but I guess I been happy some. My children they ain't done as well as I have, they have their ups an' downs, they have their arguments, an' I don't believe in that. I'm a religious man. I usedta drink, but I buried that ten or twelve years ago. I guess the Lord took it away from me. I'm Baptist, an' my wife an' the rest of 'em is Holiness. I reckon maybe the Holiness is all right, but I like bein' Baptist. The thing I like is livin' quiet, happy with God. They make too much noise, them Holiness.

India

I was seventeen 'fore I got married. I was a cheatin' li'l ol' thing, I were, always runnin' all the time. Well, I were goin' with a boy down yonder an' my mama didn't like 'im. Then Rob come over from Chinquapin, an' that's how I met 'im. When Mama saw me with 'im, I just knowed I was gonna get a lickin', but when we got up to Mama, she began to smile. Y'know what? He loved me the first time he saw me. The fourth time he come, he offered me to be his wife. An' we live a good life, close to God.

I tell you right now, I wouldn't take money for what I got. I'm poor an' I don' have anythin' other 'n what's given to me. We both been sick, can't work or nothin', get money from the welfare. We get paid just a little an' that hasta take us so long as we're paid for. But I tell you right now, the Lord goes 'n looks out for me. The way I look at it, if someone gives you a messa peas or a messa corn or sump'n, that's comin' from God. God is puttin' that in their heart to give it to you.

All the five children I have, he's the daddy of 'em. I love all my children, but see, I can't live their life. All I can do is live my life an' pray for 'em. It gets to be trouble some time.

Charles, he's the oldest boy. Him an' his wife, they live the way they live. You go down to their house, they'll be a-drinkin'; sometimes they'll be a-drunk an' they don't do nothin' about it. But they don't bother me. Joanne's happy. She give herself to

God. An' Louella, the spirit got into her up yonder in Kinston. An' J. D., I knows he's all right. That boy can sing. God give that to 'im.

Billy now, used to be he was 'bout the same as Charles. But Billy, he's tryin'. It's pretty hard to live with somebody like he's gotta live with. I don' hate that woman. I have prayed for that woman. But she tell lies, an' I don' wanna be in with somethin' like that. I got a telephone call she went over to Lola's. An' she come out an' she told 'em that she were gonna be a preacher, an' she were gonna give preachin' in Rose Hill. Well, I talked to my husband 'bout that. My husband tol' me, said, the devil's goin' on here. Robert said the devil can put that in yo to do that. You can't tell me she's livin' with God. She ain't never been a good wife to Billy. I know what I would do if it were me. I would walk right on an' I wouldn't pay her no mind. I would walk right out an' serve the Lord. I know a lot 'bout that woman. But it's way down yonder in the past, so I just let it go.

See, I'm a Christian. I can be feelin' so badly, an' when I get on my knees an' prayin' to God, I feel fine. If you feel good on the inside, it don't matter if you feel ill or what. When I got saved, that were a good feelin'. It were somethin' like bein' hit with lightnin', y'know, the first time. An' this other time I began to hear this singin' from heaven. I know'd it come from heaven, an' it were some a' the most beautiful music I ever heard in my life. That were up in Warsaw, an' I was close to God. The preacher tol' me I took a hard fall, but I didn't get hurt, got no bruise or nothin'. An' I'll tell you right now, my body an' my heart, the whole thing, everythin' I got belong to Him. I hear all the people talk about they got homes, but that belong to God. When they leave this world, they won't carry money or nothin' else with 'em.

I tol' my granddaughter, I said, "When I die, I wanna be buried in a white robe." I seen a vision about that. An' it were Jesus. I don' wanna go to torment. 'Cause I had a vision 'bout that, too. An' it were terrible. It were the hottest fire you ever seen, a fire, an' there weren't no place to hide at. An' in that place there ain't no air. No food 'r nothin' like that. You just be hurtin' so bad you wanna die an' you can't die.

An' I'll tell you one thing. Jesus is comin' back. There was just a li'l bit of a sign of it. When I were livin' over yonder, I was at the house by myself. Robert was over at Charles', an' I seen everythin' just light up. I walked over there an' they said, "What in the world is goin' on?" An' I said, "It must be time for Jesus to come." An' I wouldn't be afraid. I had a vision one night about me an' my baby boy. The Father an' his Son was sittin' in a li'l white cloud. An' this beast, now he come outta the sea. An' he had what looked like a long wooden hammer, an' there was two great long pointed things at the end, an' he was goin' to stick it inta my baby boy. But see, the Father an' His Son protect us an' none of 'em things didn't hurt us. They be all gone to Satan now, a-bitin' an' a-hurtin'. I tell you right now, did I have a time.

If you serve the Lord, there's a better place than this world. An' it's acomin'. After you leave this world, we don't go hungry, we won't be sick no more, we won't have no more pain. That's what's been showed to me. We'll all be joined together, just lovin' one another an' be happy, singin', shoutin', prayin'. I don't know what day, I don't know what hour. It ain't for me to know it, but Jesus is comin'. Won't that be a happy time up there?

Bill

In the world people die an' there's people cryin'. Well, people got it backwards. You're s'posed to rejoice when people go out an' cry when they come in. Even if you're rich, you gotta lotta sorrows. Sickness might come along, sump'n like that. An' they got all that stuff packed up in their head, y'know, how they gonna make money an' all this stuff. I know a Christian wouldn't trade his salvation for all the money, for anythin' in the world. He wouldn't take ten million dollars for it, not when he is a Christian.

Give you an example. You gotta read the Bible about Job. Job he was a rich man. He was just as rich as Nash Johnson. But he didn't love his money more'n he did the Lord. Most people, when they're rich, they let their money come before God. Like say if you had a car an' you just worshipped that car, y'know, get out there an' prettied that car more'n you loved the Lord, that's not gonna help you get to heaven.

191

In my family my mama's real religious, but not back when we was comin' up. We didn't know nothin' 'bout the Lord or God or the Devil. I dunno, seems like we didn't have much time to think about stuff like that. It'd be kinda hard to explain, comin' up poor, poor way out in the country, but my daddy seemed like he hadda move from one farm to another. An' for a right smart time he was changin' jobs. When I was a kid, I imagined all kindsa stuff, y'know, the Devil with horns an' pitchfork an' a tail. You get a picture of Jesus Christ an' hang it on the wall, an' you start to think He looked like that. Fact is, Jesus Christ He come down here as a Christian. He wasn't scared to get dirty. So there ain't no use lookin' back an' complainin'. When I was a kid, 'bout the onliest way you got outta workin' on the farm was to cry with a stomachache. One Christmas me an' my brother, Charles, got a checkerboard between us, stuff like that. But then I get to thinkin' 'bout how they killed Jesus Christ an' how they made 'im carry the cross, an' He got weakened down, they beat Him so much with a great big lash. An' see, we were lucky in my family 'cause we hadda whole lotta love. There's a lotta things I mighta done with a diff'rent start, education, better chance. But I gotta thank my daddy for what he did give us, an' the rest he couldn't do nothin' 'bout. Jesus Christ, He didn't have *no* place to call home. So my daddy—I got to where I don't blame him.

The way I see it, a man's gotta know where to put the fault on. Me, I know I brought a lotta it on myself. I just never did know much 'bout runnin' my life. I got to the sixth grade an' then I quit. I thought I knowed more'n the teacher did. After I quit, I worked out on the farm, an' I kinda got myself in a little trouble. Like forgin' checks. An' I run from the law an' went to Texas an' stayed up there two months an' a half. Got caught down there an' was brought back an' got a one- to three-year sentence. Pulled that, got out an' started to drink, caught another thirty days, got kinda to where I straightened myself out an' got runned over by a car. Had a year an' a half a' that, wearin' a cast, an' time I got straightened outta that, here come marriage. An' thirteen years a' that. Seems like I ain't never had no freedom.

I brought a lotta it on myself. But the Devil, I'll say one thing for the old boy. He stays on the job. I lived a pretty sinful life, comin' up. When you're poor, the onliest way to drown your

Highway 117

Approaches to Rose Hill
(All photographs by Reed Wolcott)

A house by the side of a road

East Main Street

West Railroad Street

Man with a wagon

Men sitting at a gas station

Life-styles

Left: Tobacco buyers

Above: Shopping—Jackie Johnson and Sara Phillips

Below: A visit to Dr. Hawes

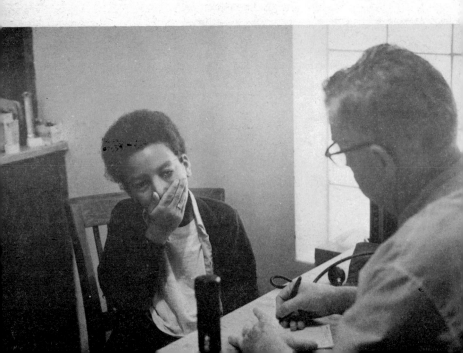

Above: Waiting—Wanda Kay Weaver

Right: Jimmy and Ryke Longest

Below: Hair Straightening—Hermetta Judge

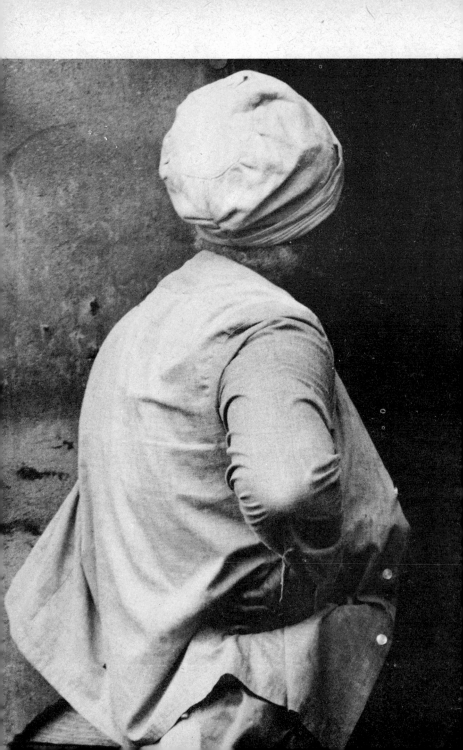

Above: Harvesters with wagon

Below: Auctioneer at farmers' market

Opposite: Woman in doorway

Interiors

Top: Portrait of Valeria Carr King

Middle: Doorway of Futrell home

Bottom: Graffiti, migrant workers' camp

Migrant workers' dormitory

Breakfast: Hugh and Helen Johnson

The Futrells: **Above:** Virginia
Below left: Tammy, Dana, Virginia, and Herman
Below right: Robert and India

Opposite page:

Above left: Robert Fussell, Jr.
Above right: Mrs. Hugh Stuart Johnson
Below left: Sara Johnson Phillips
Below right: Mr. L. B. Bradshaw

Left: Boy at tobacco auction

Below: John Douglas
Fu trell, Jr.

Opposite: Boys with a gun

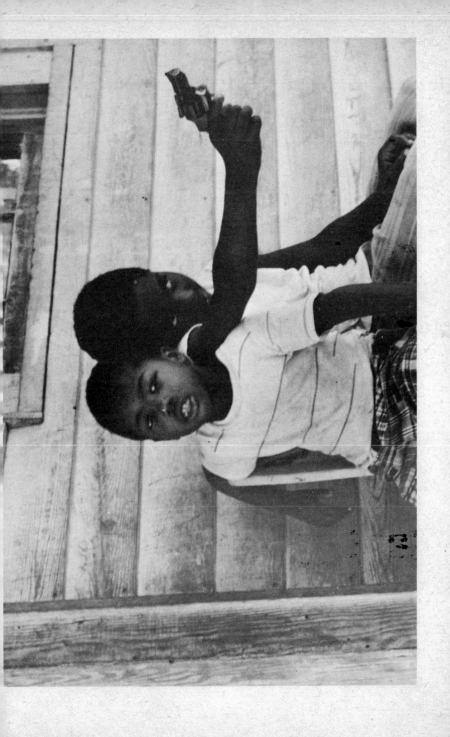

Waiting

Prayer Meeting

Laying on of hands

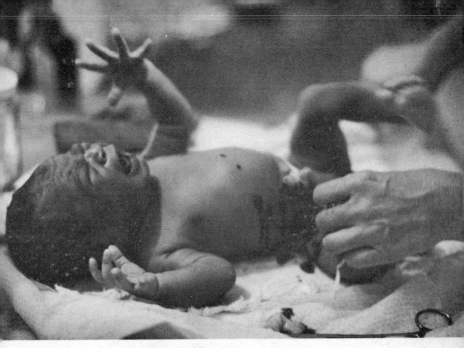

Child at three minutes

Mr. and Mrs. Clayton Rouse

Mr. and Mrs. Thurman Judge on their wedding day

trouble is drinkin'. Got to where I stayed drunk all the time. The ol' boy won his fight, you might say. An' see, if you're not saved, there ain't no need for the Devil to mess with you 'cause he's already got you, but if you got saved, he's gonna try to bring you back. 'Course the Bible say that a backslider, if he straighten up his life, really get in there, he can be a better Christian than when he started. What happened to me was, I was in a beer joint when Jesus Christ accepted me. It's kinda hard to explain. I was boozin' my beer down an' my wife, Ginny, got to this prayer meetin', which I was s'posed to go with her myself, but I left that mornin' an' didn't come back, an' they prayed that wherever I was, I'd quit drinkin' beer an' come there an' alla that. An' it seemed like somethin' drawed me, couldn't drink that beer to save my life. I couldn't understand why I couldn't drink it 'til they tol' me what happened later on. See, they prayed for me twice. It takes good Holiness people prayin' for you to get you saved. But then, if you don' pray to the Lord by yourself much as three times a day, sump'n like that, then sump'n come up an' get in your way. Then you hafta pray to Jesus Christ to remove it an' help you. If you don't, you gonna backslide.

You gotta be careful. 'Specially when you're poor. Any poor person that drinks is takin' money that their family needs an' just wastin' it on whiskey an' gas to take you to the ABC store. I'll tell you one thing. If I wasn't real religious, I'd drink beer an' whiskey an' enjoy every parta life I can. Now the other day I'd started back smokin' an' stuff like that. I mean, I'm not sayin' it's a sin to be smokin', but I made a promise to the Lord that I wouldn't smoke, an' it's the promise breakin' that's a sin. But I'll tell you. I had a li'l talk with the Lord, an' I laid them cigarettes right back down. See, you take one step an' God'll take two. If I was to renounce all religion, I'd enjoy sex an' anythin' else there was to enjoy. Reason why I say that is it would be the only enjoyment I'd have, 'cause there wouldn't be none after this world. But God blessed me. Them cigarettes cost me money an' ruined my health, an' Jesus just took 'em away from me. If I was gonna be a sinner, I believe I'd enjoy myself. But if you're a Christian, the Lord'll take the bad habits away from you.

Speakin' a' sin, a lotta people say it's wrong to be rich. Okay, Jesus Christ said it's as impossible for a rich man to go to heaven as a camel to go through a needle. But you gotta keep readin' down 'cause He also said all things is possible with the Father, an' that a rich man got a chance to go to heaven. See, it takes rich people an' poor people to make things run in the world. The Bible says there's always been poor people, an' I guess it takes whole diff'rent kindsa work to keep the world turnin'. A poor man he can do his day's work an' go home an' go to sleep. A rich man he's got it in his head twenty-four hours a day, just about. That stuff about how all men are created equal is a buncha baloney. You raise the devil, they come an' lock you up. Man with money he raises the devil, they don't do nothin' to him. An' the rich man always get richer. Like take the Pepsi-Cola company. The wages went up an' then they went up on the drinks, an' then the wages got cut down. Sometimes I get to think maybe some a' them companies cause them people to strike an' then give 'em a dime raise, an' they really go make more money offa that. An' take social security. Every time we get a raise from Washington, they get a raise in Duplin County. They ain't tryin' to help me. I see that raise comin' an' I know them groceries goin' to go up an' the price is goin' up in Kenansville for them stamps.

When my health was better, before this arthritis set in, I had a lotta low-payin' jobs. I have worked in logwood an' in farmin' an' I worked in the chicken houses for about seven years. They were all low-paid jobs, an' that's why the social security check, I'm just about the lowest-paid one on it. We get two hundred fifty-four dollars a month, me an' Ginny an' the kids. The rent is thirty dollars. An' a ten-dollar water bill, that makes forty dollars, an' the light bill usually runs about twenty dollars. That's sixty dollars. Then you add the furniture company; pay them seventeen dollars. It don't leave much. Gotta pay for the TV an' the lawn mower an' the washin' machine. I was makin' a little bit on the side, at truckin', but the man I worked for took his truck off the road. That'll tighten things up right smart. Ginny has picked up eggs, kinda helped out on that, an' I drove the truck part-time. But now we're both sick an' I dunno how we're gonna make it. Them food stamps, we was payin' fifty-four dollars for a hundred thirty-two, an' now it went up to seventy-four for a hundred thirty-two. I think if they're gonna give you sump'n, they oughta give it to you, not put it so high up there

you can't afford to get it. To get them stamps you gotta go to Kenansville an' pay somebody coupla dollars to take you up there,
an' then the prices keep goin' up. Seems like you never come out
on top. I ain't even got enough money to bury myself. So far as I
can see it, they oughta give Nash Johnson an' Ramsey the food
stamps. They can afford to buy 'em.

I got my troubles, but you'd be surprised at what the Lord can
do. Take what happened to me, for instance. I moved over here
an' I didn't have no money, no heat nowhere in the house. Everybody said, "How you gonna make it?" I said, "Well, the Bible say seek the Kingdom of God an' your needs will be ended."
An' before long a man come from the Baptist Church an' fill up
the kerosene barrel. An' other people helped here 'n there.

An' I'll tell you another time the Lord helped me. Direc'ly. I
owed some money on a bill. I was workin' in the chicken houses
back yonder. Got to where I couldn't do too much, an' it got to
where it was so bad I hadda go lay down. An' it seemed like a
voice flashed in my head an' tol' me to read a certain verse in the
Bible. I got the Bible an' I read that verse, an' it didn't seem like
it concerned me. An' I kept readin' an' it said there ain't nothin'
ain't possible with the Father in Heaven, an' I didn't worry 'bout
that bill no more, 'cause I knowed the government was gonna
pay that bill. What happened, see, I had put in for social security, but the welfare would send me a check 'til the social security
come. Okay. I got the welfare check an' on the fifth day I got the
social security check, an' so I had a chance to go 'round an' pay
that off. I believe the Lord worked it around that way. See, poor
people need so many things they get down there an' start prayin'
'bout it if they're a Christian, an' so God can help 'em.

The thing is, it's kinda hard for a poor man to get up there in
this world. Only chance you got is in education. An' a lotta them
ain't interested. I seriously hope them young 'uns finish school,
'specially Herman, 'cause mostly girls get married. 'Course lotta
times the girls need an' education, too, 'cause their husband
could get sick. I dunno. Poor children just lay around in school.
Seem like they don't got enough willpower or sump'n. They're
pretty smart kids if they get out there an' do it. But see, they
bring their stuff to me an' it's more'n I know, an' Ginny she don't
help 'em with their homework none.

A lotta times I look at Herman an' I think about myself. If Herman gets a real good education, his kids might amount to sump'n. Which now, education don't mean too much. I mean, you can keep off the welfare line, but as far as good jobs, it don't mean much at all. Now Herman, if he graduates from high school, he might not get too far. It's gonna take a lotta generations for this family to get anywhere. Sometimes I think about them kids an' I think about heaven an' I'm glad that'll be a happy time for 'em. They got golden streets an' plentya mansions, an' they say you eat honey. You could probably have nearly anythin' you wanted. 'Course the Bible don't say what they have for supper. But the way the Bible describe it, that gonna be a great place for them young 'uns.

Virginia

The first thing I got was scarlet fever. I hadda stay in the room by myself for two weeks, an' then I got scaly like a fish, an' the doctor tol' Mama to take a tub a' water, warm soapy water, an' wash me 'til them scales come off. Then I had a double case a' the red measles. Dr. Williams said he hadn't never seen a case a' measles like that in all the time he had doctored. But the first time I got really sick, I was about thirteen years old, an' I had sump'n like a seizure, a faintin' spell. I was fixin' to wash the dishes an' I fell across the dishpan. When the doctor come, he tol' Daddy that my monthlies was workin' on me an' that I didn't have enough blood. I was, y'know, anemic.

I didn't have no other real kinda sickness after I was a young 'un, not 'til I started in havin' my children. They come kinda fast. First I married Julius Weaver the fourth day a' November a' nineteen fifty, an' Robert Lee was born November the eighteenth of nineteen fifty-one. From there on it was anywhere from a year to fifteen months in the other children's ages. Mildred came along next. Dr. Newcombe said when Mildred was born, it was a wonder that hadn'ta killed me, her 'n Robert both. Then Durwood was born March the seventeenth of nineteen fifty-four. An' then there was Johnny. He was born when them hurricanes, Connie an' Diana, come through. Tommy he was born in nine-

196

teen fifty-six on the twenty-second of September. An' that was what we had, me an' Julius Weaver. Our children.

Mildred was bein' three months old an' she took sick. I thought she had a cold an' I carried her to the doctor, an' he gave her some medicine. An' then, when she died, she was right blue down one side, an' when we went to the funeral home, all the blue had left her an' had formed in the small parta her back. Dr. Westville is the coroner, an' he said that she was smothered to death. But she didn't, 'cause I had her in my arms. We weren't satisfied, an' we called in Dr. Newcombe, an' Dr. Newcombe examined her an' said she had died of spinal meningitis. You know them angels that was singin' with Mary an' Joseph when Jesus was born in Bethlehem? Well, I seen them angels before my baby died. They was tall as the door an' they had a gold circle 'round their head an' they was dressed in white. Two of 'em was standin' at the foot of the bed, one was standin' in the door. I hollered at Daddy to get the light, an' when he cut the light on, the angel in the doorway disappeared. The next time, when my husband died, I was layin' there an' I saw that angel standin' in the door. He didn't say nothin'. An' I didn't ask 'im nothin' neither. I was scared to death.

My husband always said it was his fault that Mildred died. I didn't think so, but there was no way I could tell 'im. We didn't argue 'bout that; fact, we didn't argue hardly at all. The only thing that me an' him disagreed on was drinkin'. He made me mad when he would drink that likker, an' I hemmed 'im up behind the bed one time with a big piece a' stove wood an' whupped 'is tail. But we didn't really have no trouble. An' then he went an' died out in the field. They had raised corn an' it was 'bout eight foot tall, an' he made a path all 'round that corn, just kept goin' 'round, seems like, 'til he got out in the open. He died from a epiletic fit an' ceberbal hemrage. Then he fell on 'is face an' he didn't move no more.

Robert had the fits first. An' I hadda carry 'im to Durham. They tol' me at Dukes Hospital he was havin' fits, an' then they gave 'im some phenobarbital tablets. Then Durwood started havin' the same fits as Robert, an' when Johnny come along, he was not quite twelve months when he had his first fit. Robert an' Johnny, they checked to see had it damaged their brain, an' it hadn't affected 'em in any way. They checked Durwood last year, when he was seventeen, an' they said Durwood had the mind of a ten-year-old child.

The time I carried Robert to Dukes, I met Bill Futrell. We courted with letters, an' when he came through town the third time, we was married. When me an' Bill got married, my mama an' daddy wouldn't let us have them young 'uns. I was wantin' 'em, but see, I'd stayed in my daddy's house for three years, an' they felt them kids was more theirs than they was mine. I didn't love Bill when I married 'im, an' he did the same to me, I reckon. We both wanted a home of our own. After we was married, we moved into a house with his mama for a while; then we moved to Albertson, up nexta Pink Hill. Then we moved back to Rose Hill an' lived out on the Lake Tuck Road. Then we moved from there to over behind where the ol' schoolhouse got burnt down. An' that's where we was livin' when Dana was born. We was married fourteen months when Dana was born, an' Dana was a year old when Herman was born, an' Herman like to bein' two years older'n Tammy. When I had Herman, I turned just as blue as ink an' lost my breath. Dr. Hawes tol' Bill's mama, an' they tol' me if I had another one, I was doomed. When I got like that with Tammy, I was so mad I didn't know what to do, but I had Tammy anyway, an' so he said, "Well, this is the last one." So he fixed up papers an' he sent me to Kenansville, but they couldn't operate on me then because my hemoglobins was down an' it took 'em two weeks to get 'em up to sixty percent. Then, see, I had an eatin' cancer on my womb, which they took that out because Dr. Redwine said it was the size of a silver dollar. They took out my tubes an' my womb, everythin' but my ovaries. Then, coupla weeks ago, they did what they call a cystocele, an' sump'n else I can't pronounce, a rectocele or sump'n. But anyway, they carried me to the operatin' room at quarter after seven in the mornin', an' when they brought me outta there, it was a quarter to twelve. They took out six inches a' my intestines, an' they burnt an' ulcer offa my leg an' they tightened up my bladder an' they fixed my rectum. The doctor says it's the pressure a' havin' so many children. See, I had eight heada young 'uns an' there ain't been much diff'rence between 'em.

Me an' Bill been together fourteen years, an' we got our diff'rences, but we get along as good as any of 'em. He was raised on firebread an' soppin' gravy, an' I was raised on ham 'n eggs. Back home we never went lackin'. My daddy worked three funeral homes an' then worked an eight-hour shift in the mill. I never knew a Christmas we didn't have plenty. But Bill, he tries. He gets on the mean side, which any man will. An' like most men, you can't always count on 'im. Kinda thing happens. We was married in April, an' in the last weeka May we moved to Albertson. We was stayin' at the house with 'is brother Charles an' 'is wife Fay, an' Fay's stepdaddy an' mama, an' they're all drunks up there. So one mornin' Bill he couldn't stand it an' he up an' left me. Boy, were that a time! There went Bill, home to Mama. The day Tammy was born Bill got drunk an' went out drivin' an' lost 'is brother J. D.'s automobile. Then they locked 'im up in jail when I had my hysterectomy for drivin' drunk. Now he has bad nerves, see, an' he just goes over to 'is mama's to get away from the young 'uns when they make so much fuss.

Me, I didn't have bad nerves 'til I took that hysterectomy operation. Which they don't like to give it to you 'til you're past thirty, an' I'd a been thirty-one in June an' I took it the lasta February. My first husband had an aunt, an' she took it before that time an' now she's half crazy. I'm not crazy, but I do get nervous, some. I take them little yella Valium tablets for my nerves an' also I've got a blue an' a white, an' a blue an' a white an' a yella, an' when I have a migraine headache, I hafta take two cc's of talcum. It ain't so good with two of us havin' bad nerves like we do. See, he's sick, an' I guess that's what makes 'im in the shape he's in; an' I'm sick, an' I guess that's what makes me in the shape I'm in. But we get along pretty good an' we'd be fine if other people wouldn't go stickin' their nose in our business.

Me an' Frances, which is one a' Bill's cousins, was talkin' at the clothes line today, an' Frances said she didn't see how in the world some people could be so mean, good as I was to people. But since I been home from the hospital no one else lifted a finger to help me. Usedta be when people got sick they'd go out an' help 'em with the crops, an' they'd go there an' cook for their children an' stuff like that. Nowadays you can get sick an' be layin' on the bed an' they won't even come in an' see about you. Bill's mama, that ol' lady, wouldn't even cook them young 'uns sump'n to eat. I was in that bed for three days, an' nobody bring me a glassa water. You know, God said, "An' I was sick an' you visit me not." An' He said, "When you do these things to the leasta my brethren, you also did it to me." But the Bible says do good for evil, so I won't pay 'em no mind.

Kay, which is Frances' sister, she's married to my son, Robert Lee, an' she's been stayin' with us. She's gonna have a baby, looks like pretty soon. Robert Lee, he's up in Hickory, but she don't like it. Both of 'em are 'bout as illnatured as the other. She's one a' them ill-tempered, lazy gals. She has my young 'uns cookin' for her an' totin' her sump'n to eat to that li'l ol' bed. Well, he's up yonder, workin' in a café, an' that how it gotta be, 'cause havin' them older boys a' mine around don't do nothin' for my reputation in this town. I get along pretty good with Mister Masters, the policeman, an' Mr. Fussell, the town hall man, but it got to where they wouldn't even talk to us when Robert an' Durwood was stayin' with us, they caused so much calamity. See, Durwood threwed a can at me, an' Robert Lee picked it up an' they got to fightin', so they put the law on me. Then Durwood went over to Bill's mama an' told 'er I tried to smother Bill with a pillow an' I shot a hole in 'is leg. So Mister Masters come down here to check. An' that's where all the trouble come. I don't like all them people an' all them stories. What me an' Bill do is our own business.

Them young 'uns me an' Bill got, anybody bother with 'em, I'd beat their blame tail. They was real good when I was sick. Dana really done all she could, but see, Dana's mind don't work right at times. Sometimes she acts just as normal as can be. Then again you can tell her sump'n 'r other an' she act like her mind's a million miles away. She's good with her hands, though. Her teachers tried to get me to put 'er in a retarded class an' I wouldn't do it. Dr. Owens said Dana never was retarded, an' I felt like it would ruin 'er for the resta her life. Now see, Tammy an' Herman they get A's an' B's on their report cards. It don't hurt me to work with them. But when you're talkin' 'bout school, can't never tell what's gonna happen to them young 'uns. Take Herman. Miz Allison said that Herman was a grade-A student, an' she said she didn't see how, when he got ol' lady Farrior,

200

why that ol' lady could bring his grades down like she did. She knocked the pure grease outta that boy one day an' he cried like a baby. He wouldn't even go to school. An' then she wouldn't promote him. Tammy's real smart. But how she gonna graduate from high school when she ain't gonna have the money to graduate? Johnny was goin' to school up in Henderson, an' he quit in the ninth grade 'cause he hadda pay for a gym suit an' his books, an' he was livin' with Mama an' she didn't have the money to pay for 'em. So he just quit an' went to work in the cotton mill. So that's what I mean to say. That new school out there on the Magnolia highway, I hear it's real nice an' the kids they like it fine. I know what they're doin' when they bring the papers home, so I don't go out there an' ask about 'em. Them people out there at that schoolhouse—they're doin' all they can for them young 'uns.

The thing is, I don' get out too much to go nowhere. I go down to the post office, an' I go down an' talk to them in the welfare office or over to the store. I could get out an' do as much work as any man could 'til they gave me that hysterectomy operation, but now I just do my sewin' when my eyes don't go on me. Bill says the work that God give me was singin', but I don' sing no more 'cause I get that bronchial asthma. Herman he's singin' for the Lord. One time his daddy was in the hospital, an' he was up there in front of them chicken houses while I was pickin' up eggs, an' when I come out, he was out there singin', "Well, the Lord has been so good to Mama I feel like travelin' on." Me an' Bill just sit here an' listen to 'im. When I was goin' to prayer meetin's up at Miz Brown's, there was a lady who could interpret the tongues an' she could prophesy, an' that's bein' a minister an' I think that's what I'm gonna do. I'd like to be a missionary an' do things to help people. But mostly I'm a homebody.

I got a good home, see, an' I don't wanna mess with it. Our marriage is better'n some. He don't run around an' I don't run around. He don't get drunk an' I don't get drunk. We work it out between us. We didn't love each other when we got married, maybe, but now I guess I love him. We're gettin' older, see, an' I wouldn't want anythin' to happen to him. I'm gittin' up there to forty an' he ain't much younger'n I am. If I had a dollar, I'd hafta share that dollar with 'im, an' if he had a dollar, he'd hafta share that dollar with me. I guess we have what we wanted. A home of our own. It takes two to make a marriage.

Dana

When I was little, I wanted to be a nurse. But I seen the cowboy pictures on Saturday about seven o'clock, an' there are some good-lookin' cowboys, so that's what I wanna do. First, I know I'm gonna hafta go all the way through college, an' they'll tell me howta be a cowgirl an' then I'll go on the TV. That would be fun. I dunno. I'd like bein' a nurse. Dr. Hawes is my best friend, an' if you're a nurse in the doctor's office, you get to work for him. I don't like that ol' lady he got with him 'cause she's mean. It'd be nice to wear them white clothes an' get to stick needles in an' listen to the babies cry.

I'm s'posed to be in the seventh, but I'm not 'cause I failed too many grades. But I like to go to school anyway. I got a lotta clothes I can wear. One is blue with a blue tie, an' it's slashed down the side. An' I got another one, it's blue an' white; an' I got a maxi, it's purple with flowers. I weared it to school one day an' everybody said it was real pretty. We got suites, which is sorta like classes, an' we do readin' an' writin' an' 'rithmetic an' we got some papers to take home an' do. School is fun, 'cept the teacher makes you do your work, an' if you don't have your homework, she pops you in the head five 'r ten times. She uses this ruler an' a round thing with a handle, but she don't do it to me 'cause I do my homework.

My teachers are real sweet an' nice, an' I gotta lotta girlfriends, but the trouble is the boys. We take these recesses where we play dodge ball, an' Friday they had a long time gettin' me out. They had two teams an' they had all them boys up there, an' if they hadn'ta had them, they never woulda gotten me out. The trouble with boys is they always think you go with 'em for boyfriends. An' that ain't true. One of 'em thinked that today, an' I told him I wouldn't go with 'im for three hundred dollars. He acts crazy. He tried to go with this other girl, an' she laughed at him just the way I did. I don't like him, but I like Donald Pitman. He's good-lookin'. He's my boyfriend an' he's twenty 'r twenty-one, sump'n like that, I dunno. An' I like Jerry. Every time I see Jerry he give me a lotta money, an' I think I'd go with 'im. Diana used-ta go with Jerry an' he gave her a lotta money. Then Diana said, "I'm gonna break up with 'im," an' Jerry tried to go with Tammy an' he tried to hug her. See, boys is really ecchy 'cause they're always tryin' to do these things to you.

The boys sometimes try to hit you, but in school mostly we fights with the niggers. Me an' a girl started fightin' one day, an' then her brother an' this other boy started fightin'. They call us white soda crackers an' we call 'em black niggers. They get mad about that an' we do, too, an' some of 'em got sent off the bus. In school last year they made us sing this song to 'em, an' they sang one to us. We sang, "I Must Play with My Colored Friends." This girl, Gloria, come here one day an' Mama got mad an' said she couldn't come no more. She was a nigger an' she was colored.

That don't bother me none 'cause I get to see Donna. Last night I wore my brown pants an' the red top, an' me an' Donna we got two Sundrops an' we drunk 'em when we come home from school. But see, Mama's been pretty sick an' I hafta do a lotta chores like hang up clothes an' do the laundry, an' tomorrao I got a job mowin' grass after school. Then Saturday I have housecleanin', washin' dishes, scrub the floor. An' who come along an' mess it up? Tammy an' Herman an' Frances. Frances give me enough to buy a drink an' sometimes she give me enough to buy candy. An' I like Frances 'cause she's livin' with us, an' one time Mama an' Daddy fight an' they get hurt. Mama's clock broke one time an' then Daddy left home on Saturday an' didn't even come back 'til Monday. Mama an' Daddy don't get drunk, 'cept one time they did, a long time ago when Uncle John died in the water. That was Frances' father. An' Kay's. That was after their mama she got burnt up in fronta Nash Johnson's an' she died. We was 'shamed to cry in fronta the people, an' we sneaked behind this place an' I thought I was with J. D., which is Daddy's brother, but when I waked up, I got left at the funeral home. When I got back to my house, everyone was a-prayin' an' they thought I was in a dead place, an' Mama she took my clothes an' she threw 'em away.

There was this prayer meetin' when Frances' daddy died, an' I almost fainted 'cause Brother Norris, which is the preacher, he baptized me. They didn't hold my nose 'r nothin', but Tammy she went whammy, an' they hadda hold 'er nose. The first time I got baptized I started runnin', an' they caught me an' I went under water, an' then I come back up an' the second time I went deeper an' they didn't hold my nose 'r nothin'. Not like they did with Tammy an' Herman.

I'm very busy 'cause I gotta lotta things to do. I get up 'bout six o'clock an' put me some perfume on, powders, put my dress on, an' wash an' put this medicine on my face. Then I take my rollers an' I do my hair an' I go to school. When I get home, I got my chores an' I gotta do my homework an' I gotta watch the TV. I watch *Somerset* an' then *Lassie* an' then *Daniel Boone,* an' at night I see *Andy Griffith* an' then I see *Green Acres.* I like where she's holdin' her puppy an' she goes "achoo," an' the puppy goes "achoo." The thing I really do is go visitin'. Like we went to Kinston an' we saw Durwood. There were some crazy people there, an' Mama saw this boy an' he called her "Mama." This big fat ol' boy. His legs were fat, his stomach, all over he was fat an' he can't do like the other boys did. He hadda walk real slow. An' we laughed an' laughed. Then this other time we stayed with Uncle Jimmy in Kinston an' I have this boyfriend up there an' we always play. An' I have two girlfriends. I got a girlfriend, she gave me two dresses an' a pair a' hotpants, an' one shirt got *Love* sewed on it; got *Peace,* got *Love,* got *No Pollutin' the Air* on it. An' I got some flowers on the hotpants an' these bikini drawers, which they're purple- an' orange-striped. I had fun for them days I went up there. Some boys tried to kiss us an' we kep' goin' runnin'. They couldn't catch Wanda nor me neither. This li'l girl, Bunny, they catched her an' we ran away an' went to Uncle Jimmy's house an' they didn't never find us. They came lookin' an' this lady there she called them boys "shit-asses." She said, "Them ol' shit-asses go runnin' along an' don't know howta do nothin'." An' we laughed an' laughed an' laughed 'til I was about to cry. Then Aunt Sallie's toenail fell off an' we hadda go home.

10 The Law

"The only organized crime in Duplin County's in the Duplin County Court-house."

—Duplin County deputy sheriff

The Bootlegger

In the days past, it was when I was quite a young man, I more or less kept my work a secret. I'd go to bed early 'n crawl out the window, work, makin' likker all night, an' then I'd slip back in 'fore the chickens crowed for day. I prospered, but you never gain nothin' by it. I reckon you could say I didn't use my judgment like it shoulda been used. Fast money, you don' never hold to it. Gets away from you. I made likker to sell it, now, didn't make it to drink. Kept a drunk around so's he could test it. If it didn't kill 'im, why, I could put it on the market. Didn't never kill one tester, not outright. They died in the future, not early on.

I've made quite a few friends an' I have made quite a little money, an' I've found long as I have money, I had more friends than I have any idea of. When I commence losin' my money, my friends commence disappearin'. Sorta hard to find. One time it happened I was goin' to the hospital, in the years gone by, an' I was askin' my neighbors an' friends to a barbecue farewell, not knowin' if I was a-comin' back. Sorta give 'em somethin' to think about. Well, when I got back from the hospital, they had dug up my barrel of brandy an' drunked it all up an' disposed of it, an' it come time to find out that a portion of my friends was my enemies. So I wouldn't advise nobody to trust too many people. It would be a bright idea to keep some of your secrets to yourself.

Bootleggin' was a right interestin' business. You meet a lotta folks. Farmers, school teachers, politicians. The preachers they's good fellers. Now, one time we had a mighty good neighbor was a member of the church. He had a quart bottle with a gumroot stopper in it, an' the last time I ever remember seein' that bottle, that cork stopper it looked like trimmin' with the marks from my teeth, I took it out so many times. You made a lotta money on occasion, an' other times was hard. I have sold as high as fifteen dollars a gallon an' have sold it down as low as two-fifty, three dollars. But back in the days when it was sellin' for three dollars, there was so many bootleggin' you hadda go with your shirt open so you'd know one from the other. That was the sign. If the shirt was unbuttoned, you didn't approach 'im to sell 'im none, figgerin' he had as much as you had. So one time ol' man Henry Sutton, which was the deputy marshal, accused me when I was before 'im, said, "I found out why you go with your shirt unbuttoned at the top." Said, "That's the bootlegger's sign." I played real innocent with 'im, but he was a smart feller. Thought as much of me as my daddy did, almost. He kept me posted, an' every time he'd ever find out anythin', he'd get in touch with me an' tell me all about what was goin' to take place.

Now them revenuers they was always tryin' to catch me. They seemed to think a lot of me. They was paid to catch me an' I was paid to try 'n keep from 'em. One time I had a still off in the woods, an' I was comin' out an' I met the law comin' in. I knew they had started to my place, so I run my little ol' car in the woods, jumped out, an' went barefoot through the woods an' tol' the boys the law was comin'. Rest of 'em left an' I hitched up the mule an' set through them woods, not a bit of road. I continuously kept layin' line to that mule an' I didn't look back. Few weeks after that I was over in Jacksonville an' the sheriff says to me, said, "Turn around an' let me see your back." I says, "What's the idee for that?" He says, "Turn around like I asked you." I turned around an' he says, "That's that back." Say, "You were sittin' up there in the fore part a' that cart, layin' line to that mule, an' I was back there runnin' hard as I could go an' I couldn't catch you to save my neck." I said, "You must have the wrong man." He says, "No, I ain't." So I always recommend: never look back.

Well, see, that sheriff was my friend. He didn't wanna catch me to start with. That was just his business. Probably had somebody with 'im that he hadta make a show. He pulled up to my place one day an' says, "I come to search." I said, "I ain't in no position to be searched today. If you hadda let me known, I woulda been." I said, "Come back tomorrow an' everythin'll be all right." He said, "You cut out all that foolishness an' go bring me a jar a' likker." So I went an' brought 'im a jar, 'n mighty proud to get off it that light.

I used to rent farms back then, an' they had a coupla dwellin's on 'em. Put a family in one a' them an' a likker still in the other 'n run it by kerosene stoves. Well, the ol' sheriff he got the same stove I dunno how many times, an' brought it back an' told me where he left it. Did that for years an' years. Then one time, I can remember, I had a farm raided had a tenant on it. That tenant, I done everythin' I could to assist him 'bout his crops. He just didn't pay me no mind. The grass was growin' up between the tobacco beds, an' one time he run off from Friday to Friday, didn't leave water for the mule 'n nothin'. Well, he went on, an' long about tobacco-barnin' time he said to me, "I want you to buy me a bag of ice potatoes. I want to plant me some ice potatoes." I said, "Not me, I ain't buyin' you no seed of no kind for no other crops." He throwed a fit. Ran into the house an' grabbed his gun an' was gonna kill me. I got in my truck an' come on home, got my shotgun an' went back. When I got in sight, he had dressed up an' come out on the front porch of the other house, sittin' there talkin' to his wife. Well, I'd been makin' likker upstairs, an' he'd been up there an' cut my still all to pieces an' poured the likker out, an' when I found out, he took to the river, swum out to where some people was a-fishin', an' he got in the boat with 'em an' asked 'em to put 'im across. I couldn't get in touch with 'im after he got goin'. So I come on back home.

I had a whole buncha hogs an' I was afraid that rascal would come back an' kill 'em, so I was loadin' 'em on my trailer when him an' the sheriff, highway patrolman, come in there. I stood there with my gun across myself, waitin' for somebody to shoot at. Sheriff walked up to me an' took my gun, said, "I guess you'll hafta consider yourself under arrest." I said, "I don't know what you have reference to." He said, "This man says you got a still up yonder, upstair in that buildin'." I said, "I dunno whether I have or not. I believe I rented this place to this gentleman here." Said to my tenant, "Didn't I rent you this farm?" He says,

"Yeh." I said, "He may have one out yonder. I dunno nothin' 'bout his business." Sheriff turned to 'im an' says, "I reckon you'll hafta go with me." Carried 'im right on an' put 'im in jail.

Now don't get the wrong idea. Ain't always had such good times with the law. Sheriff Williamston he killed my buddy. What happened, I was runnin' a still out to Kenansville, over there near the Grove Swamp. Seems like a colored feller had killed his wife over near Smith township, an' they had all the roads blocked, tryin' to catch 'im. Me 'n Mike had the two darkies that done the stillin' for us in the car, all four of us in the front seat an' the still in the back, an' when we come up there, right the other side of Grady School, the sheriff had the road blocked. I coulda ducked an' went 'round, but I knew I didn't have nothin' that could outrun 'im. So I stopped, an' when I did, Mike jumped out an' started runnin' right down in front a' the car. 'Course the lights was a-shinin' on 'im, but the sheriff turned right around an' shot 'im in the back. Then he drawed his gun on us an' says. "Y'all consider yourself under arrest." I said to 'im, "The hell you say, you killed my best buddy. I'm goin' to 'im." Mike was wantin' some water, an' I went up to ol' man Lonnie Gordon's well an' drawed me a bucket. Other thing was, I had a pistol in my pocket, an' I scratched a hole in the sand on the side of the well, buried it, packed the dirt on top of it, an' snatched that well bucket off of the chain to bring Mike the water. Time I come back, there was gathered up quite a crowd. So I said, "I want this man carried to the hospital." Finally the sheriff took 'im in his car an' carried 'im to Lenoir County an' he deputized his brother, Pete, to bring me an' them two niggers to jail in Kenansville.

There was no lights in that day an' time an' Pete he wasn't familiar. So they went to strikin' matches an' tryin' to get the key in the hole. I said, "Gimme the key. I believe I can open it." Well, he struck a match an' I unlocked the jail an' went on in, an' he said, "Do you want to stay down here with these niggers or do you wanna be put upstairs by yourself?" I said, "Me an' the niggers was caught together, me an' the niggers'll stay together." After he left, them niggers got pretty uppity. Said, "You're the instigation of us bein' here. He couldn'ta unlocked the darned jail without you." I told 'em we was gonna try the case right. An'

210

I explained to 'em how we was gonna handle things. Warn't no use in all of us goin' up the road. So I got ol' Sylvie Peacord, he was loggin' over here to Hallsville, an' he dated them time sheets of his back like them niggers had been workin' for him for a coupla weeks, an' it looked like they had just been hitchhikin' with us. They were right footloose after that. Me, cost me 'bout seventy-five dollars to get shut of it, an' I didn't have no idea to get my car back, 'cause they caught the still right in it, but the sheriff come to me an' give me the keys, said, "Your car's parked right around the corner here." Well, I reckon we evened up accounts. After all, I was the one that cleared the sheriff. See, he didn't mean to do it. Mike was the first one to jump out an' the two niggers was behind 'im, an' when he saw them two niggers, he figgered Mike was a nigger, too. An' nigger was what he was after. So I tol' the truth an' they didn't do nothin' to 'im.

In days past I was called to go to my neighbor in the hospital an' give a blood transfusion. After they checked my blood, it didn't match with my neighbor, but it did the sheriff's wife. An' they asked me if I would mind givin' blood to *her.* 'Course I didn't mind it an' I gave the blood, an' a few weeks later she recovered, come home an' commenced givin' her husband trouble. She wanted to go up the street barefooted, she wouldn't get along with 'im, an' there was some such talk as goin' into the bootleggin' business. Well, they got her calm, an' evidently she became very agreeable. Took some time to get her quieted down, though. I don' understand to this day why they should have that against *me.*

The Juvenile

When I was seventeen, me an' this other guy, we broke into this church an' we stole some money. It averaged to about five hundred ten dollars and twenty-five cents. It was about a month before they caught us an' they brought us back to the place where we had done it, an' they tried us an' convicted us. We had hit about two or three other places before we got caught, an' we didn't get any time on a coupla those counts, so I just knew we'd only get probation, right? Man, was I surprised!

211

Actually, we didn't go in to get the money. Just, it was Christmas an' there was a lotta presents an' stuff an' I was gonna take 'em. Anyway, the door was open an' I saw the safe was there an' I tried a combination. I was just gonna try it, right. Well, I opened it up an' saw all that money an' I took it. Y'know what really got me? The money we had stole, we bought a car with it. An' after they gave us time, me, stupid, signed the title of the car back over to the church, so that they could get their money back. I paid them back double, all right. They got their money an' I got four years. I know they got their money back outta that car because it was in excellent condition. I figger I don't owe them people nothin'.

First place they sent me was the Polk Youth Center in Raleigh. If you can make the first coupla weeks, it's okay. You've already got used to the worst part an' figgered out howta survive. It's bad when you go in there an' you don't know nobody, but I was lucky. My first cousin he was there an', see, he'd already been there before in that same camp an' he knew how the people were. So I was ready for 'em. Like there's a lotta fags in them places. An' when you first come in, they're lookin' for you. They come over 'n talk to you, say all this trash to you, just like you do to a woman. It's like a test, see? An' if they find out you take up for yourself, even if you get whupped, you won't have any trouble with 'em. You gotta be prepared to defend yourself. Mosta the time you'd get into fights if you didn't watch it. Like four hours after I got there, I got into a fight an' cut this boy. See, I had a pack a' cigarettes, an' these four colored guys are standin' around, an' one of 'em asks me for a cigarette. I figgered, "If I give him one, I gotta give all four of 'em one." An' so I said no. Man, they jumped me. I had a single-edged razor that was in a half-toothbrush, what they call a shank, an' that's what I cut 'em with. Anyway, they put me in the hole. They had me in the hole three times.

First time it was for thirty days. That was pretty rough. It's a cell about eight feet long an' twelve feet high, sump'n like that. No windows. You had a bed an' a toilet. You got six ounces of liver a day. On the third day you'd get one egg an' a slice of bread an' a cup of milk. They've changed that now. Just before I got out they were givin' 'em two meals a day, an' now they can only put 'em in for thirty days, where before it was for undetermined time if they wanted to. The first four or five days I got kinda feelin' bad, but it seems like your stomach gets strong enough an' you get used to it. If you had visitors, you didn't visit three hours a week like everybody else, they only let you visit thirty minutes. That was the only time you'd get to come outta your cell. So when you were in there, you'd hope your parents would come every week. But me, I don't think I saw my parents one time when I was in the hole. I mean, they tried 'n everythin' but they couldn't make it. I was in there on my birthday an' Thanksgivin', but on Thanksgivin' now they give you a real nice dinner, an' if there is anyone in there at Christmastime, they let 'em out. You get to take one shower a week, an' you have the Bible an' that's it. It runs you crazy, really. You think about everythin' from far back as you can remember. When you come out, 'specially in the summertime, you about have sunstroke, you been in there so long an' there's no light. If you don't watch it, your mind'll get away from you.

First there was the cuttin'. Next time I was workin' at the clothes house, which is a place where when the new guys come in, you take their old clothes an' send 'em home an' give 'em prison issues an' stuff like that. Well, I got caught stealin' a pair of socks in there an' they put me in the hole for about seventeen days. Time after that I was about gettin' my honor grades, which that's for good behavior, an' you get more privileges, like when your folks come, you get to go outside the fence, an' they caught me huffin', sniffin' this lacquer thinner stuff that gets you high. That time they threw me in the hole for just three days until they tried me. What happens is, see, they keep punishin' you right on. It's a little diff'rent now. I guess they had a lotta people comin' in there visitin', so things are gettin' better. Used to, anythin' you did in there the prison officials would try you. Now they got people from the street. When my first cousin was in there the first time, he got up without permission after the lights went out, an' the guard took 'im down to the sick bay an' slapped 'im around an' then he told 'im that if he went an' told anybody, they'd make it real hard on 'im. So he didn't mention nothin'. The second time I was in the hole this guard called me over the door an' I went to see what he wanted, an' he sprayed my face fulla mace. You talk about sump'n that burned. It took twelve hours before I could see anythin'. They still do stuff like that, but they're pretty damn careful about it with all these investigations goin' on.

I gotta say, though, there's stuff that ain't so bad. The places I was at, they had different jobs, like woodworkin', brick mason, auto mechanic, body'n fender. They also have vocational school an' they give you an opportunity to take the high school equivalency test. An' you take Kenansville, which is where I finished up my time. They take away the bars an' they don't lock the gates anymore, an' you don't even wear prison clothes; you wear green clothes, like in the service. When I was at Kenansville, one a' the guards took me out on release time. Well, he's not s'posed to let you outta his sight, an' he took me over to my aunt's house an' left me there for about six hours. Then he come back an' got me. He was a nice guy.

One thing about prison—you learn a lot in there. Used to, I didn't know nothin' about padlocks. Now there's not a padlock I can't break open. You take a radio battery, a little transistor, an' make what they calla thumb-buster an' you slip it right over just like a key. Or take a door that is locked, like on a trailer. Get a coat hanger an' fix it right, won't be no problem. You can go right in. You make contacts an' you make plans an' a lotta guys, they come back in there together. Some of 'em get straightened out, but man, some of 'em, they get to thinkin' 'bout prison like it's home.

There's other shit, too, right? Like the homosexuals. You take a guy that comes in there that's seventeen years old. Me, I don't think I weighed more'n 'bout a hundred and two pounds. He's gonna have a lotta trouble if he can't fight. I got three teeth knocked out on accounta that. There was this one boy, white boy, got raped by a buncha niggers while I was in there. Happens all the time. What it is, there's no privacy. Forty guys in a dormitory, bunk beds, twenty on each side. They don't have no curtains or nothin' on the showers. You walk to the shower, you better go with somebody. Me, after I'd been there about eight months, it was okay. They wouldn't lay a hand on me. They knew they come near me, they'd be dead niggers right on. Thing

214

is, I just don't see how any man could do anythin' like that. You get pretty horny, but after a while you don't miss it all that much, an' the way these guys act, you're watchin' over your shoulder all the time. I dunno about the rest a' the guys, but I sure as hell was.

One thing it does teach you is you gotta work. Before I pulled time, I'd go to work two hours an' I was ready to come home. Now I know if I don't work, I'll end up back where I was at. The case of a lotta them, they expect to come out here an' lay around an' take it easy. Seventy-five percent of the people that go back, they go back for not workin'. That's breakin' parole. You gotta work an' you gotta send a written report to your parole officer every month an' tell 'im what you're up to. When I got married, I got married without permission an' went outta the county without permission, an' I was drivin' a motor vehicle without permission. An' they coulda sent me back. Just for that. But see, my parole officer was from my hometown. It's like anythin'. It's who you know. Even for me.

Like take today. I passed a car, which I *did* cross the yellow line. A patrolman saw me an' gave me a break. I knew the guy. Last week this bastard down in Wallace gave me a ticket for doin' absolutely nothin'. So it really *is* who you know. The prisons is a really good example. We had a boy come in there, he was busted for drugs, they put 'im under observation ninety days, seein' a psychiatrist. All right. They send him to court. He come back to prison, served twenty-eight days, he was home. That's what I can't understand. I knew his people had money. I know that because he'd talk about it all the time an' he got plentya money while he was there. An' you take the man I used to work for. His son wrote a four-thousand-dollar bad check for a new car. He took off to California. Took 'em three or four months to catch 'im. They sent 'im up for two years; he stayed seventeen days an' he was home. See, your daddy is out there. An' he'll go talk to a judge in the county. An' he'll go talk to someone maybe a little higher, an' that man a little higher will go talk to someone a little bit higher, an' that's how it runs. Look what happened to the vice-president, what's his name, Agnew. He just disappears kinda quiet like, an' they forget the whole thing. An' President

215

Nixon. Seems like he oughta go down the road a right good little while. The way it's set up, money talks, an' if you got it an' you know the right people, it don't matter what you done.

But I'll tell you one thing. Prison changed me. I take responsibilities now. My parole officer got me a job at Nash Johnson's mill, an' the day I got out, I went on over there at three o'clock in the afternoon, an' they tol' me to come back to work at six, an' back I come. Before I got in trouble, I used to drink all the time, an' now sometimes I'll go out an' eat supper an' I'll maybe take a beer, but further'n that, nothin' else. I ain't never goin' back to one a' them places. I got three brothers an' they're headed right for it, an' I try to talk to 'em about it an' they just won't listen. See, you can't really explain how it is. It's not the beatin's or the fightin' or the food that really gets to you. It's like when they come in an' tell you to turn the TV to a certain station, you gotta do it. You gotta ask to go to the rest room. You gotta ask them for aspirin, you gotta do this an' you gotta do that, an' they're always callin' you "boy." An' you do what they tell you an' you don't draw back to hit one of 'em. You just gotta take it. An' you just think back in your mind you're not gonna make a mistake, so you won't hafta stay in prison too long. What it is, see, you don't feel like a man while you're doin' time. An' so when they told me I was gettin' out, I went out the door. I ran right into a trash can, I went so wild. Not bad, understand, but just kinda crazy. 'Cause it was sixteen months ince I was on the outside. So me, I'm gonna keep workin' an' doin' what I'm s'posed to. The trouble in my life—that's in the background. An' I wanna let it stay that way.

The Deputy

I dunno if it's an unwritten law or what, but you don't mess around in a county without seein' the sheriff. I don't care if you are a federal marshal or who you are. In other words, if an agency comes in here an' they're gonna raid someone, they'd better not go bustin' in without the sheriff knowin' about it. It's kinda like some a' them bayous down there in Louisiana; whoever's in charge of a certain parish is God. In North Carolina, now, a

216

sheriff is your highest elected official in the county. All your commissioners are voted in by districts; he's voted in on a countywide election. It don't matter how much he cares or how honest he might want to be; he goes easy on people. In a county that's your number-one man—the sheriff. An' he's gotta keep everybody satisfied.

When I first come in this work, a man told me "The only job you got is the apprehendin' of a criminal an' takin' him before the courts." He said, "If you hafta worry about what happens when you get a man in court, you won't last a week on the job 'cause it'll drive you right up the side of the wall." An' that's exactly the philosophy you hafta have. It sounds barbaric to say it, but that is the way you get to feel. My job is apprehendin' criminals an' takin' them before the courts. You forget the rest of it. Forget that the way I present my case usually dictates whether he is found guilty or not, regardless of what the truth might be. In Duplin County there's the same old game of what you got an' who you know. You just *know* when you get some people that you'll get to court an' they already been heard from an' a lesser plea's been arranged. You might spend two years workin' on a case an' it's gone.

People do a lotta screamin' an' yellin' about law'n order, law'n order, but when you're in law enforcement, they don't like you at all. In this job I'm in you get people that hate to see you because of what you represent. It's one of them things. They say you're an SOB if you do, an' you're one if you don't. You can't win. They don't want you around when they're havin' their little party or experimentin' with grass or somethin', but when somebody's breakin' in their back window or broke in their store last night, if you're not there within five minutes, they're raisin' all kinda hell. In this county the garbage collectors an' the dog warden make more than some a' the deputies. So you tell me what's important an' what ain't. An' then you gotta examine what that leads to. You got fourteen or fifteen deputies. You got about six of 'em actually workin'. The rest of 'em are too busy. They don't care. The biggest thing they're concerned about is gettin' their tobacco in, an' the least they can do, the least warrants they can sign, the least time they hafta go to court, the happier they are.

217

That is the attitude of the biggest part of 'em. They're not dedicated lawmen. They've got an easy job. They can get a little bit of extra money an' have a car to drive.

I'm a Democrat, an' I know good 'n well if I wasn't, I wouldn't have this job. That's the truth. An' I don't think it's got no place in law enforcement. A good example is what happened in our national government. That man Nixon's as liable to the law as the poor Chicano or black out diggin' a ditch. He *should* be. Well, how it happens here, see, each commissioner's kinda got his own deputies that live in his area. In the past he's the one that's been responsible for gettin' them on, so naturally they're real grateful to him. You get to know a lotta people in this job; ain't nobody else gonna see as many people in a day as I do. So you go around talkin', politickin'. Say you know one section over there, you can go get ten people an' tell 'em, "You go an' vote for so-an'-so." That's ten votes. Half the people, 'specially the blacks, they don't even know who's runnin' an' they don' care. So maybe you use a little money slid in there. You might make two trips over an' carry 'em to the polls an' tell 'em who to vote for, an' they don't know the difference. The deputies usually do it on their own because they're drivin' the county car with county gas, an' they're tryin' their best to get the man that's gotten 'em the job to stay in there. An' the people they don't care either way, or they don't know either way.

An' here's what the results come out to. We got five commissioners. Three of 'em—Gerald Quinn, Jiggs Fussell an' Willard Hoffler—are millionaires an' three of 'em, same three, are retired. How can a man that's a millionaire, retired, relate to anybody workin' about expense of livin' an so forth? I mean, he can't do it. The one or two commissioners we got that are not in that situation are so independent that they forget that somebody voted them in there just as soon as they get into office. They forget they were human bein's an' think they always walked about twenty feet over the tops of those trees. One part of this county has got a man that ain't done nothin' for four years, he's settin' there, an' all of a sudden you'll see four or five people's driveways get paved. You'll see a little street where the paved road comes up an' stop, an' they all of a sudden bring in the machines. An' he

218

ain't got nothin' to worry about 'cause he'd got his deputies haulin' 'em in on election day.

See, in Duplin County you got law an' politics, an' they're really one an' the same. For example, they got this poker house. It's real nice. Got a color TV there, they barbecue chickens, all that stuff. Well, look. Gamblin' is illegal. I'd personally like to see 'em make it legal; it's not like they're hurtin' other people by playin'. But that isn't the point. It's against the law. Well, I been in there, an' I been to see everybody I could to help me shut 'em down an' all, an' nothin' is ever gonna get done. The man that owns it is real important, an' a lotta big people go there, an' so we gotta keep hands off. That's not right. If you're gonna let a man like that get by with somethin' an' not look, well, you gotta let the bootlegger get by with makin' liquor an' not look; you gotta let the man break in somebody's house an' not look; you gotta let 'em go out an' commit murder an' walk away without a word. I dunno why it happens. I could see how a lotta men could easily take what you might call inducements. Me, I'd rather for a man to spit in my face than offer me a bribe. I got more respect for the uniform an' the badge than that. An' one day we're gonna have to be accountable anyway.

Well, there's more 'n one way of influencin', that's for sure. Take down in Magnolia. There's a private little club that gets so much a month to join, an' the man that owns it keeps women there. It's just a house of ill repute, what I call it. That's all it is. Even got a white girl stayin' there now. Has big fancy liquor stills. Let me tell you what I been told by another deputy 'bout that place. "He takes care of his own trouble. We don't never get no calls, so don't bother him." There's not a question of whether he's guilty or not guilty of breakin' the law. But you don't bother him.

Well, to me that's not the way the law is. If I knew right this minute that I could go there an' find illegal liquor or find some way to prove prostitution goin' on in that place, I'd be there fast as I could get my car to start. Only thing is, I'd hafta get somebody to go with. An' I dunno more 'n two deputies I'd trust on a raid. An' I'm not always sure about them. Besides, the people behind that joint own the county, so what you gonna do? But let some kid get caught with a stick of marijuana on him, an' if his daddy isn't rich, there's hell to pay.

I'll tell you, one profession where a man doesn't have to worry 'bout makin' a livin' is the law. What they make on the criminal cases alone is ridiculous. But with all these people gettin' separation papers, wills, all the notary work, I'd like to draw one of their checks, I'll tell you that much. There's certain things, see, an' you hafta have a lawyer. It don't make much difference how you wanna plead. You can go in there an' have a man drivin' drunk, blew twenty-five on the breathelizer. No doubt he was drunk. They get a lawyer an' pay him two hundred dollars to get up there an' say, "He's guilty." Oh, he'll act up a real storm. Tell 'em the man needs his driver's license when he drives to work or he's gotta take his wife to the doctor or somethin' like that. Y'know, kinda plead for him. But there's a lotta people can't afford it, an' the main thing is a lotta times you're payin' that attorney for nothin'. Guilty is guilty an' that's what they plead.

But the one thing you need the lawyer for is they're all friends around that courthouse. Those lawyers, judges, all went to the same college just about. All real big in the party kinda thing. They been together all their lives. So the judge an' the lawyer get together an' say, "He's a pretty good boy, y'know. How 'bout givin' him a break, he happens to be so-an'-so's son." They got a degree of punishment they're supposed to put 'em through, but they don't apply it equally.

I'll say that without hesitation. I have never sat down an' documented an' went through the cases an' proved it, but I could. If I went to court every day for a month an' wrote down each charge, the man's financial background, his race, his lawyer, an' so forth, every one of 'em, an' then started to compare 'em, same charges, I'd find it. In other words, a man gets one thing here an' two weeks from now another one, same charge, pays a different amount of money. If somebody would do that, I'll bet you my paycheck it would be cut-an'-dried. Look. It's this way. I remember one time when I was real small, I went to this man's house. He's a big judge now, an' about half of these same lawyers that's up there in the courthouse was with 'im an' they had the biggest drunk party you've ever seen. It was sump'n else. Point is, they're buddies. They got a good way of doin' things.

They're happy. Christ almighty, they oughta be. They're just playin' around with other people's lives.

The trouble is there's no standard here. You hear a lot about how there's no morals, there's no values, the country's goin' to the dogs. Well, they musta taken a good look at Duplin County is all I can say.

Now, we got probably the biggest, best, nicest landfill in North Carolina. Matter of fact, they got people comin' from Raleigh to look at it. I mean, it's a big-deal thing. Well, it happened a little time before the landfill was built, one a' the county commissioners, his son bought that land. When they decided the landfill was goin' to be there, they sold it to the county with an unbelievable profit. You can't prove nothin' on 'em. Fixed up the deeds, I guess. Here's another one. We got a dog warden. Well, this county, coon huntin', deer huntin', dogs is big-time money. People get obsessed with huntin' here like they do with playin' golf most places. There has been cases when there has been good coon dogs disappeared, an' the dog warden's truck would be seen in that area with a female dog which will draw any other dog when the female gets just right, you know. It's been told to me that they take that dog into a known neighborhood where there're some good hounds an' let her out, give that female a coupla days an' then go back there an' get some fine dogs an' sell 'em. An' one a' the commissioners is in on it. Fact is, the only man elected from this county I'd ever support after what I've seen is one from Wallace—Congressman Henderson. I followed his votin' 'cause he publishes it in our local s'posed to be newspaper. The rest of 'em they're no damn good far as my way of thinkin'. The main thing is, it's just like I think national politics was for a while. People here are satisfied with "don't bother me."

What needs to be done more'n anythin' is some way that the public has gotta know about these things. But see, the same politicians we're talkin' about has got that sewed up. The newspapers, the radio, everythin'. I know a man that went to the Duplin *Times* an' tried to get 'em to publish a letter he wanted to put in before the elections. He wasn't runnin' for nothin'. He was just makin' some statements about some things. They told him they didn't have room enough. I dunno exactly who is connected to what, understand, an' they hide it pretty good, but I can judge it by the attitude in those publications. I got sense enough to know. In the papers here I've seen how some a' the things I've had dealin' with, cases I worked, how they're reported. The fallacies an' so forth. An' you can learn a lot by readin' over a period of time. At elections each one of the politicians'll go buy him a square ol' block in the paper an' give his pitch. Then the paper itself will mention the one or two they like. Might say, "Incumbent so-an'-so is runnin' again." You won't never see nothin' about the other one. That's what I go by.

What makes me mad is there ain't nothin' you can do. Who you gonna go to for an investigation of these things? There's got to be somethin' to everythin' I see 'n hear. Where there's smoke there's fire. But a man in my position is helpless. I was gonna sit down an' write a letter. Only I dunno who to write to. 'Round here, our congressman, Dave Henderson, is probably the only one honest enough to care about it, but he's not gonna get into petty local politics. The attorney general, Robert Morgan, right now he's runnin' for the Senate an' he's not gonna cause trouble. Politicians are all parta the same little club, so who's ever gonna make a move against any of 'em? The reason it bothers me so much is I'm in the business of enforcin' the law. A lotta people, the biggest thing they think about law enforcement is carryin' a gun an' havin' a blackjack to hit somebody an' puttin' a drunk in jail. There's more to it than that. Not so much the apprehendin' criminals an' puttin' 'em in jail, which that's necessary an' I don't hesitate to do it, but you gotta think about more 'n just, "Who do I catch?" An' sneakin' up on 'em to do it. A man can't be doin' this job just for money or 'cause he thinks it looks excitin'. There ain't nothin' funny about this work. It's a bad job by most people's standards. I can convince any man in the world he'd be crazy to do this. But I put it on the same professional level as a lawyer or a doctor or a preacher. A man's gotta have a little somethin' in him that's gotta be there for him to dare to do it an' to stay with it. Maybe I'm crazy, but parta that somethin' is carin' for people an' carin' for what's right. A person in law enforcement has gotta be meant for the job. There's gotta be somethin' there.

The Judge

Since all this Watergate business came out an' everythin', people have very little respect for the law and less confidence in it. Naturally, when somethin' doesn't go their way, they'll say they didn't get justice. But actually, what they really wanted was justice tempered with mercy, or just plain one hundred percent mercy. I'd say justice is seein' that right is done. If a person should be punished, then he is punished. If he should be turned loose, then he is. If he should be found guilty an' fined, or somethin', the proper punishment or the equivalent should be found.

Any man, doesn't matter how poor he is or how influential, he'll be tried like the rest of them. You have to consider each case individually. Naturally, there are some people who are not convicted for what they are originally charged with, and that applies to people who don't have lawyers just as much as those who do. It applies to people with lawyers appointed for 'em, applies to blacks, whites, Indians—everythin' you can think of. If all the cases were tried on what they're charged with, there's not enough courtrooms in this district to handle 'em. There's not enough judges to hear 'em or enough prosecutors to prosecute. Plea bargainin' is what we're talkin' about. An' that goes on in every court in the United States besides the Supreme Court. You hafta have it.

Then, too, you sometimes acquit people because the complainant brought the wrong charge. You'd be amazed at some of the crazy charges people come up with when they're mad. They describe bein' hit with an instrument or somethin', an' when the case is actually heard, not the first word is mentioned about any instrument or anythin' beyond simple assault. But yet, the complainant went before the magistrate an' swore that an instrument was used. An iron pipe or an ax handle or somethin'. I ask him several times did he read it before he signed it. An' if it doesn't get straightened out, I hafta find the man not guilty if they don't drop the charge.

Then you got the Prayer for Judgment Continued. That's in motor vehicle violations where the judge can limit punishment to payment of costs, rather than gettin' the person's record all

223

confused an' makin' the insurance cost more. Sometimes I'll give it to them when they didn't ask for it, an' sometimes I'll refuse to give it to them when they did. Mosta the time I'll give it to them when they didn't have a lawyer or anything. We have cases of marijuana possession. If they've never been convicted on any drug offense before, they get six months suspended sentence and a two-hundred-dollar fine on the condition they don't violate any laws of the state of North Carolina for a period of two years. Everybody gets that automatically. Black, white, red or whatever, the same. Sometimes if they are unable to pay, I will put them on probation so they can pay the fine off gradually to a probation officer. That's better than bein' in jail six months. So you see, I don't believe there's a variation in the type of justice in my courtroom. There is no difference in treatment whatsoever. We try our best to be fair. That's our job.

The first thing you owe your allegiance to is the people altogether, the ones who elected you an' the ones who didn't. You're not supposed to show favoritism just because the person happens to be a Democrat and others happen to be Republican. I don't find the problem there you might think I would find. The only thing I've had some politician really before me for was on some minor traffic violation or somethin'. An' you treat 'em like you would anyone else. No problem. You don't have the conflict with bein' a judge an' a politician that I think you might with, let's say, a member of the legislature, where he's goin' to vote for appropriations. A judge runnin' for election can't make promises. The only thing he's goin' to do if elected is uphold the law as he's supposed to. That's a short platform. He doesn't have to make promises about roads, buildin' this, tearin' down that, an' that kinda thing. You don't run into a conflict at all.

Naturally in rural areas like eastern North Carolina everybody knows everybody else, an' we're all involved together. But that isn't as clear-cut as it might seem. The county chairman of the Democratic party of Duplin County isn't even a lawyer; he's Gerald Carr from Rose Hill an' he's an engineer. As far as the sheriff, yes, he's an elected official an' he's a Democrat, here an' in other counties in this district, but the involvement with the sheriff goes with punishment more'n anythin' else. A lot of times I'll call on the sheriff or some of the other officers, too. If I find

224

the defendant guilty, I'll ask whoever happens to be the bailiff that day if he knows about him before I pass sentence. I like to know if he's a habitual violator or if the problem is drunkenness, or somethin', an' if he needs some help, so we can send him somewhere. You see, you have to be very careful. It's a big responsibility. Often a man will have a family to support, four or five children maybe, an' you have to think about what it will do to them. You've got to remember you're there to listen to people an' be fair with 'em. An' that's what I do. Apply the law to the facts in the case. I try to do what's right.

Praise the Lord

"If there's ever been a time we need to grow closer to the Lord, it's the time we live in."
—A Holiness sermon

". . . and ye shall be witnesses unto me both in Jerusalem and in all Judea, and in Samaria, and unto the uttermost part of the earth."
—Acts 1:8

The Miracle I: Clayton Harris*

I'm gonna ask you a question. What are the last words that you say before you put your head on your pillow an' go to sleep at night? My last words, I say, "Good night, Lord." I get up in the mornin', "Good mornin', Lord." An' sometime I thank Him. "Lord, thank you for a good night' sleep. Thank you for a good day. Lord, I'm glad to be alive an' movin' around like I am. Thank you, Lord."

Now me, I'm not well by any means, an' I live with a fear of a blood clot, 'cause the first one I had it almost took me away. What happened, I fell when I was in the bathroom, had approximately five seconds' notice that somethin' bad was happenin' to me, an' I managed to open the door an' then I blacked out there on the tile, an' that was it. They called an ambulance an' got me to the hospital, an' all I can remember now is layin' there watchin' them machines, an' havin' all them needles an' things in me. My heart, they said it was.

Things like that make a man think, y'know. I lay there watchin' that green light an' sayin' "Lord, if it's my time, you can take me, Lord, but please, Lord, I don't think it's my time. I don't wanna go."

An' He didn't take me. Now I'm not sayin' it was one a' them miracles you hear about, but to me it *was* a miracle in some kind-a way. 'Cause life, what is it? It's sump'n God gives you an' sump'n you're lucky to have. An' when you almost lose it, an' then you're outta that danger zone, it teaches you one thing—God can do wonders.

229

The Missionary: Katie Murray

When I was about ten years old, I was sitting in the Baptist Church during a meeting, and I for the first time realized I was a sinner. I had thought before that I was a very good girl. In fact, I thought I was better than that little friend and better than this little friend. I didn't know that was pride, and that was a sin that God hates. I can remember how I deceived my mother. She told me she didn't want me to go out and get wet, and when it rained, I would like to go out and paddle in the water. So what did I do? I didn't go out the front door, I slipped to the back. See, my heart was deceitful. The Bible says, "The heart of Man is deceitful and desperately wicked." And I fooled the teachers at school, too. Well, that again shows, you see, that my heart was wicked. I found out I was a sinner, lost and condemned.

I would not let anyone know what was going on in my heart. But I went to my room and got on my knees and prayed and asked the Lord to forgive me and to save me. I would not acknowledge Him publicly for fear someone might laugh or criticize. But then I went to a meeting of the Johnson Church in Warsaw, and they sang a song—"Except a Man be Born Again He Cannot See the Kingdom of God." I thought, "Oh, I've never been born again, I can never get into Heaven." And the preacher said that day, "Do you want to be saved? If you do, come to the front for prayer." There was a great struggle in my heart, rather a struggle between the spirit of the Lord and the Devil. And I had to make the decision. Well, the spirit kept on moving in my heart until I obeyed. I went. And that day I trusted the Lord Jesus, who died for me on the cross, and He forgave my sins and gave me a great joy and peace in my heart. I want everybody to know about Jesus, who forgives our sins and saves us and comes to live in our hearts. And that's the reason I went to China.

Acts one, eight says, "And Ye shall be witnesses unto me in Jerusalem, Judea and Samaria and to the other parts of the earth." There's a promise for a Christian! I first went to China in nineteen twenty-two. After my training was over, I applied to the Foreign Mission Board of the Southern Baptist Convention, and after interview, examinations, and so on, I was accepted and went on. We first studied language in Peking for a year, and then

I was sent to Honan province, halfway between Peking and Chengchow. I went around with Bible women, visiting in homes, and that was when I really began to learn the language. There are so many tones, and if you make a mistake, it can be serious. For instance, there are four different tones that all sound like *jew* to me, and if you say the first tone, it's "pig," and if you say the third tone, it's "Lord," and if you're talking about the Lord and you say "pig," it might be too bad.

One of our most profitable times, I think, was when we were divided into groups. One group was a teaching group, another was an evangelistic group, holding meetings; another was still going into villages and places where there were no Christians. The most wonderful thing was the revival the Lord brought to China. He sent a missionary, a Swedish Lutheran, I think, and she came with the question: "Have you been Born Again?" She'd give a message on sin, maybe on stealing, maybe the next sermon on lying, maybe the next sermon on adultery. And people were under such conviction they couldn't eat, they couldn't sleep. And many times they were angry. One time they were ready to beat her up, they were so angry. But the Lord worked and there were lives changed. She'd give a message, when they were under conviction of sin, of Jesus, who had come to save sinners, and they were ready for it; they were ready to take Jesus as a savior. It seems that the trouble had been that people had just joined the church and been baptized without realizing that Jesus had come to save sinners, and they had not taken him as a personal savior. And when they did that, He came to dwell in their hearts and they became new creatures in Christ.

We don't try to change their customs, or things like that. It's a matter of telling the good news of Jesus Christ, and as they see the light, the Holy Spirit works into their hearts. They hadn't found anything like that before. You can be a Buddhist or a Confucianist and all these things at the same time. You just add on one more God. But I don't think they could receive the Holy Spirit or have any part of Christ or the true God without knowing Jesus. Of course, you've got to learn their ways and so on before you really can do much. For instance, one time the Bible woman and I were in a home, and it was summertime and the flies were so bad and it was hot and the tea didn't look very invit-

231

ing or tasty. I thought, "Well, if the Bible woman'll take some tea, that'll do for me, too." And so I didn't take any. When we got back to our chapel in a little while, the lady came in and said, "Yes, teacher wouldn't drink our tea." So I saw then that I must drink the tea whether I liked it or didn't like it, whether there were flies or no flies, whether it was hot or cold. Drink the tea. But we never felt any discomfort whatever because we were telling the glorious news—the good news of salvation. If you are sick and I know something to help you, if I don't tell you, why, that's *my* fault. And if I know something that will cure a corn, for instance, I know a little something you can put on it that will cure it, why, it's my business to tell it. And so when I know the remedy for sin, I know what Jesus Christ has done for my sins and how He's taken them, I have the privilege of the joy of telling somebody else.

The war began about thirty-seven, and we had people fleeing from the North and we ministered the refugees and had a marvelous opportunity with them. Then came Pearl Harbor. The Japanese had already taken our city and they left before Pearl Harbor, but they didn't go away from us but about twelve miles and they could have come back any time they wanted to. We stayed on, though, and we had about two years of wonderful opportunity in the ministry. One day I was coming back from early morning prayer meeting and I met a Chinese Christian who said, "The Japanese are here." I quickly went to the house and we began getting up our little things that we must take, and off we went. We were on the road, walking about two weeks, I reckon, and then finally we got to a train and out. That was forty-four, and I went home until forty-seven, and then went back for a period of one year before the communists came.

Early, even when I went there in twenty-two, young Chinese were going to Russia, and they were studying and they were coming back and planning a communistic siege. There would be strikes and a force of atheism growing. But at first we didn't know, and our people would come over and say how wonderful that the communists were bringing reforms and so on. It looked like either Japan or communism was going to take China, and we knew so little about communism that often, as missionaries, we would ask which would be the least of harm. That was our ignorance.

After the communists arrived, I went to south China, to the province of Kwangsi, the capital city of Kweilin. I was there two years when the communists came there. I didn't know what to do. Our Foreign Mission Board always said that missionaries should decide what the Lord wants us to do and they would cooperate either way. I didn't know what the Lord wanted. We gathered down in south China, the missionaries from that area, to decide. Well, as we were leaving, I didn't know still, but as I stood there waiting for the plane, the Lord seemed to say to me, "Will you stay?" I said, "Yes, Lord, if you want me to stay, I'll stay." I was there eleven months under the communists.

It meant that we were greatly restricted though there was no harm done to us. But you couldn't go to the village or you couldn't go out of town anywhere. You couldn't visit the Chinese in their homes. One of my co-workers, Miss Logan, decided she would go to see Mrs. So-and-So, and it hadn't been but a few minutes after she left before there was a communist at her friend's house saying, "Why are you having this American visit you?" So we knew then that we mustn't do it, because it would bring harm to our Chinese co-worker friends. You know, you feel your relationship with the people in Christ. But your face and your speech and everything betrays that you are an American. Sometimes your citizenship is favorable to you and sometimes it's not. Now after the Japanese War it was very favorable. You'd go down to town and the children would raise up their thumbs and say, "Very good, very good," because America had helped them win the war.

I am happy to be back in Rose Hill. We must practice the ministry wherever we go. At this time I feel not only here, but throughout this country, that there are two forces that are working. The Lord and the Devil. I have seen the signs before and I see them here now. There are many people who have come in a new relationship with the Lord, they've been filled with the spirit and they're on fire and witnessing for the Lord. And there are others, maybe, that are going with the world, though their names are on the church roll. There is a rebellion among the children,

233

off on drugs, and I think that's a terrible thing. Maybe that's in part due to many broken homes. I don't know what it is due to, except that, of course, it is the work of the Devil. And so I have much to do right here in Rose Hill to carry the Gospel and the news of Christ.

I went to China with a heart hungry to be filled with the spirit, but I didn't know how. I was ashamed to ask anybody, and I didn't hear anybody talking about it. So I was hungry. And yet there was something in me that resisted. But God, in His mercy, let me have typhus fever, and during that time I had plenty of time to think, and the Lord showed me so many things. I said, "Well, why am I not filled with the spirit? What's hindering me, Lord?"

Then one of our missionaries from north China who had been filled with the spirit came to lead meetings. Some of us stayed up praying until way into the night, but it seemed like the more I prayed, the farther I got that didn't get anywhere. And then one day as I was praying and confessed to the Lord the thing that had been holding me back, He just forgave me and the spirit fell upon me, giving me a new realization of the wonders of Christ, of identification with Him.

That's what the spirit does. He comes and He takes the things of Jesus and shows them to us. And so that's what He was doing to me. He has shown me many things. During the war the railroad was cut, and in our area the grain couldn't come in except by wheelbarrows. I've seen them—just strings of men pushing wheelbarrows; and some of them died right there, just gave out, exhausted. You'd go along and see trees that people had peeled off the bark and pounded it out, ground like flour, you know, and in the time when there were leaves, they would eat the leaves from the trees and many people died. There's an awful time during a famine. It was an awful thing to see people perishing for the lack of something to eat. But, that's a material thing, and the body only lasts a few years anyway, one hundred maybe at the most. More terrible than that is the soul that never dies, and if it perishes without life, that's forever. And that's the most terrible thing of all—to be without Christ.

The Gospel Singer:
Jennie Simpson*

You can go to any church, I don't care whose church it is, an' if
there is not much to the singin', the choir, there is not much to
the service. Usually the preacher preaches just like his choir
sings, an' if his choir don't give 'im nothin', there ain't very
much that preacher will do. Like the spirituals. They always
sing 'em right before the preacher preaches, an' if the choir really sing 'em, that give the preacher a send-off, an' the preacher
can preach a whole lot better sermon. Everybody kinda takes off.
There is sump'n 'bout that singin' that'll thrill you.

Of course, singin' really is a sermon in song. You think about
those verses an' understand 'em. A song I like to sing is "When
You Have Gone the Last Mile of the Way." Well, you think, as
you sing that song, that when you really have gone the last mile
of the way, you are goin' to rest, like the song says, at the end of
the day, an' you know there is joy that is goin' to meet you. Give
you sump'n to work for because you are workin' for that last
mile. Then there is another song I really love. "Precious Lord,
Lead Me on to the Light. Take my Hand, Precious Lord, Lead
Me On." There is sump'n 'bout those songs that's real special to
me, sump'n you don' get outta a sermon.

When I was a child, you'd be walkin' along to the church an'
you'd hear the people singin' a good little ways before you'd get
there, an' you'd be singin' as you'd go along. You learned the
song before you even learned to read. There is sump'n 'bout
singin' that the black folks is just part of. I was thirteen years old
when I first started singin' in churches. My first cousin an' two
other girls an' myself, we sang all the Negro spirituals an' we
sang without music. After I was married, my two daughters an'
myself an' my first cousin we sang together, we sang from
church to church, as far as Wilmington an' Ivanhoe. Now I sing
with a group that is called the Community Gospel Choir, an' the
chorus consists a' members from all a' the churches around close
near Rose Hill. On the fourth Sunday we are at my own church,
the Holiness, an' all the resta the Sundays we go 'round to dif-

f'rent places—Chinquapin, Wallace. It makes you feel like you're doin' sump'n special for the people. Like I was down in Wallace Sunday night an' we was singin' diff'rent songs, an' when the church meetin' was over, some a' the folks came over to me and said, "You really got us into it tonight with your singin'." Well, we rocked that buildin'. When you sing 'til you feel it yourself, then the other folks are bound to feel it. The singin' is parta the whole thing.

People are not as religious as when I was growin' up. I remember we would go to church, stay all day, an' even have dinner at the church. It was a big parta our lives then. We still do some things like that. The fourth Saturday night we have what you call a homecomin' banquet, an' we invite friends to come in an' have dinner with us. Then we have what you call a homecomin' queen. The children of each family choose a girl who they want outta their family to be representin' them, an' everybody puts in sump'n, a dollar maybe, to support their li'l granddaughter or niece or someone for the girl they wanta be queen. The money goes to the buildin' an' repairment of the church. Our buildin', we've paid for it now, an' we're gettin' air conditionin'. An' now our junior church, just this last Sunday, they furnished our music an' those children had the tambourines an' the piano an' they sang, an' it was wonderful. But I know that people feel diff'rent now 'bout religion. You go to church an' so many folks are lookin' at the watch an' clock, countin' up the hour so's they can leave an' go home. People nowadays are so busy, many of 'em don't even remember what the preacher is sayin'.

There's sump'n I always thoughta that's kinda funny, an' that's how many white people, 'specially up North, like our music, but 'round here the white churches an' the black churches don' get together at all. Everybody talks a whole lot 'bout bein' Christian, but I always thought you are s'posed to be friendly with everybody if you are a Christian, an' seems like that ain't so. All the churches here they work for foreign missions. They get up clothes, they send a lotta clothes to New York, s'posed to be boxed up an' sent overseas. Nobody thinks a' who might need them clothes right here in Rose Hill. An' then when those secondhand clothes stores opened up down here, some a' them same clothes were brought right back down an' sold from the secondhand store. Makes me think it could be the same with money; could be it never gets to Africa or Japan or wherever they are sendin' it. Seems to me like people don't really wanna be Christian, only when it please 'em to be. They still got hate holed up in 'em. If they feel that way 'bout it, they just as well can get up Sunday mornin' an' go an' shoot pool. It ain't like we are callin' for each race to be separate in Heaven, so why are we like that down here?

Maybe that's the thing I like best about music. Singin' is a people kinda thing. Most any time you could be the least bit down an' think of a little tune an' you feel better an' make other people feel better right along with you. I was workin' the other day, cleanin' a lady's house, an' I got lost in the song I was singin'—"Nothin' Between My Soul an' the Savior." Well, I was so carried away while I was washin' dishes, the lady had the television on an' she turned that television off an' she said, "I heard a little mockin'bird in there." She was really enjoyin' that singin'. There is sump'n in some a' these songs, it don't matter who you hear sing 'em. There is a song that is really true that I love— "May the Work I Done Speak for Me." That really is true, y'know. If you do good things, after you're gone that is gonna speak for you because that is what you have done here on earth an' that is the kinda person you are. Like the song says, "When I'm restin' in my grave, there is nothin' I can say. May the work I've done speak for me." That's my words, not just the song. The songs I sing, they're tellin' sump'n 'bout my life. Singin' ain't exactly like prayin', but it stands out from everythin' else, maybe anythin' religious, anythin' you wanna do. It lights me up. It's a joyful feelin'.

The Miracle II: David Fussell

. . . Helen began to relate all the trouble she had suffered because one of her legs was shorter than the other. The pains were so severe that she was unable to get out of bed. Helen went on in detail, describing all her hospital examinations and attempts to find medical relief from the dilemma.

She told me that a dentist from Fayetteville had received the baptism of the Holy Spirit and had been used by God numerous times as an instrument to give the gift of healing. Helen said that the dentist prayed for her, and immediately God answered her prayer and her short leg grew out in perfect proportion to the other.

Realizing the physical impossibility of such a thing happening, I sort of laughed politely and thanked Helen for sharing her story with my wife, Ann, and me. Just as a courteous parting statement, I said, "You know, your experience is a real coincidence, for I have a short leg myself."

Helen, grabbing at the opportunity, said, "You do? Well, praise the Lord. Let's pray for your healing right now."

The thought rushed through my head. Oh no! Now you have made a grave mistake. You just gave Helen the perfect opening to exercise her nutty Pentecostal faith. The Devil prompted me to say, "Well, it is not bothering me anymore, and I had rather you not pray for me right now. I do not believe this is the time. I don't have enough faith in this kind of thing."

I did not believe that God manifested Himself in modern times by intervening in the natural order of things. The complicated cell growth that it would take to lengthen my leg one half inch was too much to ask for. Besides, if God wanted to perform supernatural events, would he not save His strength for something really important, rather than to dissipate His miraculous strength on something as minor as a short leg?

The more I protested, the more persistent and assured Helen became. I nervously began to back away from her aggressiveness. In backing away I accidentally struck a chair, lost my balance and sat down. At this Helen knelt down and began to pray for God to lengthen my leg.

In total embarrassment I bowed my head and began to pray silently. My prayer was not for the extension of the leg; rather it was for divine help in getting out of this humiliating situation. Helen then asked that I sit up straight, place my back against the back of the chair, stick out both of my legs and show the differentiation of length between my two legs to the people who had now gathered around to watch. As soon as Helen observed the difference in length, she said, "Praise the Lord. Now everyone will be able to see God's power manifested." All of a sudden Helen began to say, "Thank you, Jesus, thank you, God."

I did not know what she was thanking God for, because nothing had happened and I didn't believe anything was going to happen. I thought, "If she had not just started thanking God, I might have figured a tactful way out of this predicament."

To my amazement a sharp tingling sensation started in my left leg. A light quiver began and I heard my wife, who had been standing by in complete horror and disbelief, exclaim, "Look, it's moving."

Ann's excited outcry gave me enough curiosity to overcome my embarrassment, and I opened my eyes in time to see my left leg move to the exact length of my right leg.

It is unbelievable. I find the manifestation of God's supernatural involvement in my life incomprehensible. However, the experience is so engraved in my life, whenever doubt of God's power begins to enter my life, all I have to do is glance down and see the living physical evidence of His power. My left leg is now in perfect alignment with my right.

The Preacher: Reverend David Moe

I'm a preacher, which covers quite a large field. Some people, perhaps, like the word "pastor" better than they do "preacher," because I'm supposed to be the pastor of my flock and help people enrich their lives and bring them closer to Christ. This is my job—to help.

I've been in Rose Hill just half of my stay, which is usually for four years. Before I came here we served in Tabor City, which is right on the border of South Carolina, and before that I was in Swansboro, where I built a new church. Wherever I go, I usually build an educational building or a church or pay off a debt. Rose Hill is a change for that: they're pretty good off financially, and we've done quite a bit of repair work, but there's no building needed to be done in Rose Hill at this time.

We have different activities, like most churches. However, other churches do not offer them during the week as much as we do. "From the Cradle to the Grave" is our motto. We have Sunday school for everyone, from the youngest children to the older people. We have visitation for our shut-ins, and I do quite a bit of calling where they're lonely and needy. We write get-well cards to the shut-ins from the Sunday school classes so they are not forgotten or neglected. In some areas where I've been, I've called on certain poor families that were really down and out and up against it, and I told a person of business who said, "Well, they're not *our* kind of people." You will not find this attitude here. If course, there's the area they call, a little jokingly, "Siberia," over across the track, because they might not get so much of the town money over there, but, for instance, our church helped one family quietly, gave them twenty-five dollars for an emergency. We bought one boy a pair of shoes so he'd come to church. The man who did it doesn't want his name known, and things like that are happening all the time. I realize there are many people who do not go to church at all, and many of these are newcomers who do not sense a welcome. I imagine it depends a little bit on what area of town you're located, whether you find true friendliness or not. We have one or two streets where migrant workers come, maybe stay a month and move. If a person lives in that area, they would not find it the Rose Hill that we know.

We do have a Board of Visitation; Membership and Evangelism it's called. When strangers move in, we give them a welcome box and we call on them periodically. If there are any prospects, I call on them myself. Then we have fellowship dinners. We have mighty good cooks here. And with the young I have quite a few counseling sessions with them before I marry them. I think it's important that they know what they're getting into and why they're marrying and of the dangers and the pitfalls as well as the blessings and the joys.

My work is with the people, trying to direct them into a deeper goal so that they will know themselves and know God. There was a man here who was having a nervous breakdown, had not darkened the door of any churches for a while, broke up with his girlfriend. Went to doctor after doctor. He was a Methodist name on the roll. I dealt with him as an individual, took him out for rides, prayed with him, talked with him, took him to the doctor myself, got him on the nerve pill and worked with him over a period of several months 'til he got himself straightened out mentally, physically and spiritually. And now he does not miss a single day in church.

Human nature is the same wherever you go. I'll agree that the pace of living is much slower down here than it would be in the windy city of Chicago or New York or any other large town. I think it's the age in which we live. Things have been happening so fast. Years ago one out of ten was hospitalized for a nervous breakdown, and I wouldn't be surprised if it's gone up much higher than that now. People tend to worry a lot. Tensions build up normally around people and homes and loved ones. Misunderstandings. I've noticed that we have people who are far too much on pills, and they demand something stronger and stronger and eventually they get it and they become addicts. I've tried to help a few, but I've had more failures than successes. I can't shoot at the whole flock and hit everyone. I have to work it one individual at a time. And this I try to do. It's not the easiest thing always to be a pastor, but it's very enjoyable. We make mistakes, too, because we're just as human as the next person. We try to let God guide us in our conversation, which we don't always do. There's too much Dave Moe and not enough Christ in what I say.

A minister is at times captive to his situation if he wishes to do good. He is never able to go as far as he is willing to go. The reason why this is—you can lead a horse to water but you can't force him to drink. If the minister at the Presbyterian church a while back had not tried to do everything in the first year and had had a long ministry, which most Presbyterians do have, for six or eight years, and had gradually led them, taken his stand and led them, he wouldn't have had so many problems. I'm not saying what he did here was wrong. What he did was right for *him.* But I believe that you need to work your ways and be accepted before you put your ideas in.

I'm just as close as the telephone, and many other members of the church are just as close as the telephone, where we are bound together as a family. I visited this morning where a lady cannot hardly hear a word. She put her arms around me and hugged me. She says that she feels a church is a family, that everyone in the church is her friend and the pastor and everyone else is her friend. I think that's how it should be. We do have a togetherness and closeness that's developed over the years, and I've noticed it. It develops not only for those who were born and reared here, but others who have come into this community sense a closeness, a oneness, a love, if you want to call it that. A fellowship where they are welcome and wanted. After a while it kind of gets hold of a person. They feel as though they would like to belong. And they do belong after a while.

The Miracle III: Lola Rouse

After I found out I was losin' my eyesight, I prayed to the Lord that it was in His will I wouldn't go blind. I knew what it was happenin' to me because there began to come shadows before my eyes. But I dunno, I always been the type a person which, if I gotta meet anythin', I always think I gotta meet it the best I can, an' I think I got along real good, praise the Lord. They wanted to send me to blind school, but I had complications an' I couldn't walk for about two years an' a half; so what I've learned, I've learned through myself an' faith in God. The doctors tol' me when they found the blindness on me that I'd never be better'n I was then. But I have been better. When you first lose your eyesight, you been usedta seein' for so long, an' you wake up in the night 'n it scares you. I mean, that feelin' comes over you, y'know. But now, I do mosta my housekeepin', an' mosta the folks that meet me tell me if they ever have a handicap, they hope they can take it the way I take mine. I feel like if it hadn't been for the Lord, I never woulda walked again.

I feel this way about it. That maybe the Lord had given me more to bear for a purpose. I think He really has been able to use me more blind than He could with eyesight. I been asked to go under tents an' around, just to testify an' let people see me with the spirit an' fire a' God in me. An' speakin' in tongues. They come here to my house an' ask me to go other places; they say it will help other people to understand if they see me up there. But I dunno, I'm kinda a curious person, an' I say I can't go unless the Lord tells me. But there's other work I can do for Him. You

242

take the prayer meetin' service. Well, the Holiness have meetin's at diff'rent people's homes, an' we make our own altar outta chairs. Holiness people find an altar almost anywhere they are. There's nine diff'rent gifts that God gives His people. An' since I been blind, I can get up an' go right to a person, the Lord'll lead me right to a person, an' I can lay my hand on his head, an' I dunno where he's been sittin' not nothin'. I heard a minister say one time, he tol' a congregation a' people that he'd never even seen me stumble. An' I'm totally blind. An' that's the gift I got. When I get the Holy Ghost, the spirit of God gets on me an' I can find my way just as good as you can. The Lord uses me to lead people to the altar. So even though I'm blind, I got my work to do.

The Baptism: Reverend Sonny Cook*

You know tonight we need to do what we can for the Lord 'cause we just got a short time. Then we're gonna be through this life an' spend eternity somewhere or other. An' they's gonna be weepin' an' moanin' an' gnashin' of teeth, praise God, so today's the day we need to get ready, children, because we don't have a promise of tomorrow, an' today's the day of salvation. Ol' Satan he's a waitin' an' he ain't got much time, brother, an' he's gonna get every soul he can, praise the Lord, he's gonna tempt everybody. An' I'll tell you right now, praise God, you gotta tear him outta your heart 'cause he's a-workin'. You gotta fall down on your knees, an' I'll tell you people tonight there's no restin' place, praise the Lord. You know, children, when people gettin' so satisfied they got a pacifier in their mouth, you gotta call on Jesus.

I'll tell you what, when they go to the water an' are baptized unto Jesus Christ, they're baptized in the family of God. I'm identifyin' with the family tonight, praise God, the family of Jesus. I'm identifyin' with His death, burial, an' resurrection, praise the Lord, an' this brother here'll be a witness everywhere he goes about this baptism. Children, I can't wait to tell you about the enjoyment, amen, that God told me about. God wants me to talk to you a little bit about the completion of the garment of Jesus Christ. It's the same garment that Adam lost, that's right. An' I don't mean just a partial garment. He's already clothin' you with it, an' it's gonna be without labels or names, amen. It's the garment of righteousness. Now you know tonight, when the Bible speaks of garments or things like that, filthy garments, then that's the filthy soul, bless the Lord, an' that ol' filthy garment it's gonna make us not fit for the Kingdom of God. There's too many folks 'as been streakin', amen, there's a lotta people that's naked. They don't have no clothes on in God's sight, but tonight, what we're doin' this for, praise the Lord, is to get the clothes back on God's people, them clean garments, amen. See, the Devil he worked through the serpent, he talked to Eve an' he made Eve pull her clothes off, so today there's ministers that're preachin' about takin' clothes off. I'm talkin' about spiritual clothes, amen, an' I want you to know this evenin' we're ministerin' to you in the name of the Lord Jesus so that you might be fully clothed in His righteousness. This is the baptism tonight unto death to finish up this brother's dyin', he'll never die no more, amen, he could be present in the Lord, amen, so brother, I'll baptize you in the name of the Lord Jesus Christ accordin' to Romans six an' three unto the death of Jesus an' accordin' to Acts two an' thirty-eight for the remission of your sins in the name of the Lord Jesus Christ, amen. Thank you, Lord. Thank you, Jesus. 'Allelujah.

Now, children, we know that Jesus said, "If my people which is called in my name will kneel down an' pray, I will hear their prayers, I will heal them, I will come to the rescue, I'll supply their needs, that's my word." But I'll tell you people, I'll tell you tonight, there's some folks so proud they don't wanna kneel down, they don't wanna get a little dust on 'em. I wanna go to heaven tonight, praise God. I want dust all over my trousers. An' I'll tell you if Satan's in my heart, he won't let me enter that Kingdom of God. Now everybody's welcome, praise the Lord. We'll welcome 'em to God's family, we'll welcome 'em to their watery grace never to die no more, praise the Lord. You know my little girl, she's passin' out some addressed envelopes; they got my name an' address on 'em, an' if you wanna pray or if you wanna help pay for God's work, praise the Lord, you just drop this in the mail, that's my box number, an' I'll pray with you, sister, amen. Praise the Lord.

Oh, Father, we're thankful to you even now for your bein' with us an' revealin' your spirit, Father. There is not a day or hour when we will not be fully clothed, fully dressed, ready to go, ready to be with you at the last feast. An' Lord, we hasten the day. May it even come quickly, Lord Jesus, as we come here to meet with these people from time to time, these brothers an' sisters, to die an' come to you, oh Lord, for our sinnin'. Help us to cast off our filthy garments, Lord. Lord, help us to please you, bless these children here an' let not one person go from here, Lord, without bein' made whole. In Jesus' name heal the sick, deliver us from our sins an' deliver, Lord, their prayers that set the captive free. Amen.

The Presbyterian: Thomas Adams*

The minute we heard about what they were doin' to our minister, Lester La Prade, we should have asked for a congregational meetin'. But in the Presbyterian Church, the Session has to call for those meetin's. So it was never actually discussed publicly. The Session consists of, I think it's nine members of the church. They're usually your older members. That is a lifetime position, an' they don't feel they have to answer to anybody. That's how things like this can happen, I suppose.

There were a few who were not aware of the petition for a week or two. I was not asked to sign, and neither were a lot of other people. I would dare say, not havin' seen the actual document, that those who did sign were members of the families, those different families who were actual instigators. But it didn't take long to get around. The way I first heard about it, I don't remember who the person was, but someone asked me had I been approached with the petition that was bein' circulated against our minister. We were shocked and dumbfounded that such a thing could happen. But no one knew what was goin' on, an' no one ever told us. *They* knew who would sign an' who wouldn't sign, so they went ahead an' left the rest of us, the people in the congregation, alone.

So, in fact, everythin' happened in such a way that Les and Laura La Prade didn't even have any idea they were disliked. Insteada goin' to him an' sayin', "Listen, Les, you are doin' such an' such a thing in the church that we aren't quite ready for yet," they did it real private, slinkin' around. An' the La Prades went on meetin' with all these so-called "Christians" as if nothin' was happenin'. Which, to me, those people are nothin' but a buncha hypocrites. Every one of 'em.

What brought about the whole thing I'll never understand if I live to be a hundred years old. He was criticized because of his mannerism that he played the piano. He played the piano like he loved it, not that he jazzed the hymns, but he just played the piano with a lot of feelin'. That was another remark that was used against him. "Well. Did you *know* that he played in *night spots,* in *nightclubs?*" Well, those kids were married before he finished studyin' for his ministry, an' he did it to pick up some extra money after they were married. What night spots they were, I'm sure they were nothin' like a honky-tonk, or anythin' like that.

There were remarks made like, "He doesn't pay enough respect when he's in the church. You walk into the church an' you hear this loud *laughter.*" Well, who says a church hasta be such a sad, sorry place? He was so happy all the time, you couldn't help feelin' good when you listened to a sermon bein' preached. He was overweight. He was criticized for the way he looked in his clothes. An' they said the most terrible things about *her.* She didn't look as if she had stepped outta one of those fancy fashion magazines. They said he acted like a child at some of the meetin's he held with the Session. I don't know about that. I wasn't there. Some people say that maybe it was because he was too liberal in his thinkin'. Well, he didn't preach about integration, he preached the Bible: "Love thy neighbor as thyself." The truth is, he was driven out by those goody-goody, self-professed "Christians," an' they didn't need a reason. They just hated him. Now this came from one of our leadin' citizens: "Well, there's one thing. If we don't get enough names to force 'im to resign, we'll just stop payin' 'im. We'll starve 'im out."

Lester La Prade was not a threat to anythin' or anybody. It's because they didn't know him. The people in this town are afraid of anythin' or anyone that's gonna bring about a change. But we are livin' in changin' times. My heavens, we've seen it more since the La Prades left than we did while they were here. Our kids are growin' up in tryin' times. I don't care how small you are, eventually it will get to you. And that what's really so pathetic about it. The kids loved him. He didn't only help in their programs, he would go to the football field every day of the week and help with the football teams. I feel like if that man could have stayed here with the influence he had on our young people, I wouldn't be afraid to bet you any amount of money in this world that the kids who have been involved in drugs, it never would have happened.

There have been very few times in my life that I have been so angry. It wasn't only what they did, but the way they did it that made me so damn mad. Yes. *Damn* mad. I wanted to go to every one of those people an' tell 'em exactly what I thought of 'em. An' yet, what good would it do? The damage had been done. To me, if they had stuck a gun in his back, so to speak, it wouldn't have hurt as much because it would have been over. Yet Lester La Prade would still get up there Sunday after Sunday, after he knew what had happened, an' go on as if nothin' was wrong. Deep down inside you knew he had been crushed.

I didn't know he was lookin' for another church, an' when he told me that he had accepted another position, I asked him if he could find it in his heart to stay. We felt the majority of the congregation would ask him to stay on. In other words, let it be brought to a public vote. But he refused. He said there was his wife, an' he knew his child would someday hear it if he remained here an' that he hoped his son would never hafta be aware of what had happened to him. It was a terrible thing to happen to a minister. He had so much more character, he was so much stronger than those weaklin's or hypocrites or whatever they are. Because the other reason he said he wouldn't stay was that it wouldn't be fair to the *church,* that it was already split enough an' he didn't want to do anythin' that would bring more discord than what had already happened. I wish I could talk about it without gettin' so infuriated still, even after all these years. I know it's not very Christian, but it makes me have feelin's that maybe I shouldn't have.

The Miracle IV: David Fussell

Granville Sheffield was a man of the world. He was a hard-nosed, hard-drivin' businessman. An' he had been a successful man. He was going his merry way of wine, women an' song at the merry age of fifty-six, until God stroke him with what he thought was the flu, an' the flu led into dizzy spells. Finally, a neurologist over in Greenville established the fact that he had a brain tumor, an' they wanted to operate on him. Well, his daughter an' son-in-law, Sonia an' Don, had friends who were neurologists at Duke, an' they wanted to carry him there, but the doctor said he wouldn't survive the ambulance trip. They carried 'im anyway, to Duke, an' they said there that absolutely nothin' could be done, the cancer had spread over his whole body. So he went home an' began to get his affairs in order. The cancer was such that he could not function as an individual. He was bedridden an' incoherent. Sonia began to read Katherine Kuhlman's books—*I Believe in Miracles, God Can Do It Again* an' several others. An' she got an inclination to carry him to Katherine Kuhlman in Pittsburgh, Pennsylvania. Well, Granville was so sick that he couldn't travel. The only way to get him there would be a private airplane. Well, who's got a private plane? Nobody but Mister Nash Johnson. So I was at Granville's house an' we got to prayin' that God would lead Mister Nash Johnson to offer to Granville Sheffield the use of his private airplane to carry him. Two weeks from then, Mister Nash came to Granville, an' as he was leavin', he said, "Granville, can I do anythin' for you?" An' Granville said, "Well, my daughter would like to take me to Katherine Kuhlman." So Nash said, "Fine, use my plane." An' it was all set to go.

This was a time when the smog was so bad all over the country the airports were closed throughout the northeast. On the day they were goin' the pilot said, "It's hopeless." But then the airport control called an' said the smog had lifted, an' if we hurried, we might get there before the smog came back. We had to give Granville somethin' to sedate him, an' right before we did, he said, "Please leave me here an' let me die in peace."

When he went to the Katherine Kuhlman session, it was a fantastic thing. People from Norway, Quebec, Mexico, other foreign countries that I don't remember the names, thousands of people. They were lined up on the steps, an' I had to get there at quarter of six in the mornin' to save Granville a place in line. When he got there, his whole complexion changed. You've seen how brown cancer patients get? Well, he became a rosy person. Goin' there he couldn't walk. We had to pick him up an' carry him to the plane. After it was over he was carryin' the luggage. I said, "Granville, you're healed." I mean, I really knew he was healed.

Well, Granville came home to Rose Hill. He went about his work to liquidate his business. He built an apartment out of the garage so that somebody could live with his wife after his death. All by himself. He never asked for God to heal him. He asked for knowledge. And he asked God to let him live to finish his work and not to die in pain. An' he died in the house, sittin' up in a chair. You never heard anybody that changed as much as he did. He went from a hardened businessman to a real compassionate individual. He completed every single thing that he had to do. An' then he died. The Lord gave him what he asked for.

12 The Crow and the Mockingbird

"If the good Lord intended the crow an' the mockingbird to lie down together, he'd a made one big bird."

—Anson Lee Baker

Doris Richardson*

When we were growin' up, there was this old man who had been a slave, an' he an' his wife lived in a little house on our land that my daddy let him live in. Didn't charge 'im anythin', just let 'em live there. An' I thought it was the most fun to go down an' see 'em. Anytime anybody come to see me an' spend the night, we'd hafta go. That was one of the fun things to do. Then, when I had a family of my own, my children would play with the colored children. They were friendly with the colored, but they didn't really socialize. It's like anything else. These changes have gotta happen slowly.

Integration's been real quiet here, but that doesn't mean people are acceptin' it fully. Not inside. The white an' the colored don't ride the school buses together much. It's been one thing that a lotta mothers have been afraid of because it's a closed-in situation, an' if there's any trouble, it could be pretty frightenin'.

So a lotta the white mothers carry their children to school themselves. If I had children in school now, I would spend the money and send them to the private school at Harrells, the Christian Academy. If a child doesn't have a good teacher, he's not goin' to learn, an' when things get all mixed up like they are right now, it's just not the best. There are some facts a law can't change. When you've got to hire a person because he's a certain color, an' not for what he can do, well, that's not for the best.

In years to come people will look back on the problems we've had with integration like we look back on slavery nowadays. Not so many years ago we couldn't even imagine bein' in the same

253

restaurant with 'em. Which of course today it's very hard to believe it coulda been that way. I mean we let 'em cook our food; I had a colored woman come an' help take care of each little baby I had. You couldn't get much closer than that, but it's the way things always were. The way it is now, no one wants to hurt anyone else, an' we know we hafta comply with the laws. But you hafta realize there are limits on these things.

Jenny Curtis*

There was this white girl in Rose Hill a few months back, went to the washer, said she come back to her car an' there was a black man in the car an' the man had a knife. Well, nobody could make *me* get in the car, not even if they had a knife. An' with all them stations open out there on that highway at that time a' night, she claimed this happened.

What really happened. She was runnin' aroun' with another man, went out between here an' Magnolia an' backed the car in a ditch. She didn't want her husband to know what she was doin' down there. On that same day they foun' a black man walkin', comin' from that processin' plant or sump'n. An' next thing, the law was sayin' that black man had that woman down there.

See, that's what she did. Said it was a black man made her get in the car an' carried her down. But still she said this man didn't touch her. After they got down there an' backed the car in a ditch, he still didn't touch her. Ain't that the stuff? Truth was, that black man hadn't even seen that woman. He didn't do a thing.

Earl Crimmins*

My little boy's got a real good friend in school, a black boy, an' they call each other three or four times a week. His father's a school teacher, a real nice man. He's not the pushy type of black man. In other words, he hasn't mentioned me comin' to his house an' I haven't mentioned his comin' here. But we're friends. There's another one, lives out here in the country, an' he's mentioned his comin' to see me an' my comin' to see him. 'Course the way I interpret the way he goes on about it, he's not really interested in me wantin' to see him or goin' to his house as he is in the fact of his wantin' people to know that he came to my house or I came to his house. I feel like he's tryin' to prove a point.

Everybody else would be a diff'rent person if they didn't hafta depend on somebody else. But naturally the world isn't that way. Say, for instance, I was wealthy, didn't hafta depend on this 'r that, naturally I'd do what I wanted to. Say, if I wanted to invite a colored person to my house, I'd do it if I wanted to. Y'know what I mean? I don't particularly wanna invite this particular man over, but I'd like to know I could if I wanted to.

Eva Newkirk

This town hasn't changed at all. The biggest problem the black people get here aroun' this town is town tax statements an' not anythin' done towards gettin' facilities of this town. We pay town tax, an' our town tax this year is seventy-two dollars. An' we don't have any facilities.

We don't get any service. You go down to the town board an' say sump'n to 'em, an' they talk nasty to you an' say they ain't got money an' a whole lotta stuff. They'll say anythin'. Well, what you pay town tax for? I thought it was for gettin' streets an' things fixed. But you don't get it. Now over in the new parta town, back over 'cross the highway, the town got busy an' put sewage an' everythin' in. The Negroes been in town ever since there's been a town an' we don't have any service.

In my house we have a bathroom. We have a septic tank. An' any time you flush the commode, you hafta stand there with a plunger to keep it from comin' back on the floor. It's right hard down here when it rains. All the water clogs right here at the end in our lot an' turns green in the ditch. They haven't opened the drain so it can go 'cross the road.

The town's s'posed to take care a' the sewage. Mister Windsor Johnson, he raised the roof with 'em. When the streets were so bad up where he lives, he went to the town board an' asked 'em why. He told 'em, "If one side a' the house was leakin', would they fix one side of it an' leave the other side leakin'?" They said, "No." He said, "Well, y'know the colored section of town is in a lot worser shape than the other." He said, "Why just fix the white section and leave the black section out?" We tried to put Mister Johnson on the town board, but they don' like 'im. He will stand for his rights, I'll tell you that. There are some others who could be pretty good, but they might be whitewashed. The white folks can bull all over some of 'em, but they don' Mister Johnson. An' they know that.

The road from town's fixed 'til you get to the coffin factory. When it starts comin' down into the black section, they stopped fixin'. Our streets last winter was so bad you couldn't see how in the world you could get in an' out through here. An' we went downtown an' asked 'em to do sump'n 'bout the streets, an' this is what they asked: "What do you want? A highway? You think you're s'posed to have a hard surface?" Then we wrote the commissioner outta Raleigh, an' within a week he was here. So the town hauled some dirt in here. Some of our people went to see Mister Jiggs Fussell, which is a county commissioner, an' he called downtown an' they gave him the same stuff—that they didn't have the money. He told 'em the thing to do is go ahead an' fix these folks' road an' get the money outta this year's tax.

A few of us try. But the rest of 'em they take it like it is. I think a lotta them 'round here are scared. Then there's one, works for the town, an' every li'l thing the black people do that's planned, like we plan to go an' meet the board, or sump'n like that, he'll tell 'em. One time we was s'posed to meet the board, an' when we got down there, the town hall was black. First time I can remember that there hadn't even been a light in there. Wasn't a person in town. An' the town cop passed on through an' didn't even stop to see what was happenin'.

The general election, there was a bond issue to build the town hall. There was books set up in another parta the town hall that they didn't let but so many people vote on, they tol' me I wasn't registered. Well, I always voted for everythin' for the town, for the resta these bond issues, for mayor an' the town board. That was some election. I registered to vote every time since they sorta made it so that blacks could vote down in the South here. I don' remember exac'ly the year, but it's been a long time.

When President Johnson was runnin', my mother got an anonymous call an' some man told 'er if Johnson got in what was gonna happen to her black self. Said they was gonna drag her out an' kill 'er if Johnson got in. She told 'im when he felt like it to come on. Of course she was scared speechless. That was a bad time. There was a rally of the Klan that put a sickness on Rose Hill I don't believe will ever be cured. I was workin' at that time for Mister Hugh Johnson, which was our State Representative from here, an' he an' the mayor, Mister Gerald Carr, when they found out about it, they went over to the county seat in Kenansville to have it stopped so the Klan wouldn't get any land here. Mr. Blount Bradshaw had already rented 'em the land, they couldn't do nothin' about that. But they did freeze them Klansmen on that lot when they had planned to march right up 'n down the black sections.

That night there was loudspeakers 'n you could hear 'em all over. We could stay right here in the house an' hear 'em like if they were out in the front yard. Talkin' 'bout the black people, said we need to go back to Africa, we use bear grease on our hair, an' they said that all the whites that voted for Johnson they was nigger lovers. Anyway, it was some terrible stuff was spoken down there. Mister Hugh Johnson wouldn't even let his children go out on the porch. He didn't want 'em to hear such as that.

Then a group of the blacks got together an' decided they would boycott the folks in Rose Hill. One white man, the black folks really did 'im wrong. He was accused of talkin' at the Klan meetin' an' he wasn't even there. People stopped goin' to his store, an' it like to drove him crazy. I've worked in his home ever since way before he was ever married, an' worked with his mother an' his aunt an' his sister now, an' really, he don' have the nerve to stand up an' say things like that. But they claimed that was him doin' the talkin' down there.

I never stopped goin' tradin'. Mosta the black folks took their trade to Wallace, but the day of the Klan meetin' the stores in Wallace was closed early so they could come over to Rose Hill.

257

Mosta the white people here in town didn't like that meetin' anyway. I guess it woulda really been sump'n that went down in history if they had let 'em march through these black sections. But the Negroes weren't as scared as they thought we was gonna be.

There was a wonderful white preacher here then, Presbyterian, an' when I saw him a week after that rally, he said to me, "Miz Newkirk, what do you thinka that mess?' He said, "I think it was a disgrace." I heard he'd get up in church an' make a prayer an' ask the Lord to bless his colored friends. I heard some a' 'is members' faces turned so red like they hardly stand it. Well, some folks went 'round an' they got a petition an' they got 'im out. We'da had a lot less dope amongst the young white children if they hadda let Mister La Prade stay here. Them Presbyterians are sorta hard-shell people.

I'm a domestic. I do housecleanin', an' I also caters for weddin's. My husband's disabled to work. He had emphysema an' coronary asthma an' he has a real bad heart condition. He gets a small disability check an' that's our income. So right now I work in about five diff'rent homes. It's general housework, at times washin' windows, moppin' an' waxin' floors. One girl I work with I worked with her mother from the time she was nine months old 'til she went away to college. Now she's married an' I been workin' for her about three years. The rest that I work with is elderly folks. They think things are just like they've always been. They wanna pay like folks paid ten, twelve years ago.

'Course the folks I work with, it gets right funny. Two places I work, they fix a meal of sump'n, they'll go in an' eat, an' they'll get through eatin' an' tell me I can come an' eat. One place, where they's nobody but the woman, she'll fix herself a sandwich an' she'll say, "Eva, you can come an' eat when you get ready." Everybody else I work with, when the food is fixed, even if I cook it, we all sit right down. When I was workin' with the Hugh Johnsons, didn't matter who was there, when the food was ready, we all sat down an' ate together. But this woman she'll fix her a sandwich an' a bowl a' soup, an' she'll sit down an' eat it an' she don't want me to sit down at the table with her. I can cook her food, but still she don' want me to sit down at the table. I says, "No thank you, I don' care for anythin' to eat." Not that I cares that much 'bout sittin' down to the table with her, but it's the way she looks at it troubles me.

The Klansman I: Blount Bradshaw

Some folks around'll try to tell you diff'rent, but back when the rally was, sixty-four, I think it was, there was Klansmen in Rose Hill. There'd been Klansmen since the Civil War an' they kept right on. I'm not sayin' it was such a strong organization. They was havin' their troubles. They was lookin' all over for a place to meet, out in the woods, down by the riverbanks, all over. They even asked for a place by the city hall, but the town told 'em nothin' doin'. An' then they came to me. Well I said, "I'll tell you, if you want a hall, I'll build you a hall." An' I built 'em one, right down where I got my shop now, alongside a' the highway. An' I rented it to 'em. I wasn't a member at that time, but they had 'em some meetin's an' I went an' I joined.

Some people might not like it, but I'm gonna tell you the truth whether they like it or not. When I joined the Klan organization in Rose Hill, they made me a Klug, which is a preacher. An' I took that real serious, 'cause the Klan is for Christian gentlemen, an' when a man goes into that organization, he goes to serve God. About that time the organization in Wallace busted up, an' practically everyone there was a gentleman. Some of 'em were real important men. The man that was Klug down there was a very high-class man, an' when he come an' join our group in Rose Hill, naturally I resigned from my position. So then they turned around an' put me on a job that every grievance that was to be handled come to me. I was the most powerful officer as far as authority was concerned. An' I was s'posed to work with three men as my assistants. So I picked three men an' the lodge okayed them, kinda like the Senate up there in Washington hasta approve the men the President appoints. The job wasn't very pleasant. One thing that happened, there was a man lived about ten miles out in the country. He was a pretty big farmer. An' he was

259

a middle-aged man. His wife was layin' up with Negroes over here 'cross the railroad crossin' 'bout three or four days a week. An' meantime, he was in his house with a Negro woman doin' it in his wife's bed. Now this report come from a woman who's qualified, truthful, honest, upright. She was a prominent woman. An' she said under no circumstances were we to let her name be used. That was the kinda thing we had the responsibility of.

I don't approve of such goin's on. No, sir. But to find out that my own organization was a party was even worse. You remember I tol' you I built 'em a buildin' down here? Well, one night I come by an' there was a whole lotta cars parked out in front, an' I come in an' they're all set up like they was gonna have a meetin'. 'Cept I noticed one thing. There was a movie projector where the altar was s'posed to be. Well, it felt like sump'n was wrong, an' I just sat around for a while, an' some of them men were sayin', "Now, Mister Blount, it's gettin' mighty late." Things like that. I said, told 'em, "No, sir, you go right on." Well they started. An' I'll tell you, I never saw such filth in my life, the things them people were doin' on that movie screen. I just turned tail an' went home. That ain't the Klan. That's a splinter organization.

Later on they come to me an' told me they wanted my field out there near where the trailer park is now for a rally. So I said, "Well, now's my time to see a cross burn." An' I gave 'em permission. I remember the night because I had been to church an' I come back an' they had mowed the place, fixed it up, put out chairs an' everythin', speaker's stand, the microphone. There was cars, cars, cars, parked all over, far as you could see. An' that's the story 'bout how that mean ol' Blount Bradshaw tried to scare the colored people outta the town a' Rose Hill.

The colored folks, I don't have nothin' to say about 'em one way or the other. They're my friends, some of 'em are. The old buildin' I built, I even rented it to one of 'em, a lady usin' it for a florist. But there are white people in this town that are such hypocrites they don't wanna say nothin' 'bout what they think an' what they done. They don't want no more boycotts. So if you ask 'em, they'll tell you, "*Me?* It never were *me*." An' anytime someone comes 'round askin' the truth about the Klan in this country, they tell 'em not to go see ol' L. B. Bradshaw. 'Cause I been around a long time an' I know who they are an' I got their names.

Tammy Smith*

When the niggers started goin' to our school, my girlfriend hadda go to the office every day 'cause she'd fight with 'em on the school bus. They'd sit in her seat an' she'd knock 'em out. An' the people down at the school would tell her to behave. When we first had nigger teachers, we'd say, "What you say?" an' "Heah Ah is." But you hadda be mighty careful or you'd flunk the subject. There were hardly any white people liked it. I hadda first cousin down in Jacksonville, an' all the black boys were all the time askin' for dates an' tellin' her they were gonna see her, stuff like that. An' me, one time they went by me in a car, said, "Come back in a minute an' pick you up, baby." An' I hadn't never said nothin' to 'em. We hadda go to school with 'em 'cause that was the law. But we sure didn't like it none. You put the bad apple with the good apple, you spoil the whole thing.

They didn't like it any better'n we did. See, Charity is *their* school. An' they don't like it when a white person walks through there, just like we don't like it when a colored person walks through Wallace-Rose Hill. Me, I never had nothin' bad happen with 'em, but they ain't got no business in our schools, an' they ain't got no business tryin' to take over an' all this mess. An' they shouldn't have the same jobs. They should be equal, but I don't think they should mix. We never had all this trouble before this integration mess come along.

Hermetta Elaine Judge

At school usually they always have white people to win things. But this year it didn't exac'ly happen that way. They had a black Miss Chorus an' a black homecomin' queen. An' some of 'em couldn't stand it. They just wasn't gonna have that. So they cheated around an' got all the white boys that used to play foot-

261

ball an' they made two queens. The nighta the game they had policemen everywhere out there 'cause someone said that some buses was comin' up from Wilmington with the Ku Klux Klan or some kinda organization. Didn't nothin' happen. But didn't nobody go to the football game, mosta the blacks an' a lotta the whites, too. We were just too scared.

We got integrated when we was in the ninth grade. It was kinda rough at first 'cause they made black children go to that school an' we didn't wanna go. We thought the white people thought they was better. That's one day I'll remember. It was the first time I had ever been with white people, an' I didn't know what to say to 'em. One a' the things was we didn't feel ready to go. Our black teachers had always told us that the white girls was way ahead of us 'cause we was so ignorant. An' that we didn't have the same books an' the same stuff they had, an' they could learn more. A lotta the school people, Mister Windsor Johnson an' some a' the teachers, thought the white kids were learnin' more, an' they wanted the rest of us to have the same rights, but most of our parents didn't like it. They thought there was gonna be fightin' an' we'd get beat up an' things like that. An' a lotta the white people started sendin' their children to private schools, even the poor white people. I knew I hadda go because I wanted to finish high school, an' it wouldn't a done me no good to quit, 'cause that's what they wanted us to do. But I didn't wanna be there. You don't feel right bein' some place when they don't want you.

It made me mad, but it was a problem I hadda face up to. An' mostly it's worked out fine. I always wanted to make friends, an' that was hard. Like if the other kids saw you talkin' to a white girl, the white kids thought you was tryin' to bring 'er down, an' the black kids thought she was tryin' to use you for sump'n. So we didn't do much mixin'. But a lotta things change, just since our class come in. This year our English teacher told us that it was the first year that the black and white kids really got along. She said a coupla years ago, when they was practicin' the play, the black kids would come in one door an' the white kids would come in the other one. They'd look at each other like they was scared to death an' neither of 'em would say nothin'. But she said our class was real good, an' I'll tell you sump'n that happened to me. I got elected Miss Chorus. I was about the only black student the white people really helped, an' meanwhile, the black kids didn't do a thing for me.

When we was doin' the play, I was real scared before I went out on the stage, an' this white boy he come over an' put his arms around me an' I was cryin' an' all an' he was tellin' me not to be afraid. An' when we graduated, I had more callin' cards than anybody else in the whole school. People give callin' cards out to their friends, an' I got 'em from everybody, black an' white. That's what people do when they want you to remember them. I guess they liked me.

Joe Maxwell*

There's one farmer out here, an' he can't stand the colored folks. He spends nine tenths a' his time sittin' up in the restaurant, runnin' 'em down while they're out there makin' his livin' for 'im. But he's a Carolina fan, the university up there, an' three fourths of 'em are colored boys playin' basketball. They may be playin' an all-white team, but he's still for 'em 'cause they're from Carolina. An' I sit an' listen to 'im. I'm just parta that crowd, an' I can't say I like the niggers much, but there's only so far you can go with a thing. I catch every word of it an' sit an' listen to 'em up there chewin' the fat, an' then I get so mad I get up an' walk out.

Windsor Franklin Johnson

When the Supreme Court order came down, they called a meetin' at the county board of education of all the leadin' Negroes to see how we felt. An' we told them how we felt. Told them that Congress an' those white judges on the Supreme Court had interpreted the laws, an' if that's what they said, that was exactly what was to be done. I was in the meetin's, but I didn't do too much talkin' that night. I wasn't, as some would say about me, "controversial" then.

Some would classify it as "militancy." Others would classify

263

it as "controversial." They use the name synonymous. That's because any person who will speak out against inequality is considered "controversial." That's why you don't have a lotta Negro fighters. We know what's gonna happen. The businessman, the political leaders, the courthouse gang. We know what they'll do. If you need credit, they cut off your credit. If you need a loan from a bank, they cut off your loan. That's how they have been able to keep the black man into segregation. They've been fairly successful over the years. They have prescribed what I should wear an' what I should eat, what kinda automobile I should drive, where I should live an' where I should go to church. An' the average black person would have the philosophy of not rockin' the boat. But I reached the position several years ago where I don't care if they tear up the boat. So they classify that as "controversial." It is when you get to the place where you can do some thinkin' for yourself.

My father was a tenant farmer, which meant that you were just a second-generation slave. The landlord furnished the land an' you, in turn, would do all the work. An' you'd go halves. An' the white man, the landlord, would invariably get *his* before you would get yours, or before the bills would be paid. It would mean that you would hafta be submissive, an' even docile, in order for the landlord to let you stay on his place.

In many instances if he had anythin' on earth that he wanted done, whether it was related to our particular crop or not, someone would come an' tell my father that I couldn't go to school that week, I hadda help with the work. That's one a' the best things that ever happened to my daddy because he was determined that I should go to school an' that accounted for him havin' to move. When my father bought his own place, I realized that in order to say what you want to, do what you want to, you hadda strive towards independence. The people where we lived, they kinda developed a paternalistic attitude towards Negroes who had been on their place, an' if ever a time came that any of 'em needed anythin', they were there. A man should get to where he doesn't need that. In a society the people who do the thinkin' for you are the people who control you.

When I graduated from college, I got a job teachin' in Calypso, an' I worked there for three years as a teacher an' I was prin- cipal there for two years before comin' to Rose Hill. I was a prin- cipal at Rose Hill Two under the segregated system for fourteen years. We hadn't traveled too far from "white water" an' "black water," where one spigot would be label "white" an' another would be labeled "black," an' when you operate two systems, one invariably is gonna come up short. All the money was in the white schools. We hadda buy the wood, we couldn't get toilet tissue, the Negroes hadda build the classrooms, make the seats, make the blackboards. That what it was like then. But on the other hand, the people in Duplin County who were least able to buy buses bought buses for their children to go to the black school. We have moved through all that, hopefully. But when it comes to bein' "satisfied," it's like the white men say: "Negroes are never satisfied."

There are some people who think that Negro teachers are not as qualified as white. Now, whose fault was that? The state was the licensing agency. Fayetteville State Teachers' College, Eliz- abeth City State Teachers' College, all of 'em are supported by the state of North Carolina. Those institutions are their babies. If they are malnourished, it was the state who malnourished them.

Another thing they've been successful in doin' is keepin' the blacks outta history. The state board of education approves the textbooks we use in the schools, an' just last year there was a tre- mendous stink because they adopted a textbook with a lotta writ- in' in it about Martin Luther King. But that was just last year. Some of the kids don't know anythin' about black history. All that they've been able to pick up is what they've got on TV an' if they read the papers. An' the editors, until recent years, they've given a negative presentation. A black man never got in the pa- pers unless he stole a chicken or a watermelon an' got put in jail. The kind of education that's been subscribed to is that anythin' with black involvement in it is not good. There might be a line about George Washington Carver or Booker T. Washington, that's the sum of it. You know nothin' about the person that was with Byrd when he crossed the North Pole. You know nothin' about the fact that the very, very first child that was born in

265

America was black. But the whole story is this: if you want to keep a group, a nation, a race down, don't write nothin' about them. They've been fairly successful in that over the years.

After we were integrated I didn't encounter any more problems than I did when the school was all black. I don't believe I had but one incident, an' it really wasn't of any consequence. The biggest thing is stayin' cool. If you stay cool, no matter what line a' work that you're in, you'll be all right. They just swore that integration was gonna bust everythin' wide open, an' there wasn't any trouble. Not a bit. I owe a whole lot to the staff. Some a' those white teachers are mighty fine ladies. It went smooth an' they all respected me. The blacks had always respected me, but it was a new experience for the whites.

The average person on the street in Rose Hill thinks that because over the years that Negroes have been the last hired an' the first fired, that there are specific jobs we hafta do. They have been able to program blacks into specific positions an' specific places in the town. Don't you normally expect that? We glorify the almighty dollar. An' sometimes people just don't have the competitive skill to get out there an' get that dollar. If everybody was given two thousand dollars in less than a year, we'd have the same situation where we started. Some people don't have an inventive, creative mind, an' that competition is rough. People always ridicule the have-nots. They say, "Oh, they just won't work. They won't do nothin'." And then they have some lady "workin'" for 'em for less than a dollar an hour. It's very conducive for people to go on welfare. That's the first time some of 'em have ever had a check or any money comin' to 'em in their lives. Who is it that wouldn't want a check? There are no jobs, an' our educational system hasn't provided some individuals with marketable skills to go out in life an' make a livin'. There's somethin' very wrong with our society where you can get more on welfare than you can make out there workin'. With all the abundance of wealth in America, everybody should be able to have a job. I think there's a worm out there for every bird.

We usedta think in terms of politics bein' the science of government, but I'd like to use the definition that Julian Bond used. He said, "Politics is to see who gets how much of what from whom and when." So Negroes need to be in politics, too. The

Democratic party in Duplin County could add to their registration considerably by havin' a commissioner of registration. They could appoint any person to start down the street with a book an' register everybody. But they haven't gotten to it. The average white politician is scared to get those votes on the book 'cause they don't know who's goin' to vote. You go out an' register 'em an' they vote against you.

The way I got in politics, at one time I was very close to my boss, the superintendent of schools, O. P. Johnson. An' about the time he got in that position superintendents didn't stay around long. So the only way O. P. Johnson could stay around as long as he did was to get votes from the colored people, an' he hadda have someone with influence to get the votes for 'im. So I got started in a program of registerin' blacks, an' I registered a lot of 'em for Mr. O. P. an' the other Democratic leaders—Dallas Herring an' Hugh Stuart Johnson. An' the Democrats communicated with me. An' that was my beginnin' in politics.

Now it came up when Robert Scott's daddy ran for governor, a cousin of my boss, his name was Charlie Johnson, ran for governor an' they wanted me to get black votes for 'im, an' I bucked an' went for Scott. An' that was the first partin' of the ways. The next time, when they really got peeved at me, Bob Scott ran for lieutenant governor, an' they wanted us to support Clifton Blue. I told them no. I was a Scott man. An' I got all the blacks in Duplin County to vote for 'im. Well, the politicians wanted me with 'em, but they wanted to wrap their fingers around me an' say, "We're gonna support this man or we're gonna support that man." But the blacks were gonna do it for ourselves. That's a principle of politics.

Some people call me radical, stirrin' up trouble. They can call me anythin' they want to. When it comes to becomin' "radical," that's based on a couple of factors. Number one, when you get older, an' number two, when you get more secure. It may be that I'm no more "radical" today then I was years ago, but perhaps I express it more. I'm a student of militant nonviolence. I think Martin Luther King coined that phrase. I'd hate to live in a country or even a town where you'd have all conservatives or even all liberals. Even the Ku Klux Klan oughta be able to exist. These freedoms are guaranteed us in the Constitution. There's no reason for the CIA or the FBI to get involved in other people's lives. It's un-American.

I hafta say that since I've come to Rose Hill, there has been some change in attitude. The stores downtown is one of the places it's changed. Of course, there's never been white money an' black money. An' the Negroes have "In God We Trust" to spend. After the famous Klan rally, the Negroes came to the conclusion that if the streets weren't safe for 'em on Saturday night, they probably weren't safe for them Sunday night, or Monday night, or Tuesday night, or Wednesday night, an' we just took our business elsewhere. It has had a positive effect. The Klan hasn't been back since.

Of course I've had some incidents. Somebody intimidated me on the telephone, but I just took the telephone off the hook. For a period of time the Ku Klux Klan would throw literature in the yard. But I have a lotta good friends in Rose Hill. One of the things that happened to change the opinion of me in this town was the two years I spent as principal of an integrated school. I think I earned their respect. What I want is their respect. I don't want their love. Love is a peculiar commodity. You don't know you have it 'til you give it away.

When you go up there to city hall to ask for justice—"What do you want? What do your people want?" That's the question they ask. Well, the black community came to the inevitable conclusion that the only way they could get anythin' was to get in the mainstream. So anythin' to bring self-dignity to my people an' to put a bottle of milk in their hands an' put some bread in their stomachs, I am for it. The Negro wants anythin' an' everythin' any other human bein' wants in the world, an' a whole lotta times just a little bit more. Because the others had freedom an' the Negroes haven't had freedom. We want that, too. It's like the little boy in the classroom. He hopped up, threw up his hands. Teacher said to 'im, said, "Siddown." Wasn't long before the little boy got back up again. Teacher said, "Siddown." Little boy got back up again. Then she scolded 'im, said, "Siddown. Siddown, Johnny." He said, "I'll siddown. But I'm standin' up on the inside."

We've made considerable amount of progress, but we can't

rest our oars on the progress we've made. We hafta try to push for the distance we gotta go.

Clara Mae Taylor*

There was a white woman here in town, 'n there was two white mens that was goin' with 'er, married mens, an' she moved outside town an' she was killed. They claimed she was raped an' killed, but I have no way of knowin' whether she really was raped or what happened. But they got this black man for it an' they carried 'im through pure torment.

When the trial come on, the lawyer made some of the white folks so mad. He said they didn't even know 'til three days after she was buried that she had been shot. The witnesses s'posed to be talkin' about what condition her body was in. So they got caught in some lies that day. But they like to accuse a black man, an' killed 'im for it. Whether he did it or not, they killed 'im.

I dunno whether he did it or he didn't do it, but this lady, she was doin' wrong things. She had lived here in town, but she lived right in front of her sister an' she didn't want her sister to see who was goin' in or comin' out. An' so she moved back out there in the country by herself in that big ol' house. Nobody knows what caused her death. But they caught this black man an' killed 'im for it.

Martha Reed*

She was a fine-lookin' woman. Day before Christmas this black man hid himself in the house. She'd gone to do her last-minute Christmas shoppin' an' he had broken in the house an' hidden himself, an' when she came home, he beat her to death. It was easy to trace, he had stolen from her an' had sold it the same afternoon. There was no question. He admitted everything. That was a horrible murder. He had beaten her to a pulp, really, and there was blood all spattered in the house an' the Negro men said, "Let us have 'im. That's all we ask. Just let *us* have

269

'im." But the white men said, "No. Maybe he deserves to be lynched, but he won't be lynched here. He will have a court trial just as any other person would have."

And that is what happened. They sped him away so that the Negro men could not get him.

Robert Ward

About nine years ago the county commissioners appointed certain ones in the community to be on the Good Neighbor Council to work together on some problems. But since it's been formed, there's very few white ones have stayed on. The ones that were on the Good Neighbor Council from the Negro race had a great deal of frustration to start with an' made certain demands, an' some of the whites that dropped off didn't wanna hear those demands. I've been on since the outset. But I guess about eighty percent of the white ones that were appointed have dropped off by now.

The Negroes wanted equal rights, equal employment in all areas. They requested the Good Neighbor Council to negotiate with different companies. They were seekin' to get into the postal service, but it seemed to be a pretty well closed shop. But most other areas have some integration now. Servin' on the Good Neighbor Council has been real rewardin' to me.

At the time of the nineteen fifty-four Supreme Court decision, people started talkin' about integration. But we never did think it would come. We thought it might at some distant point, maybe twenty, thirty years from now. We older ones weren't ready, but the children were. They were ready because of bein' exposed to television an' modern means of communication, that kinda thing.

I used to be a member of a Presbyterian church out in the country in Oak Plains, had about forty members at the time. An' even back then I was tagged as an integrationist. If it would come up in a Sunday school lesson, I didn't mind speakin' out. That church had Negro members since the Civil War, but they don't have any now, an' they're further from it than they ever were. The Methodist Church has had some Negro choirs recently, an' I understand they're gonna have an integrated revival there. But mosta the church members take this attitude, "We hafta go to school with 'em, that's the federal law. But let's not have 'em in our church, 'cause we don't have to." I can't quite comprehend anybody that reads an' studies the Bible bein' a segregationist. When you get down to the basic teachin' in Genesis an' Revelations, I can't see it.

There are people here in our community who were real energetic in helpin' the Negro race, an' they have become segregationists now since integration has started. A lady in our community, a very outstandin' lady, took these two tough colored girls about twenty years ago an' gave 'em a college education at this Presbyterian school in Alabama. She paid for their education, took 'em there, got 'em in college an' everythin'. An' she is one of our staunch segregationists now. She wanted to help the colored race, but she did not want 'em to be equal or come up. Her helpin' was a Christian thing, but yet she couldn't take integration. Now we're actually educatin' the Negro race outta welfare, we're givin' 'em some motive in life. But some of the people who were so nice before, they had helped 'em to stay in their own place.

We in the South, an' maybe the North also, have had a double standard in education for a long time. We've had one standard for white colleges an' another standard for black colleges. When we went to complete integratin', suddenly we found ourselves with a surplus of teachers. Well, people are gonna get hurt on that, whites an' blacks. That's the stand I took a few years ago on the Good Neighbor Council with some of the teachers. I told 'em at meetin's, "I'm not particularly interested in your particular feelin's. What I'm interested in is those students at the school." If we make progress, we certainly hafta sacrifice some people's feelin's on that kinda thing.

My church, the Presbyterian church, had a pastor 'bout four years ago, Mr. La Prade. Unfortunately, he was a little bit liberal on the race question an' our church wasn't ready for it. On the day of the Klan rally he was some quarter of a mile from the rally, and on the church steps he made a recordin' an' you could distinguish the words that the, waddya call 'im, the dragon, the grand dragon, was sayin'. I can't remember the things he said, but anyway, it was horrible. Even though we believe in free speech, it's terrible when anybody can turn the loudspeaker like that an' say to the people what he was sayin'. Here were people who had been suppressed for a long time, for about forever, an' here's a man standin' up there givin' 'em zip, see, an' it's a question in my mind where freedom of speech ends. After that rally the Negroes boycotted some of the stores in town, but if the town fathers an' the town board an' the business people hadda criticized the Klan an' tried to get 'em not to meet here, I don't think we woulda had any boycott after. Anyway, our minister was run off from our church by some of the families that are powerful. The minister we have now, he's scary. He's a real oddball. He carries a gun in his car with him. The church is important to me an' I was upset by all that happened. It's changed my thinkin' some.

I'm a liberal on civil rights an' I'm a conservative on social things. On the drinkin' of alcohol I'm absolutely a teetotaler. Takin' alcohol away from 'em is like takin' a hatchet away from a little child. What makes me "liberal" is that I'm for the underdog. At the Lions Club meetin's there was two of us that were outspoken for McGovern, an' I liked to argue an' discuss. I loved that. Lotta people they call anybody they disagree with a "communist." I'm no communist. I just believe what I believe. I've seen so many people in my life that didn't have a chance in the world. They were victims of circumstances. An' if the community or the church or the government can give those people a chance, I'm all for it.

We've made a great deal of strides here. I have seven children; they range in age from fifteen to twenty-six, an' they have really come along on integration. They refuse to tell me how many Negroes in their classes at school, they say it doesn't matter, that they're all students together. An' maybe the church is nearer to integration than even I dream about, 'cause two or three years ago, we couldn't even talk about it in Sunday school class without a whole lotta people gettin' upset, an' now we can discuss it. I never did get criticized too much on the thing. Maybe I got a coupla telephone calls callin' me a "nigger lover," but that doesn't bother me. I don't even think I mentioned that to my family. It was very insignificant.

272

It's all been real interestin'. On the Good Neighbor Council, for example, there's one particular Negro from Rose Hill was always repulsive to me. I couldn't bear to be around him. He was arrogant. An' since I've served on the Good Neighbor Council with 'im, he's a very, very dear friend to me. His jokes are funny. He's not arrogant anymore. He's not repulsive anymore. Well, *he*'s the same person that he was before. He's changed very little. It's *me* that's changed. An' that's the most rewardin' thing that's happened to me.

Donald Murray*

Years back yonder there were some white men 'round here havin' Negro children. There was one, never married, had a good mind for to go tradin' around. He was a miser in a way, he had a right sharp head on 'im, but he didn't even go around with white people. He just lived among the colored an' he did have several children with 'em.

I know one of 'em that's his kin, he has the ol' man's way of doin' things. He makes a good livin'. That's a hereditary thing. He's got that from the white side of him. But if a person goes around with the colored an' gets a child, he oughta be darn sorry. A person should think more a' hisself, both the Negro an' the white person. We shouldn't go across race lines that way. I don' believe in it. Both races should have more respect for themselves.

Now you take some a' the Negroes, they do real well; but you look at it, they're three-fourths white. Is that the white man comin' down or is it the Negro risin'? There's two ways to look at it. A lotta them that really get anywhere in the professions an' so forth, they're all crossed up. It's the white blood in 'em. It's what blood has he got.

Eva Pickett*

There was a girl from New York, a white girl, worked for J. P. Stevens over in Wallace. She come down here an' she'd been

273

goin' with a colored boy. An' somebody found 'em. 'Course when they were caught, she swore that it was rape. An' that boy got fifteen years. Well, he said he'd been goin' with her every summer she'd come down here. An' she was livin' in a motel an' he had no way of knowin', if he hadn't already been in that motel with her, where her room was. He mighta went to somebody else's room.

The white girl said to 'im, "If they don't kill you, come to New York." Well, they didn't kill 'im. They just gave him fifteen years. Down here a white man can do anythin' he want to a black woman. Nobody pay much attention. But a black man touch a white woman, they ready to hang 'im.

The Klansman II: Melvin Patterson*

I got involved with the Klan when the government began to fall in the early fifties. I became interested because the government was communist-infiltrated an' I felt that if we could band together, we could smoke out the liberals an' the communists. We have not succeeded. They are almost ready to overthrow our free America into a dictatorship of communists.

The Klan originated just after the Civil War. They banded themselves together. They rode white horses or had white robes on their horses to scare the colored people. They would always explain it was a ghost of the white people that were killed on accounta the war of Abraham Lincoln.

They would go to a men's home an' if he was not supportin' his family, lettin' his wife hafta do all the work an' him layin' around, maybe too drunk an' wouldn't work, they would take 'im outside. They had a doctor in the group who knew what the man could stand an' they gave 'im some rawhide. They gave 'im a sample of it an' they gave 'im a chance, an' if that was not enough, they would come back an' give 'im another taste of rawhide, an' it would take care of 'im because it would change his mind. That is one thing we need today.

To join the Klan you hafta be white Protestant an' native born. You gotta have an' above-average reputation as far as lookin' after your family, payin' your debts an' not stayin' in the courtroom with the law all the time. First thing, you hafta fill out a card application with your name, your age, your birthplace. You gotta give a complete description of yourself. You're investigated to find out from people of your community an' your home neighborhood what kind of a man you are. The point of it is, they find out where you work, are you truthful, are you a respectable citizen or are you a slum-bum drunk, won't work, that you all the time stay involved in court actions.

We have open rallies for the public an' we have our own private meetin's. Some groups meet each week, every two weeks or a month. Each community has its own meetin' place. It's in the community. No man should hafta travel more than ten miles to a meetin'.

The rallies are open to any white people of the Protestant faith. It is a Christ-believin' an' Christ-foundered organization. Now the Jewish an' the Catholic organizations are not allowed because they don't believe in Jesus Christ. Even the Catholics don't. Mary is who they worship. But they're changin' their organization to believe in anythin' they can to get more membership to get more power to overthrow. Your Klan is affiliated with people of the churches which believe Jesus Christ is the Son of God. Some of the members don't attend church, but yet they still believe in the Protestant faith. We say that the ways of Jesus Christ is true an' is right. You can believe in a thing even though you don't participate. The basic of the Klan people are Christ-believin' an' Christ-fearin' people. They hafta be, or they will never be a member of the United Klans of America.

At our rallies, main thing is there's a preacher, a Protestant preacher, he come up an' he preach. Thirty, forty minutes. Then they explain the ways of the Klan. Right at the rally. They tell the people what's goin's on, the underhanded things the average public out here don't know. There's men in this that works all the way to the top of the government, an' they find out the things that's a-goin' on.

Black Monday, the Earl Warren court, is what created the interest of the people in the Klan. Then the Warren court got nosy, sendin' down people to spy, to find out who was a member of the Klan so they could try an' intimidate people through an' by income tax. They would try to pull us in on income tax evasion.

275

They was tryin' to cut out all Protestant-believin' people organizin' together. They went to the meetin's an' would go an' sit an' see people that they knew, or would find out somehow an' come back to the community an' inquire to find out what a person's name was.

A person's got a right to attend a rally, but there'd be a highway patrolman standin' with a pad at the entrance, an' he would write down every license number that went in there. Any man is a member of the Klan gets known. That's the first thing that's smeared on the news if he's picked up or does anythin'. If he walks down the street an' stubs his toe, he's a member of the Klan. The news media an' the heads of the government kick the Klan as sump'n they don't want because they know it carries more power than they got. It is a licensed legal organization, but they know that if the people get banded together, they can overthrow anythin' that the communists are pushin' to do. That's why they don't want the Klan in this nation. They try to ridicule a man for bein' a member because he's too clean of a man for them. But this mob that goes out an' hollers, "Peace, Peace," with these communist insignias, that chicken foot that ain't nothin' but the mark of the Antichrist, the broken-down cross, that's fine. It's just a buncha rabble-rousers an' nobody does a thing to 'em.

They don't want people to talk against anythin' that the communists is pushin' in our nation. They want people to eat it, to accept it an' say nothin'. For instance, these young people that's runnin' all over the country, just like the cross-country parade in Alabama with Martin Luther Coon, that was unlawful, no good, useless as anythin' in this world. The only thing that proved, it proved that they got some white girls pregnant by niggers an' they walked several miles. An' two or three of 'em got killed. That's the only thing that proved. It didn't help. It didn't build up any morals because you saw what happened to 'im, Martin Luther King. It oughta happened twenty years before.

Now let me tell you a little story. This one time there was a buncha wild hogs. An' if a man with a packa good huntin' dogs went through this swamp an' he come out with his dogs alive, he had some very good huntin' dogs an' he was very fortunate. An' the men of the community they were scared. So one day this

276

young guy he come down with his mules an' his wagon load a' corn 'n lumber. He says, "Where's all 'em wild hogs 'at everybody scared of?" So they showed 'im where to go.

Well, he was gone down an' he was gone for nearly two weeks. An' what he did, he found those hogs an' he would throw some corn out in the open an' let the pigs come out an' git the corn an' run back in the bushes an' eat it. Well, a few days it got to where the bigger hogs would begin to come out. An' then he began to build the pen, a little bit at a time, an' he got 'em all dependent on him for their support, they wouldn't go down an' root an' hunt their grub, they were dependent on him.

This is the way socialism an' communism is workin' in our nation today. To get the people wantin' that welfare check, get them dependent on that an' then the communists will step over an' take the entire country without firin' a single shot.

Insteada doin' justice to the people, the government's a buddy-buddy system today. For personal gain is ninety percent of what public offices is used for. The only way you can change a government official is forget about his money an' vote for the man, don't vote for the party. Not some a' this buncha crooks 'n yallerbacks they got in there. Yaller all over, a man that won't keep 'is word. He'd promise you the shirt off his back an' give you a handful of sand in the face.

I'm a George Wallace man one hundred percent. Because George Wallace is standin' on his original Democratic ticket— the government of the people, for the people, by the people—an' he's the only candidate that's runnin' that has that belief. He's the only one. If them liberals can get to them doctors, then they'll kill 'im. That's my personal belief of it. Because he's too strong of a man. That man talks to the blue-collar workers, the men who's the backbone of this nation. An' that's the people. He talks to us.

I'm frustrated to a certain extent. I look at the government in one way an' I don' wanna be here. An' I look at it another way an' I don' know of any I'd trade for it. But I see it gradually bein' tore down, day by day. There's too much dictatorship in it now. They pulla guideline here an' a pile line over there an' some other kinda line, an' we pay more taxes. We gotta do this an' we gotta do that to comply. They say, "We won't give you so much more, we'll cut federal funds off or the federal aid off if you don't comply." When the government ain't got no money to begin with. It's *our* money. It's our tax money. I could use it much better, to make better use of it in my community than they are, blowin' up to the moon an' feedin' a buncha sorry people too lazy to work an' doublin' the salaries of the ones settin' up there in big offices an' havin' the big drunk parties an' so on. They think they got the average voter fooled.

I believe in standin' for America. I'm a red-blooded American an' I stand for it. I was born an' raised here. I know what freedom is: freedom of speech, freedom to work where I want to, to change jobs when I want to, to buy where I want to, to go to church in the church I want to, an' if I don't like this preacher or that preacher, I go somewhere else. I would like to see this buncha people with all these cross-country parades stopped. I would like to see the people that's able to work go to work. I would enforce the law in the courtroom to where a man would hate to go back. They shouldn't come with a lawyer, a licensed liar, an' fifty dollars an' get the case thrown out. I believe in puttin' teeth in the law an' makin' it bite. This nation was founded on a Christian belief: the laws of the land. An' I believe in them.

That's why I believe in the Klan, an' I know the men an' I stand with 'em. There's preachers an' there's a few lawyers, merchants, some law enforcement, doctors, all members. There's senators an' congressmen, several of 'em, up in Washington. It makes me know that there's somebody to represent me. An' the other people that care. If you're in a distant town an' you need help, you kin always find one a' your fellow members. We're loyal to each other. If my phone was to ring tonight an' I were needed, I would be there. Immediately.

We want them to think the Klan is dead. That's what we want them to think. Because what they don't know can do a great deal of changin' in this nation's history. The people of this land, organizin' hard enough an' votin' strong enough, they can get a job well-done. If we're gonna work for freedom, we all work together. It's the body of people to do as the body of people wish.

278

13 Growin' Up

"The kids in this area need to be involved."
—Jimmy Bowden

Robert Simpson*

When I was growin' up, there was the old community buildin'
downtown across from where the municipal buildin' is now. Up
until just several years ago, most of the men in town, or a good
portion of 'em, used to meet up there on that porch every night,
just drift in after supper for somethin' to do. There was a certain
clique that would sit up on the porch an' there was a certain
clique that would sit down at Peanut's service station. The normal division was that the younger fellas were down at Peanut's.
They were settled, but not quite as settled as the men down at
the community building. Both groups would sit outside an' talk
politics an' whatever, spread gossip. The conversations went
from all kinds of absurd stories about Uncle Remus or Brer Rabbit to politics, to who was the latest runaround. Just about anybody could take part, 'though I guess it depended on what kinda
conversation was goin' on an' if you thought you could walk in
an' not interrupt some discussion about yourself. In the summertime the sun sets late an' sometimes it goes down like a red
ball of fire behind the railroad depot, an' it would get so quiet in
those days you could hear the cars clear out to the main road. We
kids'd ride our bikes down to the community buildin' an' watch
'em talk an' listen to 'em night after night. The feelin' you got
was that this was how it was 'cause this was how it had always
been. An' how it always would be.

When I was in elementary school, the town was even smaller
than it is now. I knew about everybody, had been in every house
in town, an' could go into every house in town anytime I felt like

281

it. I know I was just a kid, an' maybe things were happenin' that I didn't realize, but it seemed like everythin' was perfect here. We used to carry on somethin' terrible an' we could get away with it. There was no law enforcement besides one man, Burtiss Fussell, who was very uneducated an' who was the constable for Rose Hill township. Dallas Herring, I think it was, appointed him for five dollars a week, or somethin' like that, to answer calls at night if there was some kinda trouble. But that would happen very seldom. He was the law, except for the sheriff's department, who would pass through maybe once every two or three weeks. Burtiss never wrote a warrant in his life, as far as I know. If anybody ever did anythin' wrong, he went over an' told 'em not to do it again, an' he was big enough an' stupid enough an' mean enough that they wouldn't. He kept things pretty well in order. We used to pull little stunts like run out an' ring people's doorbells, fill up a brown bag fulla cow manure, set it on fire, ring their doorbells an' leave it on their steps. We usedta do it to Miz Sallie Blanchard an' to ol' Miz Harrell 'cause they couldn't get you. An' besides, they were the kinda lady that would walk up to you on the street when you'd been playin' in the gutter or makin' mud pies, or sump'n, an' ask you why you didn't go in an' wash your hands. So we always liked to pick on them when we thought we could get away with it. When we got older, we stole a buncha street signs in Wallace one Halloween night an' put 'em in the back of a car. We got caught, an' the mayor of Wallace, Mister Melvin Cording at that time, made us put 'em back the next day an' write a five-thousand-word theme an' have it graded on the spot. That's the kinda law we had. They didn't put you in jail or anythin'. Just whoever had jurisdiction would decide what to do with you. If they were paintin' the town hall, that's what you ended up doin'. It depended on what was happenin' at the time.

The elementary school out here, the one that burned down, was where everyone went. It was the same building, with the same desks in it, that my parents went to school in, an' some of the teachers were still the same. It was not very progressive, to say the least. You learned a lot in several grades that had a capable teacher, an' then the next year you'd get one who was there only to get money, an' you didn't learn a thing. In the eighth grade I was in the principal's classroom. He would walk in every now an' then an' give us a readin' assignment, make sure we were behavin' ourselves. We'd have a weekly test on social studies an' there'd be two questions, an' if you'd miss one, you'd get zero; get 'em both right, you'd get two hundred. For a project we made a pile of cement one time an' put it in the roadway to fill up a hole an' made an A in science for that six-week period. So we were mighty unprepared for high school when we got there, but when we got to high school, it was about the same as grammar school had been.

Wallace an' Rose Hill had always been arch rivals as far as athletics went, an' when they consolidated the school system, we had a hell of a time. There's a little more unity between the two towns now, but when I was in high school, if somebody found out you were datin' somebody from Wallace, you were really gettin' into alien territory. It took a good four years, one complete cycle, to get things calmed down. What we did for entertainment was go to the Dairio. That's one thing that hasn't changed. The only reason the Dairio has survived is that nothin' else has been able to get off the ground. Anytime anybody had a good idea, everybody would support it in the first month or so, but then everybody would go back to the Dairio. When I was in high school, what was the thing was bobby socks an' slicked-back hairdos an' bebop music, all this kinda stuff. Doin' the shag. Even the music was real simple, a straight direct beat. You could dance fast an' then you'd do the slow ones, an' it wasn't supercool, it was romantic. Maybe we didn't know how lucky we were.

Back in the late fifties an' early sixties the U.S. economy was boomin' an' there were jobs available everywhere. Hell, you didn't hafta worry about anythin'. But the town has changed a lot now. They're movin' the stores out to the highway an' puttin' up these big shoppin' centers, an' the trains don't run through like they used to. It's hard for me to say when I think it all changed, but it did, definitely. We're still a small town, of course, an' things here are still a lot slower than in other places, an' if you're an established person, you don't really hafta worry all that much. But things are definitely less personal, y'know? I'm not a very political person, but I think that some of the

things that happened in those last years I was growin' up—
President Kennedy's assassination an' the war an' the civil rights
stuff an' all—had an effect even here. When it was all happenin',
I was into my own life, an' there were times when we were all
upset by it, but it didn't seem like it would make that big a difference. Somethin' did, though, an' I think we lost somethin'. Even
in little ol' Rose Hill, North Carolina, nothin' is ever goin' to be
the same.

Ryke Longest

My name is James Patrick Longest, Jr. I'm named after my
daddy. They call me Ryke. I don't know why, but anyway, I like
it. I like to be called Ryke because it's the only name I can spell.

I'm in the second grade an' I'm seven years old. I go to C. W.
Dobbins Elementary School in Wallace. What I like at school is
usually readin' time. We read books, mostly books that have all
sortsa stories in them. Like shinin' bridges an' enchanted gates
an' all them sorta books. I like to read a lot.

I like to read about dinosaurs. They were almost the first creatures on here. A few of 'em liked straight meat an' a few of 'em
liked straight plants. An' usually, the ones that liked plants never ate meat, an' the ones that liked meat never ate plants. I know
another thing about them. They all didn't like each other very
much. Sometimes the meat eaters would win an' sometimes the
plant eaters would win. They all started eatin' each other an' the
whole tribe was washed out. Just like that.

I like chili an' hot dogs with ketchup. That's what we had at
my birthday party, 'cept the chili was kinda diff'rent 'cause it has
mustard added to it. I had Herbie an' Forrest an' Marion an'
Luke an' Charles. After we had our hot dogs, we went outside or
played inside. Some of my friends played in my room, some of
them played in the livin' room, an' after we got done inside, we
went outside an' we got our guns an' *Pow Pow Pow.*

I got a little toy gun which the spring fell down in the barrel
part, an' I don't believe I can get it out. I can still play with it.
An' I got a dollar bill in an envelope an' I got a safe an' I got a
book an' I got a suit for my toy soldier, GI Joe. That's not all. I

got me a fishin' rod an' two army tanks, metal ones, an' I got a scrabble game an' I got a tape recorder.

GI Joe is some man that's about five and a half inches tall. There's three diff'rent kinds you can choose from. Four, actually. Five. You get one with red hair, one is a black man with black hair, another's a white man with white hair an' a mustache, an' there's another kind that's a white man, an' he's just got a mustache. But one of 'em, when you pull his dog tag, he talks. He says eight commands.

A long time ago when I was a little boy, these came out an' I was so glad because when I was four years old, there weren't any of 'em an' I wasn't able to play with 'em. Because, you see, I've liked army men for so long an' I never liked Barbie Dolls. That's the only thing you'd find in the catalogues. But finally they came up with GI Joe.

Usually that's what a boy likes because boys like fightin' a lot. Like, y'know, some of 'em like Batman, some of 'em like Superman, I like army men. You see, army men fight a lot for their country. An' I'm real interested in the past. Sometimes I'm interested way back in the eighteen thirties or sometimes I'm more interested way back in seven thousand B.C., or sometimes way back in World War II. World War I an' World War II. World War I was the first war that really was a war. It lasted about five years.

Wars is fightin' against another country. An' you know us boys, we like fightin' a lot. Sometimes we like to watch it because we like to see brave heroes do heroic deeds or help people that are in distress. I'll tell you why I like fightin'. It's so tough an' it shows that people are brave an' have courage. I don't like to see a scaredy-cat. I been thinkin' of that for a long time. That's the reason I like fightin'.

Some people are scaredy-cats because they're little. I know a boy that never eats anythin' but his dessert. An' pretty soon, after I'm in the third grade, or fourth, or fifth, he might be kinda a scaredy-cat because we'd be a little bigger than he is. Already we are.

If you're not brave, you ought not to be in the Cub Scouts because if you're not brave, then you're not brave enough to go campin'. Then you're a scaredy-cat an' you think some big snake's gonna come up an' bite-cha. I've always wanted to be a cub scout. But I'm not old enough. You hafta be eight to be in the Cub Scouts in Rose Hill.

Sometimes I wish Daddy had a million dollars. Then we could buy a big ol' yacht an' then we could buy a wind cart. I'd go to school with that. If it was a windy mornin', I would. I think he might do that someday. He would strike gold.

My daddy listens to the TV a lot, usually on Saturdays. Football games, basketball, golf, hockey. You name it, he watches it. I leave 'im alone an' do somethin' else, but sometimes I ask 'im a few questions, like, "If you could buy worms in a pet shop, how much would they cost?" Somethin' like that. Sometimes he says, "Wait 'til the commercial an' I'll tell you."

Today, when he was watchin TV an' he had his little guitar out, he said, "Wait 'til the commercial to play a little bit of it." An' I waited 'til the commercial. All the time when I ask 'im a question, he waits 'til the commercial to answer it. But Granddaddy, I never bother him because he might get grumpy. An' when granddaddies get grumpy, you know how grumpy they are. I'll tell you what makes him grumpy. There's this bird, an' every day he comes an' eats all the bugs off the fender of the car. Then he goes to the rearview mirror an' looks at himself. Granddaddy really gets grumpy about that. Sometimes he gets grumpy, but not very often. An' he never gets grumpy at me.

Barbara Connally*

In Rose Hill-Magnolia school they have the sixes an' sevens together, an' there are three suites of sixth an' seventh grades. There are seventy-one kids in my class an' there are three diff'rent groups. For some subjects we're all together, but for other ones, like for spellin' an' math, we're on what they call contracts. You get this piece a' paper an' it tells you what to do an' gives you a deadline. Then they give you a grade on that. We don't really have report cards. They just show our parents an' tell them how good we been doin'.

There are some slow kids in all the classes, not really stupid, but they can't work as fast as the other ones. Last year we were divided into levels, the slowest ones an' the average an' the highest. Me an' mosta my friends knew that we were in the highest, 'cause our teacher would say she would expect more from us 'cause we were the pick of the crop. Mosta my friends were in the same group last year, but this year we were divided into three suites, an' most of 'em are in the next suite. I don't think it was intentional. But like, my best friend's in the other suite, an' that's what got me mad. I got some friends in mine, sorta like a group, y'all hang around together. We see each other the most, 'cause we usually have subjects together durin' the day. I don't see my friends on weekends 'cause mostly they live too far away.

Our family is real close an' we spend a lotta time together. We like music an' we like playin' games. We're not that strict about anythin', but we have about three rules we live by. The first one, you hafta read the Bible every day a little bit, y'know, an' then you hafta talk to Him every day in prayer an' then confess your sins. Every night before I go to bed I ask Him to forgive me for everythin' I did durin' the day, an' if I should die in the night, I ask Him to let me go to Heaven. I think children go to Heaven anyway 'cause He said in the Bible, "Blessed are the children for theirs is the Kingdom of Heaven." But then, back in biblical times, if you were twelve, usually you were married. It was different from today. I think if I lived some life that some adults live, I would go to Hell because I think I'm old enough to know what I'm doin'. When I was little, I was fulla nuisance, y'know? An' lotsa times I'd be a little too sensitive. I'd scream at everybody an' I know it's not right, so I asked Him to help me not to do it anymore. I haven't done it anymore since. I've fibbed a little bit, sorta stretched the truth sometimes. You could say that's a sin, too.

Everybody worries about us gettin' in trouble, but there ain't nothin' to do around here. There's the Danka Theater in Wallace, but usually they just have those movies with Clint Eastwood. There used to be one in Rose Hill, where the hatchery is now, but it got shut down. You can watch TV, but there's always those stupid baseball games or basketball games or football games or somethin'. Halloween used to be a lotta fun, but it's gettin' really bad. In Wallace there's been so much trouble they put limits. If you're twelve, you can't go, an' there's a curfew after nine o'clock. People've been puttin' pins in candy an' smashin' windows, an' one time, I dunno if it was in Rose Hill'r not, but somewhere around here they cut a cat's legs off an' left him in a car to bleed to death. It was really terrible, an' so they hadda do somethin'. We don't do anythin' like that. We just go to someone's house an' eat our candy an' wait 'til our parents come.

The thing is, I don't do much of anythin', y'know. I have a lot of friends, an' I have a best friend, which is very different. We usually have the same problems an' we can talk to each other about anythin'. We have another friend an', I dunno, she still thinks like a little girl. I mean, she giggles when somebody likes a boy, that type a' thing. I get real disgusted with a lotta the girls, 'cept my best friend. Only this summer we were at the beach an' we were constantly fightin' an' arguin'.

Everybody should have a best friend. But I've learned you shouldn't depend on it too much 'cause sometimes they might be different than you are. There will always be my family, but sometimes I could do without 'em when I'm mad at 'em. Then I wish they would all go away. I would never think that I would go away, they hafta go away. I can't live with anybody without drivin' each other up a wall. But my friends an' my family, I'm glad I have 'em anyway.

Beverly Johnson

When we first got to Wallace-Rose Hill High School, even though it was supposed to be an integrated school, it was segregated. There were only certain black kids that they wanted to be around with certain white kids. An' when they put me in that position, which they did, I didn't appreciate it at all. I was always placed in classes with maybe four black kids an' the rest white. They pushed everything else on me, too, because they claimed I was a good student an' goin' to college an' all of those things. For example, I was takin' a chemistry class. I was placed in that class on accounta my average an' my IQ. And I failed the class. Well, I mean, the way I am, when I get a B, I feel I've failed, you understand? It wasn't that I couldn't do it. It wasn't that I didn't do it. I just refused to do it. There was a black chemistry teacher, Mrs. Jordan, but she didn't teach the college prep class. It wasn't only chemistry either. All the teachers of those kindsa classes were white. I guess they thought the black ones couldn't teach as well, or somethin'.

I went to the segregated elementary school in Rose Hill, an' then I went to the black high school at Charity for two years an' graduated from Wallace-Rose Hill. When they told us we were goin' over there, I didn't like the idea at the time because I was loved in Charity High School an' I wanted to graduate from there because I had already established myself. It wasn't too hard to adjust to, it's just that I felt I lost a lot of privileges, a lot of things I like to do that they didn't have. Such as, I was a majorette, an' they didn't have a band at the integrated school. I was interested in modern dance, an' in a place like Rose Hill, bein' a majorette was the only thing I could get that was at all connected with dancin'. Mostly I didn't like the idea of takin' our school an' gradin' it down to a junior high, because the two schools were supposed to be the same. We had been used to fightin' for our school an' buildin' it up, an' then to take it an' make it a junior high was somethin' we didn't like at all.

What I'm sayin' is that it's not true that the colored people were dyin' for integration. The people who were fightin' for integration seemed to mostly be the white people because they knew they would lose federal money. That's what it was. An' everybody knows this is the truth. They certainly didn't do very much to make things right when it happened. I mean, there were certain things done to help us get along, but there wasn't that much effort to try to make us understand each other, why each race does certain things. They just put us all together an' we hadda get along the best way we could.

As far as black kids are concerned, the black people do it to their own. They think the white people are so far ahead of them that they want to choose the "best" kids so they can compete, too. But they shouldn't do that because the only thing they're doin' is hurtin' the child. They've got the black kids believin', when they approach the white kids, "He's better'n I am. He knows more'n I do, so why should I try?" I'm not sayin' that mosta the black kids are necessarily on the same intellectual level with the white kids. What I *am* sayin' is that they aren't that far behind. An' if they are behind, it's not because they don't have the ability. It's because they think they've missed some-thin'. "My mother an' father didn't give me books or nothin' to read. I hadda work while *they* went on vacation." They feel the white kids had more privilege because the blacks had to work for the white man while he sent his children off to summer school or vacation in Europe, or somewhere. It really gets you off to a bad start. I always got along with people because I like people, but I must say that I never trusted the whites. And I still don't to a certain extent. I guess that's because I grew up as a black girl in the country. But the more I see of people, that doesn't bother me so much anymore.

Last Christmas I substitute taught at the junior high school and I noticed the separation very clearly. It wasn't just color separation. I had five classes a day an' maybe there would be one of those classes that cared about anythin'. The rest of 'em didn't care. There was one class with the same type of people. Everybody was on the same level, everybody was smart, everybody was interested in what got done. What hurt me was that in the classes that didn't care, the only thing I was expected to do was sit there an' keep 'em quiet. But in the "good" class I gave them their work an' I'd sit down an' talk to 'em an' explain to them an' have somethin' to do. It wasn't color. It was ability segregation.

An' it follows you right on. I have that problem even in college, even among my friends. There are some guys that don't even talk to me because I'm a chemistry major. I don't let that bother me. I used to, but when I got to where I decided if they can't cope with me because of what I want out of life, then I can't deal with them. That's one of the separations. I'm a woman. I like feminine things. I like to be pampered. But it's terrible to be a woman with brains. I'm not sayin' I have that much. I probably have more ambition than brains, but it's terrible because, for example, my father's very much the man in the house, an' that's what I look for in a man. I may be wrong, but I can't deal with a man who makes me feel superior. But even if they're smart themselves, they get uptight about the fact that you are. The guy I've been goin' with, he wants to be an architect, an' I think that's nice. But *he* always makes cracks about "my girl-

290

friend, the doctor" because that's what *I'm* gonna be. What I mean is, I have a goal, an' I'm lookin' for a man who could complement that goal, an' that's a hard thing to find.

I've thought about comin' back to Rose Hill, not so much to practice medicine, but what I want to do is build a camp, or some sort of a recreation center where blacks an' whites can learn cultural things like dance, an' other things like that. If people start to get some kinda background, the whole thing about black an' white can drop, an' they can begin to grow an' understand what it is to be a person. To be black means the same thing as to be white, to be Mexican, or any other thing. It's to accept yourself. For myself, it's to accept myself as a woman an' as a black. It's bein' able to deal with your problems, to know what's at stake, to be able to beat 'em to the punch. I guess I could be called militant to a certain extent, when I believe I'm right and I know I'm right, but I'm not goin' to go an' fight a battle 'cause I'm mad at myself. A lot of people use other people as an excuse. Black people use the white man to stay on the bottom. You hafta know where you stand an' accept it. You know what you're goin' to hafta do to get along. You know you're goin' to hafta struggle. You know you're goin' to hafta work. So why not do it?

I'd really like to set up some sorta program that would teach people that, but I know I'd hafta be pretty well on my feet to do it. The kids here need somethin'. They seem to be lost. I have younger brothers—ten, twelve an' thirteen. An' things are a lot different for them. The things kids are into now we never would have thought about in my days. You hafta realize that just a few years ago, when we were comin' up, everybody was *young*, y'know what I mean? Now there's a part of 'em that's young an' a part of 'em that's grown. They see a lot of things. They're rebellious. But I know that everythin' that I know, the morals an' the values I have, the credit goes to my parents because they taught me. They're just country people, but all the credit goes to them. So I try to help out an' pass things on. Every time I come home I sit down an' talk to my brothers on their level. Things that I think they'd like to understand. I do that because they really open up to me an' I keep a personal touch, so I guess I don't have too much to worry about how they're growin'.

Sue Ann Green*

It ain't so bad to be livin' around here 'long as you got some-body to kinda hang around with. 'Long as you got your friends with you, it's really pretty okay. Like you can ride down to Wal-lace, an' 'long as one of us got her sister's ID, or sump'n, we can get a six-pack an' get higher'n shit. Usually what we do is ride around that Dairio, an' then we go over to That Place an' sit out in the car an' talk about who's been datin' who an' who's got pregnant an' who you wanna be datin', 'cept mosta the dudes 'round here ain't worth botherin' with. Get tired a' that an' you can always go inside an' play foozeball or just mess around. Sometimes we go to the movies, which is okay if you wanna get stabbed or raped after. It depends on which kinda movie. You go see *Shaft* an' you're just askin' for trouble. Mostly what we do is get in someone's car an' go ridin'. Like you'll be goin' down some road an' someone says, "Oh, wow, they got a new house here. Remember when it was moved?" "Yeah." You go ridin' an' look at the things you seen for the last fifteen years.

It's the same way with school. School is a real drag, 'less you got a kinda group to hang out with, an' then you can raise all kindsa hell. I suppose you learn a lot, but not as much as they say you're goin' to. The teachers don't care. They'll expel you if you're fightin' a lot, 'r sump'n, but if it's only cuttin' up 'r talkin', they send you out in the hall or down to the principal, an' he ain't very strict. We all kinda help each other out. Like you're sit-tin' in some class, right, an' they ask you, "What does so-an'-so mean?" So you kinda write notes back an' forth, an' that way no-body gets in trouble. That ain't cheatin' or nothin', an' anyway, who gives a damn? It really depends on how you cheat. If you make your own cheat-sheet, that's one thing. Lookin' on some-body else's paper, that's another thing, I s'pose. But usually that's the way it is. Lookin' on somebody else's paper. Why study when you can do it that way? 'Less you get moved, an' that's a real drag.

When somebody gets caught, like on an exam or sump'n, that's a big deal, but with a pop test or, y'know, a regular test, it don't matter. If they catch you, they tell you to tear it up an' throw it in the garbage can, an' you can be excused an' go out an' smoke in the yard. The only bad thing is gettin' caught. It's like what they're sayin' about Nixon an' all those other guys up in Washington. Everybody does it. Okay. Cheatin' really gets on my conscience, but the teachers all know we cheat, an' the way they look at it, it's all right as long as they don't hafta catch us. I always usedta think if somebody ever caught me, I'd quit, but this frienda mine he's been caught three times an' he says it don't make any difference.

There are some teachers where you don't cheat in their class. Like if you get caught in a senior class an' you flunked it, you'd hafta go to summer school, an' who wants to go to summer school after your senior year just because a' cheatin'? Also, there's some people you wanna learn under them, an' then some other people it's a bunch of stupid crap, an' you don't give a damn what you do. Like I probably wouldn't cheat in math or science 'cause I like it, an' when I go to college, I wanna go into math or some fielda science. But I probably would in literature, 'cause as far as I'm concerned, literature is one big waste a' my time. An' you oughta see them dumb tests anyway. Fill in the blanks. You know, "Tommy was a.) stupid; b.) ignorant; c.) selfish; d.) jealous." An' the answer is "jealous," so you fill in the d. Junk like that. The last thing we did in literature was this story called "The Necklace." This woman she doesn't want to go with her husband to this big fancy party 'cause everybody would have all this expensive junk on, so she borrows her next-door neighbor's necklace an' loses it. She works all her life, tryin' to pay the woman back, an' then she finds out it was fake an' she falls out. Also, we did *Julius Caesar*, which usually it's a bore to do Shakespeare 'cause you go around the room an' everybody reads diff'rent parts, but now they got these records an' you follow along. Well, nobody ever follows in the book, but it's kinda fun. Far as anythin' else, it mostly doesn't have anythin' to do with my life at all, an' it's a drag.

One thing we definitely don't study in school is any of the shit that's goin' on now. We talk about what Columbus did, an' what's his name, de Soto. In my opinion that Watergate stuff's borin'. I'm gettin sick of it, 'cause that's all you hear every time you turn on the TV. Somethin' about impeachment, somethin' about the trials. I guess I'm like mosta the people around here, an' I think they oughta do somethin' about all this mess an' quit botherin' us about it. I mean, it's just so much bullshit. All of 'em do it. Like everyone thinks all of the kids were for McGovern. You wanna know what I thought? All a' that crap about legalizin' marijuana an' endin' the war was some dude's idea about how to get a buncha kids to work for 'im. I mean, how stupid did they think we were? It's all one big show. People around here act like they're concerned with a whole lotta rules, but I'll tell you what they're concerned with. Whether you're crossin' the yellow line. I'm serious. This guy got a ticket 'cause there was a mud puddle in the road an' he swerved around it. An' that's what he got a ticket for. But this other dude got caught with eight cc's a' morphine, an' they didn't do nothin' to him. I mean, they didn't do shit. I couldn't believe that. The biggest thing about gettin' busted around here is the lawyer's fee an' the court fine. An' everybody knows it. So none a' them teachers better come in to school an' start preachin' about Watergate. I feel like if they're gonna be impeachin' him, they oughta be goin' ahead an' doin' it. I swear they interrupt some good programs to put that junk on. One night they even interrupted *The Rookies*.

I don't think much about politics an' all that mess, but I'll tell you one thing I don' like about what's goin' on. I don't care what Nixon did. Those are *his* tapes, an' he's got a right to keep 'em secret. I was talkin' to my girlfriend the other day an' we started thinkin'. Lookit the kinda hell we'd get into if our parents started tappin' our phones an' all. I mean, we tell each other everythin'. I don't think it's anybody's business what I do with my private life, unless I wanna tell it. Y'know, down at Watson's Poultry there's a switchboard, an' I heard they could break into anybody's phone conversation an' listen, an' the person didn't even know. The narcs tapped this one dude's phone I know, an' they busted 'im because of his conversation. They found out where he was dealin' an' all that shit. People oughta mind their own damn business. Like some a' the girls get pregnant an' everybody always knows. They put you in a position where you gotta go sneakin' around about everythin'. Like this girl I know

294

was goin' with this dude for a long time, an' her parents started raisin' all kindsa sand about it. So they hadda be real paranoid about what they did. At first, the more they pestered her about it, the more she saw him, but after a while it ruined a real good relationship. My ol' lady she checks up in real sneaky ways. Every time I come in she smells my hair an' says, "I know you been drinkin' that beer." Okay, you kinda learn howta get around it. I got my Visine an' my chewin' gum, an' I hang my head out the winda when we're comin' home, or some shit, dumb stuff like that. I got it figgered this way. When you wanna keep sump'n from somebody, put it right under their damn nose.

The big thing everybody thinks about when they talk about the "younger generation" an' all this crap is how much do we screw an' how much do we turn on. Like we're a buncha wild animals or somethin'. Or like everybody does everythin' the same. The way it works out mostly is that I guess mosta the girls that'll be seniors next year, they're probably not virgins, an' most of 'em my age, juniors, probably are. I mean, some of us do it, but just with one guy. You don't go runnin' out an' say, "Hey, I'm horny," an' do it with *anybody*. It's a real pain to get pregnant 'cause you gotta get up with some doctor an' ask 'im to arrange it, an' all this good shit. What's really far-out is all this social pressure which actually keeps you from takin' the pill. Like if you're not married an' takin' birth control pills, it's a real drag. Can you *believe* that? I mean, if you get pregnant, they all figger you've just done it one time. But the other way it's "Well, she's been takin' birth control pills for three years." That what I mean about everybody mindin' everybody else's business. It kinda forces you to do things that aren't very good for *you*.

It all fits into the same ol' pattern. People run into a whole lot when they're young, an' then they get married an' they're sittin' home, waitin'. It's always been that way. So that's the way it's gotta be. 'Course some things change. Like I seen some pictures in the old annual about the proms an' all. Homecomin' dances were a big thing a coupla years ago, an' the girls got their hair fixed an' wore long dresses an' all. We wore jeans to homecomin' this year. We had a band, but it was just a buncha niggers playin', an' they weren't too swift. I guess everybody wears jeans now the way they wore long dresses then. 'Cept I read this article in a magazine, sayin' that's how come everybody's gettin' vaginitis, so I dunno. But it's doin' what everybody else is doin'. There's some other different things now. Like I was talkin' to this girl the other day, she was home from Carolina, an' she was sayin' how it pissed her off 'cause she thinks none of us give a damn about anythin'. Hell, what is there to get all excited about? Alla them movies about how the law hassles you if you got long hair is a buncha bullshit. Only one who gives the boys any trouble 'bout that is Doctor Hawes. So I told 'er if all those people who were our age five years ago wanted to go get busted, that was their problem. But we ain't got nothin' to protest. An' maybe we're too fucked-up to care.

When I get outta college, I'm gonna travel if there's still some gas left to travel with. Then I'll probably get a job doin' somethin'. I dunno. A lotta people go to school to be certain things, an' they ain't doin' it. They want security. Well, I don' care about that. I don' particularly wanna settle down. I know what I *don'* want. I don' want no young 'uns naggin' behind me all the time. "Gotta make wee-wee, I'm hungry, give me sump'n to drink." Maybe when I'm fifty, I'll want 'em. Or maybe I'll have 'em when I'm thirty-five. But one thing, I ain't gonna have no kids 'less I can raise 'em right, talk to 'em honest. Like the people here, they're a buncha hypocrites. The kids get drunk an' the mothers get mad an' raise all kindsa hell, but any time *they* can scratch up some dough an' go sneakin' down to Wallace to get a bottle, they will. Far as I'm concerned, dope is better'n drinkin' a fiftha likker anyhow. I mean, you don't hafta piss all the time, an' all you get is the munchies. When people get drunk, they wanna dance an' raise all kindsa hell, but when you're stoned, all that happens is you're so down you just wanna go home an' go to bed. But you can't tell 'em anythin' about that. Mention turnin' on, they think you're some kinda dope fiend.

You oughta have dinner with us sometime. First, nobody says anythin'. Then my mother asks my father if he's had a bad day. Then my father starts in, givin' one of his speeches, usually about the "younger generation." Talkin' 'bout all the "bad" kids, all the dope an' the screwin' an' all. What's funny about it

is he never asks questions. Neither does my mother. Not direct-
ly. I mean, she knows I used to knock on doors an' run, an' drag
junk across the road an' leave it so cars would hafta stop, shit
like that. But they aren't really into what I'm doin' now. My ol'
man'll ask about my report card. Long as I'm passin' everythin'
an' keep my hair clean an' don't get pregnant, long as I'm still
goin' to Sunday school an' don't mess around with the car,
everythin's fine. It makes me feel sorry for 'em because they're
so innocent. Only sometimes I feel like if I could tell 'em, it
would be off my conscience. Sometimes I wish they would find
out what I am.

14 **Whisperings**

"What you expect from yourself is the important thing."

—Expectations

The Bride

I knowed a lotta boys, like any girl would, an' I guess I been in love, 'specially with this one boy I went with, but this time it's for real an' I'm gonna get married. I met 'im in Warsaw. They got this club where the black kids hang out at. Anyway, every time I'd go in there, he'd be tryin' to get me to dance, an' all this stuff, but I was in love with my boyfriend, an' I didn't pay 'im no attention. An' then he kept callin' me an' wanted me to go ridin', so I thought, "What's the use a' just sittin' home doin' nothin'?" So I went an' I fell in love. It took four months. That's a pretty long time.

I dunno what happened. It was the way he acted, the way he talked to me an' the way he treated me an' all. He was always askin' me to marry him. We'd be sittin' in the car sometimes, an' he'd ask me an' I'd say, "Boy, you just go somewhere." An' I'd laugh 'cause I thought he was kiddin'. An' he tol' me one night, after I had fell in love with him, he said, "I want you to be mine forever." I said, "You know what you gotta do." He said, "What?" I say, "Ask me to marry you." I was bullshittin', y'know, 'cause I didn't believe him. But he says, "Will you marry me?" An' I said, "Yeah," an' that was it. We was engaged.

It's funny how people treat you. Everybody starin' at you all the time. You can't let that bother you. I don' mind when *he* stares at me 'cause I like for him to look, 'specially when I'm lookin' half cute. But other people keep askin' all sortsa questions an' things. I got some sisters, an' we ain't never got along

301

so good, to tell you the truth. But seems like since I been engaged, they really turned against me. I dunno if they're jealous or what it is, but they talk to each other all the time an' don't let me know what they're talkin' about an' don't let me go out with them. That don't bother me so much right now 'cause I got lots to do, an' anyway, if they don' wanna be my family, they don' hafta. I'm gonna have a family of my own.

Havin' a family's the best thing a woman can do. I mean, there's other things I wanted to be, but a family always been the most important thing. I wanted to be a singer one time, an' I know I sing pretty good, but that takes you away from home. Artist. That's what I wanted to be at one time. Artist. I drew this picture outta this book an' sent it to Minneapolis. An' this man come to see me an' gave me this whole big thing, an' I started workin', drawin' pictures an' sendin' 'em, an' they'd send 'em back to me an' give me a grade an' all. The man said you could do this an' take your lessons at home, an' he told me I could get married an' have children an' still do my drawin' work. An' make good money. But I got tired of drawin' an' I changed my mind. Before I got engaged, when I was goin' to high school, they was askin' what we wanted, an' we talked to some of them people from James Sprunt Institute over in Kenansville. I didn't wanna go for a nurse an' I didn't wanna go for one of them ladies that fix your hair an' stuff, a cosmetologist, an' I started thinkin' about art again. They got them art classes up there, but now I don't think I'm gonna go. I got me a job anyway down at the sewin' plant, an' I'm gonna work there 'til I get pregnant an' start showin', an' then after, maybe I'll go back. Most factories around here you hafta stand up all day long an' you don't get to talk to nobody, but at the sewin' plant you get to siddown an' you can talk to your friend sittin' next to you. You get two breaks an' a lunch period, so it's real nice there. My boyfriend's workin' down at the military base in Jacksonville, sump'n to do with brickmason stuff. We're gonna get us a little trailer, fix it up real nice. So we both gotta be workin', at least at this time.

It wasn't so excitin' at first, but it sure is gettin' to be now. I can't wait 'til that weddin' come. Everyone say that's the big day in a young girl's life. But the thing that's good about it to me is what come after. Like I wanna have children of my own. I wanna have 'em real bad. We both love children an' we're gonna have one as soon as we can. I know what's gonna happen. When a young black person gets married, people say she's marryin' 'cause she's pregnant. Well, I don' care what they say 'bout me. I don' want people talkin' 'cause my mama, it'd hurt her, but I guess we'll have one as soon as we get married, even if people are doin' their month countin'. It's my own business what I do with my life. I'm gonna live with somebody I love an' that loves me. I'm gonna feel like a woman 'cause when I'm at my mama's, I got her to baby me an' I feel like a child. I'm gonna really be a wife. I'm gonna be a woman. Gettin' married's gonna change a whole lotta things.

A Young Man

Every time the high school graduates, it's marryin' time, y'know. After May twenty-first 'til 'bout the middle of August, it's live dove season. *Bam. Bam. Bam.* I never go on dates. People try to con me into it, people try to persuade me into it, they trap me into it, an' I get up an' walk out. I despise underhanded tactics. So I say no. You get into situations on a date that can be perplexin' an' also that could hurt you. When I think of a woman, I think of shadows an' skeletons in the closet because there are always rumors, an' I despise that. It offends me.

A woman has her place in the world, an' when I decide that I want a woman, I'll decide to go out an' hunt. But that's the furthest thing from my mind. That's a reason I don't like to get in conversations with women. It kinda disturbs me because I get so damn rough an' they get upset, an' I hate to see people cry, an' that disturbs me. The thing about it aroun' here, the parents go away for the weekend, and the kids invite about twenty people, whoever walks through, y'know. The morals, in my opinion, are corrupt as hell. Intercourse—people have it for fun. It's nice an' all that, but it don' make a lotta sense.

I've had my chances several times an' I just can't do it. Damn it, it's not right. The way I've been brought up an' the way I look

303

at it is: there's a stoppin' line, an' you hafta say, "Well, I'm goin' to enjoy life, an' when I get married, I expect it will be one of the happiest moments of my life to have sex." Intercourse is somethin' you can wait for.

One of the things that kinda turned me off on women in many ways, I was in about the sixth grade, an' we were havin' a birthday party somewhere, an' we had this little slap, hug an' kiss. It came my turn an' I was up there waitin', y'know. The girl closes her eyes, she points, y'know, an' it came to me as "kiss," an' I despised it so much I got up an' walked out. The ones I could have had got everywhere but *there*, they were really diggin' it. If I wanted to, I could go out tomorrow night with about anyone I want who's eligible, do whatever I wanted to an' have a good time. It's like every day I go to work. Well, every night I could get out an' have sex all night long. Matter of fact, I've been told by several people I kiss better than anyone in town. It's just I don't want to. When I want to, I will.

The Divorce

He asked me to marry him when I was a senior in high school, but I wanted to go to college. So when I finished high school, he gave me the diamond in the summer, an' I accepted an' went on to college in the fall. About two an' a half months later he came to school to see me an' asked me to marry him an' come on home. Well, college is somethin' that's a whole diff'rent life because you're meetin' diff'rent people, an' you're bein' with 'em an' you're makin' somethin' outta your life, too. But I wanted to be with him, so I came home an' got married. It wasn't such a bad thing to do. I mean, if that's what you really want, you sacrifice that much.

I still think that is what a woman is made to do or should do. Most women think they should be liberated. Well, I'd rather depend on him an' live a life like they did back there in the old days. I don' mean bein' tied down, an' that you're supposed to stay at home while he does what he wants to do. But I'd rather give my whole self to my husband an' my children an' to help them make a life of their own. That's not puttin' yourself down. How can you be puttin' yourself down when you're givin' your whole self to him?

Anyway, I was in love an' I couldn't wait to get married. I had a formal weddin' at eight o'clock an' everybody wore formal clothes, an' I had trumpets play an' then, for the reception, we went to the country club an' had champagne an' an orchestra an' a band. We went to the beach, an' then we went to the mountains an' to see some of my friends. When we came home, the trouble started right away. I still dunno why. It wouldn'a been so bad if we hadn't been so close to his parents. It's hard to make a life of your own when you have them on your back.

I don't think my husband realized how, that when you get married, you're s'posed to move away from your family an' start a family of your own. I guess it sounds like maybe he was more or less dreamin' about the marriage an' I was believin' in it. An' I don't think he liked it once he realized what life really was. See, I knew that marriage was more than a dream in life an' a play toy. That there was a lotta responsibility an' a lotta hard knocks, but it was a matter of how much you loved each other which would count on whether you stick it out. When I think about it, I don't understand why he wanted to get married at all.

When we first got married, he had a job of his own an' I had a job. He wanted me to work. But when I started workin', he wanted me to be back home at a certain time, which was impossible when I had responsibilities to finish. Then the place I was workin' at went broke, an' I decided to go back to school 'cause that was what I wanted to do in the first place. I wanted my time filled up. But he objected an' he said he wasn't gonna pay my way. Well, how was I s'posed to carry on a job to pay for school with all the hours I had in class, an' then get back an' fix his meals? An' he wasn't even home anyway. I'd be at home on my break from school, fixin' lunch, an' he would go to his mother's house an' eat there.

One a' the big things was we came from diff'rent ways of livin'. I didn't go out there an' crop tobacco an' do things like that. An' I wasn't about to do it. I wasn't raised that way. Not that I had anythin' against it, but we had talked about it, an' I tol' him

305

before I married him that I wouldn't be able to cope with it. I mean, if he wanted his own farm, I'd help him to do anythin' in the world, but to have his parents tell him what to do an' run our life, no. An' he said he didn't want me to work tobacco. That was *before* we got married. But when his parents started pressurin' him—"Why ain't she out in the tobacco field? Does she think she's too good for us?"—well, that kinda put a damper on him. But if he'd really loved me, he'd say, "Listen, she's my wife an' I love her, an' I don't want to hear you talk about her anymore." An' that woulda prevented the whole thing.

I noticed one thing. He would come home from work sometimes an' we'd get along real well. But as soon as he would go to his family's house or out around his friends, he would come home cussin' me out. Like here's an instance. I hadda friend that come out to see me, an' he was a boy. But my husband knew him really well, an' he knew that we were real close. Just friends. Well, I got this boy, this friend of mine, to carry me to my husband's granddaddy's house to get his truck. His grandmother saw the boy an' went back to my husband an' tol' my mother-in-law that I was runnin' out on him with some man. An' that wasn't true at all. If I was goin' out with some guy, I wouldn'a gone to that house to pick up that truck, right? I come home from school an' then he come home all mad. I didn't even know what he was talkin' about, but I figgered it out. I knew his mother had told him. So I decided to put an end to it once an' for all. So I went up there an' I came right to the point. She tried to deny it, an' I caught her in a lie. You know what happened? He got mad at *me* for goin' to his parents an' defendin' my marriage. I politely told them to keep their big fat noses outta my marriage, 'cause if they didn't, it was gonna bust up an' I didn't want it to because I loved him. I begged him. I pleaded with him because I knew if we moved, we'd be happy. I knew it. I even went to counselors to see what they'd say, an' they said the same thing. But he wouldn't move away.

Another thing his parents ruined was sex. When we come back from our honeymoon, we wanted to be together. But with his parents livin' right up the street, there wasn't any way. I don't think that his parents even knew what a honeymoon was. An' we needed time. I was a virgin before I was married, which it's an honor really, 'cause you know that you're able to wait that long for your husband. I guess it's kinda old-fashioned now, but I'm a kinda old-fashioned person anyway. One of the things about bein' a virgin, you depend on the man about knowin' what to do in sex. Sex is a lot of marriage, along with love. Because everyone needs to release their feelin's one way or another. But that isn't what happened. I got to thinkin', "Maybe it's because he's under the pressure of his parents, not knowin' when his parents are gonna be comin' in." He shoulda been man enough to say, "I'm on my honeymoon. Leave us alone." But I noticed that he didn't wanna have relations, 'cept like maybe twice in every two weeks. Which was kinda funny. I dunno what the problem was. He didn't wanna talk about it. Every time I started to get down to the real stuff about where the problem was originatin' from, he'd change the subject. It's so funny 'cause you always think men know it all an' they're gonna be teachin' the women. I guess that's not the way it is. Maybe in some cases the men have been abused. I mean they don't like to admit it, but maybe they've been brought up that sex was nasty an' dirty, an' things like that. With us it was like when you go to these little parties when you're six or seven years old, or twelve or somethin', an' the girls sit on one side an' the boys sit on another side. Some people never grow out of it.

I wouldn't leave until I knew for sure he didn't love me. No matter what he did to me, I'd try again an' I'd pray about it an' all of that. I was patient through the whole thing, until he was man enough to tell me he didn't love me anymore. He never hit me. There were probably times he felt like it, but there's ways to get around that. Like keepin' your mouth shut while he's losin' his cool. There are times when you felt like pullin' out your hair, but you didn't because you realized that this other person has feelin's, too, an' you hafta try to understand them an' get your head together an' think this thing out. But there are ways of tellin'. Like him not comin' home at night until the early mornin'. An' stayin' all night long with his friends an' not includin' you, or bein' out with his family an' not includin' his wife. An' such things as when you would want to rub his back or make him feel comfortable when he comes home, an' he says, "Leave me alone an' get away from me. I don' want you around me." Just a lotta things, where you can see that he doesn't wanna spend time with you an' that he doesn't show his respect for you, an' there are a lotta excuses he'll put up because he's not man enough to tell the truth.

Finally he told me. I stayed that night, an' he woke up in the mornin' an' he told me to be outta the house, but I stayed one more night to make sure that was how he felt. An' he told me if I didn't get out, he was gonna take my face an' bury it in the dirt an' he was gonna kill me. All I could do was look at him an' hug him good-bye an' tell him that I loved him. An' turned around an' walked out. The next day he went to work an' I went to school, an' after school I went out an' got my clothes. I haven't seen him since.

I didn't wanna tell my family because I'd quit school to marry him, an' now my marriage had fallen through, an' I thought, "Here's another disappointment." But I talked with my lawyer, an' she said the thing for you to do is to move in with your parents for a while. An' my parents said the same thing 'cause you dunno what's gonna happen until you get separated. Durin' that period of time someone could say you're committin' adultery before you sign the legal separation papers. So I agreed. It doesn't matter anyway. The best way is to kinda stay to yourself.

In the regular group I went around with when I was single, sometimes the parents think, "Don't go around with her because she's a divorcée." Some of them think it would be a bad influence on their children, that their reputation wouldn't be as high. An', too, you hafta be very protective of your friends because you dunno if your husband is gonna cause some trouble an' bring you into court an' drag your friends into it as witnesses. I didn't have any desire to go out anyway. Once you have a disappointment like that, you might have a reaction where you forget it, an' that's it, have a good time an' start all over again. But I don't think I can or I want to.

For me it's not that easy. A long time after, I still loved him. When you love somebody, you love somebody. An' when love is dead, there ain't nothin' as bad as dead love. It's a matter of gettin' used to it. An' it's easier to get used to it when you know they don't love you anymore. There isn't anythin' you can do about it, 'cept go out an' make a life of your own an' start again.

My plans now are unpredictable. I mean, so far. I'm takin' my time an' I'm not gonna jump into anythin'. Because now I know whatever I go into, it's gonna be for the resta my life. I'd like to specialize in somethin', like maybe business or modelin' or stewardess because I wanna be with people. But the thing is, I want a home of my own. I don't hate marriage because my marriage didn't work out. That's one a' the hard knocks you get along the way. I'm the domestic type. I loved bein' married because it's the greatest feelin' in the world to really know what love iş all about, an' to take care of someone an' to show your need for him an' to fulfill his needs. It's wonderful because you look up to him an' he's smilin' at you, an' you want to do everythin' in the world that you can for him to make him happy.

I took a lot. But I know now what I want out of life, an' I know what I can live with an' what I can't live with. Next time I'd more or less want someone that had been brought up the way I had been brought up an' was used to the same life-style I was used to. You can't be bitter. I want a family. I want little babies. I mean, that's a pride an' joy—to have your own children, to see yourself startin' all over again. I want it to be with the right person. An' I won't be mistaken next time.

The Ladies' Man

There ain't no harm in knowin' a lotta women. It gives me pleasure an' I hope it gives them pleasure, too. There ain't nothin' beats ol' true nature. Ain't a thing in this world. Why would the Lord make a man an' a woman? Give 'em the passion an' all, an' then not expect 'em to use it? Doesn't make much sense, does it? I don't understand why so many people try to make such a big bugaboo about it. It's always been simple to me.

If I see a woman, an' she appeals to me an' I do to her, I don't think there's anythin' wrong, if I don't cause no trouble. It's as essential as food. That's why you see so many old people go crazy. They can't do it anymore. Best thing for you when you're feelin' down an' out, go out an' have intercourse with a woman. It don't do 'em no harm, an' some of 'em they like it just like a man. Now you take some woman, the reason why their old man runs around, they're as cold as a cucumber. Them women don't care nothin' about it. Only reason why they have intercourse with a man is to try 'n please 'im. But other women, well, shoot. There's women around beggin' for you to slip it to 'em. Me, I like a sexy woman.

Lemme tell you one thing. There's as many married women goin' out as single. A woman got herself a blind when she got a husband. Sump'n to hide behind. Here's what happens lotsa times. A woman gets married an' her old man is simply no good. Now what do you expect that woman to do? An' there's women, one man ain't enough for 'em. An' they sit around thinkin' about it all the time, itchin'. You can tell when you meet a woman like that. Now what's the best thing for her to do? Split up her home an' take off, or go on an' rear her children an' do things normal, an' slip out every once in a while an' get her some? Same as for a man. You gotta understand what you're doin'.

Thing you gotta be careful about is the ones that take it too serious. You gotta set 'em straight from the very beginnin'. Say you meet a woman, real pretty woman, an' she turns you on, y'know? Well, you go on an' start in talkin', an' then later on you call her an' meet her somewhere. She knows you're married, an' you make sure'n tell her 'bout your wife an' lovin' your wife. Even if that's a lie. But you gotta do it that way. Everythin' starts off fine. Pretty soon you find out you're real sexy with each other an' you start wantin' it more'n you should, can't keep your mind on business. That's when you get in trouble an' you gotta take off.

I never did see the reason people make a big deal outta the thing. Me, I keep it pretty quiet. I don't wanna cause any damn fuss. Most men hafta cut a pretty fine line with it. You want the women to know you're available, but you gotta protect your reputation, an' you don' wanna break up your home. Politicians gotta keep it quiet. Preacher gotta keep it *real* quiet. But you show me a man'll tell you he ain't gettin' it on the side, or he ain't lookin' or hankerin', an' I'll show you a man that's a damn

310

liar. It's good for a man to try out diff'rent women. Each a' them does a little sump'n diff'rent for you. Thing about women, they like it all diff'rent kindsa ways.

My wife knows me well enough to know that if the right woman come along, I like women an' sump'n might happen. That's the way I am. She's a good woman, all right. An' I been good to her. She never wants anythin'. If she wants to buy anythin', she can get it. I've given her a good home, an' everythin' a woman needs. I imagine she don't like it much when she knows I been tomcattin'. But hell, she'd never find a man that wouldn't. Not one that's worth anythin'. 'Course she hasta be true to me now. I'm biased in that way. I ain't sayin' it's fair. But my wife she ain't a sexy woman. She gotta lotta good characteristics, but that ain't one of 'em.

Sex has always been what I enjoyed. More'n anythin', I guess. I bedded down real good when I was a younger man. It wouldn't be so bad gettin' older, 'cept for that, y'know? You're not like you were when you were young. Used to, I could keep goin' five times, six times. Nothin' like it when the woman gets satisfied. I still enjoy it, but I can't always give 'em what I'd like for 'em to have. But damn if I ain't gonna do it. Gives me pleasure, right on. An' I'll tell you another thing. I like the way the younger generation thinks about the thing. They're admittin' there's a use for it an' a place for it, an' it should be used. I've seen people that would get off on the wrong road an' abuse themselves, self-abuse an' things like that. Why should anybody do that with so many women, good-lookin' women, pretty women, women that really needs it from you? If I could have anythin' in this world, I'd order me a new one an' keep it goin' like before. Can't do that, but I still get pleasure outta it an' I give 'em what I can. When you get right down to it, there ain't nothin' better in this world.

The Deer Widow

It's not the huntin', understand? It's all that goes with it. Fixin' up the camp. Buyin' an' breedin' an' trainin' the dogs. Huntin' an' fishin' an' politics. The whole crowd of 'em. They go to the camps, go to diff'rent places. Seems like they think more of those camps than they think of their own homes. I don't mean there's anything funny goin' on. I'm sure none a' them would even think of havin' to do with another man. But they got their own little world, an' a woman's not part of it. My husband could live very well without one in a personal sense. Least this is the impression he's given me.

Talk to him, he says he has to have sump'n in life. He has to get away from the pressure. It unknots him. In the meantime, he takes off four days a week an' comes home eleven o'clock at night an' expects a hot supper. A year or so ago I think he had sump'n more than gettin' away for a while. I caught him in so many lies it was perfect. But I wouldn't care about other women because then you know what you're fightin'. As it is, it's hard to tell what pulls him. All I know is I'm resentin' it more an' more. He'll leave sometimes to go huntin', an' what he's really sayin' is kiss my behind an' the devil with you. If you don't like it, lump it. I'm gone. Then he come back an' he's worn out, an' he want me to be good to him. I hafta get home by five an' fry chicken an' cook a vegetable an' make a salad, an' then sit an' wait to see what time he'll come in. It's got to the point I'm so disgusted I go play bridge or go to the movies an' leave it on the stove. Or he can go out an' get him sump'n. He don't like that much, but I don't even care.

The trouble is this is sump'n that goes back to how things have always been done. When they're kids, they get spoiled rotten. Just because they're boys. Everyone always told him he was special. Somewhere along these men are fightin' a battle against somebody or somethin' in the first years of their lives. My husband's mother was a good woman. But she was scared to open her mouth about anythin'. She was absolutely subdued, an' the only way she ever got anythin' she wanted was to manipulate. I guess my mother was the same way. So that becomes the pattern. There's a lack of responsibility. There's no sense of bein' partners. Like he takes six hundred dollars for the dogs an' I've got six hundred dollars worth of bills to pay. You can't sit down an' say, "Listen, we need to use that money for so-an'-so." He'll spend it when he's ready, doesn't get together to make a deci-

312

sion. He'll let the car go empty an' I better remember to get it filled up, or somebody's gonna end up stuck out in the middle of the road. It's like havin' an extra child. I can't even send him to the store for a loaf of bread. He won't go. He'll do some things if I have it set up for him. He'll sit with a pencil an' figger out a lotta stuff that I don't do. He does that because he thinks that's *important*. That's the *smart* person. He says that. Bein' smart is not workin' with your hands. He says I'm not smart because I do it. He thinks I work because I like to, not because there's stuff that's gotta get done.

The older he gets, the more distance there is. An' I'm not sure he's even conscious of what he's doin'. These last five years have really been somethin'. There's a certain amount of tormentin' they do to you. 'Course he could be upset about business problems. Could be. But try talkin' about it. "No," he'd say. "Are you crazy?" That's what I'd get. Give a problem out an' don't get two cents worth of words back. "Now if you really wanna talk about it, c'mon, we'll talk about it. Now you get out here tonight an' figger out what we can do about the business. What's the matter? You aren't happy? C'mon. I'll take you to the huntin' camp with me. Well? C'mon. What's the matter with you?"

I guess he's tryin' in his own way. But it doesn't seem to do any good. Not anymore. It's like there's a hole in me. It's like I'm a widow. Well, maybe I am. A deer widow. When you live with someone, there's got to be some kind of touch, some kind of contact. He's so distant. It's almost like he's disturbed. He keeps lookin' in the mirror. He must comb his hair thirteen times a day. He wants to be left alone. All the time. "Leave me alone." All that talk about men bein' aggressive. It isn't that way at all. Well, I can't push anymore. I have pushed an' pushed an' pushed, an' you get sick an' tired of bein' rejected. He's goin' to go too far one of these days. He's goin' to say one time too many he doesn't want to be here. An' that'll be that. Nothin' left.

When you get married, you oughta hold that person up high, more'n anybody in the world. I've always tried to do him like that. I wouldn't talk to his friends or any of his people or even my friends. I've tried to fill the time. I work in the church. I've raised my children. As far as other people are concerned, we have an ideal marriage. But there's no way to make up for it.

313

What you've lost, you've lost. You never really want to admit you've failed, so you keep goin'. You're always thinkin' if you really had an opportunity to talk to him, to touch him, to understand, you could work out all the problems. Then one day you wake up, an' the years have gone by an' you're older an' your hands are gettin' rough an' your skin is saggin', an' where has it all gone? You've let it go by without stoppin' to talk because you thought, "That's how men are. He's afraid to be gentle. He's afraid to be kind." You wait for him to see. He never does. What you've become, you're two strangers occupyin' the same space. What's left? Twenty years? Thirty years? No matter how many, they should be good ones. But how do you do that? You've lost sight of your life, you've lost yourself.

When things get more straightened out, I'll move on maybe. I'll live out at the beach. Or I'll find a larger town. I could do that. I'm pretty strong. The thing is there *have* been good times. A coupla years back we did seem to be workin' things out. Everythin' we did we talked about. An' then I think my leavin' would kill him. If somethin' happened to me an' I should pass out, I mean go away or die, period, I think he would have a hard time adjustin' to anybody or anythin'. He wouldn't have anybody takin' care of the little unimportant things he thinks happen without anybody doin' them.

Or maybe I don't have the nerve. After all, what's in it for me? A little bit of spark sometimes. Attached to a man's name. Havin' him there when he comes in, an' there is a feelin' of at least protection, even if there is no love life. I've been through these thoughts a million times. I say to myself, "I'll go into a home for crazy people. That's what I'll do if I can't find any other way out of here. They will take care of you. They will feed you." Then I laugh at myself, say, "Lady, you really *are* crazy." You know, if he'd come in every once in a while an' just kiss me hello an' say, "Hey, I did all right today. Here's what happened. What happened to you?" A little dab of a touch. Who knows? It might make a difference. Anyway, I'm in the process of thinkin' about it. I'm finally thinkin' about myself, like a person, I mean. Maybe I'm stuck, but I don't think so. I can start walkin' as straight as those pine trees. I could walk right away if I make up my mind.

The Plan

Underneath all of this there's another part of me. I s'pose a lotta men say that kinda thing, but for me it's true. An' it comes up at bad times. Like I'll be sittin' in church or at one a' the men's club meetin's, an' I'll look around the room an' think, what in hell would they say if they knew what was on my mind? No. I'm lyin' about that. What I think is this: what in hell am I doin' here? An' then I wonder sometime if some a' them aren't thinkin' the same things an' tryin' to figure out the same plans.

The last coupla years I been developin' a strategy, kinda escape route, y'know. The way it works is I keep earnin' a good livin' an' make sure the kids get through school, wait an' see that they're all settled, an' maybe let 'em get my wife busy with some grandchildren, an' then I'll get up one mornin' an' take off. I like to play around with it some, sit back an' imagine the places I'd go. Sometimes, when the pressure gets on me, I think about one of those islands, lotta sun an' pretty girls. That's crap. That would drive me crazy. I'm a man who likes to keep busy. Trouble is, busy as I am, I don't feel I'm doin' anythin' at all.

Let me tell you one thing about feelin' guilty. It kinda goes in a circle, 'cause the more guilty I feel, the more I get to considerin' the plan. 'Cept, of course, I haven't got one. Not really. But I consider it just the same. Then I think like this. What kinda man up an' leaves his family, his town, the whole thing? My wife is a good woman, understand? A Christian woman. She made me a fine home. We have fine children. An' I guess you might say I've done pretty well. But it's those other things, the kindsa things you think about that you might be missin'.

I've been workin' all my life. An' I've done things like you're supposed to do them. 'Course I've had my little mistakes, but any man will. An' those times, those type a' women they never satisfied me. Sure, I like sex. An' that married parta our homelife has never been what you'd call very satisfyin'. But that's not what I'm talkin' about, understand? I guess the only way I can put it is that I'd really like, just once in my life, to feel like I'm my own man. Don't know as that makes any sense or not, but that's what I'm feelin'. I s'pose you might say that's what I'm lookin' for.

The Affair

There's not much beatin' around the bush about this love affair. Right from the beginnin' we had problems. I mean, hell. You spend your whole life listenin' to all of this crap about how sex is dirty, how nice girls don't do it, how it's all a duty to satisfy your husband, how a man won't respect you if you give in to him. An' most of all, how you float down that carpeted aisle to never-never land 'til death do us part. So when you finally start cheatin', what do you expect? Fun 'n games? I'm not talkin' about guilt, understand? I don't feel a damn bit guilty about anythin', 'cept maybe what I'm doin' to mess up my own life. But that first time we got into bed, well, it wasn't exactly like alarms goin' off an' bells ringin' an' all that stuff. We were two very scared people, let me tell you. Not because of what would happen if we got caught, but because of *us*.

I had my first orgasm with him. Can you *believe* that? I had been married a right good while, an' I didn't even know what an orgasm was 'til I had been married three years. Then it was only because I had a bridge group over one night an' one of the women said, "I just had my first orgasm," an' dumb me, I said, "What's that?" Well a coupla them laughed, but everyone got real quiet, an' if you wanna know what I think, mosta them didn't know an' never will. All I can tell you is that after I had mine, I knew that anythin' that good couldn't be not only not all bad, but wasn't bad at all. Feel guilty? Hell. I felt marvelous.

When I was a kid, we never talked about "it." I hardly knew where babies came from. All I knew was I was supposed to get into bed with this man, this stranger called my husband, an' whatever he wanted to do, we were supposed to do. Well, he didn't want much an' I sure didn't, an' we did it enough to have some kids an' that's been that. I don't know what he does with other women, but I can make a guess that what he does is he goes on trips an' he finds himself a whore. Or at least some woman he doesn't have to think of as "nice." You know, ME he always puts on a pedestal. I've been married for ages, an' he still thinks I'm a virgin. Maybe parta that's been my fault. My ol' lady sure did some job on me. An' the other day my daughter asked me what to do if a boy kissed her. An' I heard myself tellin' her, "You hafta realize that when you put your mouth next to someone else's mouth, what a personal thing that is." Then I felt awful about it. I thought, "Maybe I just talked the poor kid into never kissin' anybody." But she'll learn for herself. All of us do.

Personal is really the point of it. Personal is where it's at. My "friend" really changed my attitude about that in a lotta ways. Like kissin' him is much more meaningful than it would be to go to bed with somebody else. A kiss is a very intimate thing. I'm lucky because I've got a man who understands that an' who taught me that. He's at an age now where he's goin' through what could be a difficult time, so he worries about satisfyin' me. Sometimes he asks me, "Did I satisfy you? Did you come?" I wish he wouldn't ask. Because as excitin' as those orgasms are, that really isn't what counts. Not to me anyway. It's absolutely not important to me that he's not a Hercules. He's no prize. He's actually kinda funny-lookin'. But bein' close to him is fantastic to me. For a while I thought, "It's me. He's lost interest in *me*." But then we talked about it, an' he made me understand. It isn't as easy for a man as it is for a woman. Frankly, he sometimes has trouble gettin' erections. An' so we do other things. But no matter how much pleasure he gets from it, it worries him that he's not bein' a man, whatever the hell that's supposed to be. What's a man? Walkin' around with a hard-on? Chasin' every piece of pussy you see?

I suppose I'm very ambivalent about marriage. I have a lousy one. An' I believe so much in the possibility of a good one that I'm afraid to risk it an' try. I hear about all of the playin' around an' I think, "Not *us*. That sordid, cheap, ugly stuff has nothin' to do with *us*." An' it doesn't. We don't even think about it as an affair. Sometimes I start to get angry with his wife, but then I think, "Well, it's not her fault. She's not holdin' him." I mean, face it. A man can leave any time he wants to. I think both of us basically feel that if we got divorced an' married each other, it would ruin the very nice relationship that we have. It's hard to be with somebody day after day. Like if he was goin' someplace, I would say, "Where are you goin'?" He doesn't like that. He wants to be independent. An' with the wife he's got now, he is. She never knows where he's really goin', an' she could care less.

An' that's the problem. Too much love. It's the kinda thing where I constantly am thinkin , "I want to make his bed an' bake his bread." Do things for him. It's a struggle about givin', that I want to an' he won't let me. He told me one time, he said, "One of the reasons I stay married is I'm married to a woman who doesn't really love me, an' if I divorced her, I'd marry you, an' you love me too much an' it would be the worst thing in the world." I suppose it's true. I couldn't stop doin' it. I'm never goin' to change. I mean, I'm a liberated woman an' all. But I still believe what happens in the home is up to the woman. She's the thermostat of the family, an' if I was married to my "friend," the temperature would be hot to stand.

Sometimes I think what I'll do is get a divorce an' move away from here, not because I mind livin' with my husband—you can't be hurt by nothin'—but because I'm sick an' tired of the fool I've become. It's not the situation. We don't hafta worry about the gossipin' 'cause we're perfectly covered. An' after so many years there's still no staleness to it. I can honestly say it's more excitin' an' more pleasure an' more closeness all the time. To feel so much love for another human bein' is incredible. So much that I always feel these days I have a choice—explode or run away.

So I stay here an' hold onto my little secret. I can't leave. I'm under lock an' key of my own choosin'. I don't cook his food or raise his children or get myself deducted on his income tax. We don't smile together at parties or send out Christmas cards. There is nothin' official an' there is everythin' bindin'. It's as simple as pie. I am his wife.

Expectations

I'm a real oddball, I guess. One thing, to show you how much of an oddball I am. I taught a Sunday school class some years ago. I went in one mornin' an' I gave those boys pencils an' paper an' envelopes, an' said, "Boys, today I want you to write a letter to yourself to be mailed ten years from now, sayin' what you expect out of your life from now until then." Last year I took 'em out of the safe in the church an' mailed 'em to the boys.

Some of them had really accomplished what they had set out to be, an' they had forgotten about it. But some of 'em had gone down a bit, an' I'm sure that it sorta shook 'em into takin' a little bit of inventory of themselves. I also sent one to myself, an' I was a little shocked when I read what I had written. What you expect from yourself is the important thing.

The Widow

I used to be petrified of dyin'. Jimmy an' I used to talk about it, an' I was scared to death of dyin' an' he never was. I always kept sayin' that I wanted to die before he did because I thought he would get along better than I would. Jimmy was smarter than I was. He didn't hafta live a sheltered little life. All in all I had more faith in his ability than I did in mine. Now I find that I have more than I ever dreamed of. But I still don't have all that I need.

I was a very pampered person. My life was very easy. For example, one time I had shingles. It's terribly painful, an' I think I was embarrassed that I had somethin' so unromantic. My friend, Mary, went to my bridge club an' she came home so tickled. She said they said, "Well, somethin' has finally happened to Emily Sue. Nothin' bad ever happens to *her*." An' they were right. I lived a very secure life. But also, I never complained about things. I hear other people complain about normal things like "My children cry. My children fuss. My husband gets on my nerves." I have no patience with it. I don't think they know what a problem is. A problem is somethin' that is done unto you that you can't do anythin' about. You can do somethin' about your own immaturity or your own lack of judgment, but when you are done unto, you have a problem.

I guess as a child I thought mostly about gettin' married. Girls are conditioned, y'know? I never thought of myself as bein' a mother. I never liked children until I had my own. I guess I probably thought of myself as doin' typical ladies' jobs. I majored in English at Queens College in Charlotte, but Jimmy was at Carolina, an' when we got married, I had three hours to go, but it was never convenient for me to finish. There were times

319

when I thought, "I must find somethin' to do. I must go to Katharine Gibbs." But it wasn't the most important thing. I tried to be superwife an' then I tried to be supermother. I guess before we were married I tried to be supergirlfriend. I was not a lady driven with ambition to get into a man's world.

Maybe I do make things between us seem more right than they were, but they were about as right as two people could make them. We started datin' when we were seventeen, an' I think from the very time we started, we really loved each other an' understood each other. We dated other people, an' there were times when I wouldn't see him for a month or two months or six months, but when I saw him, nobody ever said, "Where have you been?" Nobody ever got mad, nobody ever said, "I'm sorry," or demanded anythin'. You gotta understand that we went through an awful lot when we were young. Jimmy was sick with a rare lung disease, an' I would drive back an' forth to Chapel Hill, an' I would think about things. I decided, "I'm gonna live the resta my life with Jimmy, so that if anythin' should happen, I won't regret it."

Our whole relationship was what you might call chauvinistic, but I liked it that way. I would say sometimes, "I reserve the right to be myself. I am not an extension of you." But in our house I always did the traditional things. I could talk women's lib all I wanted to, but I loved doin' what a wife always did. He was the man who took care of his family, an' there were times when, if I had worked, we could have afforded more things than we did have. But when it came right down to the idea of me gettin' a job, he finally admitted that he didn't like the idea that he couldn't support me an' give me what I needed. Jimmy always gave me credit for bein' an intelligent human bein', but at the same time everythin' I had was from him. *He* could get *me* nice things, but I never worked an' I didn't have my own personal income to buy *him* things. He never held it over my head—"Okay, I support you. I give you everything. I do everythin' for you. I take your golf bag out. I get your golf shoes out." All I'd hafta do when we went to play golf was maybe find my socks. I never carried my own tennis racket out to the country club. I mean, somebody was there to open the door for me. Somebody was there to pack the car when I got ready to go away. I never knew about money an' I never wondered about money. If I wanted somethin', I got it. I have been a child an' I have been a wife an' I have been a mother. Now I'm havin' to be an adult. It's the difference between night an' day.

For a long time the actuality of what happened when he died was on my mind. But I don't really know how it happened an' I don't think I will ever want to know. I do know that it was a tornadoey type day, with a very strong gust of wind, an' it had somethin' to do with that an' with a wall fallin'. Jimmy got out early that mornin' an' he kissed me good-bye, an' he left an' went out the door an' he came back an' he kissed me good-bye again. From that very second that he walked out I thought, "I'm goin' to eat lunch with Jimmy today." I went on an' took the children to school an' got dressed to go eat lunch with Jimmy. Then I was at my parents' house, an' all of a sudden I was sittin' there an' I thought, "I've got to eat lunch with Jimmy." It wasn't, "I'm goin' to." It was, "I've *got* to." An' that was about the very time it all happened. I was at my parents' house when Mary Teachey, Jimmy's mother, called. Everybody was sayin', "Now wait 'til you're calm to get the children here." But I hadda have the children. Finally I said, "If you don't go get the children, *I'm* goin' to get them." I just had to have them with me.

Adjustin' was different for them. I could lull around at home, an' if I wanted to, I could stay in my bathrobe until noon an' I could sit here, listenin' to Neil Diamond for an hour at a time. I could stay away from anythin' that bothered me or grated, or anybody that was unpleasant. But the children were thrown out in their same school situation. One night we were eatin' supper an' one of the boys said, "There's a new word for what happened." An' the other said, "Don't tell her because it'll make her sad." When they said that kind of thing, I had to find out what they meant. There was a new code word—bricks, bricks bricks—for the sound of a wall comin' down. Children can be cruel sometimes to other children. They don't mean to be, but "bricks, bricks, bricks" is cruel. To the other kids it was just like somethin' you see on TV.

At first I was gonna be all things to my children. When Jimmy was alive, we did so many fun things. We tried to take them places, out to eat or to the movies. They'd go with us to play golf an' tennis. Jimmy always wanted them to have the best. I can still do those things for them, but we can't do them together anymore. And at first the children had a hard time understandin' that I was the final authority. I kept sayin', "Mama's the king of the mountain. Just remember, Mama's the king of the mountain." I was always too careful about them, but I have noticed that maybe in the past month, say, I'm better than I used to be. I couldn't leave them for a long, long time. I couldn't let them alone. They had kept mentionin' goin' to see Hank Aaron hit his home run, an' somebody said, "Well, why don't you put 'em on the plane to Atlanta an' let 'em go?" But I decided, "No, if the plane crashes, I wanna be on it, too." I decided then it was the last time anybody was ever gonna leave me behind.

For a long time after I felt so hard. I didn't think that for the rest of my life I would care what anybody else said or thought or did, except for my children. I was absolutely stripped emotionally. I was a vacuum. Jimmy was my very best friend, an' when he was killed, I missed him in so many ways that normal people don't. One night, two or three months ago, I had kissed the boys good-night, an' I had gone through all of the motions of what a devoted mother is supposed to do, but it was *motions*. An' all of a sudden Timothy just reached up an' hugged me, a little bear hug, an' it hit me then how long it had been since anybody had touched me in any way. I don't mean physically. But I had just built up such walls that I didn't want anybody near me at all. Then one day I laughed. I had come home from my mother's house an' Charlie Watson, one of our friends, an' Philip, Jimmy's brother, were up tryin' to patch my roof, an' my friend, Mary, came over from next door, an' we stood there an' laughed, the whole thing was so hysterical. I was really surprised to find out that I could laugh. It shocked me. Then I finally found out I could smile, an' sometimes the smile would even come from the inside. I guess I thought that would never happen again.

I get more independent every day, but I have a long way to go. I'm an adult now. I knew nothin' about money, an' when I say "nothin'," you don't understand the nothin' I knew about money. The men I know, Jimmy's family an' all, try to take care of me. It's sweet, really it is. It would be better for me to be more on my own, but I try to understand that it's all done out of love an' concern. An' I'm not ready to take on the whole world. There have been times when I felt like I'm almost up, an' then I'd get knocked down again. So I have been lucky in not havin' had to be on my own financially. A lotta times I hear about other people an' I think, "Well, I'm not in *that* situation." Maybe I make myself sound a little bit Pollyanna, but in every situation, if you look hard enough, you can find somethin' worse.

About a week before Jimmy was killed I went in to tell the children good-night, an' I came back an' I was tryin' to explain to him how much I loved all three of them, an' I said that I loved them so that normal livin' was a hurt. Just normal everyday livin'. I usedta think, "If only I could stand in front of all of them forever." But you can't do that, can you? For a long time I was afraid to be in this house by myself with the children. I would wake up every thirty minutes. I'm not afraid anymore. Time takes care of a lotta things like that. I've never called Allied by myself, an' that's what I'll do if I move to Raleigh, which I'm thinkin' of. I have never taken the initiative myself to pick up an' leave anywhere, but in time I wouldn't hesitate if I thought it was the right thing. I had always assumed from the time we lived here that I would step from this house into my dream house. If I move, I'll step from this house back into an apartment. I am an adult woman now an' it's time to grow up. I will never let normal livin' hurt me again.

Old Woman

I don't want to live with my children. It takes away their privacy an' it takes away ours. We took in my sister. Well, we couldn't go anywhere. We had to find out that she was taken care of; we had to see that she had somebody to watch over her. We didn't say nothin' about it, an' she was able to pay us a little somethin' for ourselves. But we were not free to go an' come like we woulda been if she had been in a home, or somewhere. Then she went into a home, an' I think she was happy. Anyway, she was up there three years. She would get awful cross with the nurses, but I seen them come in there an' bend down an' kiss her an' pat her on the head an' tell her how sweet she looked with her hair curled. I love all my children an' I love all my grand-children, an' I don't want 'em to feel we're a problem to 'em, me an' my husband. I remember how it was with my sister. It took a lotta our life away.

Now my children, I think they respect us. They want us in a way. But they got their own lives. We don't see 'em too often, but maybe that's the way it should be. Anyway, that's the way it is. When I was raised, my grandmother lived with us an' we never thought to mind about it. But it ain't like it used to be. There is not a child in the world now that has got accommodations. I'm not complainin'. The children have moved away from here, an' it's a long way for 'em to go. My son came down here an' spent all of his vacation buildin' things for us. My other son he gives me enough money to buy somethin' for my room. They are al-ways doin' somethin' for us. Sometimes they bring us a messa fish when they go down to the beach, an' when my husband was in the hospital, I couldn't ask for anybody to be any better than my children were. There is a little sign on our back door, a wel-come sign. Well, that is hand-carved an' hand-painted, an' my son made that himself. An' he also made the frame for the pic-ture hangin' up there on the wall. An' my granddaughter went an' picked up shells at the beach an' brung 'em home to me. They are always bringin' me some little memento of some kind, some little somethin'. I come to the conclusion if I hafta break up my home, I'm goin' to pack everythin' that each one has giv-en to me an' give it back to 'em. I won't be able to move it around an' care for it. It might be hard to do that, but if somethin' got to be, it got to be.

It's not so scary to get old, like people think it might be. It is a happy time because when you get old, you know the Lord has blessed you so that you could get to that age. 'Course there are changes, you know? I'm not readin' like I used to. My eyes go on me. I used to like to look at *Ironside*. Now he's in the chair, but he was a lawyer when he was on one a' them shows, an' I liked to look at that. I still try'n watch a few of the stories they have, but some of 'em are so disgustin'. I try not to mind the way things change.

People here are real nice when you're old. My husband don't drive an' I don't drive, an' the neighbors an' diff'rent ones take me to the store when they're goin'. But I never ask 'em to take me anywhere. They will not even take any money if I ask 'em to do anythin' for me. I asked this one lady, when she got off for lunch, if she would bring me some bread that I was short of, an' she did. An' she wouldn't let me pay. When my sister died, the Eastern Star served the first meal, an' the day after, the Baptist ladies served a meal, an' the Methodists the next day. It was real nice. But sometimes I am ashamed. We can take care of ourselves.

Way back we decided if we didn't want to live with the children an' we didn't want to go to a hospital, we would get a little house. Now we have our little house, an' my husband an' me, we don't agree. He worries more'n I do about it. He don't like to sit here blind, an' sometimes, like yesterday, I was feelin' poorly an' he couldn't do a thing for me, an' he says there has got to be a change. But me, I think this way. We built this house an' this was our place to come when we got old. I can go anywhere in this house at night without turnin' on a light an' I can usually put my hand on anythin'. We burn a little light on a table that reflects into our bedroom, but if I want to, I can go all over the house in the pure darkness. So long as we can live this way, I'm not goin' to move with any of 'em.

15 A Good Life

"It may be that this is what we want: a place to live in, a good community in which we can all live together an' live in peace, rather than the hustle-bustle that you've got to do this an' you live for money an' money alone."
—D. J. Fussell, County Commissioner

The Jaycees:
James "Knott" Teachey

The Jaycee creed prob'ly sums up with the first two or three lines: "We believe that faith in God gives meaning and purpose to human life." We got a group of boys, they all feel like a family, an' we enjoy doin' things for the town that people can appreciate. We have leadership programs an' those type things. To me, every young man should be a Jaycee. You lose somethin' whenever you get to be thirty-six an' you age out.

We have twenty-six boys in the junior chamber of commerce right now, an' they represent from rich to poor, from a truck driver to an executive. Anybody can join. If they come in an' ask us, we'll more'n welcome 'em. We have a Jaycee buildin' that's been loaned to us, down east of Rose Hill at a fishin' pond. Right now we're meetin' at the park, an' then sometimes we'll meet at the Rose Hill Restaurant. About once a month we have a Jaycee party. Last Friday we had a shrimperoo. This is where you boil shrimp, an' we had chicken 'n pastry an' that kinda stuff, an' some of 'em take social drinks an' dance some, sit around'n talk, that kinda thing. Just bein' social. 'Course the basic thing we do is try to help our community to be a better place to live in, an' we take diff'rent projects to do this with.

The Poultry Jubilee is the biggest project we have. This is a poultry town, an' the reason the jubilee was put on was to show 'preciation to the poultry industry an' to promote poultry. We elect a North Carolina Poultry Queen. She travels all over the country, rides in all the parades an' all this kinda stuff. It's sorta like a country fair. We have a beauty pageant an' we bring in entertainment, like this year we're havin' Pat Boone. We cook chicken in the world's largest fryin' pan. It's fourteen feet in diameter an' it'll cook two hundred sixty-five chickens at one time. An' it takes a hundred sixty-five gallons of oil to fill it up. We serve about five thousand people every time. We have a cake bake sale where the local women bring cakes, an' we auction 'em off to raise money for the retarded children. Last year the grand champion brought over a hun'red dollars.

The park in Rose Hill, over where the ol' schoolhouse burned down, we did a lotta work on this, an' we contribute seven hundred fifty dollars a year to the recreation program, an' anyone can participate. There were some colored boys out this year, playin' with the white boys, an' I was glad to see that. We've got some swings out there, an' we're tryin' to start a little park. We try to add somethin' every year.

At Christmastime we went to the Rose Hill School an' we got the teachers to tell us who the poor children were, the underprivileged children, an' they gave us fifty or sixty names, an' we gave each one a' those children a gift certificate to spend like they wanted. We didn't give 'em any money because we didn't want their ol' man to take it away from them, but they could go into three or four stores in town an' spend that gift certificate like they wanted to. If they wanted to buy all the bubble gum in town, they could buy it. We put up Christmas lights, we put up Christmas trees, an' Lord knows what else we do.

A community or town can never progress without industry. We have two major industries here—Ramsey Feed Company, which is where I work, an' Nash Johnson. There is also a little sewin' plant here. I'd like to see more money get into people's pockets in Rose Hill, but you've never seen a town with an industry wanted to see another industry come in, have you? What happens, they start competin' for the labor.

Now here's exactly what's been goin' on. Them Yankees bring them textile plants down here an' pick up cheap labor, an' that's the reason we don't get anywhere. They cheapen our labor, as far as I'm concerned. Sure, they put money into lower-class people's pocket, which helps, but they still cheapen it. Now, I don't like a union. If they were run honestly, they'd be the best thing, but they're crooked an' everybody knows it. But those unions are gonna get in here sooner or later, an' it's gonna break that little piggyback ride all them Yankees got. I wanna be aroun' an' see that happen.

Now listen, we got jobs down here to catch chickens. An' that's the nastiest, dirtiest job in the world, an' I wouldn't do it. But some of 'em boys can make a hun'red fifty dollars a week. Just gotta go out an' work. That's a lotta money in this area. 'Course this is basically colored work. I mean, it's not designed that way, but this is usually who catches chickens. But what happens? I'm not knockin' the colored people now, but you can't get 'em to come in steady. They get enough for the family to eat, an' that's it. Now why can't they think like me, accept this job an' have pride in it, come five nights a week, catch the chickens, go home an' lead a decent life? I know I got a good job an' I wouldn't wanna do that kinda work, but I would before I'd go on welfare. That's what I'm sayin'. There's a job available if they'll come in an' go to work.

I wish these people were red or blue or white or any other color but black, because it's been blown up so much. If you say anythin' about anythin', someone says, "Well, you hate the colored people." This is not so. This is really not so. An' it burns me up. Who's got the most civil rights now? I don't think because they're a minority they should jump up an' down an' say, "My cat needs his toenails clipped." That's not right. I'm a minority. Hell. I'm just as minority as anybody else.

Now, we're gonna talk about white people. We ain't gonna talk about colored people. You can take a white family that's growin' up, an' the parents don't care. So the children aren't gonna care. You can give 'em a hun'red fifty dollars a week salary, an' he still ain't gonna have anythin' because he don't want anythin'. So you're not goin' to change anybody like that. You hafta change the child. There's only one way to eliminate some a' these problems, an' that's to raise the child in a diff'rent environment. I'm not advocatin' it, because if I was in that position, I wouldn't give away my children. But you gotta do somethin'. The Bible says you'll always have the poor. An' you always will.

The thing I'm sayin' is there ain't no easy answers. I wish I could change an' be like the young people, see how it feels. I don't see how anyone could turn against their country. I get tired

331

of watchin' the news media. They show four thousand people walkin' around an' cuttin tires, but they never show anythin' like a youth crusade; they never show anythin' that's good. You see all those people marchin' on the Capitol, an' all this stuff. Why don't you see people like me that's in favor of patriots? That's what you call it. *Patriotism.* Why don't you see *us* up there? Because we gotta work for a livin', an' we ain't got time to go lallygaggin' around.

The best thing could happen to both the boys an' the girls, get 'em through high school an' give 'em military service. This gives 'em somebody to be over 'em. I went in the service when I get outta high school, an' that helped me more'n anythin' I know. I was one year in Norfolk, one year in Charleston, two years in California. We made two cruises, to China an' the Philippines. I went in the Navy in nineteen fifty-six, right after the Korean War. An' let me tell you one thing, I missed the fightin', but as long as you live an' as long as I live, there will always be war.

You know why the Civil War was fought, don't you? Well, the same situation in Vietnam. The North Vietnamese invaded the South. One is a democracy, or is s'posed to be, which it is not a very good democracy. But the other is under communist control. I don't see how anybody can justify one group of people tryin' to impose a life on another group of people. If we hadn'ta stepped in, Hitler woulda taken over Europe. An' the same is true here. All you hear is one side. You don't ever hear about what the North Vietnamese do or what the Viet Cong do. If you pick up a *Reader's Digest,* or any book that's not biased, you can see that they go in there an' rape women, cut chieftains' heads off, an' they're terrible. Yet all you hear is "Ho Chi Minh's a god."

I've been to these places. I've been to the slums of Peru. An' you know how these Indians live. Why should those people be subjected to somethin' they don't want? We've got an obligation by bein' so powerful an' strong to help those people. To protect 'em. It'd be the same thing if you came to me an' said, "Listen, we're real good friends, I need five dollars," an' I said, "You're on your own. I ain't givin' it."

I was in the Navy four years, an' for two years we were stationed in California, an' hell, you couldn't even get anybody to speak with you across the fence. An' me, I'll just talk with everybody. Here, everybody knows everybody else an' everybody's good to you. I'm divorced, an' if you get a divorce in this town, everybody's gonna know about it, everybody's gonna know basically what the problem is. But people tend to forget quickly. They talk about things for a while, but then soon it blows over. This is more of an ideal community than any I've ever been in.

It's a good life here. I've got a good job. There's really not much entertainment, but we get along. In the summer the church leagues an' the Jaycees have a ball team. We get together an' meet an' talk. On the weekends we go to the beach. Right in Rose Hill you don't have a movie to go to, you don't have a bowlin' alley. You gotta ride fifty miles to Wilmington to do any of those things. But we gotta lotta pride an' a lotta feelin', an' we try to make things more right. A community to me is like a big family. Naturally we don't have mothers an' fathers; we don't live in the same house. But everybody treats everybody the same way. If I was in trouble, I don't think there's anybody in this town I couldn't call. It's just a feelin' of security an' belongin'.

Sally Ryan*

Some people around here they keep a perfect garden. They take a lotta pride in it, an' that's fine for *them.* But much as I love it, I just don't want to break my neck an' spend the whole summer keepin' every little weed out, neglectin' my children, neglectin' my husband, neglectin' my house, neglectin' myself. 'Course there are times you gotta pitch in an' do it. Like freezin' corn now. That's an all-day job. We dream it an' talk about it an' complain about it, but really it's good because it takes you one full day an' then you're through.

You hafta fix the corn just as soon as you pick it, 'cause if you don't, it gets too old. I like to pick my own 'cause my husband takes everythin' in sight an' I sorta pick the good ones. You get out there early in the mornin', say about six o'clock, pick it, come back in, shuck it, start soakin' it, an' put it up. You might be through by five o'clock if you're lucky an' know what you're doin'. I can usually do two or three hundred ears in a day.

The trouble is you really gotta keep goin', an' it's hard to keep

333

goin' when you got a lotta other things on your mind. I gotta stop an' change somebody's pants or wash a tub a' clothes or cook supper, all these other things. Right now we're doin' butter beans, which is easier than corn. But I stayed out in the bean field all yesterday afternoon, an' then I had a lotta other things to do in the house, so I was up shellin' butter beans 'til Johnny Carson went off last night. Every summer I tell myself I'm not goin' to do it again, an' every summer I'll plant everythin' I can find. I know I can't tend to it right an' put it all up an' freeze it all, but I can't imagine not havin' a garden. I may not do it perfect, but I do it every time.

Margaret Patterson*

When my children were growin' up, every year the PTA would have a king an' queen contest to raise funds to improve our school buildin'. Each class would vote on a representative for that class, an' then the child that got the most votes in the school would win the contest. People paid a penny a vote to the child they were supportin'. Well, of course, this cute little doll baby would come up to you an' say, "Would you give me a vote? I'm runnin' for king or queen from my class." Insteada givin' the child a penny, you'd give a quarter or fifty cents or a dollar, an' the little one that got out an' worked the hardest an' made the most money would win.

The nights of the Halloween carnival they would put the votin' up on the blackboard. You could vote up until nine o'clock, an' the child in the elementary grade that had the most votes would have the most money an' be crowned king or queen for the school.

Then there was the high school contest. *That* would really be nitty-gritty. The boyfriends would be pressurin' their fathers, "You gotta vote for my girl." I don't remember any kid from out in the country ever bein' elected. It was always one of the boys or girls from the little clique in town. Once in a while there would be a cute little girl that all the other children really liked, an' she would become queen, but it would usually be the one that the daddy had the most money. Of course the money did go

334

for a good thing, but it was not always the child that was the most popular, or the smartest, or the prettiest child. It broke many a little girl's heart, an' it created a lotta ill feelin's. But that was one of the things we hadda do to raise money for our school.

The Musician: Goldie Alderman

I reckon I was about seven when I started playin' the piano, an' I was gonna practice an' have music, regardless. Mrs. Boney, Judge Boney's mother, was my first teacher. I would go there an' pick out tunes, an' she'd say, "I'll teach you." Mrs. Boney couldn't sew a stitch, just like me, so Mama would sew my tuition out. She never had a pattern or nothin'.

Every time Mrs. Boney'd have anythin' big, she'd have me to play. You know, when you're along about twelve, that means a lot to you, an' every time there'd be somethin' in the county, she'd have one of her children play, an' it would be me. I do the same with my students now. I went to Lenoir-Rhyne College an' I made the dean's. That was good, out of a little town like this. I wanted to go on, but I had no money. I could have borrowed it, an' I would have done, but I decided to get married. That didn't phase me with the music. I've had a good time. Just made me love it that much better.

Now let me tell you. We used to put on concerts. My goodness, we had wonderful things! We had some of our concerts in the auditorium of the high school, which was right down on the big lot, the school buildin' that burned down. Our music club sponsored anythin' in the world, just like the one they have in Raleigh. Sometimes we could run our tongue out, that's the truth, tryin' to get somethin' beautiful from somewhere. The artists would come down an' say, "This is beautiful. This is a lovely, cordial place." We had *nice* things. But now there's been a turnover of those we depended on. An' the young people aren't goin' to do it. They want that bang-bang music. That "fuss" is what I call it. Now, I love rhythm. But the new stuff, sometimes you don't even know the theme. They get careless. It's just a fuss, an' they turn it as loud as they can.

Trouble is, they can get by with that today, where we couldn't.

335

If people don't learn discipline when they're young, when are they goin' to learn it? Everyone that I've talked with all my life will say, "Why didn't I practice like Mother wanted me to? Why didn't I continue?" I say, "That's the sixty-four-thousand-dollar question. If you ever find out, will you let me know?" "*Why*, Miss Goldie? *Why*?" An' then that ends it. But I know why. Their mothers say to me, "I would like them to take piano, but they won't practice." Now watch gonna do? You have to have the basics. When I go in there an' I improvise, some of 'em say to me, "When we improvise, we don't sound like you." I say, "Sure. You don't know your arpeggios." An' they don't understand why they can't play like I do.

When I had my family, music was natural as eatin' in my house. I had two girls an' a boy, an' those girls would practice before they went to school. They couldn't get in here an' do that bang-bang music 'cause I wouldn't do a thing but go in there an' just knock. That's all I had to do, let me tell you. I taught them for the first five years, but after that Miss Marshall, she was a conservatory graduate, she took interest in my children 'cause she knew I was goin' to make 'em do it right, an' she'd have 'em in all the contests. They were good for a little town. People'd say, "Where you from? Where's Rose Hill?" But they knew after my children'd leave 'cause they'd hear those girls play.

I've been playin' the organ at church for more than forty-two years. We had an' old pump organ back then, used to do the swells an' all. Every year the church sends me to Montreat, North Carolina, for the music conference, but I can't interest anyone else in goin'. Dallas said, "Miss Goldie, nobody can bring back the things you can." Well, he does that to flatter me 'cause he knows I like to be flattered, but I have all this choir material from Montreat an' it gets frustratin'. On weekends the children are away to the beach, or somewhere, an' you can't depend on a choir like that. I wouldn't care to play a service at that church unless I had three hours' practice on the organ. Every Wednesday night our preacher, Mr. Porter, gives me the theme he's gonna preach on an' everythin', so I can kinda go along with what he has. We won't have any fuss. If we have any misunderstandin', we work it out.

I was organist under Mr. La Prade, an' he never did mention

anythin' to me, but I'll tell you why he left. They did that man ridiculous. I'm not goin' to mention any names, but our own members they run that man away from here. An' let me tell you, they are gonna suffer for that. They made life miserable for that poor man an' his wife. They did. It's the people you'd least expect. The congregation wanted to stop it, but how you goin' to do it when *they* do it in such a sneakin' way that you don't know, you can't put your finger on it? There were people who left the church when he left Rose Hill. They liked him an' he was, he was fine. An' I remember she was kinda stout, an' she looked sometimes as if she would cry, but she had to come to church, she had her husband preachin'.

Now they're startin' in on Mr. Porter the same way. It's the devil is what it is, an' it's terrible. They're pickin' some of 'em now, an' you can just pick into anythin'. When you know a little bit about the insides of the thing, the excuses they give for it is frivolous. I'll tell you. I get upset. I don't think that's the thing to do. An' Mr. Porter he preaches the nicest sermons. He told me the other day, he said, "If I can find a place, I'm gonna leave." When you hear such things like that, it kinda upsets you when you've been here all your life an' worked with these people. It's the devil, that's all it is.

I'm gettin' old, but I'm not goin' to think about that. I'm just goin' to be doin' somethin'. That's the best way to get old. Everywhere I go I learn somethin', an' I still love to play the piano. I play classical. I play jazz. I play popular music. When my girls would come in way back, an' those boys would come with 'em, I'd let 'em dance an' I'd play for 'em. An' they thought that was the funniest thing in the world. I would rather have played concerts than anythin', an' it was pathetic because I certainly didn't have many finances, an' I had a lot of talent. But I've had a good time with my music. You see, I know my music. Not like today, where they don't have any real trainin' or discipline. Art is the same. You see it, it's not deep like it used to be. The young people should be takin' my place, an' I can't even get an assistant down there. It's not that I'm so good as an organist. It's they are not goin' to take responsibility for somethin' nice, so I have to do the work myself. Well, I love it. I wouldn't do it if I didn't love it. But supposin' I wasn't there. If one day I didn't show up.

That's goin' to happen sometime, an' when I think about it, I'm not thinkin' about myself. I want there to be music. I'm doin' it for the Lord an' the church as a whole.

Patsy Maxwell*

A dark person is easily offended if a lighter one calls him "black." I guess the reason is that there was a time that the whites accepted the lighter blacks, an' the dark ones they didn't. I dunno the reason. But after the blacks learned that it *mattered,* then the lighter ones, what you'd call the "black bourgeoisie," tended to marry lighter ones an' kept it goin' on that way. It was a sign of prestige.

Myself, I always made it a policy never to date a light. It mighta been that I felt insecure, I dunno. But I think it's all changin' for us. The first time I realized it was when I went over to Fayetteville, to the base, an' we were in one a' the clubs an' James Brown recorded his record that went ". . . I'm Black an' Proud." Maybe before that people were seein' somethin' good in the darker blacks. But for me that was the first time.

C. R. Lawton*

When my son hit sixteen, he wanted a car. Well, I coulda bought it for him or loaned 'im the money to buy it. I coulda helped him in a lotta ways. But I wanted 'im to pay for it himself. He appreciates it a whole lot more.

Of course if he gets in a spot, I'd help 'im out. But that hasn't really been necessary. He even pays his own repair bills. The first time he had to have anythin' looked at, he wanted to borrow mine while his was in the shop. He also wanted me to go by an' pick his up that night when I got off work. Well, he was tryin' to con me, see. He thought I was gonna pay that bill. So I brought him home the bill, an' he looked at me real funny, didn't say a word. The next day he went around an' paid it. I know if I had paid that bill, he'd think it was home free an' he'd keep it buildin' right on.

Then we had a little problem with his license. I told 'im, when he got that car, that if he got a ticket, he'd hafta sell the car an' I'd take away his license for thirty days. Well, wasn't long before he got a speedin' ticket. I felt just terrible. But I'da never been able to do anythin' with 'im the resta my life if I had backed down on my word that time. He didn't think I'd make him do it, but I told 'im to get his car cleaned up so I could sell it. It took 'im a week. He'd wash it a little bit today, wash it a little bit tomorrow, clean the engine one day, just hopin' I'd back out.

It killed me, but I did it. I sold his car an' put his license in my pocket for thirty days. I believe it hurt me as bad as it did him. I had gotten used to sendin' 'im to the store at night, an' he did little runaround jobs for me, an' there I'd be on the couch an' I'd hafta get up an' do it myself. But I knew if I gave 'im his license back to do somethin' for me just one time, he would want it the next night for himself. So I stuck it out, an' I think that was one a' the best things I ever did. This whole car experience has been good for 'im.

Kenneth Wexler*

There's some people in this community who have had the courage to admit they've got problems an' go for help, but mostly you aren't supposed to confess to havin' inner troubles. There is a story I've heard about what happened to one man who had a serious drinkin' problem. The man was in real bad shape; he had drunk some rubbin' alcohol, or somethin'. So his family called some deputies to come an' carry 'im to Cherry Hospital in Goldsboro. All right. First they took 'im to the hospital in Kenansville to get one of the doctors to sign the papers so they could go on over to Cherry. Doctor says, "I don't have time. I've gotta go to lunch. I'll be back about two o'clock." Well, the man was havin' the D.T.'s. They weren't s'posed to do anythin' for him, but one a' the deputies gave the man some liquor to calm 'im down. That mighta been wrong, but hell, it's better'n havin' a man bite his tongue off. Then a nurse comes along an' says, "Well, you know the doctor's got diff'rent priorities." So the deputies took the guy up to the third floor an' told the nurses to call when he had been examined by the doctor. The man was left sittin' out in the hall by himself. Finally, about two-thirty the doctor showed up an' signed the papers.

The mental health clinic, we got that about six or eight months ago. It looks very nice, but as far as I can see it, that place is for these women 'round here that live on nerve pills an' these rich drunks to go an' dry out so they won't hafta go through the process of goin' to Cherry. The beds were full a week an' a half after it opened. They have what they call counselin' or therapy, or somethin' like that, but it's kinda like puttin' on a Band-Aid, y'know? There's a lady in this town, rich as the devil, who's had a coupla nervous breakdowns, shock treatment, the whole thing. I saw her one day, drivin' with a neighbor of hers, an' she was starin' out the winda like she was seein' some awful sump'n, or maybe like she wasn't seein' nothin' at all. All right, she's had a lotta troubles an' she's a real bad case, but there's a lotta people who get worried, an' there ain't even a place for *them*. They've probably got some guidance program down at the high school, but these kids aren't goin' to talk to anyone like that. They go to youth groups, some of 'em, but in a small town like Rose Hill, who's gonna open up an' say anythin'? Used to, lotta the kids went an' sat in Jackie Johnson's house an' talked to her. Well, she's a real fine woman an' she's been a mother to a whole litter of 'em, but Mis Jackie she's not a psychiatrist. It's too much responsibility for one person who isn't even trained.

Then there's the alcoholics. Which we're not supposed to have 'em see 'cause nobody drinks in the town of Rose Hill. That's gotta be the biggest joke goin'. Hell, you see a man drivin' home, weavin' his car from one side a' the road to the other, what you s'posed to think? He's got a real bad headache?

Around here a person that's got problems, he's a weak person. Say you got a relative that's a little off in the head. You keep 'im locked up in the house. Or say you got somethin' worryin' you. You kinda push it down an' wait for it to go away. There's been times in my life when I got real pressured, an' I knew I was makin' it worse for myself, but I didn't know what to do about it. So I got some nerve pills, an' after a while I was feelin' so slow I hadda stop that. I still get real nervous sometimes, but I'm not goin' to take the money an' ride to Goldsboro or Wilmington an' start lookin' for a doctor. An' I'm sure as hell not goin' to sit down an' discuss my personal business with Dr. Hawes. The fact is in Rose Hill you know everybody, but you ain't got nobody to talk to.

The Hunter: Reuben Teachey

You hunt to kill the deer, but that's just a small part of it. There's a joy you get out of it, the fact that you get away from other things you detest doin'. We can only hunt two an' a half months here, but the resta the time we're breedin' dogs an' trainin' dogs, developin' our land, buildin' new roads, burnin' undergrowth or plantin' feed for our deer. You get all kindsa benefits out of it. I figure the money I throw away on huntin' saved me a million headaches or a million sicknesses. Some call it a hobby, but it's not like just goin' out there an' killin' a trophy buck an' hangin' it on the wall. Or goin' off to Africa an' killin' an elephant. To me that is not a sportsman.

The big ol' buck deer got his big rack of horns through the fact that he is very cunnin' an' wise. The idea is to jump him an' run him out by the people who have been placed strategically around the area that you're huntin'. You usually have bush-hogged access roads right through the woods, so you can get in. The deer is a creature of habit. If you jump 'im an' he has a favorite way to escape through the thick vegetation, you have got to discover that place. He'll take it time after time if nothin' bothers him. But if you shoot an' miss 'im on that path, his getaway, then he'll switch. That ol' buck is just as educated as a turkey. He can't see very well, an' if you stand perfectly still, he don't pay any attention. What he depends on is his nose an' his ears. His sense of smell is so keen it is fantastic. Just fantastic.

The younger bucks, first an' second years, are not so mindful of these things. The older they get, the more sensitive they are to any abnormal sound or abnormal smells. A buck has a special place that he likes, an' he stays away from the other deer. He will come out an' mingle with 'em at night, breed an' feed with 'em, but then he will go back to the sidelines behind the does. A buck deer in the ruttin' season his neck will swell up an' he'll fight.

341

The older he is, it seems to be the meaner he is. I don't mean he'll attack human beings, but he'd just as soon stop an' fight the dogs as not. Stick his horns right through 'em. When you're after a big ol' boy, you wouldn't want one of your men to have after-shave lotion on, an' you shouldn't be smokin' or drinkin'. That's kinda far out, an' a lotta the men don't observe it, but I always want 'em to. If you don't jump 'im with the dogs, an' he's already heard your racket or smelled you comin', he slips off to another place. Then the driver hasta take the dogs into the woods an' drive that buck towards where you've placed the men who are your standers. What I enjoy as much as anythin', I guess, is jumpin' that nice buck an' runnin' to your friends or guests, or one of the other fellas, an' let 'em kill 'im.

I enjoy it all, the shootin', the trackin', the fixin' the roads. I enjoy a man's company. I don't mean to say "a man." I mean a good hunter. We get enjoyment outta teasin' each other, tellin' jokes an' tall tales, expand on that thing, enlarge on everythin' that happened. You're always jokin' about somethin' an' it's a free atmosphere. We just rile the devil outta somebody if he misses a deer, charge 'im three dollars, that kinda stuff. We have a good dinner a lotta times, feedin' offa the deer, sittin' down, eatin' with a buncha your friends. You have mutual respect, somethin' in common. You can't imagine me bein' interested in an ol' crooked lawyer, but that's the way it goes.

We are one of the most exclusive clubs in North Carolina. We have our rules. There are bigger clubs, an' they have a lotta undesirables. We can reject anybody we want to. It might make us appear to be selfish; we aren't. We are our own boss. We don't hafta depend on anyone. Of course it's very expensive. We spent thirty thousand dollars in about two years. The dogs, well, I don't even like to talk about it. A thousand or two thousand dollars in dogs all the time, not includin' feedin' them an' waitin' to see that they're all in so they won't get lost. It's a big headache sometimes, but you get a lot out of it. It isn't easy to find a way to relax. Just sittin' around, doin' nothin', doesn't accomplish anythin'. You work at your office an' get to the point where you can't solve a simple problem. You don't want to stay home with your wife every minute. An' she doesn't want to stay home with me. Well, then it's time for a change. I like to go to the woods, not just to look at the trees an' the sky, but it's really gettin' to yourself. You're close to nature an' your problems are small, you don't have any pressure. It's somethin' that seems like it was born with me.

'Course there are things wrong with it. It costs too much to do it like we do, an' it takes most of your time away from your business. An' your family. But if it were fishin', it would be the same thing. Or what if it were bowlin' or gamblin' or women? You see, there is a bad side to everythin', advantages an' disadvantages. I have done too much of it, an' I have tried not to let it get control of me all the time. We go huntin' today, an' somebody comes along an' wants to go tomorrow, an' you know you can only afford so much unless you are a millionaire. But it's like takin' a bath or talkin'. It's relaxin', gettin' away. It's necessary. Nobody can walk in on you. No phone is goin' to ring.

Most of our forefathers were free when they came to this country. America's heritage goes back to the hunters, the explorers, the people who loved the outdoors. They were in close contact with the wilderness. The people in the cities don't look healthy to me, an' maybe that has somethin' to do with lack of freedom. Now a deer, as all animals are, was born an' bred in the wilderness. He is not afraid of that limb fallin' out of that tree, the animals an' the hunters. We cherish our freedom above all else.

Marguerite Blanchard

Before we moved to our house, we had a Cape Cod house out in the country, and I redid it I don't know how many times. Then, when I decided I wanted to put this house together, I wanted it to suit Billy, I wanted it to be *us*. You don't have to have a lot of money, you know. You can be a good observer of nice things, an' with your own ingenuity you can come home an' do it yourself. I knew what I liked, an' I had a pretty good knowledge of color an' what color did for you an' how much you could use without overdoin'. An' so I used what I had learned an' observed an' I did it.

I've been studyin' an' teachin' ceramics for years, an' when you go to the kiln, you learn a lot about color. The combination of heat an' glaze an' clay, an' what it produces, is always a surprise. I also enjoy paintin', an' when you start paintin', you find out what one color does next to another, or how a color affects you. A lot of people don't know that color influences your mood. You can be in a room that's real heavy an' dark, an' it's depressin'. Psychiatrists know this. Now, I like red a great deal. I painted a red flower, an' when I did that, I had a feelin' that I wanted to do somethin' dynamic an' strong. I had a feelin' that I wanted to burst a flower open, an' so that's what came out. I did a lot of it with a palette knife. I'm no artist. I just take a brush an' brush a little bit. I think of Margaret Cooper as an artist. She really *paints*. An artist is somebody who can just zip-zip-zip. But I guess there's a certain amount of art in anythin'.

Most people here have comfortable houses. Mine may be a little bigger, but I'm not really aware that I live differently from other people here. I know there is poverty in this town, but that's not *Rose Hill*. And it makes you think of the question, "Who is a rich man?" Well, everybody's rich to somebody. A rich person is somebody who has more than you. I don't think of myself as an elegant person. I'm the kind that can get my hands in too many things to be elegant. Of course, you need to do everythin' in elegance, I suppose.

Maybe people who live in other ways are as happy as they would be livin' here with me. An' if they did come here, this house would be like where they lived in a little time. They wouldn't know how to adjust themselves. I mean, I live here an' I enjoy this, an' somebody else might live in his house an' it might not be like this, but he has the same feelin' about enjoyin' his life that I have. So I don't feel like I'm livin' above anybody else. What other people have is right for *them*. Whatever a person has, that is his thing.

Barbara Jean Ryan*

When my kids were babies an' I was tied right here, all I did was mostly tend to the babies an' keep the TV runnin' all day long. I'd sit down before I was through with whatever I had to do an' I'd watch the television. I couldn't stop doin' it, I'd get so

344

involved. I could see it wasn't doin' me any good. I already had little babies screamin', an' that was enough to keep me in a bad mood. But I'd be glued to that TV all the time. The thing about it is it keeps you from reality. The folks in those stories can become your people. They're your friends. You don't care about goin' out an' doin' anythin' or visitin' anybody else. You turn on that TV. Even when I was sittin' there an' I had the kids or I had my sewin', or doin' somethin', it's like a brainwashin'. An' it started to scare me.

I hadda cut it out altogether, an' now I got to where if I've had a busy mornin', I can take a break at lunch time an' sit down an' turn on *As the World Turns*. I gotta admit it. I've watched *As the World Turns* ever since *they* were kids on there, an' I feel like I grew up with 'em. I like that one especially, but I really try not to listen to all that stuff. I think I finally got it under control.

The Artist: Margaret Blanchard Cooper

I never thought I'd be teachin' art here in my home the way I do. But it's worked out very well for me. My first student was a lady who called an' said could I teach her at any hour, any day, at my convenience. We hold our little class right over in the corner. I had two little boys who had to take naps upstairs, an' they would wake up before the lesson was over an' come runnin' down. Then my class grew to about three, an' soon it really mushroomed. I had several classes, an' I'd set up little life studies all over the house, an' there were paint smudges everywhere. Well, we had built a little buildin' outside to store tobacco, but it gradually came to be a studio. So it worked out that I could do this an' still be home with my children.

I don't think I'm unusual or irregular, or anythin' like that, but every little town doesn't have someone who can teach art. I mean, we didn't twenty years ago. When the James Sprunt Institute came along, I taught art there, an' I guess I was the first art teacher they ever had. I had twenty-five students in my class at one time, an' I had four or five classes of pupils. So you see how many people here have had a little bit of art in their lives. There's really a great deal of interest. Some of the women started

345

what we call the "clay play club," where we meet every Wednesday we can an' do things, cultural things you might say, that we're all interested in. We learned to do ceramics an' we had our own little studio. We go to Wilmington or to Raleigh an' visit the museum or the craft shops or shop around. In Duplin County we have the Tarheel Fine Arts Society, which I've been a part of since it was organized, and was president the last two years. We bring three or four concerts or programs to the country, like Jack an' Sally Jenkins, an' what's his name, Liebert, the organist from Radio City Music Hall. We've had him twice. We're tryin' to promote that kinda thing in the community. They can have a country music program in the auditorium at Kenansville an' fill the house, an' when we started, we had only a handful of folks which were almost embarrassed to be there. An' now we have filled the house, too.

For a year an' a half I've been goin' down to the university at Wilmington an' takin' a course. Because after you teach an' teach an' teach, you feel you're drained an' you've gotta have some inspiration. Another woman in town an' I have been goin' for one day a week, an' that gives us at least seven or eight hours of homework to do. The problem is I never seem to find the time. I've still got my classes to teach, an' I think havin' a clean house is important. An' I do my cookin' an' my gardenin'. Then, too, we have a house down at the beach an' we've decided to remodel it a bit, an' we spend a lot of the weekends there doin' the work ourselves. My husband, Jack, works very hard, an' then all of a sudden he's got to get away an' relax. We haven't been to Europe, or any place like that. Jack likes it down at the beach, an' I spend my time there or in my yard or paintin'. I don't know. Time gets so filled up that you don't even know about leisure time. An' you know there are other things, problems in the world, but you get so wrapped up with your own business that you tend to forget them.

We go on in our own happy way. I mean, we're not faced with terrible things, except in the news. Like with Vietnam we can sorta put it out of our thoughts, long as we don't have a boy over there. In World War II Jack was in the Philippines an' my brother, Billy, was in Korea, both of 'em in the Army. That was terrible. We'd get the news on the radio. Now we get the news at suppertime, an' sometimes I think that it doesn't make the food taste any better. Jack says it beats all he's ever seen, just the kinda war it is. I'll tell you, Vietnam has been a question to myself. The last war we fought 'cause we had to, to protect ourselves because they attacked us. I think probably if we hadn't helped the Vietnamese, that there'd have been another front that we'd have had to work against communism. An' I suppose that since we have fought this long, that we can't just walk right out; we're doin' right by gettin' out gradual. But Vietnam has been somethin' none of us knew how to feel about. I think we just got in it an' didn't mean to.

We're happy here in our own little world, an' I hope it lasts. I usedta think that my life had been so happy or so lucky or somethin' that I knew that I had to have somethin' happen to me. Well, our son, Brian, was just fourteen, an' he was out ridin' with a friend. They were goin' too fast around a curve on a paved country road, an' he was thrown out an' hit his head on a little stump or somethin' an' it killed 'im instantly. It could have been more tragic in other ways, I suppose. An' I didn't fail to see that. I said if a drunk or some mean person killed him, that'd be a lot worse. What I mean to say is that with everythin' the way it is, you hafta know you're gonna have somethin' happen to you that's not perfect. I've never been bitter. I imagine the Kennedys' religion helped them a lot, too.

I've always thought it was really kinda nice that I could keep house an' raise my family an' do my art right here. I hardly know how to say this, but if I had never gone on with art an' had done housework, I don't think I'd have been nearly as happy with my life. I guess I spend a lot of my time in a way that satisfies me. I feel like that I have touched a lot of other people, and if I hadn't been teachin', there are so many all over the counties that I would never have known. I don't have the talent Dallas has, really. I just taught the basics an' I've used my time helpin' others an' criticizin' their work. Maybe one of these days I'm goin' to stop that an' get busy an' paint myself.

Jack thinks I would miss the association with people. I don't know I would still take a course down in Wilmington, an' that would keep me in touch. One of these days I might set up a little shop of my own work. For example, I have a lamp that I painted, a real old antique that someone brought me so I could paint the globe to match the bottom. I get called on to do these things quite a bit, an' most times I don't charge. Once in a while I'll sell a painting, or someone'll ask me to paint somethin' specific an' I'll do that for them. But I don't feel right about chargin' a lot of money. You see, I'm not that much an artist. I don't call myself an artist, an' if anybody says that to me, I feel like it's not really the truth. I've always been interested in paintin', an' you have to have an interest. I have a little talent for design, maybe. An' if I applied myself, I might be a little better than I am. I wonder. Because I think an artist, a real born artist, is gonna find time to paint, no matter what, an' I wonder if everythin' would get in my way an' I still wouldn't find the time. I do have Florence to come in once a week to help me with the housework, an' my husband has always been a very good critic an' very cooperative, so I really have no excuse. But even if I didn't have these times fixed to teach, I might make my other work so important, my housework an' a little church work an' other things, that I just might not do it. Maybe I'd always just keep hopin' I'd find the time.

Dave Harris*

Fightin' with animals is illegal, but it's no worse'n boys gettin' out there boxin' around. You gotta do it on somebody's farm way out in the country, an' you gotta have it in some county where the sheriff an' mosta the deputies is out there lookin' at the fight an' joinin' in. You get that part of it lined up right, can't let it get out where you're havin' the fight an' so forth. Just let it stay inside.

The dogs'll go down there in the pit, an' the one that lives longest is the winner. A lotta times you'll have a fight an' your winner'll die within an hour or two. But if he breathes any time longer'n the other one, he wins. You're cockfightin', you gotta be in a ring. Those gaffs they use on the fightin' cocks, I don't think they oughta do that. You cut the spur off a little, 'bout quarter of an inch, an' put a metal gaff on, stickin' out like a natural spur. An' they get down an' fight 'em, an' whoever lives longer is the winner, like the dogs. They get cut up pretty bad.

348

I went down to Florida one time, went down for a vacation. They had a fight there lasted a whole week. One man got up, said he'd bet ten thousand to eight thousand on his fightin' cock. Man on the other side of the pit said, "I'll take you all of it." An' when they met in the center of the pit, they fly up there slingin' those gaffs right an' left, an' the very first lick the rooster that had the ten thousand bucks bet on him, he got hit right in the back of his head where the first joint is. Died just like an atom bomb had hit him good an' hard. Didn't lift a feather 'r nothin'. That feller hollered. Ten thousand gone.

There were about fifty, 'r sixty professional gamblers follerin' the deal. Some of 'em didn't do a thing but go down an' gamble. I heard a feller ask one a' the boys when they were lockin' up, "How'd you come out today?" "Well," he said, "at noon I was nine thousand dollars ahead." Said, "I've lost that an' twenty-seven more thousand. Better make a comeback tomorrow or I'll be in bad shape."

That's frightenin' 'cause it sorta gets to you, y'know? Gets to the animals, too, I reckon. Some of 'em like to fight so much they stay right in there 'til they die. I never did see one of 'em run. It happens sometimes, an' people say it's the bad blood in 'em. To tell you the truth, I hafta be careful I don't get too far in it. I'm afraid of myself. I like it too good.

Alice Carter*

Some a' the older black people are havin' a tough time adjustin' to the way some a' the younger black people are livin'. It's diff'rent times. Like my husband an' I live in a trailer. We have two cars an' a fancy stereo set an' the whole thing. We'd like to have our own house an' we're thinkin' about buildin'. Right now we're discussin' about what kinda style we want that house to be. Well, all of this was unthinkable about fifteen years ago. I can remember havin' electric lights, but we didn't have a bathroom. My father worked as a laborer an' didn't make but fifteen dollars a week. When we were lucky. We were outta school three months in the summer an' we'd always look forward to that because we could pick strawberries startin' out, an' then we'd pick

349

blueberries an' then beans an' then we'd work in tobacco. It was the way we'd get by.

I was tellin' my mother the other day that we had just about as much to eat then as we have now, an' how lucky we were that we always had decent clothes to wear. That's one big way you can see that things have changed. There's a store in Wallace an' they have a racka cheap clothes. They usedta associate Negroes with buyin' cheap clothes, flowers 'n plaids together, that type a' thing. One time we did, but now we buy what everybody else does. If you see somethin', no matter how much it costs, you can buy it. Or charge it. Or lay it away.

You know what the biggest diff'rence is now? Used to be you needed the word of a white man to get credit. Now you can go to a store an' get yourself in all sortsa trouble, runnin' up bills. An' you can do it without havin' to get a white person to sign for you.

John Henry Wilson*

My family has always owned property here an' there, an it's been a real pleasure to me. But every time I get to enjoyin' it, build a cabin or somethin', the public comes in. To me privacy means to be able to own somethin' an' be able to control the use of it. But here's the kinda thing that happens. Somebody went in on Saturday night or Sunday mornin', took my boat out onto the pond an' used it. They put it back an' I'd never have known, but they ate some tuna in it an' spilled the tuna, an' that tuna sure wasn't in it when I used the boat Saturday. If you're a fisherman an' you have a body of water, you want to have the first scoot around that pond. I'm pretty much a conservationist. I more or less play with the fish, catch one, look at 'im, say, "See you again, buddy," an' throw 'im back. I used to go, say, four or five times a week. Since it's gettin' to be almost public, I don't spend a great deal of time over there.

It's a loss to me as a person. For instance, I own a place, I like to be able to say who uses it with me. But I can't do that. I'm afraid to even go out there now unless I have some way to protect myself. Even a lock doesn't make things private anymore. If I leave the lock off of my shed, they don't bother it too much, but if I lock it they'll tear the lock off of it an' tear up what's inside. They have stolen outta my cabin everythin' that could be carried off: the dishes, part of the light fixtures, everythin'. It doesn't make any sense, wantin' to destroy somethin'.

I'm fixin' to start buildin' another cabin now. I'm gonna build it myself. I did the last one that way, took the old frame an' did all the work—sanded the floors an' took out the walls an' put in the bathroom, built the septic tank, put in the sewer. I can, in a fashion, do a little bit of it all. There's always somethin' else pushin', but you gotta take the time an' go. We have our own deer club an' we go down there, talk a lot, sleep a lot, eat more'n you can imagine. Have a real ball. But sometimes I go by myself and spend the night with all the bear an' deer an' coon an' all. My wife doesn't think too much of it, but nevertheless, it does you good to get off by yourself where you don't hear anybody else talkin', an' you can think what you wanna think if it's ugly or if it's good. Some people can't bear to be alone, but I've been this way mosta my life. I don't think I'm what you'd call a hermit. I have my family an' I have my friends an' I enjoy them an' I hope they enjoy me. But solitude is real important to some people. There's always somethin' pushin', but you let it push you too much, you get pushed right away from yourself. So sometimes I go off by myself where all you hear is the dog barkin' an' the owls hootin'. There's no particular reason for it. I just decide I want to go. Take off.

The Athlete: Jimmy Jerome

I played ball all my life, ever since I can remember, in the backyard. I've never been pressured or anythin', but my father played ball an' I guess you could say he encouraged me. He never forced me. There's a diff'rence in force an' encouragin'. I went up through the little leagues, through the midget football deal into junior high, played all the sports in high school an' went on to Chapel Hill, the University of North Carolina, an' now I'm playin' football there.

I did all right in high school an' I was recruited by a few colleges here an' there. I lucked out an' made all-American high school player. You gotta have the statistics. I don't think I'm such a hero. You gotta have the breaks an' I was fortunate. A back's only as good as his line. In high school it was the best line I've ever seen in a two-way conference like we have. If it hadn't been for them, I probably woulda been another run-of-the-mill ball player. But if you have a line an' you have any ability whatsoever, you're able to walk an' chew gum, you can do it.

The recruitin' was kinda fun. They've changed the rules a lot since then 'cause now, when they come down, they can only do it a certain number a' times an' take you out to eat a certain number a times, an' you only visit the school once in an official visit. But when they were recruitin' me, it was unlimited, an' they would keep comin' an' you would keep goin' out to dinner. They'd call you up, "How ya doin'?" An' they'd keep on doin' that. You hear about these guys gettin' all kindsa offers under the table. Well, I never did. I only got a scholarship. But it sure makes you feel good. It's always nice to be wanted. I tried to keep my feet on the ground. My father an' mother helped me to do that, an' I don't think I ever got bigheaded. I hope I didn't anyway because that's the mark of an idiot. Somebody that gets blown up over sump'n like that can't see things for what they are.

When I got up to Chapel Hill, I first tried out for quarterback, an' as it happened, there were thirteen quarterbacks that showed up when we were expectin' three or four. So after the fiasco of a few days of quarterback, I tried tailback, an' after about a week of tailback, I broke my arm, of all things, trippin' over a dummy. Well, I got over that an' I made it through prespring practice. Then we got into spring, an' eight days into spring practice I broke my arm again in the same place. So my freshman year at Carolina was rather dismal, to say the least. I guess it made me that more determined to make it. The next year I was healin', convalescin', an' I was redshirted. That's when they keep you outta eligibility an' you go to school. The next spring started an' I was doin' all right, an' then I happened to hit the arm again, didn't break it or anythin', but my elbow was inflamed an' my arm was swollen, an' I was in the hospital for about three days with the thing propped up. When I got out I said, "How about changin' me to wingback?" An' wingback I've been ever since. I guess I'm lucky. If I had broke my arm a coupla times in high school, I mighta quit, you know, wouldn'ta done nothin'. But with a little luck here 'n there, a little determination, you can come out all right.

In some places football players are bigger than others. At Carolina you're no celebrity or anythin'. A few more people might know you because they happen to see you in the program, but you don't get any special privileges, an' some professors are actually harder on a jock than they would be on a regular student. You hear about football players bein' big and dumb. Well, every now an' then you might find one like that, an' if they can find one, they're gonna stereotype everybody else. But we got some kids that are Phi Beta Kappa on our team. One kid from New York he's got about a 3.8 average.

I think I've gotten a total education. 'Course I need to go in the library an' stay there a little more, but I'm makin' my 2.4 an' doin' a lotta other things, too, an' havin' a good time. I'm enjoyin' myself. I went through a rush my sophomore year. It was kinda like recruitin'. They come up to you, "How ya' doin'?" They never seen me before in my life. "How ya doin'? We sure would like to have you here." An' you'd know it wasn't sincere 'cause ten minutes later the same guy would come up and say, "How ya doin'? We sure would like to have you here." After the third time they did it, you knew you were about ready to leave.

A fraternity's all right if you wanna be in one. You can make a lotta friends. But when you play ball, you're automatically in with a hundred ten guys or a hundred twenty. You get close to a few of 'em, they bring in some of their friends, an' it's like playin' dominoes—you gather 'em in. 'Course you find a few sorority girls that only date fraternity men, an' you find a few jock sniffers around, an' little cliques here an' there. But on the whole you don't find a whole lot of it, an' I go to the fraternity parties anyway, so why pay all the dues? At college you learn to meet a whole lotta people, an' I get a kick out of it. Sometimes I like to sit down an' think, but I enjoy bein' around people. I don't like stayin' by myself in a room all the time.

I hope I'm gonna get a professional draft when I graduate. But if not, I'm gonna try out for some team, either in Canada or in the NFL or the WFL. They have plenty of teams to try out with.

If I don't make any of those, I'll go into teachin' or coachin', or somethin'. I'll hafta wait an' see. I try to work out every day, doin' sump'n. Sometimes I run a mile. I've been runnin' with a weighted vest. I do some sprints. I try to catch a little football, do sit-ups, work out with weights twice a week. There's a coupla guys workin' out with me, an' I throw ball with Donny Buckner, whose father owns the restaurant. But besides those boys, mosta the people my age are gone. The home cookin' keeps you satisfied for a while, but when there's no one to hang around with, it kinda makes you ready to go back to school. I guess I'm just waitin' around.

When I was a kid, we had a recreation program, but when I was twelve, that was the last year they had it. Then after five years, a group of men got together an' decided they wanted to try again. They organized an' hired me to be the athletic director for a summer recreation program, an' I've been in charge of it for four years. The programs we've got now consist of three Little League teams an' one Pony League team.

It wouldn't be so embarrassin' if they'd go out an' play another team from town, but we've got an eight-team Little League, teams in Faison, Beulaville, B. S. Grady, Warsaw, Kenansville an' Wallace, an' we've had dismal luck in the past few years. In the last three years we've won three games. Now this year I hafta admit they had spirit an' we had a lotta fun. We won our one game for this year an' had a big celebration after that, jumped up an' down, did this an' that. Usually we kinda reconcile all the hurts after we lose by stoppin' in at some place like Tastee-Freeze, an' they cool it down with ice cream. The sting of defeat lasts only about ten minutes after the game.

Sports are fun to me, although after you've done it for a while, you quit thinkin' about it bein' fun exactly. Spring practice, now, that's not fun. I dread it. I hate that more'n anythin'. But in the fall you get into the swing of things. You get geared up an' it's very excitin'.

To people not involved in sports it's just a game, but you're puttin' everythin' you have into it an' it's very important to you. In the program we have for the kids I try to take as much emphasis off winnin' as I can. In a lotta sports it's come to the point,

354

"Win at all costs." I don't believe in that. Sure, I believe in winnin'. But it's more important for these kids to learn the sportsmanship an' the fundamentals than it is for 'em to get all concerned.

The truth is once you taste competition an' you enjoy it, you're hooked. It *is* how you play the game, but you still wanna win. Let's rate an athlete on ability, one to ten. You give me an athlete with, say, number six ability, an' on the same scale number ten desire, against an athlete with, say, number nine ability an' number five desire, an' I'll whip you. If you give me a man that wants to learn, that wants to do it, that's got his heart in it, he's the one you can work with. He's not the kid that grumbles over this an' that, just 'cause sump'n didn't go his way. He'll bounce back. They call it guts. You gotta have one hundred percent all the way.

Lawrence Brown*

I was here a coupla years before I was asked to join the Jaycees. Margaret Cooper came to see us when we first got here, Welcome Lady, but other'n that not too much was done. It's human nature, I guess. I wasn't asked to join the Jaycees 'til I bought my new house, an' then I started goin' out, diff'rent things. But the Jaycees, they've been one a' the brightest spots in my life since then. It's helped me, far as havin' friends. In this parta the country, it's social standin' an' nothin' else. If you dress real nice, don't hafta get dirty to work, maybe they'll accept you. They kinda look down on you if you hafta work with your hands. As far as drinkin' coffee with you, that's all right, but as far as invitin' you over to the house to play bridge or anythin' like that, it'd be in a diff'rent category. Some of the ones that think they're real well-off, they act like they are, they're some a' the ones that're livin' from paycheck to paycheck just like everybody else. But they give you the impression that they're not. People here live all right, but they live more in a financial strain than they think they do. Or than their neighbors think they do.

355

Adele St. Clair*

In big cities money might mean more than character, or the fact that people have known a person and they know he's honest. You don't get to know people as well in a big town. They'd be known more for their money or position.

People in a small town certainly wouldn't have to be more than average to have other people think highly of them. They could be the most humble. Some of the most important people here don't drive new cars. They don't want us to think, "Now, doesn't he think he's the stuff." You don't have to put on a fancy show here to be of this class I'm talkin' about. It's a fact of life, isn't it, that there are people who have proved to be, what would you say, of good character? Proved to be worthy of respect.

16 Three Young Men

"We always have to seek alternatives. The people who become frustrated are people who can't find them."

—Dennis Ramsey

Billy Saunders

I've never seen anything that I didn't want to know everything about. That's what I feel my function is—to inquire about things. I'm so damn curious that I don't get headed in one direction as long as I should. Tomorrow morning I may fall into something that I'd like to do for the rest of my life. But I'm not security-minded enough to the point that I would stay at a job simply because of the security it offers. As long as my wife and I can do the things we want, then I'm secure as I want to be. My desire is to retain my freedom.

What got me about the educational system was that you have to stay in the same direction for at least a year to get anywhere. When I got to college at Carolina, I had my own opinion of what an educational environment was, and I thought it was an atmosphere of pensiveness where you mulled over your secret thoughts. I didn't find the work all that difficult, but there was too much of it and I didn't want to do it. The first semester I was there my advisor gave me twenty-one semester hours, including physics, chemistry, German, analytical trig, English literature and civics. There I was at the University of North Carolina at Chapel Hill, coming from Wallace-Rose Hill High School. I had four hundred some people in my physics lecture. You couldn't even see the damn professor. They had television monitors suspended near the ceiling for the people in the back. You were a number and you answered to your number and you could send any damn body to answer for you. I flunked out after two semesters. I don't regret it, except that it was quite a calamity to be a disappointment to my parents. And for five years I had worked as a soda jerk in Sam Cavenaugh's drugstore, and I had worked for my uncle Bob Herring in construction after school and during the summer time to try and save money. Then I went up to Carolina and blew every dime of it. It hurts me that folks were really scraping to send me there.

After that I got prodded into goin' to Central Piedmont Community College as an industrial design major. I didn't know what I was doing there either. I certainly never expected to come back here and work with my Uncle Dallas in the casket company business. It was nice to learn how to design things, and drawing, drafting, art composition. But it appeared to me to be more of an avocation than a vocation. I had an art instructor up there, his name was Gene Rubin. He was a Jewish fella from Cleveland, and he and his wife were regular, A-number-one, one hundred percent forerunners of the hippie movement. Everything in the house was pillows and real low stuff, and they had incense burning all over the place. They lived close to where I did, and I got to hang around them a lot. I didn't agree with their philosophy, so I decided to get the hell out and find something better. Which is the same thing I did at Carolina, really. I came back home and was down at Wrightsville Beach one Saturday, drunk, or somewhat so, and I decided to drive into Wilmington and join the service. I went into the Postal Building with a wet bathing suit on, walked into the Navy recruiter's office. He wasn't there. A guy stuck his head through an adjoining door, said, "Come on over an' talk to me." About an hour later I had joined the Air Force and was leavin' on the followin' Thursday.

You only have a very ill-conceived notion of what it's like somewhere else until you go there. My idea of what a people would be like or what a foreign land would be like was certainly different from what I found it to be in Germany or England or Pakistan, which were the places I was stationed. I didn't think the people would be purple or eat dirt or anything like that, but it was amazing to me how similar society in Western Europe was to ours around here. If you took someone from Wallace and put him on the street in a town in Germany, and in place of the German signs put English signs, I daresay he wouldn't know he was in Germany until he heard somebody talking. I bought an old Volkswagen while I was over there, and four of us would get together on our four-day off-shift. We had passes to go everywhere except to the Iron Curtain countries. England, France, Italy, Spain, Switzerland, Sweden, Norway, Denmark—we went to every one of them. Quite often we were invited to stay in someone's home, camp out in their barn, or whatever. At other times we'd stay in some youth hostel, where you'd pay a buck a night. We got to see a lotta stuff.

I was in Peshawar, Pakistan, for just a few days over fifteen months. It was a small base; there may have been four or five hundred people. That's including local personnel, U.S. support personnel and people in communications. The nearest westernized city was Rawalpindi, which at the time was the capital city of West Pakistan and was about a hundred twenty-five miles from where we were. The Air Force made an attempt to entertain us. They had a bowling alley, a movie theater that showed movies that were a couple of years old. There was a swimming pool and one little refreshment stand where you could get something that was similar to a hamburger. We had a monthly supply flight when they brought in our mail and a supply of food. We were to stay on the base at night at all costs; even the natives who worked for us had to travel back and forth to the base armed because they were always getting ripped off. It was not because the people were mean; they were trying to survive. The base was located outside of town in a rural agricultural area. The people grew wheat and sugarcane, grass crops, raised sheep. There was one brick factory, each one made by had. The above average home there was a one-room stucco job with no furniture, just a grass mat that was about a foot and a half off the floor. We could hire a man for three dollars a month to make up our beds every morning, shine shoes, dust our room and all this. He'd have eight or ten guys on the same floor on his list and he was making thirty-five or forty dollars a month, which made him upper middle class. The man that worked for me, Mubaark, had thirteen kids, and I went out to their house to eat with them twice. The roof structure of his house was supported by saplings with mud on top of it. The mud was very cohesive there. You could build a beautiful house out of it, like you do a sand castle on the beach, except it stuck together, and once that dried in the sun, it was like a brick.

I spent a lot of time tryin' to see what it was all about. Some people've got a little plot of land that they're squatted on, an' they stay there until somebody makes them move on. They'll have what little belongings they do own gathered up in that one little area. And that's it. Maybe people do something, but it doesn't appear they do anything but exist. That was especially evident in Peshawar. If you went downtown in the summer, you couldn't breathe. There were no sanitary facilities at all, and it didn't bother them. You'd walk along a canal in town, just actually a ditch is what it was, and you'd see some guy run his flock of sheep or goats in there, and then further downstream a ways there's a lady washing her clothes, and then further down a man relieving himself, and a little further down there's a guy with a bucket of water to drink out of. They're walking around, some of 'em with no clothes on, and they just squat right in the middle of the street. When you're talking about a street, you're talking about an expanse of maybe twenty or thirty feet full of people all the time. In the day people stumble over some guy takin' a crap in the street; at night it's like the Dark Ages in Europe. There are herds of sheep and goats bedded down in the streets, camp fires which people huddle around, cooking and talking.

In Peshawar there was nothing more to be had than a very casual relationship with a Pakistani. They were very hard-line Muslims, and you didn't even look in the direction of a woman. Not only was she covered up, you didn't even look at her covered up. The Pakistani people I associated with in Rawalpindi were the wealthier ones. The Westerners I met in Rawalpindi were very high up in somebody's embassy, so the Pakistani nationals that came to their parties were what the natives referred to as "Christian." That doesn't necessarily mean their definition of that word is the same as ours, but it meant they weren't Muslims. The women didn't practice purdah, for one thing. At one of the parties I attended I met a girl whose father was Colonel Tommy Blackham, who was the air advisor to the British high commissioner. His home came complete with a doorman, a molly who made the beds and swept the floor, a cook, a waiter; about six servants. The man who was president of Pakistan at the time would have breakfast with the Blackhams, and I would stand there talking to him just like I would to you. It threw me for a loop. I was a staff sergeant in the U.S. Air Force and was about as low on the totem pole as you could get. It was quite an experience.

So I've really had the opportunity to meet a lot of different people. I hope I've gotten to know them. It's hard as hell to get people to talk to you actually, just to *talk.* I have close friends who are living differently, and sometimes we go for long periods of time without seeing each other. But when we do get together, we can talk about the most intimate things. We trust each other implicitly. We don't necessarily have a whole lot in common. But can we be human beings together? That's what turns me on.

In a place like Pakistan we had nothing to do, and I read nine books by Lobsang Rampa. There are nine dimensions, and one project I had was to read those books and try to conceive an understandable concept for each of those dimensions. How do you conceive of a dimension beyond time? Most people probably can conceive of a fourth dimension being time fairly readily. But how do you go to the fifth? What would it be? You think of things like this. You're sitting in a chair in a room. And you say, "Well, here is a hemp place mat. Coffee cup. A match. Et cetera. How many different things could I do with what is right here to interest myself, and how long could I involve myself with what's available to me?" If you tried to make a list of the possibilities, there would be myriads of things you could think of doing that would occupy your time. What if you were in a jail cell and this was all you had? I could go for ten years. What I'm saying by that is life is so short and there are so many things to do in it. Why in hell keep right on doing the same thing over and over and over again?

You know what I'd like? I wish there was a university right across that highway which offered every course which has ever been conceived from the beginning of everything. And I could go over there and take it all. Hell, if somebody knows how to do something, I don't care how unrelated it is to my present activities, I want to learn how to do it. If a lady can make a cake, I'd like to know how to make one. Think of somebody that can do

363

something. Take painting, not as an artist, but house painting. The painter was here yesterday and he went upstairs and did that damn room in three hours, beautifully. It took me two and a half weeks to do one. Why? How did he do that? Well, he taught me something about white paint. Always put a little black in it. It covers more easily and doesn't leave streaks. That's the kinda stuff that some people would say, "Well, the hell with that. What good is that?" I think, go ahead, clutter your mind with trivia. You never know when you're going to use it. And you don't have to remember it all the time. When you need it, it'll come right back.

Cornell Chasten

Some people might think it ain't much in this day 'n time, wantin' to be a farmer, but it's the one thing that means sump'n to me. It's not a job that everyone can do. The man that build Disney World, let him go out in the woods sometime an' look at a tree. Or a man could cut down that tree an' use the wood to build 'im a fancy motel. But he can't even grow a leaf. Sometimes I like to go out in the field an' pull one leaf or look at one hill of grass. A man can use it all up, ruin everything with his work. But a farmer he can say, "Look, I've prepared a place for it to grow."

My daddy was a farmer an' that's where we lived, right on that farm. What he growed was for half. He did all the work an' the other man got half, the man that owned the land. They furnished the seeds an' the fertilizer an' all the material, an' you furnished the labor. In the summer he grew tobacco an' corn for half of the profit, an' in the winter he growed turnips, which all that was his. Really, now, he was my granddaddy, but my mother never married and she an' my two sisters an' I, we lived on his farm along with the resta his children. I guess that's where I started thinkin' 'bout the idea of havin' my own farm someday.

Always workin' other people's land, you don't feel good about it. But it takes money to buy land. I started to do farmin' after I got outta high school, an' I started to work at J. P. Stevens. So I was doin' two jobs. I was leasin' just about anywhere I could get land, an' I was farmin' tobacco with Billy Blanchard, tendin' his tobacco. After a while I quit at J. P. Stevens an' went to farmin' altogether. Then I had a bad year, started gamblin' bad. So I quit farmin' an' went to workin' in Southport at a construction job. I was gettin' a pretty good salary, but then all of a sudden I got the urge to move. Sump'n in me, I reckon. So I left all of a sudden, didn't let anybody know. It was sump'n that'd stayed on my mind a couple a' months an' I kept sayin' "I'll go tomorrow." Well, one of 'em days I found myself doin' what I'd always intended on doin' in my mind. I drove my truck to Raleigh, parked it, got on a bus an' left. I dunno what finally made me do it. Coupla weeks playin' poker bad, wife mad, comin' home with no money. Y'know, you hear so much talk about New York, an' when I wound up, that's where I was.

I started workin' at the Waldorf Astoria. My job was to keep the womens outta that motel. The prostitutes, y'know. It were pretty rough. They'd pay you, beg you, an' turn you on just to get in the motel. I didn't get much headache, but after a while, 'bout three months, it got to be too much an' I quit an' went to work for this boy from down home who had a down-home country store. Cured ham, sausage, stuff like that.

I liked it up in New York. There's more opportunity in a way a' speakin'. If I got a dollar in my pocket an' somebody gonna come by with a hustle, I can make two or three outta it. So I was better-off there. Less work, more money. Here you do anythin' illegal, everybody gonna know it. But after a while I didn't have no choice but to turn around an' come on home. My wife likes it down South, an' I didn't wanna break up with her. Me, I liked it fine up there.

Sometimes I feel like I shouldn'ta come back. Come back an' got myself busted down in Wallace. What happened, some a' the boys I went to school with were home, an' I was over talkin' to 'em an' they said, "C'mon, have a drink." Well, I had some marijuana with me, y'know, an' I wanted to go get ridda the stuff. An' they said, "Well, you're too good to drink with us, ain't ya?" I said, "It ain't that. I just got sump'n to do this mornin'." See, anytime I got sump'n to do, I like to keep a level head. Well, they had Ol' Grandad an' I started drinkin' right outta the bottle. 'Fore I knowed it I was pretty high, an' there I went, ridin' around in Wallace. You know how you get so high you get to talkin' to yourself? I said to myself, "Stop. Put this stuff out 'til you come back alone. If you go into Wallace, the law'll get you." Then I said, "No, the law'll get somebody else. It won't be you." Well, time I pulled up by the Dairio I seen the law make a circle, pullin' round behind me, an' I couldn't get away from 'em. So I stopped an' sat in the car. They pulled me out, throwed my hands on top a' the car, handcuffed me, read me them rights, carried me on down to the police station. Had me blow the breath-elizer. While I was doin' that, they went outside an' searched my car. An' when they come in, they had the stuff. Policeman said, "I reckon we better write up a search warrant so we can go out there an' search that thing."

Well, I wasn't gonna say nothin'. Then they searched me three times. Well, I had two little rocks, pretty little rocks I found. I said, "You took everythin' I got, but these two little rocks I'm gonna keep 'em." I shouldn'ta said that. This one grabbed me an' took the rocks, an' then I turned around an' musta pounded him one. Kept right on. Got to where there were two or three of 'em with their blackjacks. It was sump'n, I'm tellin' you. I hadda play dead, near about. I fell out like I was hurt bad to get 'em to stop. An' it wasn't so much fakin'. I was all beat up, eyes closed tight, head all bloody. They handcuffed me an' carried me down to the doctor, said, "Look at that. Look at the tracks on his arms." An' there ain't never been nothin' on my arm. An' I'm listenin' to all their shit, y'know. Anyway, they put me in jail over there an' my granddaddy come down an' stood my bond. Got me a pretty good lawyer.

There's people say, "I don't care 'bout goin' to jail." Well, they ain't never been there. I pulled six months an' I stayed there eighty-six days. The judge tol' me if I'd plead guilty, he'd give me six months. It was eight counts. Drivin' under the influence, resistin' arrest, assault on two police officers, possession of marijuana, failin' to stop for the blue light, careless an' reckless drivin', everythin'. Lemme tell you, jail is sump'n else. You get in there an' you think you ain't gonna take this, an' you ain't gonna take that. Well, there ain't nothin' for you, nothin', nothin', nothin'. Anythin' you do the guard can near tell what you're doin'. I mean you steal from a man, they know you're stealin'. An' you fool around with any of that funny stuff, they know that, too. Then they ain't gonna help you get out. But you do like you're s'posed to an' they help you. A lotta fights go on an' all sortsa shit like that. Everywhere you look there's somebody tryin' to suck your thing, an' all. Them types you don't wanna mess around with. I was in there to do my little time an' get out, know what I mean? I just tried to be on the amen side.

The way I feel, I'm a lot diff'rent now since I pulled time. I'm a lot more conscious about things you do wrong 'cause you can't do wrong an' get away with it for ever an' ever. When I came outta prison, I turned over a new leaf. The big thing I changed was gamblin'. When I first started playin', I'd go by a little while, win a hun'red dollars, go right on 'bout my business. Then I got to the place where that hun'red dollars would make me feel I could go get more anytime I needed it, keep goin'. You go there an' stay an' stay an' stay there. But if you stay, somebody gonna get you. An' you get to love it. Win or lose, you wanna be there for the game on Friday night. I started losin' worse when I got married. Before that we went together a coupla years, an' I couldn't stay at the gamblin' thing too long. I always hadda go by, check in, one thing an' another. But then, when I got married, I'd stay out all night, stay out all weekend, one thing an' another. The only way I broke myself of it was when I went to prison. I mean, they were playin' cards in there an' I swore to god I wasn't gonna play, an' I found myself playin' right on. An' then I said, "When I get out, I ain't gonna play no more."

Right now that ain't one a' my troubles. But I gotta say I sure got an understandin' wife. She's had her ups an' downs, left a coupla time. She's got a pretty good job an' she's a pretty smart girl. I guess some guys might not like it, her goin' so well an' all. Way I think, a job is like an asshole. Everybody's got one. I'm workin' an' she's workin' an' we got the things we need. All the things I said I was gonna have back yonder when I was a little boy. Soon as I got outta school, I got my own car an' always kept some money in my pocket. When I was a little boy I'd see somebody come by with a car an' a record player an' it really meant sump'n. An' when I came up tape machines was comin' out, an' I got me one a' them. Things is funny 'cause they mean more before you get 'em. Everythin' means a lot before you get it, an' when you get it you feel like you oughta get a pat on the back or sump'n, an' then you find out you don't get no special pat nor nothin'.

The important thing is I don't want it to look like that nobody gave me nothin'. For the last two or three years, without my granddaddy's help I couldn'ta made it, but I don't want nobody to give me nothin' really. I wanna get it for myself. I don't want nobody to come back an' say, "If it hadn'ta been for me, he'd a' been here, there, somewhere 'r other." When I get to the top of the mountain, I wanna say, "I made it on my sweat." See, I'll try anythin'. An' success lies there.

I got this kid, see, an' he's the spittin' image of me. When you say "love," you can't say enough. My wife took 'im to visit her cousin an' I can't ever say how much I miss 'im. I still like to gamble every once in a while. But then I remember how I felt when my wife brung him to see me when I was in jail. I felt so ashamed. The first day I came home I had him walkin' behind my leg, holdin' on. An' it seems that's all he wants to do now. I come in the door an' the first thing I do is put my hat on my head an' go into the bathroom an' pee an' he sees me with that hat on, anytime, an' he just runs to the bathroom. You think kids don't notice things, but that ain't true. If sump'n's wrong, they gonna know, so you gotta see there ain't nothin' wrong.

There's certain things you want more an' more an' more all the time. It don't matter a damn how much money I got. I'd like to be successful at farmin'. What I want is to grow things better. To come in a size larger or come in a day earlier than anybody else. I dunno. All I want is enough to get a little house an' some cows to eat the grass up in front of the yard. I don't really know how I'm gonna do it. But how don't matter. I'm gonna do it anyway.

Robert Fussell, Jr.

About the time I finished school I got drafted. Guys would go up to Kenansville an' worry the clerk at the draft board every day. Sometimes I thought she'd go ahead an' draft 'em to get them away from her. There was thousands a' questions, an' then rumors had a way of gettin' started, like "They need men bad. We're all goin' next week." That type a' thing.

Well, I let 'em draft me. I probably woulda joined anyway. I felt I had an obligation, not in the sense of the enemy invadin' the beach shores on the coast, or anythin' like that, but there was a coupla guys I know who were over there or had been over there, an' I felt like if they had gone, I certainly should go. At the time I was not clear-cut on the war, an' I kinda felt like maybe I'd know really what it was about if I got over there an' got involved with it.

The basic trainin' I took wasn't that oriented towards Vietnam. It woulda been the same no matter what war it was. I went to Fort Bragg in Fayetteville for basic trainin', then to Fort Polk, Louisiana, for infantry trainin', an' then I went to NCO school in Fort Benning, Georgia. In a way the trainin' at Fort Polk was created for Vietnam. But it would not have been humanly possible to have really trained someone to go over there an' find themselves in a combat situation. When you went to Vietnam, that was another world.

We're limited in the type of military operations we have. Politicians could come up with objectives, with Vietnamization, but what it boiled down to was the soldier on the ground. I was a Specialist Fourth Class with A Company of the First Air Cavalry Division. The only purpose I found for bein' over there, in the sense of what was my objective, was to do my job an' try to stay alive. There was no feelin' "We're goin' to go liberate this province today an' these people will be free forever, an' history will record what we've done." I felt like I was justified in bein' over there. But there wasn't this sense of havin' a goal.

There was a set pattern to everythin'. It was gettin' up at the same time every mornin', doin' the same thing over an' over again. If we didn't get into a fire fight, we just walked all day long, or humped, as we called it, an' you had about nine pounds strapped on your back, an' when a fire fight came, that became repetitious, too. The real action we saw was after we moved outta the DMZ to along the Cambodian border in the jungles in that area, an' in particular, a rubber plantation. It was a huge thing an' we walked an' we walked an' we walked through it, an' I always thought what a pitiful circumstance it was that there was this war goin' on when there was all this lovely country. You couldn't imagine how beautiful it was. There was right many paved roads in the plantation, but there hadn't been any government troops in there for four years. The U.S. Army was the only ones dumb enough to go out there. We had a new company commander an' he volunteered our company, an' we would hit the enemy all day long an' they would hit us at night.

The only association we had with civilians, we'd come in about once a month outta the jungles to guard the fire base for five or six days. In the mornin's the Vietnamese would be outside a' the fire base, an' they were industrious people. They'd sell you anythin'. From radios to lewd pictures. I think in that type of situation you didn't get to know the people. You wasn't s'posed to be havin' any dealin's with them anyhow. I remember after we'd caught some prisoners there was one boy about twelve or thirteen years old, an' there's this type a' combination French, English an' Vietnamese you speak an' you can communicate to some degree. We were gonna leave an' we were waitin' for the tanks to get straightened out an' Cambro, this hillbilly guy from Tennessee, he was talkin' to this boy, say, "Well, now how many children in your family?" an' all this, an' wanted to know what his mother an' father did, an' it was like he was talkin' to somebody on the other side a' the hill. The boy was real interested in Cambro's machine gun an' Cambro was goin' to show the kid how it worked. That's when I put a stop to it. It's all right to talk to 'im, but you don't hafta show 'im how to operate our weapons.

There was really a sense a' belongin' between the individuals in the company. The same thing every night, sittin' around in a group, tellin' stories. You get to learn a lot about each other in a situation like that. It wasn't the rank you had, it wasn't the position you had, it was just this feelin' that every man counted in a way. The day I was shot was probably one a' the most memorable of my life, not because I was hurt so doggone bad, but because when the guys in my platoon found out I'd been shot, every one of 'em volunteered to come an' get me. They wasn't accustomed to doin' things like that, 'specially after so many people had been shot up.

The way I got wounded, I had just got back from R and R. I had gone through the complete cycle by this time—carried a grenade launcher, walked point, an' then I was squad leader. Then our lieutenant he got his foot infected an' I hadda play lieutenant for ten days. This was right before I went on to R and R, so when I came back, they made me the platoon sergeant for the first platoon.

We was checkin' out what we called an arc-lighted area, where the jungle was torn up from the B-fifty-twos. Our company commander carried one platoon up ahead of the rest of the company an' he was pinned down. Then another platoon went up an' tried to help them out, an' before they could get to 'em, they got pinned down. By this time I was gettin' pretty disgusted with the whole affair. We couldn't seem to make no headway. The company commander called back an' asked for six volunteers from our platoon to help get the wounded out. The lieutenant told the two squad leaders to each give him three men. These were volunteers, see. An' so I was sittin' down there, smokin' a cigarette, an' all of a sudden here they come, they had picked six of the newest guys in the whole platoon. They had never been out in the jungles before, an' I hated to see 'em guys gettin' into somethin' like that. So I went along with 'em.

I was leadin' 'em out an' there was a little clearin', an' the fightin' was ahead of me. I saw three guys wounded over this clearin'. I told those six guys to get down an' I went walkin' up, an' about the time I got to the first wounded man, the first bullet hit me an' went right on through my leg. It didn't even knock me down. But then when he shot me again, that was the one that broke the bone. It was like gettin' hit by a truck. About three hours later I was evacuated.

After I was shot there was the operation to get the bullet that was lodged in my leg. An' then when I was sent to Okinawa, I received another operation, an' I had two more while I was in the VA hospital. If it had just been my leg, I probably would have enjoyed my hospital stay, but the bad thing 'bout it was that the bullet that went through my leg damaged a nerve an' the pain never let up. The way the good Lord made people, we can't remember pain like it was, but I can remember sufferin'. There was no medication that would knock it out or anythin'. That last operation I had they went in my back an' clipped some nerves right down to my foot an' that relieved the pain. An' that was after eight months. After they had done this operation, three days later I was up. I have paralysis of the left leg an' I hafta wear a special shoe because the bone was shot up so bad it wouldn't heal, an' then they hadda overlap it. I ain't complainin'. I'm walkin'. I was glad to see that day come around.

Those guys I served with were pretty decent human bein's. Even goin' through a hell like Vietnam wasn't goin' to change 'em that much. Just as long as they survived. I was irritated by the Calley thing. There were so many people around me who were applaudin' murder. These people couldn't have realized what they were sayin'. I personally can't pass judgment on Calley. I think he was a person who was in the wrong place at the wrong time. An' I have this feelin', too, that although the evidence was presented against him, the Army was probably lookin' for someone. Maybe they thought they were doin' the right thing by puttin' him on trial, but I'm sure that there are a lotta people who probably committed things just as bad, or maybe even worse, that have not today received any type of trial or accusations brought against them.

I think in a situation like that, if the orders had been given in my platoon, I cannot see anyone hardly that I worked with committin' atrocities like that. I'm sure that a person could be driven to doin' it. I know we were driven pretty far sometimes an' things become pretty frustratin', an' perhaps a person would do somethin' that he normally wouldn't do. I dunno. Those guys who did the shootin' were boys next door, you know. The boys you an' I grew up with in high school. I reckon we can say that, well, that was their situation that they were in, an' I reckon we can trace that all the way back to the citizens over here for ever allowin' this thing to happen to begin with.

The point is that even now or in years to come, the people will get to askin' themselves, "Who can we blame for this war?" A person might say, "I'm not against our involvement there. Although I'm not that clear-cut on the issues, I think we should stand up an' fight." Now this type a' person will be lookin' for somebody to blame. An' the people who were for peace all the time—who are they gonna blame? Matter of fact, what it boils down to, it's sorta havin' to point fingers at people. We oughta point 'em at ourselves.

When I was in Ohio, I went an' visited the parents of a boy that was killed. He an' I became real good friends. I reckon he was the best friend I had while I was over there. He was a Christian. I never heard him use a foul word. I think everybody admired 'im because he was a devoted Christian an' he was able to just put himself above all of it, an' still yet was a part of it. I don't know where it makes much sense.

Anyway, I went to his home. He has a brother an' I met his mother an' his father an' his grandfather. An' in the den they had a case. They had all of his medals an' various things.

There were so many things goin' through my mind. Even after this long a time it was still a painful thing. I could think back, why in the world did a thing like that hafta happen? I mean, why did he hafta go over there an' be killed? He certainly had never been involved in politics. He wasn't the type of person that was bitter about bein' over there. He realized he had a job to do an' he was doin' it. He didn't try to find any easy way out of it. That's why I keep sayin', "Why him?" There was probably no finer human bein' in this country than he was. I have tried to answer some questions about it, an' I really did some deep thinkin' about it after talkin' to members of the family while I was in Ohio. An' to this day I've never had it black or white in my mind was it worth it. An' I probably never will.

17 Coming Home

"No matter what I do or where I go, I'll always want to come back."

—Leona Roulette

Changing Things: Donald Lawrence*

When we were in high school, a number of us always talked about going off to school so that we could come back and maybe do something for Rose Hill. We didn't really know what we were going to do, but we were products of the late fifties, early sixties, an' I guess even back then we were thinkin' that what we wanted to do would be to create a more open type of society. We were naive. We thought there was a possibility of changin' things from the grass roots up. It was still the ol' American dream type of thing. Now some of us are slowly filterin' back into the area an' tryin' to do somethin'. An' if there were more job possibilities, there would be more of us. But I don't know whether it will amount to anythin'. As you get older your dreams sorta fade. You put up with things wherever you happen to be.

The advantage I have is I grew up in this area and I understand it very well. I know a lot of the people and I know how they think. There is a meanness in Rose Hill. I don't know how to describe it, but it's there. And that is very frightening. There is a shortcomin' that people have, that is very typical of this town, which is they're very prone to overlook things. They draw into themselves an' build up all sorts of feelin's of hate rather than get out into the open with it. Then it comes out in all kindsa ugly an' subversive ways. They spend years tryin' to get back at you. Okay. How are you gonna deal with that? Attack it head on?

Let's take a specific example. Let's take the Mt. Zion Presbyterian Church. I would like to see that organization used for what is the function of a church, instead of as a ladies' gossip club an' a back-stabbers' operation. How do you do that? It's very complicated. The only way you can do it is that you hafta go unnoticed. Because if anyone knows what you're doin', you're goin' to lose them along the way. You hafta understand the influences of the churches here. Some of them are the central sources of a lot of our problems. I damn sure think so anyway. There's a place down in Wallace which it's a hellhole, but it used to be the only place you could buy beer in the whole county. And if you crossed the door of that joint, you were really a sinner. But what went on in that pool hall was so much more innocent an' aboveboard than what goes on in some a' the meetin's at some a' the churches. Well, I might like to walk into my church an' tell 'em to cut out all the foolishness, that I don't think my church should be a political an' social organization. But those Christians are likely to kick me in the tail an' I could never go back.

The point is that you hafta let people know in a subtle way that there is a possibility of change. Then wait an' let events an' people move. There are a lotta folks here who are tired of all the bullshit, an' it won't take a whole lotta doin' to clean things up. It doesn't take an education to feel this way. Maybe some people are beginnin' to realize they have options. Let's take the town government. C. T. Fussell has been the town clerk as long as I can remember. An' I don't know why Ben Harrell ran for mayor except to keep C. T. in there. They're such close friends they even went on their honeymoon together. I'm serious. Anyway, they're very, very close an' my personal opinion is that they're also very lackadaisical an' nonenergetic, an' neither of them is doin' anybody in the town of Rose Hill the least bit of good. For a long time the only salaried position in this town was C. T.'s. Now there are a couple of laborers to fix the streets an' a girl they hired to be a kinda secretary down at the town hall. But for years all we had was C. T. an' he moves at a snail's pace. He even t-a-l-k-s l-i-k-e t-h-i-s. An idea would bust his head right open, an' the same with Ben Harrell. Well, people learned a lot when Perry Whaley came so close to beatin' Ben for mayor. In a symbolic sense that election is the most positive thing that's happened in this town in a long, long time.

But you hafta understand what we're up against. In another type of environment we could do more. Organize some sorta political campaigns maybe. Not just against Ben an' C. T., but against the whole packa them, the commissioners, representatives, everybody we got in there. Or we could go around givin' speeches. Well, what good would any of that do us? My idea isn't to tear this community apart, or to make it over into my image of what a town or a county should be. I have options. I can leave anytime I want to. My family and I could move on to Raleigh or Richmond or Washington, D.C., or New York City, and we'd feel perfectly at home. But I guess every human bein' has some desire to influence his or her surroundin' human bein's to some extent. Either by action or nonaction. Maybe by just bein' around. I want things to change here an' I'd like to be parta that. I'd like to ride down the roads in this county an' not see children who look as if they've never had a real dinner or taken a bath. Hell. I'd like to ride down the streets of Rose Hill without havin' to dodge the damn potholes because the town government's so sloppy an' inefficient they can't even do a pavin' job correctly. Maybe I'm not talkin' about commitment. Maybe I'm not talkin' about a long term thing. It could end tomorrow. But while I'm here, I don't want to just *be* here.

I don't mean I want to be a leader. An' I'm not a radical or anythin' of the kind. I guess it's a question of helpin' people identify what they want, of crystalizin' their own values. The way I see it, it's like a chemical reaction. We've got the components. We've got the people. They've got problems an' they know it. It's a community situation. It's sorta analogous to the play, *Our Town,* where you're standin' there an' you see yourself in the same situation, but somehow or other you can look objectively at it. Maybe I'm idealistic, but I think it might work to try to show people that there are people who are involved and who do care, who have some kind of personal freedom for themselves. The idea is to build up confidence and a sense of community. It's a situation that has all sortsa possibilities.

Leona Roulette: Coming Home

I was very young when I first moved to New York. Sixteen or seventeen. My big sister was there, but it was difficult in the beginnin' because none of the things I was doin' I had done before. My whole life-style was different. I was used to walkin' through the trees an' watchin' things change in the fall, all this business. Here, you're comin' *here,* an' this is your destination an' there *is* an end. In New York it seems you go downtown shoppin' an you never stop goin' around an' around. I think that's the difference. It's just which way you wanna live. You know what I mean?

I have one boy an' he's sixteen, same age I was then. There's a big difference in how we grew up, an' it bothers me. I had more advantages than he did. I had the yard to play in, swingin' from trees, all that stupid stuff. That was great to me. But my son, he's more or less patterned. Like he goes to the park. He stays there 'til ten. He comes back in an' he has lunch. He goes back to the park. This is a routine thing he's doin' all the time. But we didn't do that. What we were doin' came natural. We would get up an' go out in the yard an' we played, an' that was a big difference right there. My son didn't get the fun outta life that I got. Never will. An' that's what I regret. I regret it. Because he doesn't know a whole part of what's happenin' in this world. He comes down here an' says, "Oooooooo! A bug." Well, what's so big about a bug? These are simple things that he really should know.

My job in New York City is that I work for Social Services, doin' children's counselin'. The problems the kids have in New York are a lot different than they are here. Their behavior pattern is not the same. There's no discipline. I can go into a classroom here an' I get the students to listen to me. Try doin' that in New York City, an' see what happens to you. Some people think it's because the families here are closer, but that's not necessarily the reason. The environment is different. You see what I'm sayin'? In a classroom here you don't walk in and knock a teacher down, an' things like that. Right? But in the city you do. An' it's all ignored or excused away. As far as prejudice, there's as much in New York City as there is in Rose Hill. One thing I can say about North Carolina is they integrated when they had to. An' as far as that goes, things are a lot better than they used to be. Used to, the black schools didn't have the materials that the white schools had. But those things have changed. Some of it is the law, an' some of it is the struggle our people have gone through. An' some of it is plain people bein' people an' learnin'.

380

You hear talk about the North bein' the promised land, an' maybe that's true for some folks, but I'm movin' back here next year, soon as I can get my pennies together, soon as I can. My husband loves the idea because he's from the city part of Kansas City, so he never had what we had. An' far as my son is concerned, I feel he's been crippled by missin' out on these things. So much I have experienced that he'll never know. Lookin' at the corn. Silkin' the corn. Takin' the grasshoppers apart. That was great 'cause I knew how. We did everythin'. It was science an' a whole lotta other things combined. We taught this to ourselves.

I know what livin' here was like before, an' that has never left my mind. But now, some of those little things that tend to press against your brain tellin' you "Uh-uh, you can't do this." Well, I don't hafta listen to that no more. If I want to go in someplace, I go on in. Far as treatment, you're not talkin' about a passive thing. I can *demand* to be treated better. If the Supreme Court tells me, "Yes," there's no way you can stop me. The way I look at it, this is my country. I was born here. This corner here, we always lived here. We grew up here. We played in the yard. I come back, four times a year maybe, an' I can't wait to drive up to my daddy's house an' drop off my suitcase an' go outside an' look at the yard. To check out the garden an' see how the corn is growin'. Maybe it's good to get away, an do your workin' in some place like a city, an' maybe I won't be comin' back as soon as I'd like to. But I know I am comin' back here. An' no matter what I do or where I go, I'll always want to come back. Rose Hill is always gonna be my home.